A History of the University of Michigan School of Social Work

A History of the University of Michigan School of Social Work

PHILLIP FELLIN

Published by
The University of Michigan Social of Social Work

ISBN 978-0-9823953-0-1

Contents

Foreword

It is with great pleasure that we write the foreword to Professor Fellin's history of the University of Michigan School of Social Work. In collaborating on the foreword, we represent the span of the school and its history and future. Laura Lein is the new school dean (as of January 1, 2009) and John Tropman has been a professor at the school, interim dean, and currently associate dean.

Phillip Fellin is the perfect person to write a school history. He was in the first cohort of graduates from the school's innovative Joint Doctoral Program in Social Work and Social Science. He spent some time at the School of Social Work at St. Louis University and then returned to the University of Michigan as a professor, assistant dean, and then dean. He held the latter position for ten years, after which he returned to the role of professor until his retirement. Consequently, his perspective is relevant to students, alumni, faculty, and administration alike. He has seen the school from many points of view, and that is reflected in the inclusiveness of this volume.

Fellin's history is an important part of the history of the school itself, and that history is important for several reasons. Professional education is a touchstone in our lives, and we value the opportunity to revisit it, recreate the community and connection it created for us, and re-examine the knowledge we gained from it. Therefore, one of the history's most obvious values is what it means to the people personally involved with the school over the years—alumni, current students, faculty, staff, field instructors, donors, and other friends of the school. For them, this volume evokes memories of people who were meaningful and influential in their personal and professional lives, as well as signature courses that provide guidance to this day. One particularly impressive aspect of the book lies in the rich detail Professor Fellin has provided about the faculty who worked at the school. We all have our favorite teachers and professors, and the chance to review the history of their roles in the school is a real pleasure. For current faculty, this opportunity is valuable as well. It connects us to, and recalls, our predecessors. For staff, many of whom have been with us for years, the history also provides a reflection on the meaningfulness of the workplace then and now.

Furthermore, the book evokes more than just personal connection. If a hallmark of "thinking like a social worker" is the concept of people-in-context, the book also serves to locate the people and the school in the larger social context—the Depression, World War II, the 1950s, the 1960s, the 1970s, and so on, into the 21st century. National and global events have always played an important role in curriculum considerations and student interests—for example post-WWII readjustment for veterans, the rise of civil rights leaders, and the importance of the student voice. Professor Fell-in highlights the crossroads between social events and social work education, noting, for example, that the first "teach-in" was organized at the University of Michigan and involved many social work faculty. The theme of activism in response to social justice issues has been and continues to this day to be a major part of the fabric of the school, and this history book recounts that legacy.

Another reason this book is important—apart from its discussion of historical details—is its focus on the ways in which the school's programs, and by extension, social work education, and indeed the profession of social work itself, have evolved over the years. The book is more than a history of the school—it is also a lens on the evolution of social work pedagogy and the field of professional training in general. While social work has always had a focus on helping the person and the family (micro), and working for positive social change, better social policies, and promoting social justice (community organization, social policy, management, evaluation), the book shows how the school enlarged and enriched each of those areas for the field as a whole. In this sense, it is the story of a flagship school—the influence of which is still growing through its commitment to the highest quality social work education.

The University of Michigan School of Social Work is a leader school. For many years it held the formal number one spot, which tended to reflect the string of social work innovations that have characterized the school over the years.

Michigan led and continues to lead in doctoral education. As one looks at the special chapter on the Joint Doctoral Program in Social Work and Social Science, it is important to remember that at the time of the program's founding in the middle 1950s, social science and social work did not experience much interaction at all. In fact, at the time, there tended to exist a kind of mutual suspicion between and among disciplines that prevented collaboration. Thus, the blending and combining of social work with other disciplines was a major invention, and though somewhat scorned at the time, has changed the field and opened the way for ongoing rich and valuable collaborative efforts. The maintenance of this "fruit" requires constant gardening over the years.

Michigan led in the provision of quality interpersonal practice education (micro) through the introduction of therapeutic group work and behavior modification, among other areas, and this focus continues in importance today.

Michigan led and continues to lead in the macro area through vigorous and full courses of study in community organization, administration and management, and policy methods.

And we continue to innovate in areas of diversity of faculty (the school now has the most diverse faculty at the University of Michigan), students, and staff. The school now engages in a wide range of valuable sponsored research efforts in areas such as preventing domestic violence, assessing the impact of physical punishment on children, and working with young adults who have aged out in the foster care system, to cite only a few.

Finally, the book also reminds us of how much things have changed in the last three quarters of the 20th century, and now into the 21st. When the School of Social Work began, there were no televisions, no cell phones, and no computers. Faculty members used pedagogical methods popular since at least the 12th century—class notes were in a notebook from which the professor lectured. Students took notes with paper and pencil and studied in traditional libraries. Today computers and modern communication tools provide web-based class systems, advanced forms of research, and new possibilities for promoting social justice. It is a new world but with many of the same problems as the old one. This book allows us to reflect on the past and learn from our history, allowing us to apply some of the wisdom gleaned from previous mastering of challenges in order to call upon our ongoing dedication to leading the charge to serve those who need our help.

Laura Lein   John Tropman
Ann Arbor, MI   June 2009

CHAPTER ONE

The First Thirty Years

Social work education as a degree program at the University of Michigan began in 1921, some 104 years after the university's founding in 1817. This chapter covers social work programs at Michigan from 1921 to 1951. During the first fourteen years of this period, a Curriculum in Social Work was offered at the undergraduate level in Ann Arbor in the university's College of Literature, Science, and the Arts. In 1935 the university opened a graduate program for social work in Detroit, where the program leading to a master's degree remained until 1951. In 1951 this graduate program was moved to the Ann Arbor campus, where it has continued its master's program, with the Joint Doctoral Program in Social Work and Social Science initiated in 1957.

Part One, Historical Context, presents highlights of the early years of the university as a context for this history of social work education at Michigan, especially in regard to university goals, such as teaching, research, and service. The activities of faculty members at the university who were active prior to 1921 in connecting the fields of economics, philosophy, and sociology to "charity work," philanthropy, social work practice, and social work education are noted. As a historical context, early "training" schools and programs in social work education in the United States are cited. Part Two, Curriculum in Social Work: 1921–35, describes features of the university's program in social work education at the undergraduate level in Ann Arbor from 1921 to 1935. Part Three, Graduate Social Work Programs: 1935–51, covers the graduate program in social work offered by the university in Detroit from 1935 to 1951.

PART ONE   Historical Context

The University of Michigan
The founding of the University of Michigan in 1817 was the result of an education law developed by William Woodbridge, secretary of the Michigan

Territory, Judge Augustus B. Woodward (appointed to this position by his friend Thomas Jefferson), Judge John Griffin, Father Gabriel Richard, and Reverend John Monteith. The governor of the territory at this time was Lewis Cass. Judge Woodward was the principal drafter of the education law. He had published *A System of Universal Science* in 1816, a "classification of all knowledge by departments, classes, orders, and specifics, to each of which he gave original names," based on a Napoleonic concept of a university (Peckham, 1994). The model for the new university was "the Imperial University that the first Napoleon gave to France in 1806–08, which was not, in fact, a University at all, but rather a highly centralized organization of State instruction, having its centre in Paris" (Hinsdale, 1906). The draft of the education law became a territorial law on August 26, 1817.

> It is to this date that the University of Michigan traces its origins. There was created a "Catholepistemiad, or university, of Michigania," to be composed of thirteen didaxiim or professorships, including Universal Science, Literature, Mathematics, Natural History, Natural Philosophy, Astronomy, Chemistry, Medical Sciences, Economic Sciences, Ethical Sciences, Military Sciences, Historical Sciences, and Intellectual Sciences.
>
> In subsequent acts passed that day and later, the tongue-fluttering Catholepistemiad was omitted and "University" or "University of Michigania" was used as the name of the public organization in the Territory of Michigan over all grades of instruction. Two weeks after the establishment of the University, the Territorial government appointed the Rev. John Monteith as president and gave him seven professorships, or courses. Richard was named vice president and was given the other six professorships. (Peckham, 1994)

According to Hinsdale (1906), the Act of 1817 establishing the university stated that the president should receive an annual salary of $25.00, the vice-president, $18.75, and professors, $12.50. In another reference to salaries some fifty years later, in 1869–70 the president of the university was paid $3,000 and a house, full professors in the Literary Department, $2,000, assistant professors, $1,300, acting professors, $1,500, and medical and law professors, $1,300.

Fr. Gabriel Richard, a native of France and a graduate of the Sulpician Seminary at Angers, had arrived in Detroit in 1798, creating a parochial school for boys, a school for girls, and a school primarily for Native American children at Springwells. "By 1808 he reported that he had eight schools operating in the area and petitioned for a school building. Then he went East and brought back an organ, a piano, a printing press, and a printer to publish bilingual textbooks of his own selection" (Peckham, 1994). After the founding of the university, "The good French Father could be heard on various Saturdays yelling, *Allez les bleus*" (Gavrilovich, 2001). Rev. John Monteith was a graduate of Jefferson College in western Pennsylvania and of the new Princeton Seminary. He came to Detroit in 1816 at the call of the Protestant residents. "Incidentally, these Protestants, to whom Richard had preached occasionally, held their first services in the new Ste. Anne's Church . . . at the invitation of the priest!" (Peckham, 1994).

Shortly after its founding, "the University" (Monteith and Richard) established public primary schools in Detroit, Monroe, and Mackinac Island and a classical academy in Detroit. As university historian Peckham (1994) observed,

> These were not free schools; a small fee was charged, although poor children could attend at public expense . . . presumably after declaring their poverty. On October 3, 1817, the University bravely established . . . or, more accurately, called for the establishment of . . . a college in Detroit, which was also to have a board of trustees and visitors. At the treaty of Fort Meigs which Governor Cass was conducting while the university got underway, he persuaded the chiefs, who still owned most of Michigan, to grant six sections—3,840 acres—half to Ste. Anne's church and half for the new college at Detroit. (Peckham, 1994)

Peckham also observed,

> The vision of Woodward, who drew the plan, and of the young minister and the older priest was remarkable. They had given substance to the clause in the Northwest Ordinance of 1787 that read: Religion, morality, and knowledge being necessary to good government and the happiness of mankind, schools and the means of education shall forever be encouraged.

While the University of Michigan dates its founding back to 1817, in fact, only education at the primary and secondary levels was offered until the university moved to Ann Arbor in 1837 (Peckham, 1994). It was in this year that the State of Michigan was admitted to statehood by Congress, the state legislature reorganized the university as a state university, and a plan was approved for purchase of forty acres of land in Ann Arbor as a site for the university. The town of Ann Arbor had been planned in 1824, with John Allen as the town's principal founder. Governor Cass established Ann Arbor as the "seat of justice in the new county of Washtenaw" (Bidlack,

1998). In naming Ann Arbor, John Allen "had chosen the word 'arbour' to follow his wife's first name, it being commonly used in Virginia for a bower of trees" (Bidlack, 1998). By the time the university moved to Ann Arbor in 1837, the town had a population of about 2,000 people (Peckham, 1994).

In 1837 control of the university became vested in a Board of Regents, which "had power to grant degrees, regulate courses, and prescribe textbooks; they could appoint and remove professors and erect buildings; and they could recommend to the superintendent and legislature the branches that should be established in the counties" (Peckham, 1994). Henry Philip Tappan was appointed president of the university by the regents, making him, arguably, the first president of the University of Michigan. At this time, the regents set about borrowing money to erect buildings for classes and for homes for four professors. By 1840 some buildings were completed, and, as Peckham (1994) noted:

> At last, courses at the collegiate level were offered beginning in September 25, 1841, with six freshmen and one sophomore and twenty-three in the preparatory school. The ratio of one professor to 3.5 students was never achieved again. The freshmen had been examined for admission in mathematics, geography, Latin, and Greek and made to furnish satisfactory testimonials of good moral character. Each had paid an entrance fee of $10.

The regents declared that:

> The fee of admission to the University should never exceed $10 and the institution should be open to all persons resident in the state who might wish to avail themselves of its advantages without charge of tuition, and to all other persons under such restrictions and regulations as the Regents should prescribe. (Hinsdale, 1906)

Admission to the university was limited to men until 1870, when the regents took the following action:

> Resolved, that the Board of Regents recognize the right of every resident of Michigan to the enjoyment of the privileges afforded by the University, and that no rule exists in any of the University statutes for the exclusion of any person from the University, who possesses the requisite literary and moral qualifications. (Hinsdale, 1906)

Miss Madelon L. Stockwell was the first women to enter the university as a student in the Literary Department, as well as the first female graduate in 1872.

As a part of the university's reorganization in 1837, three departments were established, including the Departments of Literature, Arts, and Sciences; Law; and Medicine, each with a number of professorships. The Department of Law did not open for students until 1859. Throughout these early years various departments, schools, and colleges were established, sometimes linked together (such as Engineering and Architecture) and often beginning with professorships, moving to departments, and then to schools or colleges. For example, a program for dental education began in 1875, leading to the School of Dentistry in 1927; a professorship in architecture and design in 1876 became a department in 1913, a College of Architecture in 1931, and later the College of Architecture and Urban Planning; a school for nurses, with a two-year course, in 1891 became the School of Nursing in 1940; a chair of the science and art of teaching within the Department of Literature, Science, and the Arts in 1879 became the School of Education in 1921; the Department of Forestry in 1903 became the School of Forestry and Conservation in 1926; the School of Natural Resources in 1950 was later the School of Natural Resources and the Environment. The School of Business Administration started in 1924 as an outgrowth of courses initiated in 1900 in higher commercial education, accounting, land economics, and social insurance and offered in the Department of Economics (University of Michigan, 2001).

In order to provide some consistency in the names given to educational programs at the university,

> In 1914, the faculty recommended a new nomenclature for the divisions of the University. Those which granted first degrees to students were to be called colleges; those which gave professional degrees were to be schools. Departments were to be subdivisions of colleges and schools which taught a given subject in several courses. Thus it was proper to speak of the College of LSA, the Literary College, the College of Engineering and Architecture, the Medical School, the Law School, the Department of English and the Department of Philosophy. The Regents adopted the new terminology in January 1915. (Peckham, 1994)

The College of Literature, Science, and the Arts included departments, as well as special curriculum areas. In 1921 the regents of the university approved a formal Curriculum in Social Work within this college.

Social Work Education and University Goals

In first developing an undergraduate social work curriculum, then graduate professional study, the university sought to contribute to meeting social
service needs of people in Michigan and the United States and throughout
the world. The intermingling of these goals has been a dominant feature of
the history of social work education at Michigan. The interest in social welfare, the social work profession, and social work education on the part of
citizens, providers of health and social services, and university professors
led to educational programs that involved service through degree program
fieldwork components and the active involvement of faculty members in
community and the society.

The University of Michigan's goals of teaching, research, and service
provide a framework for examining social work education programs in the
university. As Peckham (1994) has noted:

> Throughout the long history of the University of Michigan runs a cord that
> thickens as time passes. First there was only a single strand representing the
> University's aim to disseminate knowledge. Meanwhile a second strand was
> turned around this first line. By the 1890s, the University saw it must con-
> tribute additions to knowledge, which was not a static, fully known body of
> facts and accepted interpretations. Now there is a third strand wound with
> the other two. The University touches more than just its young students and
> faculty. It gives services to the state that help maintain it; it aids citizens who
> never enroll.

Peckham concluded: "Teaching . . . research . . . and service. These are the
warp and woof of the University today."

The history of social work education at Michigan involves all three
strands: teaching, research, and service. The goal of public service was incorporated into the undergraduate Curriculum in Social Work in 1921 and
emphasized by the director of the program, Professor Arthur E. Wood.
Social work educational programs have followed the university's long tradition of providing professional and semiprofessional training for service
purposes, such as in education, psychology, medicine, dentistry, psychiatry, nursing, and public health.

Public service has been a major theme in the university's Extension
Service, the University Musical Society, the Museum of Art, and the university libraries. Of special significance for social work is the Extension
Service. "The University Extension Service was established for the purpose
of providing educational opportunities for residents of the state who are

not in a position to pursue programs of study in residence at the University" (Soop, 1977). From the time the social work program was offered in Detroit in 1935 and in Ann Arbor in 1951, social work courses and summer institutes have been offered through the Extension Service in communities in Michigan and Ohio.

Faculty Forerunners: Before 1921

Prior to the establishment of the Curriculum in Social Work in 1921, several University of Michigan faculty members were interested and involved in the education of students for positions in philanthropy, charity, and social work. These faculty members were in the fields of economics, sociology, history, and philosophy; prominent among them were Andrew Dickson White, Henry Carter Adams, John Dewey, Charles Horton Cooley, and Arthur Evans Wood.

ANDREW D. WHITE. Andrew Dickson White joined the Michigan faculty in 1856 as a professor of history. White resigned his position at the University of Michigan in 1867 to become the first president of Cornell University, while also serving as dean of the College of History and Political Science. In this capacity, White pushed for instruction in political economy and social science and emphasized the "importance of men receiving education and training in order to fulfill positions of social usefulness" (Broadhurst, 1971).

In 1890, as president of the American Social Science Association, White urged members to engage in courses of instruction "as to the best dealings by towns, counties, states, and the nation, with pauperism, crime, inebriety, and other vices, lunacy in its various degrees, the organization and maintenance of Health Boards and hospitals, general sanitary measures, and the like," and "the need for special schools for the study of the science of charity" (Broadhurst, 1971).

HENRY C. ADAMS. Henry Carter Adams began his career at the University of Michigan in 1880 as a lecturer in political economy under a dual contract with Cornell University. "He was appointed chair of Michigan's Department of Economics when his criticism of American railroad conglomerates forced his departure from Cornell. . . . One of his principal causes was shaping a proper curriculum of business education for Michigan. He supported the study of business as an academic pursuit. An idealist and an iconoclast, Adams was known to agitate his colleagues with his zealous defense of labor unions and other principles. At the same time, he was a traditionalist and promoted ideals like hard work and personal integrity as a means to advancement" (University of Michigan, 2001).

Along with Professor John Dewey, Adams had studied at Johns Hopkins. They were members of a History of Politics Seminar at Hopkins before leaving to take positions at other universities. These individuals were considered to be "apostles of social science . . . spreading the word on historical scholarship throughout the United States" (Broadhurst, 1971). Hopkins was known as the "Baltimore atmosphere" for social science and philanthropy, with professors from Hopkins helping to create the National Conference of Charities and Correction in 1879. This conference was organized "to provide an opportunity for program managers and civic leaders to discuss common concerns," such as "training workers in urban charity agencies and improving the efficiency of charity administration" (Austin, 1997). At the same time, some economists who trained and taught at Johns Hopkins in the late 1800s had qualms about the nature of "sociology," viewing it as a mixture of economics and psychology. "Social work was looked upon as merely 'palliative,' narrowly focused on the techniques of handling social pathology rather than being concerned with the economics of poverty. Less politely it was referred to as organized gossip, participated in by fuddy-duddies" (Broadhurst, 1971).

While at the University of Michigan, Professor Adams served on a committee at the 1893 International Conference of Charities in Chicago that petitioned for a permanent section of the Conference on Sociology in Education. Professor Adams administered a university fellowship in sociology, begun in 1897, as a field assignment in settlement work at Chicago Commons. In 1904 Annie Huber held the scholarship, with Adams stating that "an intelligent interest in the work of social settlement is a part of University life and an intelligent sympathy with this enlarged idea of a University as a part of education" (Adams, 1904). Adams described the nature of this assignment in the October 18, 1904, edition of the *Michigan Daily*.

> The Chicago Commons is a social settlement under the direction of Professor Graham Taylor of Chicago Theological Seminary. No place affords a better opportunity, either for the rendering of social services, or for the analyzing of social forces than Chicago Commons. The interest of the student in social settlements is found in the fact that they afford an outlet for the spirit of broad and discriminating brotherly kindness, which is one of the choicest fruits of University life; they afford, also, an opportunity for observing at first hand the social conditions from which spring some of the most dangerous tendencies of modern times.

Adams (1904) went on to say in the *Michigan Daily* that "no one who believes in the University of Michigan can regard it as a misfortune that it is situated in a small town. It is, however, something of a disadvantage that students are deprived of contact, at first hand, with some of the conditions respecting which, as good citizens and educated men, they will be called upon in after life to have an intelligent opinion."

JOHN DEWEY. In the fall of 1884, a 24-year-old philosophy instructor "deeply rooted in philosophical idealism" joined the faculty at the University of Michigan (Williams, 1998). This was Dewey's first college-level teaching position. He served on the Michigan faculty from 1884 to 1894, departing for the University of Chicago, and hence to Columbia University. At Chicago, Dewey lectured at the Chicago Commons to employees of social agencies in Chicago. While at Michigan, Dewey influenced the emergence of the disciplines of sociology and psychology. "Although a philosopher, he made significant contributions in psychology, including encouraging the founding of the first psychological laboratory at Michigan" (Frantilla, 1998).

In 1888 Dewey published an essay, "Ethics in Democracy," where he "began to apply the organic concept of the individual to the broader context of society and systems of government" (Williams, 1998). This essay suggested "an intellectual link to his Michigan colleague and friend Henry Carter Adams," who was teaching a political economy seminar on industrial society at Michigan at the time (Williams, 1998). In 1889–90, Dewey drew upon sociology in his lectures in political philosophy and the "Theory of Institutions of Social Organization" lectures attended by Cooley during his graduate study at Michigan (Angell, 1951).

CHARLES H. COOLEY. Charles Horton Cooley was born in Ann Arbor and completed his bachelor's degree at Michigan in 1887. He began teaching at the university as an assistant professor in political economy in 1892, finishing his Ph.D. in political economy at Michigan in 1894. Cooley gave the first courses bearing the name "sociology" at the university in the academic year of 1894–95, "Principles of Sociology" and "Problems of Sociology" (McKenzie, 1951). Social work historian Frank J. Bruno (1957) notes that in the 1880s, prominent sociologists such as Franklin H. Giddings of Columbia University, Charles H. Cooley of the University of Michigan, William H. Brewer of Yale University, and Harry H. Powers of Smith College discussed the relationship of sociology to charitable work. "This period might be called the honeymoon stage of the interrelationship between theory and practice; between the teaching of sociology and the practice of social work.

. . . It also became clear that the art of helping, in common with all professional arts, is dependent not on one science, but on many, including such diverse subjects as biology and economics."

In 1904 Professor Cooley was one of thirteen members of a Committee on Training for Social Workers, organized at the National Conference of Charities and Correction and chaired by Rev. Graham Taylor of the Chicago Commons and the University of Chicago. Committee members from universities and charity organization societies were instrumental in having papers presented at subsequent conferences on the need for training of social workers, thus demonstrating how "social science and philanthropy had come together in developing education for social work" (Broadhurst, 1971). At Michigan, Cooley authored a classic trilogy: *Human Nature and the Social Order* (1902), *Social Organization* (1909), and *The Social Process* (1918). He taught the first social work course at the university, entitled "Seminary in Principles of Social Case Work" in 1913. He taught courses in the 1921 Curriculum in Social Work, including the basic sociology course and a course on social process.

ARTHUR E. WOOD. Professor Arthur E. Wood joined the faculty in 1917. He was a graduate of Harvard in 1906. He also earned a bachelor of sacred theology degree in 1911 from Harvard. He earned his Ph.D. degree at the University of Pennsylvania in 1920, completing a dissertation on "Some Unsolved Problems of a University Town" (Wood, 1920). In 1921 he taught a sociology course on social casework first taught by Cooley, "intended for those who mean to follow some phase of social work as a profession" (University of Michigan Catalogue, 1921–22). At this time, sociology courses were taught in the Department of Economics and Political Economy, as the Department of Sociology was not established until 1931. Before the Curriculum in Social Work was formally established, Professor Wood was developing courses on social problems and social work. He taught courses entitled "Criminology," "Community Problems," "Problems of Poverty," and "The Family" and arranged for a few students to receive credit for fieldwork in social agencies.

An indication of Professor Wood's interest and expertise in the field of social work is found in his publications. In 1919 Wood, as an assistant professor of sociology, and Harry L. Lurie, director of the Research Bureau of the Associated Charities of Detroit, published *Trouble Cases: A Study of the More Difficult Family Problems and the Work upon Them of the Detroit Social Agencies*. In this book, Wood and Lurie called for the training of social workers in Detroit. The study focused on "a disconnected system into which drift thousands of men, women, and children, with varying degrees and kinds of need, insufficient income, ill health, disruptions of family life" (Wood & Lurie, 1919). A significant part of this study was a review of cases in social agencies and the methods of social workers, principally the technique of casework, including investigation, diagnosis, and treatment. A major finding of the study related to social work education:

> The defects that have been revealed in the social work upon these "troubled cases" point to a very definite need for more trained case workers in Detroit. The administration of relief, medical, and other services, required competent social workers, and it is desirable that more and better trained case workers be brought into the specialized fields of social service such as the courts and institutions.

Wood was appointed director of the Curriculum in Social Work in 1921 within the College of Literature, Science, and the Arts. In making Wood professor emeritus in 1952, the regents noted that:

> Professor Wood's career has been an unusually varied and significant one for its impact both upon this University and upon the social structure of the State. The provision of opportunities for our students to gain professional experience in social work are largely due to his initiative, and his long-continued studies, especially in criminology, penology, and community social service, have made him effective alike as a teacher and as counselor on the social problems of governmental units and of organizations, such as the Ann Arbor Community Fund, the Ann Arbor Family Welfare Society, the Detroit Community Fund, and the Detroit Council of Social Agencies. (January 1952)

The Early Years of Social Work Education: Context
The faculty members at the University of Michigan just identified attended to philanthropy, charity, and social work in their teaching and professional activities. As formal social work education programs were developing in the United States, Michigan professors—especially Adams, Cooley, and Wood—interacted with faculty members at other universities as well as with community leaders. They played important roles in national welfare organizations concerned with education in the social sciences. A brief discussion of the nature of social work education prior to 1921 provides a context for examining the initiation of a formal program for social work education at Michigan in that year.

Most social work historians attribute the beginning of social work education in the United States to the early 1890s (Coohey, 1999; Feldman & Kamerman, 2001; Wenocur & Reisch, 1989). While apprenticeship programs were conducted prior to this time, conferences and summer sessions were organized to meet the educational needs of philanthropic workers more fully. With a strong practice orientation, these programs were soon supplemented by formal one- or two-year programs, usually for college graduates and/or persons with social welfare/charity work experience. Hence, some current schools of social work date their "establishment" to these early forms of "training schools" sponsored by social agencies and charity organizations, loosely related to academic institutions but not offering academic degrees (Steiner, 1921).

Calls for the training of social workers came from the leaders of the settlement movement and the Charity Organization Societies of the late 1800s and early 1900s, as well as professors in educational institutions. The most often-quoted calls were at National Conferences—for example, presentations by Zilpha Smith of the Boston Associated Charities in 1892, Anna L. Dawes of Boston in 1893, Jane Addams of Hull House, Chicago, in 1893, Mary Richmond of the Baltimore Charity Organization Society in 1897, Philip Ayres of the New York Charity Organization Society in 1899, and Jeffrey Brackett of Baltimore in 1901.

In 1897 Mary Richmond, secretary of the Baltimore Charity Organization Society, presented a paper at the National Conference of Charities and Correction entitled "The Need of a Training School in Applied Philanthropy." In this presentation, Richmond noted: "The question now is how to get educated young men and women to make a life vocation of charity organization work. We must educate them" (1897). This proposal was linked closely to the creation of the Summer School in Philanthropic Work in New York City in 1898 (Pumphrey, 1956). Richmond's book, *Friendly Visiting Among the Poor* (1899), was used in the Summer School in New York in 1899 (Kahn, 2001). Richmond further developed her ideas on education in her book *First Steps in Social Service Treatment: A Textbook for Caseworkers* (1911), followed by the publication of *Social Diagnosis* in 1917, and *What Is Social Case Work?* in 1922.

In Chicago, Jane Addams, founder of Hull House, called for education for social workers in a book entitled *Philanthropy and Social Progress* in 1893, in the essay "The Subtle Problems of Charity" in 1899, and in *Democracy and Social Ethics* in 1902. Addams' experiences at Hull House are described in her book *Twenty Years at Hull House* (1910).

In Baltimore, Amos Warner, associated with the Baltimore Charity

Organization Society and Johns Hopkins University, wrote what is regarded as the first social work text, *American Charities*, in 1894. In it, he discussed philanthropy, poverty, charity, the dependent classes, philanthropic financing, and the supervision, organization, and betterment of charities (Broadhurst, 1971). Wenocur and Reisch (1989) have observed that "Warner's book . . . attempted to distinguish charity work from philanthropic benevolence and arm its practitioners as educated, knowledgeable men and women."

Among other prominent leaders in the fields of charity, philanthropy, and settlements who supported education were Julia Lathrop and Graham Taylor in Chicago; Edward Devine, Porter Lee, Robert deForest, and Homer Folks in New York; and Roger Baldwin and W. H. McClain in St. Louis. Many other community leaders were involved in the emergence of social work education and the development of schools of social work. An extensive coverage of pioneers in social work education and social welfare can be found in the *Encyclopedia of Social Work* (Lurie, 1965), *Some American Pioneers in Social Welfare* (Abbott, 1937), the *Heritage of American Social Work* (Pumphrey & Pumphrey, 1961), *A History of Social Welfare and Social Work in the United States* (Leiby, 1978), and *Social Welfare Pioneers* (Stroup, 1986).

The First Schools
Five organized programs for training social workers are generally regarded as the first schools. In 1898 the New York Charity Organization Society's Robert W. deForest, Edward T. Devine, and Philip Ayres led the establishment of a Summer School in Philanthropic Work "for volunteers who wanted to deepen their understanding of the poor people they were dedicated to helping" (Columbia University, 2001). In 1904 this program became a year-long certificate course of study called the New York School of Philanthropy, with Edward T. Devine the first director, followed by Samuel McCune Lindsay, Devine, and Porter R. Lee as directors. In 1919 it became the New York School of Social Work, with "working linkages" with Columbia University until becoming formally affiliated in 1940 as the New York School of Social Work of Columbia University under Walter Pettit as dean (Austin, 2000; Feldman & Kamerman, 2001; Kahn, 1998; Meier, 1954).

The School for Social Workers in Boston was organized in 1904 through an arrangement between the Boston Associated Charities, Harvard University, and Simmons Female College. Jeffrey Brackett, a graduate of Harvard and Johns Hopkins and a social work leader in Boston, directed the school. He discussed the training of social workers in *Supervision and Education in Charity* (1903). Students from Harvard and Simmons took a pre-professional curriculum in their first three years of undergraduate study, followed by a senior year of courses and fieldwork in the School for Social Workers. The association between Simmons and Harvard dissolved in 1916, with the formation of Simmons College School of Social Work (Channing, 1954).

The St. Louis School of Philanthropy developed from a series of meetings in 1901–02 of workers in the St. Louis Provident Association directed by W. H. McClain. In 1907 a set of courses was offered in St. Louis, affiliated with the University of Missouri. These courses became a one-year program in 1908, with the program named the School of Social Economy in 1909. The program was given yet another name, the Missouri School of Social Economy, in 1916. This school was "shuffled back and forth between the University of Missouri and Washington University in St. Louis" and was dissolved in 1924 (Kendall, 1978). In 1925 the George Warren Brown School of Social Work opened at Washington University under the direction of Frank Bruno, and a school of social work was established at the University of Missouri in Columbia (Kendall, 1978).

Precursors and antecedents of the School of Social Service Administration (SSA) of the University of Chicago date back to the early 1890s, with the Chicago Institute of Social Science organized in 1901 as a part of the extension program of the University of Chicago (Abbott, 1941; Coohey, 1999; Diner, 1985; Wright, 1954). Diner (1985) dates the founding of the present-day SSA to 1908 when the Chicago School of Civics and Philanthropy was established with a two-year diploma-granting program. This program was brought back into the University of Chicago in 1920 through the efforts of Edith Abbott and Sophonisba Breckinridge as the School of Social Service Administration (Diner, 1985; Wright, 1954). "The SSA emphasized broad social science education and research. Over the course of the 1920s, Abbott argued not only that social workers needed the social sciences, but that social work was a social science, which she called 'the social science of social welfare'" (Shoemaker, 1998). This school also emphasized training personnel for public welfare services.

The Philadelphia Training School for Social Work began in 1908 as a short course of lectures within the University of Pennsylvania. According to Porter R. Lee, general secretary for the Philadelphia Society for Organizing Charity, this led to development in 1910 of "a definitely organized school with a curriculum providing for both class work and field work and for definite tests for graduations" (Steiner, 1921). The school was incorporated as the Pennsylvania School for Social Service in 1916, becoming the Pennsylvania School of Social and Health Work in 1922–23, and the

Pennsylvania School of Social Work in 1933 (Robinson, 1960). Virginia P. Robinson (1960) has provided a history of this school in *The University of Pennsylvania School of Social Work in Perspective: 1909–1959*.

The Expansion of Social Work Education

During the decade from 1910 to 1920, social work education was offered in a number of new programs, in addition to the initial five schools of social work. By 1919 there were fifteen U.S. and two Canadian schools that belonged to an Association of Training Schools for Professional Social Work. Social work education at Michigan was one of the very early programs in a public university, with only nine schools established in public universities before 1921 (Universities of Missouri, Ohio State, Minnesota, North Carolina, North Dakota, Oklahoma, Indiana, Nebraska, and Washington). These were mostly undergraduate social work programs in social science departments, usually developed "with a particular commitment to social services in the public sector" (Dinerman & Geismar, 1984).

It is unclear whether some of these early programs were at the undergraduate and/or the graduate level. The programs at the New York School, Bryn Mawr College, and University of Chicago were clearly at the graduate level, with the latter two schools offering a master's degree. The Bryn Mawr Carola Woerishoffer Graduate Department of Social Economy and Social Research, begun in 1915, offered both a master's degree and Ph.D. in social work. Some historians, such as Coohey (1999), regard Bryn Mawr as the first graduate school of social work since the program required a bachelor's degree for entry into the school and offered a graduate degree.

Austin (1997, 2000) has identified some common characteristics of the early programs.

- The earliest schools were established under private, nongovernmental auspices, followed by a number of schools in public universities.
- The curriculum was strongly influenced by agency staff needs.
- Some schools were undergraduate programs, but there was a move toward schools with one- or two-year graduate programs.
- Teachers in the early schools were mostly practice professionals, not social scientists.
- Most of the field training was in direct service voluntary nonprofit organizations, with casework as the primary practice method. (Austin, 2000)

As Kahn (2001) has noted, "The social work school had to be invented." The early schools began with lecture series by practitioners and professors, and

as Wright (1954) observed in relation to the program at Chicago, "Most of
the courses were series of lectures on one subject given by almost as many
different people as there were sessions in the series. One looks in vain for
any semblance of a curriculum or an integrated program of study."

PART TWO   Curriculum in Social Work: 1921–35

At a meeting of the regents of the University of Michigan in January 1921,
the Committee on Educational Policies

> reported that a hearing had been held with representative citizens of the
> state in regard to the establishment of a School for the training of social and
> civic workers. Upon the recommendation of the Committee, and a mo-
> tion of Regent Lelend, the following resolution was adopted: Resolved, that
> the President in cooperation with the Deans and other persons concerned
> make a careful study of the needs for the training of social workers in the
> State of Michigan, and the best methods by which the University could un-
> dertake to meet these needs, and that they report their conclusions to the
> Regents' Committee on Educational Policies. (Board of Regents, 1921)

Based on this study and report, in May 1921 the regents authorized
the establishment of a Curriculum in Social Work.

> On motion of Regent Murfin the Board adopted a plan for correlating
> courses for prospective social service workers in general accord with the
> following outline: A special curriculum will be provided in the College of
> Literature, Science, and the Arts of the University of Michigan for the train-
> ing of social workers, such curriculum to include the usual requirements
> for the Bachelors degree and to be subject to the approval of the Dean of
> the College of Literature, Science, and the Arts. Dr. A. E. Wood is to be
> appointed Director of the Curriculum for the training of social workers.
> (Board of Regents, 1921)

In terms of university organization, a "curriculum" was "a group of courses
selected from various departments and so arranged as to constitute a uni-
fied program centering about a given subject" (Wood, 1951).

The regents' action to create a Curriculum in Social Work also stated
that a master of arts degree could be completed, with requirements beyond
class work: "a considerable amount of field work will be assigned under

supervision and in connection with the social agencies in Detroit and Ann Arbor" (Board of Regents, 1921). Documents examined in the regents' proceedings and university catalogues do not show that curriculum requirements for such a master's degree were ever developed or that any person was granted this degree from 1921 to 1935.

The 1921–22 *University Catalogue* stated:

> The curriculum for the training of social workers is designed to meet the increasing demands for training persons in the various fields of public and private philanthropy. Among the different agencies are Associated Charities or Family Welfare Agencies, Public Welfare Departments, Hospitals, Medical and Psychiatric Clinics, Child Welfare Societies, Industrial Welfare Departments of Factories and Stores, Institutions for Dependents and Defectives, Financial Federations, Recreation Courses, Settlements, Civic Leagues, Chambers of Commerce, Research Bureaus, and many other organizations of similar or allied purpose.

Students from Michigan enrolling in this 1921–22 academic year paid a $10 matriculation fee, nonresidents, $25. Michigan residents also paid annual fees of $82 for men, $77 for women; nonresidents, $107 for men, $102 for women (Hinsdale, 1906).

The Social Science Influence
By regental action in 1921, Arthur E. Wood directed the social work curriculum, teaching both social work and sociology courses. He had a close association with Professor Charles H. Cooley, who taught sociology courses for social science and social work students. Cooley's writings in sociology related to the social work curriculum, and his influence on Wood are apparent in an article in the *American Journal of Sociology* in 1930: "C. H. Cooley: An Appreciation." In this article, Wood reflects upon Professor Cooley's manner of thought and his personal qualities. Wood (1930) recalled that Cooley "valued sociology as a means for the interpretation of life-situations." Cooley was known for reading literature and philosophy, and from this broad reading he "sought wisdom, criticism of life, currents of thought, and clues to the understanding of personality and human behavior."

According to Wood (1930), Cooley defined sociology as "the science of man in the group" and believed "that the materials for this social science must be chiefly derived from a study of the ways in which individual behavior . . . are socially determined by the behavior patterns of the group."

Cooley's interest in social work was apparent in his establishing "the foundations for the modern study of child behavior through the case histories of our Child Guidance Clinics." Wood asserts that Cooley was the central figure in the establishment of courses in sociology at the University of Michigan between 1894 and 1917.

In *The Philosophy of Community Organization*, Wood (1922) recognized two approaches to defining community organization: (1) "the whole broad field of community life," including "the structure, functions, and interrelationships of organized groups and institutions" or (2) "the efforts of social workers to organize constructive forces on behalf of improved standards of living." It is this second definition that Wood linked to philanthropy and the efforts coming out of the Charity Organization Society movement, and the development of financial federations, consumers' co-operatives, health organizations, and recreation/leisure-time organizations. Regarding community organizations, Wood concluded: "Fifty years of social work have not been in vain if as a result an increasing number of people have begun to see the community and the value of effort on its behalf."

In *Community Problems*, Wood (1928) examined "a variety of ways by which communities of different types are planning and organizing to further the efficiency and socialization of their inhabitants." In the preface to this text, Wood notes, "The author makes 'no bones' to confess that his interest in general problems of social organization and control was first aroused through direct observation from the angle of a social settlement of the ill health, delinquency, disorder, and squalor that is to be found in an impoverished city area." In this text, Wood goes on to identify a role for social science in social work:

> Unless social science has constructive suggestions to make concerning the problems that infest such an area, we might as well return to a mumbling of outworn theological shibboleths. . . . However we are not restricted to such a dreary prospect. The humanized social science of our day is delving to the roots of social maladjustment as it affects both communities and individuals therein. The correlate of social science is social work. The former is normative, giving us a rational basis for community efforts; the latter has an ameliorative purpose, but seeks a scientific basis.

The First Social Work Curriculum

The 1921–22 *University of Michigan Catalogue* indicated that the new Curriculum in Social Work "referred to three groups from which recruits for social work are drawn. These are undergraduates, graduate students, and mature students who may not have the A.B. degree, but whose training and experience qualify them for certain positions in the field." Undergraduates taking this curriculum were "subjected to all the requirements governing admission, election of studies, graduation, etc. of the College of L.S. & A." As this catalogue noted: "It is expected that undergraduates following this curriculum shall do their major work in the social sciences, including Sociology, Political Science, Economics, Biology, Psychology, History, and Philosophy." The following program of studies was suggested:

> *First year courses*
> Rhetoric, Mathematics, History, Foreign language, Botany or Zoology or Geology
> *Second year*
> English, Economics, Political Science, Zoology, Psychology, Philosophy, Sociology, Foreign language
> *Third year*
> Mathematics (statistics), Political Science, Zoology (heredity), Psychology, Philosophy, Sociology, Foreign language
> *Fourth year*
> Economics, Political Science, Sociology, Psychology (race differences), Psychiatry, Public Health, Electives

Sections of the basic sociology course were taught by Professor Charles H. Cooley and three sociology instructors—Roy H. Holmes, Lowell Carr, and Karl W. Guenther. A range of courses were offered under the title "sociology," including Social Process, Rural Sociology, Social Evolution, Immigration, Criminology, Family, Principles of Social Work, Community Problems, and Problems of Poverty. Economics courses included Principles of Economics, Principles of Accounting, and Labor Problems. Political science courses included American Government, Municipal Government, and Municipal Administration. Psychology courses included General Psychology and Individual and Race Differences. Philosophy courses included Introductory to Psychology, Introduction to Systematic Ethics, Political Philosophy, and Seminar in Contemporary Philosophy.

Elementary courses in sociology, economics, political science, psychology, and history could be taken in the second year. In the third and fourth years, students took social science courses and courses related to social work, including electives on casework, medical social work, psychiatric social work, and child welfare. Students could also choose a course in supervised fieldwork.

As stated in connection with the description of courses in Sociology, a few
of the hours of the senior year may be spent in Field Work in Ann Arbor or
Detroit by students in good standing who are enrolled in Sociology courses
of a practical character. If the Field Work is done in Detroit, three hours a
week, exclusive of the time spent in travel between Ann Arbor and Detroit,
and continued throughout a semester, will entitle the student to one hour of
University credit. The same arrangement holds for Field Work done in Ann
Arbor, that is, one hour's credit will be given for three hours of such work."
(*University of Michigan Catalogue*, 1921–22)

Fieldwork credit was limited to six hours during the senior year. The Ann
Arbor agencies in which students could engage in fieldwork included social
service departments of the University Hospital and the State Psychopathic
Hospital, the Ann Arbor Family Welfare Bureau, the Ann Arbor branch of
the Michigan Children's Aid Society, the Washtenaw County branch of the
American Red Cross, and the Ann Arbor YWCA. Some scholarships were
available to pay expenses for weekly travel between Detroit and Ann Arbor.

By 1932 members of the Sociology Department staff directly concerned
with the Curriculum in Social Work included Professors Arthur Wood and
Mildred Valentine as well as the following individuals in the community:
E. W. Mallory, Psychopathic Hospital; Dorothy Ketcham, Social Service De-
partment of the University Hospital; Fred R. Johnson, Michigan Children's
Aid Society; Leon Frost, Detroit Children's Aid Society; T. Raphael, University
Health Service; and Louis A. Schwartz, Juvenile Research Clinic, Detroit.

Organizational Membership

According to Wood (1951), the University of Michigan Curriculum in Social Work was admitted to the Association of Professional Schools of Social
Work in 1925 as a "school."

In June 1927 the regents of the University of Michigan authorized
granting a special certificate to those who had completed the requirements of the Curriculum in Social Work and had "performed a definite
assignment in field work, most of which will have to be completed after
receiving the degree of Bachelor of Arts" (U-M Catalogue, 1927–28). The
regents' action includes reference to completing "two months of field work
with the approval of the director of the social service curriculum and his
advisory committee" in order to obtain the certificate (Board of Regents,
1927). The suggested program of studies for the special certificate in social work appears under the heading "Social Service" in the 1927–28 U-M
Catalogue, with most of the fourth-year courses listed under sociology,

including Social Psychiatry, Case Work, Social Process, The Family, Community Organization, Field Work, and Psychology for Social Workers.

PART THREE   Graduate Social Work Programs: 1935–51

In the 1935–36 academic year, the University of Michigan initiated a program of graduate education in social work in Detroit in response to a 1934 report to the regents by a committee of prominent Detroit citizens, including Henry S. Hulbert, William J. Norton, and Tracy McGregor. For several years, civic-minded groups in metropolitan Detroit had urged the establishment of a school for training social workers. These civic leaders believed that "mere apprenticeship on the job was proving inadequate and that departments of sociology could not train students for competent practice in this difficult field" (U-M Announcement, 1946–47).

The view that evolved was that "the best method, if it could be had, was a professional school which would offer an adequate course of study and preparation on a graduate level" (U-M Announcement, 1946–47). The committee report to the regents "requested the University of Michigan to undertake to fill this need through the establishment of a school of social work in Detroit" (U-M Announcement, 1946–47), and the committee emphasized the need for a professional school at the graduate level. The University of Michigan had sought to meet the need for "trained" social workers through its undergraduate Curriculum in Social Work initiated in Ann Arbor in 1921. Also, Wayne University in Detroit had offered an undergraduate Curriculum in Social Work within the Department of Sociology and Social Work beginning in 1928. In 1936 Wayne University extended its education in social work to a fifth year of study and a graduate curriculum in social casework in the School of Public Affairs and Social Work (Dillick, 1984).

A third social work education program in Michigan began at Michigan State College in East Lansing in 1936 through a technical course for undergraduate seniors, designed primarily as training for emergency relief work. In 1940 a one-year graduate curriculum was introduced within the Department of Sociology. In 1944 a two-year program leading to the master of social work degree was introduced at Michigan State University (Austin, 2000).

The University's Institutes for Social Work Education
Graduate-level social work education at the University of Michigan began in 1935 as a program within the Institute of the Health and Social Sciences.

The program was offered under various organizational entities, academic requirements, and locations from 1935 to the present. These include:

1935: Institute of the Health and Social Sciences, Detroit, M.A. in social work (24 credits)
1936: Institute of Public and Social Administration, Detroit, M.S.W. (48 credits)
1946: Institute of Social Work, Detroit, M.S.W. (48 credits)
1951: School of Social Work, Ann Arbor, M.S.W. (48 credits)
1960: School of Social Work, Ann Arbor, M.S.W. (56 credits)
1996: School of Social Work, Ann Arbor, M.S.W. (60 credits)

The Institute of the Health and Social Sciences: 1935

In 1935, the University of Michigan Board of Regents took two actions related to social work education at the graduate level. First, it authorized the creation of a Center for Graduate Study in Detroit. This center was located in Detroit "in order to meet more fully the needs of students who are qualified for graduate study but who are unable to do their work on the University Campus" (U-M Center for Graduate Study, 1935). The center required a minimum of twenty-four hours of graduate work for a master's degree and was placed under the control of the Executive Board of the Graduate School, with details of class organization and financial matters handled by the University Extension Division. Second, the regents established the Institute of Health and Social Sciences within the graduate center, which included educational programs for study in two areas, public administration and social service. Robert W. Kelso was appointed director of the institute. At the opening of the Institute of Health and Social Sciences, the Executive Committee of the institute consisted of:

> Alexander Grant Ruthven, Ph.D., LL.D., President of the University of Michigan
> Robert Wilson Kelso, A.B., LL.B., Professor of Social Service and Director of the Institute, Chairman
> Clarence Stone Yoakum, Ph.D., Vice President in Charge of Educational Investigations, and Dean of the Graduate School
> James Deacon Bruce, M.D., Vice President in Charge of University Relations
> Carl Eugene Guthe, Ph.D., Director of the Museum of Anthropology, and Chairman of the Division of Social Sciences
> Henry Schoolcraft Hulbert, LL.M., LL.D., Detroit, Michigan

Clarence E. Wilcox, LL.B., Detroit, Michigan
Roderick Duncan McKenzie, Ph.D., Professor of Sociology
Roland Haynes, A.M., Professor of Community Organization

The Institute of Health and Social Sciences was first located in offices of the Children's Fund of Michigan and rooms in the Detroit Children's Aid Society (Institute of Social Work, 1946). In the summer of 1935, Tracy McGregor purchased a building at 40 East Ferry Street, the former home of the late Henry G. Stevens, and gave to the university the free use of the building. This building housed the institute classrooms and offices, and "the annex which was servants' quarters was converted into a library" (Andriola, 1940). Funds for the new institute came from McGregor and his wife, Katherine Whitney McGregor, as well as from the Horace H. and Mary A. Rackham Fund. Tracy and Katherine McGregor had established the McGregor Foundation in 1925 with a mission statement: "To relieve the misfortune and promote the well being of mankind."

Tracy McGregor had moved to Detroit around the turn of the century to run a mission for homeless men that was founded by his father. Katherine Whitney was born to a wealthy Detroit family but was not content pursuing the social pleasures of her class and became directly involved in helping people who were less fortunate. Katherine met Tracy while volunteering at a children's hospital and the couple later married. The McGregors were always concerned about the welfare of the less fortunate. For example, they established a haven for homeless children in their first home. Tracy McGregor wrote several nationally recognized essays on social issues. His efforts helped him to become one of Detroit's influential citizens, and he organized a group of civic leaders that met weekly to discuss and find solutions for community problems (School of Social Work, McGregor Commons, 1998).

Robert Kelso, director of the institute, was a 1907 graduate of Harvard University Law School. He was recruited to become the director from the Colorado State Relief Administration, a unit of the Federal Emergency Relief Service (Board of Regents Exhibits, 1935). The process of his appointment is recorded in the deliberations of the Board of Regents of March 1935. University President Alexander Ruthven sent the following letter to the regents in regard to the appointment of Mr. Kelso.

> For some time it has been evident that we need a member of our staff who can live in Detroit and keep closely in touch with the various agencies in the city which are working with us. At various times such men as Judge Butzel,

Judge Hulbert, and Mr. William Norton of the Couzens Fund, to mention only a few, have urged us to add an experienced man to the staff who could direct this work and, at the same time, give them advice in the matter of educating social workers in practice with their staffs. We have been unable to do this for two reasons: first, a lack of funds, and second, the difficulty of securing a man. Both of these difficulties have now been overcome.

Mr. Tracy McGregor has been so much interested in this work and in improving instruction in social work that he has agreed to contribute $10,000 to its support.

It happens now that Mr. Robert W. Kelso, a nationally known figure in the field of social work, a writer of distinction, and a lecturer of experience, is willing to take the position of Director of Health and Social Sciences in our Graduate Study Center because he is very much interested in educa-tion. Mr. Kelso is 54 years old, and in addition to his scholarly qualifica-tions, has had an extensive practical experience. I know him personally as does Dr. Bruce and Mr. Norton. Mr. McKenzie (R. D. McKenzie, Professor of Sociology) knows him by reputation. These men, together with Dean Yoakum and Dean Kraus recommend his appointment for one year with the title of Professor of Social Service and Director of the Institute of Health and Social Sciences, Graduate Study Center, Detroit. The appointment is to be at $7,000 a year on a 12 month basis.

This salary is higher than usually paid to a professor, but, since we are giving him additional responsibilities and a limited term of appointment, we feel that the amount suggested is not excessive.

It is understood that Mr. Kelso's salary is to be paid from a contribution to the University made by the McGregor Foundation, and it is specifically recorded that Mr. Kelso is to understand that this appointment is for one year only, unless funds can be found for the payment of salary beyond that date and that this salary is contingent upon the receipt of funds from the outside source already indicated.

I am, personally, satisfied that this is a remarkable opportunity to add a distinguished man to our staff for important work and the recommenda-tion has my unqualified endorsement. (Board of Regents, 1935)

Most of the regents responded in favor of the appointment, usually adding a qualification, "as long as compensation is contributed" and not from uni-versity funds. One regent noted, "The donation of Mr. McGregor toward the expense of putting a highly skilled man in Detroit in charge of directing graduate social work and educating social workers would seem to be of the highest importance" (Board of Regents, 1935).

Another regent, however, raised questions about the appointment of Mr. Kelso. In a letter to President Ruthven, the regent said:

> I scarcely know how to vote on the Robert W. Kelso matter. The "Who's Who" detail is so meager, with no length of service anywhere, and routine work in City Welfare, which does not indicate any special ability, or permanency, or continuance. One year he is in Washington, another in Colorado.
>
> I wish I could know what "Graduate Study Center, Detroit" means.
>
> However, the main thing is his proposed salary of $7,000, which will be $8,000, when we get back to the old salary base. When we have so many older faculty men at $4,000, $5,000, to $6,000, I wonder how they will feel. Can we satisfy them by saying this is from new money given us, when they can only see the comparisons?
>
> I realize our Sociology Department is weak, but hesitate to put a man at the head of it who is no teacher, and at such a salary. If you can enlighten me about him and the good he can do, it will be appreciated. (Board of Regents, 1935)

President Ruthven went ahead with the recommendation of appointment, stating, "Mr. Kelso is a nationally known expert in social work and will bring great prestige to our Department of Sociology and the Graduate School" (Board of Regents, 1935).

ROBERT W. KELSO. Robert Kelso earned his A.B. in 1904 and his LL.B. in 1907, both at Harvard. He practiced law from 1907 to 1910. He was an instructor, lecturer, or honorary lecturer at several institutions, including Harvard College, Simmons College School of Social Work, and Washington University's George Warren Brown School of Social Work. He held several positions in social service agencies, including secretary of the Massachusetts State Board of Charities; commissioner of Public Welfare, State of Massachusetts; secretary of the Boston Council of Social Agencies; director, St. Louis Community Fund and Council; director, Federal Emergency Relief Service, Colorado State Relief Administration. He was president of the National Conference of Social Work in 1922.

Several publications demonstrate Kelso's expertise in the field of social welfare, including *The History of Public Poor Relief in Massachusetts 1620–1920* (1922), "County and City Homes" in the *Social Work Yearbook* (Hall & Ellis, 1930), and *The Science of Public Welfare* (1934).

At the time of his retirement in 1950, the regents of the university noted: "Professor Kelso has served the University of Michigan well in the shaping of its programs in social work and in the training of young people for professional careers in this field" (Board of Regents, 1950).

The Social Work Program in the Institute
The Institute of Health and Social Sciences' specific purpose was

> to coordinate the teaching and research of the University in these fields (health and social sciences) in the City of Detroit and to cooperate more advantageously with social, educational, and research agencies in the metropolitan area. The general objectives are to equip men and women for professional social and public service, to offer fundamental courses at the graduate level in the social sciences, and to train investigators in methods of social research. (U-M Center for Graduate Study, 1935)

Professor Kelso's recommendation that the institute be funded over a guaranteed five-year period at $50,000 per year with a ten-member, full-time faculty proved impracticable within the university's means. The first-year budget was only $25,723—including $20,000 from Rackham and McGregor Funds, $200 from personal gifts, and $523 from student fees—and the staff did not exceed two full-time members and one secretary until the second year (U-M Announcement, 1946–47).

The institute included programs of study related to public service within "two general but closely interrelated fields: public administration with particular reference to governmental work and administration, and social service work and administration which is more or less nongovernmental or voluntary in nature" (U-M Announcement, 1935–36).

The 1935–36 U-M announcement of the institute's opening described a plan for a master's degree program in social work that would cover two academic years and a summer session. This plan called for the establishment of "training-center" standards for fieldwork, stating that an internship "must be performed under conditions of supervision, leadership, and training fully equivalent to the standards required in the faculty instruction of the Institute. Every assistance through field supervision and circuit-riding by members of the Institute faculty will be rendered to the student during his internship."

This announcement (1935–36) also set admissions requirements of a baccalaureate degree and at least 30 undergraduate hours in the social sciences, "provided they intend to make a career of social welfare service, and show themselves mentally apt and physically fit for this exacting profession." A personal interview and a physical examination were required of all entrants. It was noted that "only students who expect to enter professional service in the field of social engineering as a career will be accepted as candidates for the degree."

At the same time, the institute provided professional courses for public and social service workers "now in the field who desire to improve their training and to obtain certificates or degrees in public and social service work and administration" (U-M Announcement, 1935–36). The two-year program described in this announcement was not implemented; the program introduced was one year of graduate study (24 credit hours plus a semester of fieldwork) leading to a master of arts in social work degree.

The announcement of the institute for the second term, 1935–36, indicated that qualified students could obtain a doctor of philosophy social work degree and stated that "courses of study are provided to properly qualified students, leading to the degrees of Master of Arts in Social Work and Doctor of Philosophy in Social Work." There is no indication in university documents that any student ever pursued or was granted the Ph.D. in social work under this institute or within the Graduate Study Center.

The Master of Arts in Social Work

In its first year, the Institute of Health and Social Sciences offered a Curriculum in Social Work that led to a master of arts in social work degree. The degree requirements for the master of arts in social work were the following:

1. At least 24 credits in graduate courses at the Institute which yield credit for the degree.
2. Credit for all courses required for candidates for degrees.
3. Minimum of one academic year of full-time residence, or equivalent (part-time courses).
4. Satisfactory completion of a schedule of study worked out by the student with his faculty adviser.
5. Equivalent of one semester of supervised field work at a social agency approved by the Institute as a training center. No course credit is given for field work. Ordinarily study will not be permitted to carry field work simultaneously with full-time class work (6 courses).
6. Submission of a satisfactory thesis on an approved subject.
7. The candidate must pass a comprehensive oral examination which may cover material related to courses which he has taken, his thesis, and his field work experience. (U-M Announcement, 1935–36)

The social science course requirements for admissions are described further in references to the preprofessional background of the applicant that could be obtained at the University of Michigan, including sociology (principles, human ecology, community problems, poverty, social statistics, social institutions, social psychology), anthropology, economics (labor), philosophy (ethics, social philosophy), psychology (abnormal psychology, mental measurements), and zoology (heredity).

The curriculum for the master of arts in social work degree were required and elective courses. The required courses were Social Engineering, Principles of Case Work, Medicine and Case Work, Psychiatry and Social Work, Community Organization, Introduction to Social Research, Law and Social Work or Public Welfare. Some of the elective courses offered were Family Case Work, Children Under Foster Care, Techniques of Supervision, Nature and Varieties of Human Behavior, Mental Measurement, Organization of Public Welfare Programs, Social Legislation, Criminal Law and its Social Application, Social Planning, Public Health Nursing, Administration of Social Agencies, and Welfare Resources in Detroit and Michigan.

Electives in the social sciences as well as in education were offered in the Center for Graduate Study, of which the institute was a part. Students interested in social work in schools could take a course on the public school and social work, with such topics covered as "Relationship between the educational processes and the organization of welfare services. Health education. Play. Organization of out-of-school time. The school visitor and the home" (U-M Announcement, 1935–36). Another course related to school social work was Playground Management: "Principles of playground organization and management. Physical equipment studied with reference to safety, economy, and efficiently. Health protection" (U-M Announcement, 1935–36).

One of the electives available to social work students through the graduate center was a course in anthropology, Primitive Society, described thus:

> How do primitive peoples live? This course will describe in detail the technological, social, political, ethical, intellectual, and artistic aspects of the cultures of a number of representative primitive peoples. Why are societies organized as they are? Why do they behave as they do? These are questions the study will endeavor to answer. (U-M Announcement, 1935–36)

This course was taught by Leslie A. White, who became distinguished in the field of anthropology through his teaching and writing at Michigan, authoring classic books on culture such as *The Science of Culture: A Study of Man and Civilization* (1949), *The Evolution of Culture: The Development of Civilization to the Fall of Rome* (1959), and *The Concept of Culture* (1973).

Fees of the Institute

Announcements for the Center for Graduate Study and the Institute of Health and Social Sciences note that a matriculation fee was required of all applicants for degrees who had not previously matriculated at the University of Michigan. This fee was $10 for residents, $25 for nonresidents. The tuition for full-time work per term was $55 for Michigan students, $75 for nonresident students. In these announcements no distinction was made between residents of Michigan and nonresidents. The summer session tuition was $34 for both residents and nonresidents. Fees for part-time students were the same for residents and nonresidents—$15 for students enrolling for not more than 3 semester hours, $25 for part-time students with 6 hours of credit.

In 1940–41 full program students were entitled to health service and athletic privileges. Students could obtain the privileges of outdoor physical education for $3.75, Michigan Union for $5, and Michigan League for $7.50. The tuition for one term had been raised from $55 to $60 for residents and from $75 to $100 for nonresidents; summer rates were raised from $34 to $35 for residents and from $34 to $50 for nonresidents.

These rates remained the same until 1946–47, when the per-term rate was raised to $70 for residents and $150 for nonresidents. Summer rates for nonresidents were raised to $85. In 1950–51, just prior to the creation of the school in Ann Arbor, the rates were $75 for residents per term and $200 for nonresidents; for the summer session, $40 for residents, $100 for nonresidents.

Institute Faculty

The first bulletin providing information about the Institute of the Health and Social Sciences did not list faculty members for 1935, but stated:

> The teaching staff for the professional as well as the Graduate Study Center courses is in process of construction. It is impracticable, therefore, to announce the faculty in this prospectus, or to offer assurances further than the guarantee that the teaching in this new Institute will be of the quality which the University of Michigan maintains in all of her other professional units. An announcement of professors and instructors will be made in later bulletins (School Bulletin, 1935–36).

The Institute's U-M Announcement for the second term, 1935–36, lists as faculty two professors who appear to have been full time, Robert Kelso and Arthur Dunham. Eight lecturers were listed as faculty, two of whom were associated with the university's Law School (John B. Waite, A.B., LL.B.) and Sociology Department (Richard C. Fuller, A.M., J.D.). Waite taught a course on criminal law; Fuller, a course on social legislation. The remaining lecturers were with social agencies in Detroit, including Harry E. August, M.D., Children's Center, Detroit (Psychiatry and Social Work); Pauline Gollub, B.S., Jewish Social Service Bureau (Case Work); Ruth M. Hubbard, Ph.D., Consultation Bureau (Mental Measurement); Fred Johnson, A.B., LL.B., Michigan Children's Aid Society (Case Work); Claire M. Sanders, A.B., Council for Youth Service (Social Service); and Maud E. Watson, Ph.D., Children's Fund of Michigan (Behavior Problems).

ARTHUR DUNHAM. Arthur Dunham, born in St. Louis, Missouri, earned his A.B. at Washington University in 1914 and his master's in political science from the University of Illinois in 1917. He joined the Michigan faculty in 1935 as a professor of community organization. He was acting director of the Institute of Social Graduate Study Center in Detroit from 1949 until 1951 and remained on the faculty until 1963.

Before joining the social work faculty, he was the assistant director at Boyle Memorial Center in St. Louis; visitor and registrar at St. Louis Provident Association; secretary of the Philadelphia Social Service Exchange; secretary of the Central Council of Social Agencies in Newton, Massachusetts; secretary of the Child Welfare Division, Public Charities Association of Pennsylvania; director of the Pittsburgh Child Welfare Study; director of the Department of Special Studies, Family Welfare Association of America; and field director of the Pennsylvania State Emergency Relief Board.

Dunham also held several teaching positions at highly regarded institutions, such as the New York School of Social Work, University of Chicago School of Social Service Administration, Pennsylvania School of Social Work, University of Washington School of Social Work, Fordham University, Rutgers University, and the University of Pittsburgh. Dunham was the co-founder of Friends Meeting in Ann Arbor in 1935.

On August 20, 1935, Kelso wrote Dunham as follows: "Thank you for your letter of the 17th. . . . I expect all of the full-time teachers on this faculty to write, to develop their national reputations, and to keep up an interest in civic affairs. . . . I have declined to accept teachers from the University of Michigan simply for the reason that they lack understanding of our field and are spoiled forever for usefulness in our method of teaching because of the dogmatic rote method of teaching which they have followed so long. . . . It would be a great joy to work with you. I would count myself very fortunate not only in having your personality, but also in having your clear insight into administrative things, and your wisdom in the rather delicate job of preserving the right tutorial relationship with the student" (School Records). Dunham responded by telegram accepting the position at the institute, with a twelve-month appointment at a rate of $5,500 (Bentley Library Collections).

Although the institute was in Detroit, Dunham and his wife, Esther, decided to live in Ann Arbor. In their 1935 Christmas letter to friends, they said: "Arthur is now Professor of Community Organization at the Institute of Health and Social Sciences in Detroit, but we decided to live in Ann Arbor, 38 miles away, because it is a beautiful little city and has many advantages found in a University town. The commuting is long, but Arthur has certain days each week at home for writing and study and this eliminates some trips back and forth. . . . We are told that Ann Arbor ranks among the highest cities in the country in living costs; so from that point of view we came to the wrong place! Ann Arbor is well named. On these glorious fall days we drive through streets of gold; gold arching above us, gold drifting down upon us, with here and there a magic burst of scarlet . . . almost an enchanted village. We wish you might all enjoy it with us" (Bentley Library Collections).

The regents of the university appointed Dunham Professor Emeritus of Community Organization in 1963. The regents noted: "During his tenure at the University, Professor Dunham enhanced his national stature by conducting institutes for the personnel of community agencies in various parts of the country, by serving as chairman of the Advisory Committee of the *Social Work Year Book*, and by publishing, in 1958, an authoritative text, *Community Welfare Organization: Principles and Practice*. His own humane concern for the well-being of persons was made evident in his warm friendship with international students and his active social ministry on behalf of the Religious Society of Friends" (Board of Regents, 1963).

In 1974 the School of Social Work established a named professorship in honor of Professor Dunham, with Professor Robert Vinter designated the Arthur Dunham Professor of Social Work.

The Institute of Public and Social Administration

In 1936, one year after establishing the Institute of the Health and Social Sciences under which the graduate social work program was offered, the university absorbed this institute into a newly created Institute of Public and Social Administration. Only sixteen students completed the master of arts in social work degree offered under the Institute of Health and Social Sciences, with the remainder transferring to the two-year Curriculum in Social Work within the new institute. The new institute included a curriculum in public administration leading to the degree of master of public administration (M.P.A.). The move from the one-year study for a master of arts in social work to a two-year program of 48 credit hours leading to the master of social work degree occurred during the 1936–37 academic year.

This new institute was created to ensure the integration of professional study programs in public and social service fields, especially in light of their interrelationship in public and social questions and the common purpose that "arises from the need to develop the social structure for more wholesome living" (Institute of Public and Social Administration, 1936–37). One goal of the new institute was to "seek to encourage a deeper and broader understanding of public affairs" and to emphasize field training, research, and investigation. The two major divisions of the institute were the Curriculum in Public Administration and the Curriculum in Social Work, in which students earned the master of social work degree.

The committee in charge of Curriculum in Social Work in the Institute of Public and Social Administration consisted of Max S. Handman, chairman; William Haber, professor of economics; Robert Kelso, professor of social service; and Arthur E. Wood, professor of sociology. In addition to Professors Haber, Kelso, and Wood, the faculty for the Curriculum in Social Work were Arthur Dunham, professor of community organization, and Richard C. Fuller, instructor in sociology.

Six lecturers were affiliated with the program: Harry August, M.D., Children's Center of Detroit; Hugo Freund, M.D., Children's Fund of Michigan; Pauline Gollub, B.S., Jewish Social Service Bureau of Detroit; Robert H. Haskell, M.D., Wayne County Training School, Northville; Ruth M. Hubbard, Ph.D., Consultation Bureau of Detroit; and Maud E. Watson, Ph.D., Child Guidance Division.

WILLIAM HABER. William Haber joined the faculty of the University of Michigan in 1936 as professor of economics. He was actively involved in the social work programs in Detroit and Ann Arbor through his teaching and committee work. Haber earned a bachelor's, master's, and doctorate degree from the University of Wisconsin. He came to the University of Michigan after teaching at Michigan State College from 1927 to 1936.

In 1936 Haber served on the committee in charge of the Curriculum in Social Work in the Institute of Public and Social Administration. Each year he taught the following courses: Institutes on Social Insurance, Labor Problems in Relation to Social Work, and Economic Problems and Social Work.

Once the School of Social Work was established in Ann Arbor in 1951, he remained in the Department of Economics but continued a relationship with the school until his retirement in 1971. During the period of 1953–54, he was a member of a faculty seminar on the Research Basis of Social Welfare. This seminar, staffed by David G. French of the Russell Sage Foundation, engaged in discussions that led to the establishment of the Joint Doctoral Program in Social Work and Social Science. Haber served on the Coordinating Committee on Social Welfare Research in the School of Social Work from 1955 to 1970 and, once the doctoral program was established, on the Supervising Committee of the Joint Program.

Of special note regarding his relationship to the social work programs at Michigan, Haber co-edited with Wilbur J. Cohen two books on social security: *Readings in Social Security* (1948) and *Social Security: Programs, Problems, and Policies: Selected Readings* (1960). The second book was written while Cohen served on the faculty of the School of Social Work, having come to the university in 1955.

Master of Social Work Program

The specific purposes of the curriculum for the master of social work degree first offered in 1936 were: (1) to provide a definite professional education for those who were planning to enter public welfare work and private social agencies and (2) to provide opportunities for research and an understanding of the efforts to improve social practice (U-M Announcement, 1936–37).

The requirements for admission to the Curriculum in Social Work remained the same as those in the Institute of Health and Social Sciences. The new master of social work degree required 48 hours' credit, including credit for course work, fieldwork, and thesis work. Course credit of 12–18 hours was given for fieldwork, with an internship carried out for an uninterrupted period of at least one semester (U-M Announcement, 1936–37). Students with satisfactory field experience could be exempted from part or all of the fieldwork requirement. Six to eight hours of credit were granted for seminar courses in connection with the thesis. A grade average of not less than a B was a degree requirement.

Courses required for the M.S.W. degree were Social Statistics, Law and Social Work, Field and Trends of Social Work, Community Organization for Social Work, Introduction to Public Welfare or Public Welfare Administration, Labor Problems in Relation to Social Work, Principles of

Social Case Work, Medical Information for Social Workers, Psychiatric Information for Social Workers, Mental Hygiene and Social Work, and one of the following: Group Work, Children under Foster Care, Case Work with Juvenile Delinquents, Psychiatric Case-Work Treatment, Family Case Work, or Medical Case Work.

The social work program remained at 40 East Ferry Street in Detroit until January of 1942. At that time, the Institute of Public and Social Administration moved to the Horace H. Rackham Educational Memorial Building, at Woodward and Farnsworth Avenues in Detroit. Despite the obvious beauty of the new building, negative views were expressed about the new quarters.

> In this new building the Institute has quarters with insufficient space for its faculty and administrative offices, but with ample and highly appropriate arrangements for classrooms and library, but less accommodation for larger seminar groups. Space also exists for research laboratory work, but the Institute still lacks any research laboratory equipment for thesis and other research stridence. There is also no locker equipment for students, nor any lounge room for either faculty or students. (Institute of Social Work, 1946)

The Institute of Public and Social Administration, reconstituted as the Institute of Social Work in 1946, remained in the Rackham Memorial Building in Detroit until the School of Social Work was created in 1951 and the program moved to the Ann Arbor campus. The new School of Social Work was first located on campus in a small house at Washington and Thayer Streets, then in the Frieze Building until 1998, when the school moved to a new, dedicated building at 1080 South University.

The M.S.W. Curriculum: 1936–51

The curriculum for the M.S.W. degree remained substantially the same from 1936 until 1949. Forty-eight hours of course credit were required, distributed over four major areas: required courses (18 hours), elective courses (12 hours), fieldwork (12 hours), and thesis (6 hours). Courses continued to be classified functionally—that is, general courses, special fields of service, technical methods, informational courses.

Other requirements established in 1936–37 continued. In subsequent years, there were some changes in the course hour distribution, as a range of hours was permitted: in-classroom courses (22–30 credits), fieldwork (12–18 credits), and thesis (6–8 credits). The distribution of courses was usually pictured as required (16), electives (14), fieldwork (12), thesis seminar (6).

Beginning with the 1938–39 academic year, students with satisfactory field experience were exempted from an appropriate amount of the fieldwork.

Transfer credit is mentioned for the first time in the U-M Announcement of 1939–40. A candidate for the M.S.W. was permitted to transfer a substantial amount of approved graduate training for social work from another institution and "be given advanced standing as the facts may warrant." Under these conditions, the student was required to have a minimum of one year's residence and a minimum of 24 hours of credit at the University of Michigan. A list of cognate courses that could be taken by candidates for the M.S.W. degree in the Graduate School included Economics, Education, History, Hygiene and Public Health, Landscape Design (city planning and civic improvement), Philosophy, Political Science, Psychology, and Sociology.

In 1939–40, the institute introduced a Program in Public Welfare and Public Administration, which recognized "that many administrative positions in the field of public welfare require basic equipment in public administration" (U-M Announcement, 1939–40). The program awarded a degree of master of social work with a specialization in public welfare and public administration. Part of the work was taken in Detroit, part in Ann Arbor, with a total of 52 semester hours required: 16 hours in the required courses in social work, 8 hours in elective courses in social work, 12 hours in courses in the public administration curriculum, 10 hours of fieldwork (partly in social casework and partly in administration or community organization), and 6 hours for thesis.

In the academic year of 1940–41, the institute announced a summer session of eight weeks "to provide opportunity for study in regular courses to those whose plan of study makes the taking of such courses difficult when postponed to the fall semester" (U-M Announcement, 1940–41). Part-time students could take one course during this session, full-time students not more than three courses. From the beginning of the Institute of the Health and Social Sciences, content had been included in the curriculum related to psychiatric social work and medical social work, terms applied to social work practice in hospitals and clinics. The first courses were labeled "Medicine and Case Work" and "Psychiatry and Social Work."

In 1943–44 the strengthened training was available to students specializing in medical social work. The course in medical casework was replaced by Medical Social Work I, and a new course, Medical Social Work II, was added. Students interested in this area of social work were expected to complete a special project in medical social work, which was to be integrated with work in the thesis seminar.

The concept of specialization had been used in the early planning for the master's degree in social work but was not implemented in the early years of the program. The idea of specializations was once again introduced and implemented in 1949–50. In this academic year, courses were organized under sequences or specializations. Specializations were organized according to practice methods and occurred in the student's second year of study. Thus, the 1949–50 Institute of Social Work Announcement stated:

> All candidates for the degree receive broad basic training which it is believed is needed by all who practice social work. During the student's second year, however, it is expected that his program will be planned in accordance with his major interest in some specialized area of case work, in group work, community organization, research, or in the case of certain students with previous experience, administration. Special requirements and sequences of courses applied to each of these areas of specialization. The student was advised to work out his program with his faculty adviser in the light of these special requirements.

Beginning in the academic year 1949–50, all candidates for the degree were required to take the following basic courses in the first year: Introduction to Social Work as a Profession, Community Organization for Social Work, Public Welfare, Economic Basis of Social Work, Social Case Work, Research Methods in Social Work, and Mental Hygiene in Social Work.

In 1950–51 specializations were offered by the institute in the following areas: generic and family casework, child welfare, medical social work, community organization, research, and administration. In each of these areas two or more specialized courses, together with fieldwork, were offered. Basic courses were offered in other areas as well, and substantial advanced work was offered in the field of psychiatric social work. The institute made plans to develop full programs of specialization in psychiatric casework and public welfare.

New Faculty

In 1936 Eleanor Cranefield was added to the faculty. She was the first full-time faculty member to have a degree in social work, having completed her master of arts degree at the University of Chicago School of Social Service Administration. In 1941 Ralph Fletcher, a specialist in social research, joined the faculty as associate professor of social work. The next year Clarice Freud, a specialist in child welfare with a master's degree in social work, came to the faculty. Kelso, Dunham, Cranefield, Fletcher, and

Freud made up the faculty until 1948, when they were joined by Mary N. Taylor and Leonore Gottfried.

ELEANOR G. CRANEFIELD. Eleanor G. Cranefield earned her Ph.B. in 1929 and her M.A. in 1930, both from University of Chicago. Before she joined the U-M faculty in 1936, she was a social worker for the Crane Fund in Chicago and taught family casework at the University of Chicago School of Social Service Administration. Cranefield was on the university faculty for thirty-two years. She coordinated fieldwork courses and taught basic and advanced methods in social casework, as well as courses on child welfare and family casework. During her tenure at Michigan, she also lectured in the School of Public Health and in the Sociology Department, and she continued to lecture occasionally at the University of Chicago.

Cranefield was an expert in the field of corrections, and in her professional and public role she was a consultant to state and federal departments and an officer in social welfare associations. The regents noted: "It may simply but accurately be said that she became a national statesman (if the solecism is allowed) of the profession of social work. To this gracious and accomplished lady, the Regents of the University tender their most grateful and most respectful esteem as they appoint her Professor Emeritus of Social Work" (Board of Regents, 1963).

RALPH C. FLETCHER. Ralph C. Fletcher received his A.B. from Washington University in 1924. He was a fellow at the Brookings Institution from 1924 to 1925, attended graduate school at the University of Wisconsin in 1926, and received his M.A. in economics from Washington University, St. Louis. Before joining the U-M School of Social Work faculty, he held academic positions in institutions such as Washington and Duquesne Universities; the Universities of Indiana, Pittsburgh, California, and Wisconsin; and the Carnegie Institute of Technology.

Being an expert in techniques of social inquiry, upon joining the faculty in 1941 Fletcher taught the research courses required of master's candidates and chaired the school's Thesis Committee. He also taught courses on Budgeting in Social Agency Administration, Programs of Social Security, Labor Problems, and Social Legislation. He supervised or personally conducted studies of deprived persons in Toledo, of probationers and parolees in Saginaw, and of children committed to Michigan mental hospitals.

In 1966 the Board of Regents noted in the memoir making Fletcher professor emeritus, "And not only was he widely known and consulted here in the Midwest, but his personal geniality and comprehensive intellectual interests won for him a respectful professional acquaintance far beyond the purview of his immediate duties. . . . His colleagues gratefully admit the precision and rigor which he lent to the programs of instruction and research in social work here, and his students are deeply indebted to him for his close personal concern" (Board of Regents, 1966).

CLARICE FREUD. Clarice Freud studied at the Connecticut College for Women from 1926 to 1929 and received her A.B. from the University of Michigan in 1930. She did graduate work at the University of Chicago and received her M.S.S. from the Western Reserve School of Applied Social Sciences.

Before joining the U-M School of Social Work faculty, Freud was a caseworker for the Jewish Social Service Bureau in Detroit and the Jewish Children's Bureau in Chicago. She held supervisory positions at the Eloise Parole Clinic and the Jewish Social Service Bureau in Detroit, where she was executive director from 1941 to 1944.

Freud was born and raised in Detroit, the daughter of a prominent family engaged in real estate development. Detroit continues to have a street named after the Freud family. As Joyce Carol Oates, the novelist and poet, has noted, the street is correctly pronounced the Detroit way, "frood" (McGraw, 2001).

In 1960, Freud was responsible for Michigan's report to the White House Conference on Children and Youth. In 1964 Governor George Romney presented her with a certificate of appreciation in "recognition of outstanding public service." She received a merit award from the American Association of Social Workers "as a beloved and inspiring teacher of social work, and as a courageous professional leader." As director of the School of Social Work Office of Field Instruction in the 1960s, Freud organized numerous educational programs for field instructors.

In the 1974 memoir naming her professor emeritus, the regents noted that Freud "was an active and valued participant in the development and expansion of this School. She helped to develop curriculum in child welfare, social casework, and supervision. She served in the demanding role of Secretary to the Governing Faculty for many years. As a classroom teacher she imparted her own special enthusiasm, open-mindedness, and sense of values. Field instructors benefited from her strong investment in assisting them in carrying out their role in social work education. She had undeniable impact upon the social work field through her many institutes, workshops, and conference papers. She was cited by the Governor of Michigan for outstanding public service as the Chairman of the Michigan Youth Commission. She was a member of key committees of national organizations such as the Council on Social Work Education and Family Service Association of America" (Board of Regents, 1974). Freud's interest in and commitment to supervision and field instruction were expressed dramatically by her large bequest to the School of Social Work, with the intent that field instructors could benefit from educational programs and students from scholarship support for field placements in child welfare.

MARY TAYLOR. Mary Taylor was born in Ash Grove, Missouri. She earned her A.B. degree at Wilson College in 1931 and her M.S.W. at Pennsylvania School of Social Work, University of Pennsylvania, in 1937. Prior to joining the U-M School of Social Work faculty, she was a caseworker and supervisor at Children's Aid Society of Pennsylvania, a Humane Society supervisor in Cleveland, a caseworker for the American Red Cross in Cleveland, and a casework supervisor at Methodist Children's Home Society in Detroit.

Taylor moved through the ranks to full professor in the school, beginning with her initial appointment in 1947 as instructor of social work in the Institute of Social Work, Graduate Study Center, Detroit. She taught courses on the field of social work and school social work and was responsible for the development of field instruction placements in the public schools. She brought distinction to the school through her dedication to quality education for students in the most remote parts of the state through extension courses, and through her contributions to teaching at the graduate level as well as her role as concentration advisor in social work in the College of Literature, Science, and the Arts.

Taylor was the school's expert in school social work, exemplified through her training of visiting teachers and her affiliations with the Department of Public Instruction and the School of Education. Her memoir acknowledging her as professor emeritus of social work noted, "No one person has been so instrumental in furthering the cause and practice of visiting teachers–social workers in the State of Michigan. From Ann Arbor to Grand Rapids to Gaylord to Boyne Mountain to Mackinac Island, Mary Taylor has moved actively and forcefully to promote social work education" (Board of Regents, 1978).

LEONORE GOTTFRIED. Leonore Gottfried was appointed to the faculty of the Institute of Social Work as assistant professor in 1948. She came to the institute with practice experience in medical social work and taught courses in this area. Her professional and civic activities included membership in the American Association of Social Workers, the National Foundation of Infantile Paralysis, the Michigan Welfare League, and the

American Association of Medial Social Workers. She continued on the faculty through the academic year of 1952–53.

Summary of Faculty: 1935–51

Six faculty members continued with the School of Social Work when it moved to Ann Arbor in 1951, with Dunham having been on the faculty since the inception of the social work program in 1935, Cranefield since 1937–38, Fletcher since 1941–42, Freud since 1942, Taylor since 1947, and Gottfried since 1948.

The following professors served on the faculty between 1935 and 1951:

Eleanor G. Cranefield, Ph.B., A.M., Professor of Social Work
Arthur Dunham, A.M., Professor of Community Organization
Ralph C. Fletcher, M.A., Associate Professor of Social Work
Clarice Freud, A.B., M.S.S., Assistant Professor of Social Work
Leanore V. Gottfried, M.S.S.A., Assistant Professor of Social Work
William Haber, Ph.D., Professor of Economics
Robert W. Kelso, A.B., LL.B., Professor of Social Service
Mary N. Taylor, M.S.W., Instructor in Social Work
Mildred A. Valentine, A.M., Assistant Professor of Social Work
Arthur E. Wood, Ph.D., Professor of Case Work and of Sociology

Lecturers: 1935–51

At the start of the Institute of Health and Social Sciences in 1935–36, eight lecturers provided instruction. In the following years, the program continued to rely heavily on lecturers from health and social welfare agencies in the community, usually including university professors, physicians, lawyers, and social workers and social service agency administrators. Social work lecturers included the following individuals.

Of special note is the involvement of Professor Selma Fraiberg with the social work program through her teaching and her supervision of students in field placements. Fraiberg was also a professor in the Medical School and director of the child development project of Children's Psychiatric Hospital, University of Michigan Medical Center. Fraiberg authored the classic book *The Magic Years: Understanding and Handling the Problems of Early Childhood* in 1959, as well as a number of other books, including *Every Child's Birthright: In Defense of Mothering* (1977) and *Clinical Studies in Infant Mental Health* (1980).

Another lecturer of special note was Bertha Capen Reynolds, who taught in the institute for the winter semester of 1942. Reynolds, who had a distinguished academic career at the Smith College School for Social Work, notes in her book, *An Uncharted Journey* (1963), that in 1942 she took on "a temporary position as teacher of casework classes for a professor on leave from the Institute of Public and Social Administration of the University of Michigan, then located in Detroit." Reynolds noted that she spent her mornings working on a book, to be published in 1942 under the title *Learning and Teaching in the Practice of Social Work*, and her afternoons lecturing and visiting social agencies.

The Extension Program

From the beginning of the graduate program in social work under the Institute of Health and Social Sciences, courses have been offered through the University Extension Division in Detroit. Under an arrangement between the Center for Graduate Study and the Extension Division, in 1935 extension courses carried credit that could be transferred to the student's graduate record, but such credit was not counted for meeting residence requirements. A limit of 6 hours of extension was established, with a fee of $5 per credit hour for all students taking extension credit courses.

Because of the demand for instruction by social workers employed in distant cities, the faculty and lecturers providing the social work curriculum from 1935 onwards taught regular institute courses through extension, in which the majority of students were college graduates, eligible for admission to the graduate program in social work. The cities included in this extramural service over the first ten years were Flint, Grand Rapids, Kalamazoo, Pontiac, Saginaw, and Toledo. More than 500 students took courses in this manner during the first ten-year period. One purpose of the extension courses was "to provide training for groups of social work students on a graduate level, who were unable, because of their professional occupation, to come to Detroit for training" (Institute of Social Work Announcement, 1946–47).

Special Programs

In 1944 the institute developed a cooperative program with the Michigan State Welfare Commission to provide special preparation of caseworkers in the child care field in Michigan counties. Three courses were taught on an intensive schedule through a six-week period, after which students participated in supervised fieldwork. At the same time, students took two courses at the institute. Credits earned in this program could be applied toward the requirements for the master's degree. During the 1944–45 academic year, the institute initiated cooperative arrangements with the Merrill-Palmer

School and the Children's Center. Under these arrangements, courses could
be taken as cognates for the master's degree in social work.

A program of special studies sponsored by the institute was inaugu-
rated in the summer of 1945 in cooperation with the Michigan State Normal College and the American Foundation for the Blind. The program,
given at the Michigan State Normal College at Ypsilanti, was designed as
"a special summer course of training for both blind and seeing persons,
to fit them for positions as case workers, public assistance investigators,
and rehabilitation agents working with the blind" (U-M Announcement,
1945–46). Courses taken in this program could be used for advanced credit
toward the degree of master of social work. Courses in the program included:

> Fundamentals of Social Work
> The Field of Social Work
> Fundamentals of Educational Psychology
> Psychological Effects of Blindness
> History and Philosophy of Work with the Blind
> Causes of Blindness and their Social Implications
> Vocational Adjustment
> Administration of Social Agencies
> Medical Information for Social Workers
> Problems of Administration of Aid to the Needy Blind

Early Graduates

Suzanne Dayton Copland (A.B., Vassar College) was the first person to be
awarded the master's degree in social work from Michigan in 1936. Other
early graduates were the following.

> *Graduates in 1937:*
> Wilda F. Bolles, B.S., Michigan State College
> Joseph Bockall Cherry, A.B., University of Michigan
> Cora Elizabeth Shoecraft, A.B., University of Michigan
> Caroline Ruth Welz, A.B., University of Michigan
> *Graduates in 1938:*
> Eleanor Butzel, A.B., University of Michigan
> Agnes Derry, A.B., Wellesley College
> Virginia Faricy, A.B., Michigan State College
> Barbara Gilbert, A.B., Vassar College
> Hildred Jarvis, B.S., University of Michigan

Dorothy Jennings, A.B., Michigan State Normal College
Graduates in 1939:
Florence Booth
Marjorie Decker
Bernice Farley
Mildred Fritz
Nelson Jackson
Helen La Croix
Barrett Lyons
Wilma Wickstrom
Virginia Wolf
Graduates in 1940:
Zelma Arney
Clarence Clohset
Ray Johns
Louis Newmark
Beulah Whitby

A list of the names of graduates through October 1948 appears in the Institute of Social Work Announcement of 1949–50.

Financial Support, Budget, Financial Aid

Financial support of $25,723 for the Institute of Health and Social Sciences in 1935 came from the Rackham and McGregor Funds, personal gifts, and student fees. In the institute's first year, "the University paid nothing directly to the support of the enterprise" (*First Ten Years Report*, 1946). The second year, the university contributed $26,900 and received back $4,836 in student fees. The McGregor fund added $15,000 that year and the following four years. During the following years, the university increased its support to $39,710 in 1944–45, with $12,933 from student fees.

During the first ten years of the institute, 306 single-semester scholarships were given to students for tuition and living expenses, "especially during field work activities." Sources of these scholarships included the Michigan State Welfare Department, Veterans Assistance Program of Michigan, the American Foundation for the Blind, the Community Fund of Detroit, the Wayne County Consultation Center, the McGregor Fund, and the Children's Fund of Michigan. *The First Ten Years Report* (1946) notes that "the McGregor Fund, always a friend of the Institute, selects a few especially worthy students for scholarship aid." These scholarships were viewed as "some measure of the increasing appreciation by agencies and the public generally of the value which the Institute has been rendering to the community."

Institute of Social Work: 1946

In 1946 the social work program in Detroit was changed from the Institute of Public and Social Administration to an independent unit, the Institute of Social Work. "At the moment of entering a new decade, the Institute has been reorganized as the Graduate Institute of Social Work under the director and the faculty as formerly, but with the addition of an Executive Committee responsible to the Provost of the University in problems of policy and development" (*First Ten Years Report*, 1946).

The Institute of Social Work Announcement of 1946–47 described the social work program as follows:

> The Institute is a graduate unit of the University of Michigan to provide a professional curriculum in education for the practice of social work, and to provide facilities for research in the field of social work practice. Headquarters of this unit are in Detroit. Supervised field work is offered there and in other centers affording field training facilities. The program is conducted at the Horace H. Rackham Educational Memorial, 60 Fransworth Ave., Detroit, Michigan.
>
> The Institute offers a specifically professional program of education for social work at the graduate level and seeks to encourage a deeper and broader understanding of public affairs. Field Training is emphasized. Research and investigation are planned to play an essential part in the program.

The curriculum of this new Institute of Social Work sought "to enlarge the technical side of training for work in the general field of social and public welfare and to relate it to the broader aspects of political and social life." The institute's specific purposes were:

> (1) to provide a definite professional education for those who are planning to enter public welfare work and private social service work; and (2) to provide opportunities for research and understanding of the efforts to improve social practice. . . . The majority of students find it necessary to carry on their studies in the Institute while employed, and because of the extreme fluidity of social work employment they are scattered to the four corners of the nation. . . . Facilities for field work are available in the social organizations of the metro area of Detroit, in intermediate and smaller towns in the vicinity, in rural communities, and in state and private institutions in

which the necessary training may be provided under suitable supervision. (Institute of Social Work Announcement, 1946–47)

Graduate Assistants in the Institute of Social Work

The Institute of Social Work provided financial aid through graduate assistantships. "These graduate students assist with many details of faculty duties other than teaching, and are selected because of their high standing and their efficiency" (Institute of Social Work U-M Announcement, 1947–48). Graduate assistants for the years 1946 to 1951 included individuals who later became leaders in the social work profession and in social work education. For example, Charles Lebeaux became a professor of social work at Wayne State University and coauthored with Harold Wilensky of the University of Michigan the classic text *Industrial Society and Social Welfare* (1965). Graduate assistants included Dwight S. Adams, Linda Akutagawa, Barbara Alleman, Josephine Blum, Flora I. Burgess, Antoinette Debler, Patricia D. Getz, Jean Haymans, Howard L. Kitchener, Agnes MacKinnon, William R. Miner, Jack Mitchell, Shirley Pearson, Martha L. Rupp, Jerry A. Shroder, Willie V. Small, and Lucile Turnquist.

Student Enrollment and Student Relationships

Prior to the move of the program to Ann Arbor, the Institute of Social Work U-M Announcement of 1950–51 noted that since the social work program at the graduate level was established in 1935, over 2,000 students had taken courses, with 265 recipients of the master's degree in social work. Enrollment was increased considerably through offerings by the University's Extension Service. The 1950–51 announcement stated: "The Institute, as a part of the University of Michigan feels a special responsibility to serve the state in every way possible. Close co-operative relationships are maintained with state social welfare agencies and institutions, as well as those in Detroit, and courses under the sponsorship of the Institute and the University's Extension Service are frequently given in key communities of the state."

During World War II, enrollment decreased in the graduate level social work program at Michigan and throughout the nation, particularly among male students. However, following the war, GI Bill funding for military veterans brought about an increase in enrollment of men in social work education. The National Mental Health Act, with the creation of the National Institute of Mental Health in 1949, brought about a program of student stipends and faculty support in social work education. This funding program had particular significance for the development of the new School of Social Work in Ann Arbor from 1951 onwards.

The Institute of Social Work Announcement of 1950–51 describes student relationships as follows:

> The student plans his program in consultation with his adviser, and the adviser feels a responsibility for keeping in touch with the student's progress and in counseling with him and assisting him, so far as possible, with problems that arise in connection with his work at the Institute. In most cases it is possible to keep classes small enough so as to provide for a generous amount of participation and group discussion. The faculty and student body, moreover, are of a size that makes it possible, ordinarily, for the full-time student to become acquainted with all or nearly all members of the faculty and many of his fellow students. An active student organization promotes social life and extracurricular professional interests among the members of the student body. A strong Institute alumni organization was established in 1948 and carries on an active program, including close and helpful co-operation with faculty on matters of mutual concern.

The Transition Years: 1949–51

Professor Kelso took a retirement furlough in the academic year 1949–50, and Professor Dunham was appointed acting director of the institute for the 1949–51 academic years. During his years with the social work program in Detroit, Dunham had gained a reputation for leadership in the area of community development at local community, state, national, and international levels.

During these transition years, Dunham and the faculty considered ways of improving social work education in Michigan. Alternatives considered by the University of Michigan and Wayne State University were merging the two schools of social work, expanding one school to handle the total program of graduate education in social work in the Detroit area, or moving the university's program to Ann Arbor. As a result of months of exploration, Wayne State announced plans to strengthen its program in Detroit. At the same time, the University of Michigan established the School of Social Work, to replace the Institute of Social Work, transferring the operation of the school from Detroit to Ann Arbor, effective July 1, 1951.

The regents' deliberations regarding the move from Detroit to Ann Arbor are recorded in a number of meetings. At its February 1949 meeting, the minutes of the regents note: "A proposal for the joint operation of the Institute of Social Work of the University of Michigan and the School of Social Work of Wayne University was referred back to the executive officers for further consideration and recommendation."

The March 1949 meeting minutes of the regents note: "The Board discussed a proposal by the executive officers for a collaborative plan between the University of Michigan and Wayne University in the operation of a school of social work in the City of Detroit." No action was taken, but the regents approved a policy statement: "The Regents share the view that collaborative efforts on the part of the University of Michigan and Wayne University will serve useful educational purposes and the public interest. They believe that the conduct of professional training in the field of social work offers an opportunity for such collaboration" (Board of Regents, 1949). However, they concluded that they could not share their constitutional responsibilities for complete control of any educational function performed in the name of the University of Michigan. Still, they authorized the executive officers to continue exploring ways of collaborating within legal limitations.

In June 1949, "the Regents authorized the appointment of Professor Arthur Dunham as Acting Director of the Institute of Social Work for the period of August 28, 1949 to June 30, 1950, with the understanding that during the fiscal year 1949–1950 final conclusions are to be reached regarding the University's purposes and plans with respect to participation in this field of educational activities" (Board of Regents, 1949).

The November 1949 proceedings of the Board of Regents indicate that "a progress report by the Provost on the discussions with Wayne University regarding the social work program in Detroit was received." The next mention of social work in the regents' proceedings came in February 1950: "The Provost made a progress report on the program of social work now being carried on in Detroit. All action was deferred, except that authorization was given to continue the program through June 30, 1951, and that at present no commitments will be made to any of the faculty beyond that date." During this period, the activities of some of the regents in regard to the future of the social work program were reported in the *Detroit Free Press* (1950). Under the heading "UM Considers Ending Detroit Social Work," Regent Stevens said, "These two social work schools in Detroit make for needless duplication."

Kenneth M. Stevens, Detroit member of the Board of Regents, "maintained that either UM or Wayne U. should carry on a social work program in Detroit, but not both." Stevens said, "I'd like to see one first-class school, not two like we've got." Regent Charles S. Kennedy said, "We feel that the program should be improved. Both schools have graduate students seeking advanced degrees in social work" (*Detroit Free Press*, 1950). The *Detroit Free Press* (1950) reported: "High UM officials have for months been studying 'what to do with the Institute,' which had a annual budget of $71,685. Long conferences between UM and Wayne officials on the possibility of joining the two social work programs failed to pan out, it was disclosed."

In 1950 Wayne State University made a structural change in the School of Public Affairs and Social Work, resulting in the establishment of a new School of Social Work as a separate entity. Charles Brink was appointed the school's first dean (Dillick, 1984). In this same year, Michigan's Institute of Social Work was reconstituted as a School of Social Work. Alexander Ruthven, president of the University of Michigan, announced that "the school will continue to work with Detroit agencies" and "the school will direct more of its attention to the educational needs of other communities in the state." President Ruthven said that "moving the social work school to Ann Arbor will enrich its educational program and allow it to use other campus facilities more completely"(*Detroit Free Press*, 1950). President Ruthven also noted,"This action by the Board of Regents is a recognition of the importance of social work as a field of public service. This should make possible the further development of a distinctive program related to the over-all interests of the University and the needs of the state" (Board of Regents, 1950).

CHAPTER TWO

The Fauri Years

The opening of the School of Social Work at the University of Michigan came about when the Board of Regents decided to reconstitute the Institute of Social Work, a part of the university's Center for Graduate Study in Detroit, and move this graduate degree program to the Ann Arbor campus. With this regental action in 1950, social work education at Michigan gained the status of a school within the university system. The school began operating in Ann Arbor in September 1951 in an old frame house at 320 East Washington, where the Modern Languages Building now stands. The old house held faculty offices and a small meeting room. Classes were held in Angell, Mason, and Haven Halls, with a library in Mason Hall. According to Professor Emerita Katherine Reebel, "The house was eventually torn down, but we used to affectionately call it the little gray house in the West. Others dubbed the house, less affectionately, as the shack." The school remained on East Washington Street until it was moved across the street to the Frieze Building in 1957.

PART ONE   The New School of Social Work

Regental Action of 1950
In keeping with the recommendations of the Executive Committee of the Institute of Social Work, in May 1950 the Board of Regents made the following decisions.

(1) That the Institute of Social Work be reconstituted as a School of Social Work under the administrative direction of a dean.
(2) That the School of Social Work continue to offer a professional educational program on the graduate level leading to advanced degrees.
(3) That the School of Social Work be a "state focused" program designed to serve the needs of the state as a whole with such operational arrangements

with the social agencies in other parts of the state as to give effect to this purpose.

(4) That the School of Social Work be situated in Ann Arbor, with such subsidiary operations in Detroit as may be necessary in order to draw upon the educational fieldwork opportunities there and in order to provide a minimum number of basic courses to the convenience of students residing in Detroit.

(5) That the educational program be so developed that it draws upon the large and varied resources of the university, through its agencies in Ann Arbor, in order to achieve a distinctive educational contribution to this professional field.

(6) That the educational program be maintained on a high quality basis and that special consideration be given to the field of public welfare.

(7) That an effort be made to encourage more well-qualified undergraduates of the university to look forward to this graduate educational program and professional work in this field.

(8) That the university plan upon a budget of $90,000 for this school in the year 1951–52, subject to the availability of funds.

(9) That an advisory council be established in connection with the school, representative of related interests within the university and outside, in order to strengthen the position of the school with the state.

(10) That this plan be given effect on July 1, 1951. (*School Bulletin*, 1950–51)

At this time, University President Alexander Ruthven stated, "This action by the Board of Regents is a recognition of the importance of social work as a field of public service. This should make possible the further development of a distinctive program related to the over-all interests of the University and the needs of the state" (Board of Regents, 1950). The regents' action was based on additional factors, including the desire to make more readily available the outstanding resources of the university in related fields of study and to bring the social work program into closer association with undergraduate programs related to the school's goals.

By-Laws of the School
Building on their action creating the School of Social Work, in February 1951 the regents established by-laws for the new school as follows:

> *General Purpose*. The School of Social Work shall be maintained for the purpose of conducting instruction, research, and service at the graduate level in the field of social work.

The Dean. The executive functions of the School of Social Work shall be performed by a Dean.

Powers of the Governing Faculty. The governing faculty of the School of Social Work shall be in charge of the affairs of the School. It shall provide the necessary courses of instruction. It shall prepare suitable requirements for administering proper curriculums, and appropriate requirements for graduation, which shall become effective upon approval by the Board of Regents. It shall recommend to the Board candidates for degrees. It shall exercise such other powers as are ordinarily exercised by school or college governing faculties.

The Advisory Council. There shall be an Advisory Council for the School of Social Work consisting of citizens of the State interested in the work of the School. The Council shall include some persons identified with both private and public social welfare agencies, either as members of governing boards or in professional capacities. The members of the Advisory Council shall be appointed by the Board of Regents recommended by the President. (*School Bulletin,* 1951–52)

The New School's Personnel

At their meeting of January 1951, the regents named Fedele Frederick Fauri dean of the school and professor of public welfare administration, effective March 1, 1951. Born in Mansfield, Michigan, in 1909, Fauri grew up in Crystal Falls, Michigan. After his graduation from the University of Michigan in 1930 and the university's Law School in 1933, Fauri practiced law in Crystal Falls. He worked in the area of rural resettlement and became a legal advisor to the O.A.A. Bureau in Lansing in 1937. In Lansing he worked in the state Social Security Office and became director of the Michigan Department of Social Welfare. He served the U.S. government in Washington as senior specialist in social legislation and specialist in Social Security for the Senate and the House of Representatives, general counsel of the U.S. Senate Finance Committee, and chair of the Advisory Council on Public Welfare for the U.S. Department of Health, Education, and Welfare.

Shortly after Fauri's appointment as dean of the school, the faculty set about planning a reception "in the form of an informal tea, a more formal reception to be given later. . . . Miss Gottfried, Miss Schroeder, and secretary Miss Glowski were appointed to the Planning Committee" (Faculty minutes, February 12, 1951). An item in the March 5, 1951, faculty meeting minutes noted: "Tea for Mr. Fauri. Miss Gottfried reported that the banquet hall in the Rackham Building (Detroit) has been reserved for April 6 from 3 until 6 for the reception to be held for Mr. Fauri. It was decided that the reception should be held from 4 until 6, rather than from 3 until 6. Faculty are urged to check the invitation list."

The faculty in the new School of Social Work included individuals who had appointments with the Institute of Social Work in Detroit: Arthur Dunham, Eleanor G. Cranefield, Ralph C. Fletcher, Clarice Freud, Leanore Gottfried, and Mary Taylor, along with new faculty Fedele Fauri, Helen Pincus, and Dorothy Schroeder. In a faculty meeting on April 2, 1951, Dean Fauri noted, "The Regents' by-laws call for a secretary of the governing faculty. Miss Freud was elected to take the minutes of the faculty." Irene Glowski remained secretary to the dean and faculty. In an April 23, 1951, faculty meeting, Dean Fauri "reported that he met informally with the regents last week. They expressed interest in the developments of the School and its move to Ann Arbor. Mr. Fauri expressed the opinion that although it is, of course, up to individual faculty members where they make their residence, he thought that from a University point of view, it would be desirable for as many faculty members as possible to live in Ann Arbor" (Faculty minutes, March 2 and 23, 1951).

The First Years in Ann Arbor

Dean Fauri opened his first annual report to university President Alexander Ruthven as follows: "Sir, I have the honor to submit herewith the report of the School of Social Work for the year 1951–52." Dean Fauri noted that the offering of courses in Detroit and Ann Arbor had placed an increased workload on the faculty. Fauri stated that "the willingness of faculty members to accept additional responsibilities and to give freely of their time beyond normal expectations has enabled us to make this transitional year a successful one." Fauri also observed that curriculum changes had been made in regular and elective courses "in order to strengthen the curriculum and to reflect current levels in regard to the social welfare field" (Fauri, 1952).

In commenting on activities of the faculty during the first year in Ann Arbor, Dean Fauri indicated that "throughout the year attention was given to the development of a more state-focused program with increased attention to the needs of communities throughout the state in accordance with the action taken by the Board of Regents when it created the School of Social Work." Fieldwork placements were established in thirteen Michigan communities. The school's faculty and special lecturers collaborated with the university's Extension Service to offer "certain of the regular School courses in graduate study centers and other localities outside Ann Arbor and Detroit." The Extension Program was expanded to include ten courses taught in nine communities in the state, with an enrollment of 186 students in these courses.

Educational programs were initiated with the cooperation of the Michigan Department of Social Welfare, including summer institutes for employees of the department and workshops for child welfare consultants and county child welfare workers taught by Professor Clarice Freud. Dean Fauri noted in his annual report that these educational activities represented "a supplementary but vital function of the School in assisting agencies in child services throughout the state to improve their social work services" (Fauri, 1952). The school also developed cooperative arrangements with the Merrill-Palmer School in Detroit for use of courses as cognates for the M.S.W. degree at Michigan. The school also continued its summer program of special studies for social workers with the adult blind, offered at Ypsilanti in co-operation with the Michigan State Normal College and the American Foundation for the Blind.

In his annual report for 1952–53, Dean Fauri stated, "It is now apparent that the decision to establish the headquarters of the School on the campus was a wise one." He then cited a number of activities occurring on campus, including faculty members from other university units teaching at the school; students taking cognate courses in other units; social work courses being taken by students enrolled in other university programs; a close cooperation between the school and the Sociology Department in carrying out the pre-professional program in social work; and faculty participating in an interdisciplinary seminar on the research basis of welfare practice, sponsored by the Russell Sage Foundation and staffed by David G. French.

Organization of the School: 1951–71
In creating the School of Social Work, the regents specified the responsibilities of the dean and the faculty. Membership criteria for the governing faculty, along with its responsibilities, were detailed in a manual of policy and procedures. The governing faculty included professors, associate professors, assistant professors, and instructors and resident lecturers with professorial rank who had served beyond one year. The faculty participated in the formulation of educational policy and program development through several channels: (1) as a total group, (2) through an administrative committee elected by the faculty, (3) through the committees of the school, and (4) as individuals. Faculty members participated in developing the school's curriculum through a structure of programs and areas. Program committees operated in the concentrations for students: casework,

group work, community organization, social welfare administration, and research. Other sequences of courses offered included human growth and behavior, social services, and social research. These programs and areas were administrative units, composed of faculty teaching in the sequences, with one faculty appointed by the dean to serve as head of each program/area. In addition to participating in curriculum sequences, faculty members were on standing committees in regard to admissions and scholarships, field instruction, thesis, extension, and library.

The pattern of administration and faculty governance established at this time continued through the next twenty years, with some notable exceptions. In 1964 a position of associate dean was established, followed in 1969 by creation of the position of assistant dean. In 1969 the school created a faculty council, with membership elected by the faculty and with an advisory function to the dean. In 1971 this council became an executive committee, with increased responsibilities and jurisdictions. Membership consisted of two faculty members from each rank and two at-large members.

A major responsibility of the dean was to propose and administer the school's budget under the direction of the vice president for academic affairs. A second major area of responsibility was in relation to the hiring of new faculty. All faculty appointments were by action of the Board of Regents, upon recommendation of the dean and approval of the vice president for academic affairs and the president. During the early period of the school, it was the "practice" of the dean to "seek assistance and guidance from faculty members in searching for new faculty" and to "secure consensus before recommending an appointment." As the size of the faculty grew, faculty still provided input to the dean on faculty appointments, but not all faculty members were involved in this process.

The dean engaged in numerous administrative functions, including convening and presiding over faculty meetings; chairing the Administrative Committee; making appointments of faculty to all committees except the Administrative Committee; formulating the budget; recommending new faculty appointments, changes in ranks, and merit increases; administrating educational policies adopted by the faculty; and representing the school within the university and at state and national levels. The associate dean's functions included chairing the Curriculum Committee, managing course assignments to faculty and faculty workload, developing grant proposals for outside funding, overseeing research grant proposals, and providing leadership in searching for new faculty and personnel.

Fedele Fauri served as dean of the school from 1951 to 1970, when he was appointed vice president for state relations and planning at the university, serving in this capacity until his retirement in 1975. Associate Dean Robert Vinter became acting dean in 1970, serving until the summer of 1971, when Assistant Dean Phillip Fellin became dean of the school.

> *School Administration: 1951–71*
> Dean Fedele F. Fauri 1951–70
> Associate Dean Robert D. Vinter 1964–70
> Assistant Dean Phillip A. Fellin 1970–71
> Acting Dean Robert D. Vinter 1970–71

Irene Glowski and Jean Berkley Parker were longtime secretaries to the dean and played crucial roles in the school's operation. At the time of Glowski's retirement, Jean Berkley Parker became the dean's secretary, hence accompanying Dean Fauri to the vice president's office in 1970. Roy Gaunt served as an assistant to the dean for several years as a financial officer, retiring in the 1970s.

In 1956 Shirley Anderson joined the staff while an undergraduate student at the university, hence becoming an assistant to the dean. Shirley "Stevie" Anderson spent her entire professional career of thirty-six years at the School of Social Work, working for four deans (*Ongoing*, Fall 1992). According to Anderson, her position of assistant to the dean required "almost anything and everything that deals with financial matters. If money is spent, one way or another it crosses my desk." She was responsible for the school's budget, personnel, startup and oversight of grant accounts, space allocation, and equipment and facilities. At the time of her retirement in 1992, Anderson noted, "The School reflects the values that I have. It is personally satisfying to be part of an organization that is trying to do something to make life better for others."

The Move to the Frieze Building
Through the diligent efforts of Dean Fauri, in 1957 the school was moved across the street to the Frieze Building. The Frieze Building provided the school with five classrooms, a small auditorium, administrative and faculty offices, and a student lounge. Dean Fauri noted in his annual report, "The new quarters in the Frieze Building have received the enthusiastic approval of students, faculty, alumni, and friends of the School." In the spring of 1958 a divisional library for social work was approved by the regents and located in a large room on the second floor of the Frieze Building. In 1966 the library was relocated on the north side of the Frieze Building in a large space that once housed a Carnegie Library operated by the Ann Arbor

Public Schools. Cristina Neal, A.M.L.S., served as head librarian of the social work library for many years.

The Frieze Building had an interesting history, having served as Ann
Arbor High School prior to purchase from the City of Ann Arbor by the
university. The university named the building after Henry Simmons Frieze,
who served as professor of Latin beginning in 1854 and as acting president
of the university on three different occasions during the period of 1869
through 1888. University historian Hinsdale (1906) has noted, "Dr. Frieze
stands as a charming figure, a man of the broadest literary culture in rare
combination with musical talent and a taste for fine arts." Hinsdale goes on
to say about Frieze, "The visitor meets his name and his face in the music
halls, art rooms, and library." For over forty years students and faculty at
the School of Social Work—as well as students in theater, drama, and communications (including Madonna) and several All-American athletes—
met Frieze's name as they attended classes at the university.

National Context

At the time of its opening in Ann Arbor, the School of Social Work was accredited by the American Association of Schools of Social Work (AASSW),
the organization under which the graduate program in Detroit had been
accredited. In 1944 the AASSW established a curriculum policy statement
that guided accreditation in this area. Social work programs were required
to include a curriculum with a generic foundation for all social work
practice. This curriculum included a "basic eight" set of knowledge areas:
public welfare, casework, group work, community organization, medical
information, research, psychiatric information, and social administration.
The school's program in medical social work was approved by the American Association of Medical Social Workers. Accreditation of the program
in psychiatric social work was granted by the American Association of Psychiatric Social Workers at the close of the 1951–52 academic year. Graduates
of the school were eligible for membership in the American Association of
Social Workers. Upon its founding in 1952, the Council on Social Work
Education (CSWE) became the accrediting body for social work education. Michigan's School of Social Work was among fifty-nine accredited
schools becoming constituent members of the new council. In 1954 Dean
Fedele Fauri was elected president of the council, serving a 1954–56 term.

The Call for Expansion of Student Enrollment

Dean Fedele Fauri was a leader in the Council on Social Work Education in
promoting recruitment for social work education. The expansion of the size

of the student body in the school at Michigan was the result of a clear direction established and carried out by Dean Fauri and the faculty. Dean Fauri's presidential address at the Third Annual Program Meeting of the Council on Social Work Education in Chicago in January 1955 set the tone for this expansion. This address was published as "The Shortage of Social Workers: A Challenge to Social Work Education" in the *Social Work Journal* in 1955. At the annual program meeting, Fauri noted, "To end this conference on a note of satisfaction with past accomplishments, however, does not strike me as appropriate in view of the many urgent problems confronting social work education. So I have chosen to focus my remarks on what I think is the most pressing problem before us, namely, the failure of social work education to meet the growing demand for trained social workers."

Given Fauri's background in the law, his remarks in this address about the profession of social work are notable. "Professions, it seems to me, develop by stages. One of the problems of those who would lend direction and guidance to professions is to know when one stage has been completed and another one is ready to begin. It is my guess, and I do not claim it is much more, that social work has completed that stage in which the task was to establish the identity of the profession and to differentiate it from other activities. To dwell at this stage too long brings with it many dangers. A profession can become so intent on its inner development that it loses its sense of accountability to the society which supports it and which it has been created to serve."

Some eleven years later, Dean Fauri restated more forcefully and fully this last idea. He articulated the continued need for expansion of enrollment and creation of new schools in the *Social Work Education Reporter* in 1966. In "Achieving the Great Society: The Contribution of Social Work Education," Fauri recognized the range of social welfare programs advocated by legislation that would lead to the "Great Society" proposed by President Lyndon B. Johnson. At this time Fauri served as chair of the CSWE Deans' Advisory Committee to Federal Social Welfare Agencies. He noted: "The major responsibility of social work education in furthering the 'Great Society' is to augment the social work manpower pool by making it possible to increase the number of qualified social workers. The social work manpower shortage is a concern in every community of the nation. The unprecedented rate of expansion of both governmental and private social welfare programs has caused a greater demand for social workers than ever before" (Fauri, 1966).

In his "Achieving the Great Society" article, Dean Fauri recommended that "social work education must expand at a more accelerated rate if it is to accommodate the rising number of students seeking admission to its schools and if it is to meet the rapidly increasing demand for professional social workers. I believe that it is possible to speed up the growth of graduate social work education without lowering its quality or making radical modifications in its present educational methods." Fauri went on to propose that enrollment be doubled by 1970. He noted, "Expansion of such proportions would, of course, require additional teachers, field placements, and facilities. Of these, I think the most difficult to obtain would be competent teachers. Doctoral programs must be expanded to help meet the need for larger faculties. In addition schools of social work should recruit faculty members directly from the practitioner ranks as they have done in the past."

PART TWO   The School's Students

Admission to the School
All faculty members in the Institute of Social Work played an active role in the admissions process. They created the criteria for admission into the School of Social Work and the application procedures, and they also participated in the selection of students. Faculty members continued this role in the early years of the new School of Social Work, with overall coordination and administration assigned to a director of admissions. Professor Clarice Freud was director of admissions from 1951 to 1960. She was succeeded by Professor Rosemary Sarri, who served in this position from 1960 to 1967, at which time Professor Sheldon Siegel became director, serving until 1972.

Admission Classifications
The *Institute of Social Work Bulletin* of 1950–51 defined full-time and part-time students as follows:

- A full-time student is one who is taking ten credit hours or more in class work, field work, or thesis research, or any combination of these, under the Institute, in a given semester.
- A part-time student is one who is devoting less than ten hours to work under the Institute. The amount of work which he may carry depends upon his employment or other responsibilities.
- A student employed in a full-time position may not register for more than four credit hours during any semester without special permission.

Such a student could not accumulate more than a total of 12 credits for part-time study before enrolling as a full-time student.

Students were classified as a candidate or an unclassified student as follows:

- A student is a candidate for the degree when he is admitted to the Institute either regularly or provisionally and expresses his desire to work for the degree.
- An unclassified student is a graduate student who is admitted to specific courses in the Institute but who is not a candidate for the degree.

The Institute of Social Work's classifications for students were used by the School of Social Work in Ann Arbor until a revised classification system was introduced in 1958–59. The school bulletin for this academic year stated that students were admitted to the school in the following classifications:

1. Regular admission. Granted to a student who is admitted unconditionally and who plans to work toward the Master of Social Work degree.
2. Lack of Preparation. Granted when the student has not completed, with acceptable grades, required courses in social and biological sciences. Readings will be assigned to make up this lack by the end of the first semester of registration.
3. Low Record. Granted admission on a trial basis for one semester.
4. Nonaccredited Institution. Granted admission on a trial basis for one semester.
5. Unclassified. Persons in this classification are admitted to specific courses in the School but are not candidates for the Master of Social Work degree and may not take over twelve hours without faculty permission.
6. Tentative. Granted in situations where the records are not sufficiently complete to warrant a permanent admission status.

In 1963–64 the definition of full-time student was changed from registration of 10 credit hours or more in the school in a given semester to 8 credit hours, with a part-time student defined as one taking fewer than 8 credit hours. These definitions remained the same through the 1970–71 academic year.

Admission Requirements

In 1951–52 admission requirements for the new School of Social Work included:

1. An undergraduate degree from an accredited college or university.
2. Completion, with acceptable grades, of at least thirty credit hours of introductory work in the social and biological sciences, representing a reasonably well-rounded preparation for advanced training in social work. Introductory courses in sociology, political science, economics, and psychology are particularly important. Other courses in these subjects and in anthropology, history, and biology may be counted toward this requirement. A student who lacks some of these foundation courses may be admitted conditionally, subject to special arrangements for meeting the requirements.

   Completion of an undergraduate course in the field of social work or its equivalent and of a course in social statistics is especially important.
3. Adequate training in English composition, even though courses in English composition are not a part of the thirty credit hours required.
4. Probability of success in pursuing professional education for social work at the graduate level based on the applicant's record in undergraduate and any previous graduate work. A student who is a graduate of an unaccredited institution or who lacks certain prerequisites can be admitted only on a provisional basis. In such a case he must make a satisfactory record in his work during the first semester in the School in order to acquire graduate residence credit in the courses elected.
5. Satisfactory evidence presented by the applicant that he possesses personal qualifications essential to the successful practice of social work.
6. A personal interview with at least one representative of the School before final admission and completion of registration. If a student lives at a distance, special arrangements should be made in advance by correspondence regarding this requirement.

Admission requirements remained the same from 1951 to 1952 until 1958–59, when the previous requirement for "adequate training in English composition" was changed to an expanded statement for applicants whose native language was not English. In such instances, the student was required to take an English proficiency examination during the process of admission, along with a second test upon arrival in Ann Arbor. Alternatives for students not showing proficiency included opportunity for study of English at the university's English Language Institute.

The 1958–59 statement of admission requirements remained the same until 1961–62. At this time, item five above was revised to read: "He must possess personal qualification considered essential to the successful practice of social work such as sensitivity and responsiveness in relationships, concern for the needs of others, adaptability, good judgment, creativity, and integrity" (*School Bulletin*, 1961–62).

A new admissions requirement was added in 1961–62: "All students entering the University of Michigan for the first time are required to have a medical examination prior to admission. It is essential that the applicant make his own arrangements for this prior to coming to Ann Arbor. Applicants will be sent a form on which a confidential summary report of this examination is sent directly to the Health Service of the University" (*School Bulletin,* 1961–62). This requirement continued until removed for the 1969–70 academic year. In 1962–63 there was a modification in the requirement regarding "probability of success," adding the sentence: "Skill in oral and written communication is important."

Admissions requirements for 1961–62 remained the same until 1964–65, when the personal interview was no longer required, and the wording was changed to "A personal interview may be arranged with a representative of the School before final admission. If the student lives at a distance, special arrangements for interview nearer to the applicant will be made by correspondence regarding this requirement." In 1965–66 the *School Bulletin* stated, "A personal interview with a representative of the School may be requested when the Admissions Committee requires further information before reaching a decision on an application. Applicants who wish to visit the School to discuss educational plans are to make arrangements through the Admissions Committee."

These requirements remained the same until 1967–68, when the *School Bulletin* stated, "A student may be requested to take the Miller Analogies or other test by the Admissions Committee." In 1970–71 this statement was revised to read: "Applicants are required to take the Miller Analogies Test. Other tests may be requested by the Admissions Committee. The Miller Analogies Test will not be required of applicants living overseas or from countries other than Canada." This requirement of the Miller Analogies Test was discontinued in August 1974.

Expansion at Michigan: The School's Students and Faculty
Student enrollment in the Institute of Social Work in Detroit in 1950 was 203 students (72 full-time, 131 part-time). With the move to Ann Arbor, the total enrollment decreased by 16 students, to 187. However, the Ann Arbor enrollment showed an increase in full-time enrollment, from 72 to 91, and fewer part-time students, from 131 to 96. Once in Ann Arbor, the school's full-time enrollment continued to become considerably higher than the part-time enrollment so that by November 1960, of a total enrollment of 250 students, 152 were full-time, 98 part-time.

There was a dramatic increase in full-time student enrollment from 1960 to November 1970, when the total enrollment was 769 students (581 full-time, 188 part-time). Increases in enrollment were due partially to the availability of federal student training grants and to additional university funding. Beginning in 1957, doctoral students are included in these figures, from 6 students in 1957 to 31 students in 1970–71. Enrollment figures are taken from reports of the American Association of Social Workers (1948) and the Council on Social Work Education (1954).

Along with the increase in student enrollment, from 1951–52 to 1970–71 faculty size grew from nine to sixty. This count of faculty is based on faculty appointed at least one-half time with the school, thus including some faculty with joint appointments in other schools and colleges. The faculty count does not include adjunct faculty or other part-time lecturers. Full-time equivalent faculty time figures were not available as a basis for computing the number of faculty members, so faculty counts are taken from *School Bulletin* listings.

Student Enrollment*				*Number of Faculty*
year	full-time	part-time	total	
1951	91	96	187	9
1960	152	98	250	20
1970	581	188	769	60

*Figures are for student counts on November 1 of each year. Academic year counts are higher, but reports of these counts are incomplete. The counts presented above do not show the increase in full-time enrollment for calendar years following 1965 when the school began a year-round operation.

The gender distribution of the full-time student body in 1951 was 43% male, 57% female; for 1960, 48% male, 52% female; for 1970, 40% male, 60% female. Data were not available to make comparisons in terms of minority student enrollment.

In 1965 the school's faculty determined to actively pursue the recruitment of students and faculty from minority groups in order to enrich its programs through racial and cultural diversity and to provide increased educational opportunities for minority group students. The faculty began to implement the recommendations of the Minority Opportunities Committee, under the leadership of Professor Harold Johnson, which included increased efforts in recruitment, financial aid, supportive services, and curriculum development relative to minority group and disadvantaged students. By 1970 the school's full-time enrollment included

76% White, 24% minority, foreign, and other students. The school led all university units in the enrollment of Black students, 15.7%, and also included Chicano and Puerto Rican, American Indian, and Asian American students. The faculty at this time included one Asian American and six Black members.

Full-Time Student Enrollment, Fall 1951–Fall 1970

1951 (91)	1956 (81)	1961 (167)	1966 (419)
1952 (96)	1957 (121)	1962 (194)	1967 (429)
1953 (85)	1958 (141)	1963 (234)	1968 (502)
1954 (87)	1959 (136)	1964 (272)	1969 (539)
1955 (98)	1960 (152)	1965 (346)	1970 (581)

In 1951 the school ranked sixteenth of fifty-one schools of social work in size of full-time student enrollment for the M.S.W. degree. By 1960 the school ranked seventh of fifty-six schools in full-time student enrollment. And in 1970, the school ranked first of seventy schools in full-time master's-level enrollment. The size of Michigan's social work faculty in 1970–71 was the largest of all schools of social work in the nation.

In 1970 the school's full-time student enrollment was 31 doctoral students and 550 students in the M.S.W. program. The M.S.W. students were enrolled in several methods specializations. The number of students enrolled in the casework program (165) was ninth highest in the nation. Compared with other schools of social work, Michigan was first in size of enrollment in group work (95 students), community organization (96 students), administration (73 students), and research (12 students). One hundred and nine students were in a program that combined social casework with group work or community organization.

Graduates of the School

As the student enrollment increased during the period between 1951 and 1971, there was a corresponding increase in the number of graduates with an M.S.W. degree. During the first ten years of the school, the number of graduates each year ranged from 47 to 67, with a total of 550 graduates. From 1961 through 1971 the range was between 74 and 306, with a total of 1,790 graduates during this ten-year period. By 1971 the school had graduated 2,340 students with an M.S.W. degree. Looking back, the University of Michigan's social work program granted 348 M.S.W. degrees in Detroit from 1935 to 1951.

Graduates by Academic Year

1951–52 (56)	1956–57 (44)	1961–62 (74)	1966–67 (205)
1952–53 (48)	1957–58 (47)	1962–63 (79)	1967–68 (228)
1953–54 (54)	1958–59 (69)	1963–64 (109)	1968–69 (233)
1954–55 (54)	1959–60 (61)	1964–65 (104)	1969–70 (279)
1955–56 (50)	1960–61 (67)	1965–66 (173)	1970–71 (306)

Fees and Financial Aid: 1951–71

Fees, the term used for tuition, for the full program in social work in 1951–52 for each semester were $75 for residents, $200 for nonresidents. Part-time student fees per credit hour were $20 for residents, $50 for non-residents. By the 1960–61 year, fees had risen to $125 for residents, $300 for nonresidents. By the academic year 1970–71, the fees (tuition) in the school per semester were $270 for residents, $824 for nonresidents. By comparison, for the academic year 2002–03, per-semester tuition was $6,538 for residents, $11,958 for nonresidents.

The relationship of resident to nonresident fees changed over this time period. In 1951–52 the resident fees were 37.5 percent of the nonresident fees. By 1970–71 resident fees were 32.7 percent of the nonresident fees. In the early years of this twenty-year period, the increase in nonresident fees was similar to that of resident fees. However, from 1960–61 onwards, the dollar increase in nonresident fees was considerably higher than the dollar increase in resident fees. For example, the change in resident fees from 1968–69 was $230 to $270, but for nonresident fees, from $700 to $824.

Throughout this twenty-year period, the *School Bulletin* listed a number of field scholarships, fellowships, and stipends available through state and federal social work training funds, community and agency programs, and graduate assistantships by the university. Many of the health and welfare organization scholarships involved "a commitment on the part of the student to accept a suitable position in the area for at least a year following the completion of his work at the School." A number of fellowships were available to second-year students in psychiatric agencies—for example, agencies related to field placements in child guidance clinics and mental hospitals and the Michigan State Department of Mental Health. Scholarships in medical social work were provided by the National Foundation for Infantile Paralysis, National Tuberculosis Association, Veterans Administration, and Wheat Ridge Foundation. In 1952–53 graduate assistantships provided through the university usually carried a stipend of $200 a semester and required 200 hours of service in connection with the activities of the school. By 1970–71 these graduate assistantships carried a stipend of $600 for a term and required 120 hours of service under the direction of one or more faculty members.

By the academic year 1956–57, there were a number of traineeships available to students from federal and state agencies as well as national foundations, including traineeships for psychiatric social work from the U.S. Public Health Service and the U.S. Department of Veterans Affairs; for medical social work from the National Foundation for Infantile Paralysis, the National Tuberculosis Association, and the U.S. Department of Veterans Affairs; and for rehabilitation services from the U.S. Office of Vocational Rehabilitation. By 1965–66 there was an increase in traineeships available from the National Institute of Mental Health and the U.S. Children's Bureau.

Year-Round Operation

In 1965 a change was made in the summer session to permit students to take a full term's coursework during the spring/summer session of the university. The spring/summer term was split into two equal parts. Beginning in the academic year of 1965–66, enrollment was permitted twice each year, with applicants choosing between two time spans. In the winter-term plan, a student could begin study in the winter, spring/summer, or fall term, completing the degree on an uninterrupted basis in one year and four months. In the fall-term plan, the student could begin in the fall or winter term, have a summer recess, and continue for two more terms. In previous years students were able to enroll in the fall or winter terms but could take only part-time work through regular courses in an eight-week summer session.

Student Relationships/Student Organizations

Faculty minutes of 1951 and thereafter contain reports on a range of student matters, including identification of student progress, students in difficulties, requests for waivers of time requirements, students with low grades, admissions decisions, thesis plans, scholarships, assignment of advisers, development of field placements, library issues, and book ordering.

The 1952–53 *School Bulletin* stated: "As soon as a student is admitted to the School, a member of the faculty becomes his adviser. The student plans his program in consultation with his adviser, and the adviser keeps in touch with the student's progress and is available for counseling and assisting him, so far as possible, with problems that arise in connection with his work." This *School Bulletin* made other observations about student experiences, such as the following: "Because of the size of the School, classes are usually small enough to provide for a generous amount of participation and group discussion. . . . Also, the full-time student is thus able to become acquainted with all or nearly all members of the faculty and many of his fellow students."

The bulletin noted that "an active student organization promotes social life and extracurricular professional interests among the members of the student body."

By 1965 students had created a student union. In later years, students created a number of student organizations representing special groups, including the Association of Black Social Work Students, Trabajadores de la Raza, Coalition of Asian Students, and the Women's Caucus. In 1969 the faculty of the school formalized student participation in the school's affairs by approving an arrangement of fifty percent student-to-faculty ratio of membership on school committees, with one faculty member serving as chairperson. The faculty council and governing faculty were not included in this arrangement. This plan for student participation was known as the "fifty-fifty plus one plan."

PART THREE   The School's Faculty: 1951–71

Introduction

The size and composition of the faculty of the School of Social Work changed dramatically during the period from 1951 to 1971. The number of faculty members increased from nine to twenty between 1951 and 1960–61, and to sixty by 1970–71. The characteristics of the faculty changed from individuals with social work practice backgrounds and master's degrees in social work and related degrees to a faculty with more than half of its members also having doctoral degrees.

During the period of 1951 to 1961, nineteen new faculty members were hired, with one retiring and four departing for other positions. Three of those leaving the school were on the faculty only one year, with one for five years. In 1960–61 the faculty of twenty included ten men and ten women. Thirty percent (six of twenty) of the faculty members had doctoral degrees, and sixty-five percent (thirteen of twenty) had social work master's degrees. There were no members of minority groups of color on the faculty at this time. From 1957 through 1961, four faculty members were hired to be involved in teaching and advising in the school's Joint Doctoral Program in Social Work and Social Science. There was considerable turnover in the faculty during the period of 1961–71, with over sixty new hires and nineteen persons departing or retiring. In 1971 the total faculty of sixty members consisted of forty-four men and sixteen women; thirty-nine had doctoral degrees and forty-nine had social work master's degrees; and seven were minority group members.

In the late 1950s and the 1960s, the increase in the size of the faculty was influenced by the school's receipt of federal grants for social work education. Funding during this period came from the U.S. Vocational Rehabilitation Services, U.S. Public Health Service, U.S. Children's Bureau, and the U.S. Administration on Aging. By 1968 twenty-two faculty were fully or partially funded by federal funds. Most of these faculty members were full-time on grant funding, usually teaching one course and engaged in field development and faculty liaison to field instruction sites. By this time there was also an increase in university funds for faculty, especially in the appointments to faculty associated with the doctoral program. The following chart shows the gradual and steady growth in the size of the faculty from 1951 to 1971, doubling from 1951 to 1961 and tripling from 1961–62 to 1970–71.

Academic Year/Number of Faculty

1951–52 (9)	1956–57 (14)	1961–62 (21)	1966–67 (48)
1952–53 (11)	1957–58 (15)	1962–63 (27)	1967–68 (54)
1953–54 (10)	1958–59 (17)	1963–64 (29)	1968–69 (56)
1954–55 (11)	1959–60 (19)	1964–65 (34)	1969–70 (57)
1955–56 (13)	1960–61 (20)	1965–66 (46)	1970–71 (60)

Profiles of Faculty Members: 1951

At the time the School of Social Work opened in Ann Arbor, six members of the faculty had served with the Institute of Social Work in Detroit: Eleanor Cranefield, Arthur Dunham, Ralph C. Fletcher, Clarice Freud, Leanore Gottfried, and Mary Taylor. Profiles of these faculty are provided in chapter one. In 1951 three new members were added to the faculty: Fedele F. Fauri, Helen Pinkus, and Dorothy Schroeder.

FEDELE FAURI. Fedele F. Fauri served as dean of the school from 1951 to 1970, when he became vice president for state relations and planning at the university. In 1975 the regents named Fauri vice president emeritus and professor emeritus. At this time, the regents of the university noted, "During his tenure as dean of the University's School of Social Work from 1951 to 1970, the School experienced both phenomenal growth and recognition as one of the nation's best schools. He was both indefatigable and indomitable in achieving the high objectives which he set for the School."

During his deanship, Fauri served in a number of national leadership roles, including president of the Council on Social Work Education, president of the American Public Welfare Association, and chair of the Editorial Committee of the first *Encyclopedia of Social Work*. In 1955 Fauri received the National Conference on Social Welfare Distinguished Service Award and in 1957 the W.S. Terry Jr. Memorial Merit Award from the American Public Welfare Association. The Terry Award citation noted, "Through his inspiration and skill he has built one of the outstanding schools of social work in the nation and has given new meaning to public welfare as a profession." In 1968 he received the Distinguished Service Award of CSWE "for his wise, far-seeing and effective leadership in addressing the problems of social welfare manpower and in opening the doors to lasting solutions through the promotion and support of social work education."

The Fedele F. and Iris M. Fauri Memorial Lecture in Child Welfare was established in 1985 through gifts from alumni, faculty, friends, and members of the Fauri family. A professorship named after Dean Fauri was awarded to Professor Edwin J. Thomas. A seminar room in Fauri's name is located in the School of Social Work, where a plaque notes that "his accomplishments in the field of child welfare and social work brought national and international acclaim to the School of Social Work and the University of Michigan." At the time of Fauri's retirement, the regents noted, "His matchless record of public service at community, state, and national levels foretells excellent and sure-handed administration in the sometimes controversial Sport of Kings. His experience in driving and training horses from boyhood in Crystal Falls insures a commissioner who loves the sport he has been called upon to administer" (Board of Regents, 1975).

DOROTHY SCHROEDER. Dorothy Schroeder joined the faculty as assistant professor in 1951, retiring as professor emeritus in 1973. Schroeder came to the university as a specialist in mental health with a broad range of experience as a teacher, researcher, and practitioner, including director of Girl Scouts and director of a guidance center. She held an A.B. degree from Vassar and an M.S.S. degree from Smith College. At Michigan Schroeder provided leadership in the social casework program, teaching courses in this area and in mental health services. Nationwide, she was a member of the commission on accreditation of the Council on Social Work Education and chair of the psychiatric social work section of the National Association of Social Workers. The regents named Schroeder professor emeritus of social work in 1973, noting, "Her career was marked with a particular ability to translate social science theory into a rational practicum for the social work student. She shared her rare talents generously with her colleagues in numerous professional associations and governmental agencies."

HELEN PINKUS. Helen Pinkus was appointed to the faculty in 1951 as lecturer under a U.S. Public Service grant, holding a B.A. degree from Stanford and an M.S.S. from Smith College. She formerly had been a caseworker and supervisor in the U.S. Department of Veterans Affairs and a supervisor of social work students at Western Reserve School of Applied Social Sciences. At Michigan Pinkus played a leadership role in the development of a specialization in social casework and psychiatric social work. Her teaching areas were psychiatric information for social workers, psychopathology for social workers, and social casework. Pinkus left the school in 1956 as assistant professor, moving on to completion of a doctor of social work degree at Columbia University and a distinguished teaching career at Virginia Commonwealth University and Smith College.

LEONORE GOTTFRIED. Leonore Gottfried was appointed to the faculty of the Institute of Social Work as assistant professor in 1948. She came to the institute with practice experience in medical social work and taught courses in this area. Her professional and civic activities included membership in the American Association of Social Workers, the National Foundation of Infantile Paralysis, the Michigan Welfare League, and the American Association of Medical Social Workers. She continued on the faculty of the School of Social Work through the academic year of 1952–53.

Faculty Lecturers
In the early years of the School of Social Work, a number of courses were taught by lecturers who each usually taught one course. Serving as lecturers in 1951–52 were the following eleven individuals active in the field of social work:

> Maynard Allyn, M.A. (Washtenaw County Bureau of Social Aid)
> Rachel Andresen, M.S.W. (Ann Arbor Council of Churches)
> William Avrunin, B.S. (Jewish Welfare Federation of Detroit)
> Ara Cary, M.S.W. (Grand Rapids Child Guidance Clinic)
> Cecilia Craig, M.S.W. (Ann Arbor Community Chest)
> James Cunningham, M.D. (Children's Center of Metropolitan Detroit)
> David Gage, M.D. (Saginaw)

Paul Kniskern, M.D. (Grand Rapids)
Faye Portner, M.S.W. (Ann Arbor Council of Social Agencies)
Clare Toppin, LL.B. (Attorney at Law, Ann Arbor)
Betram Zheutlin, M.D. (Battle Creek)

These lecturers taught courses in social casework, group work, interpretation of social work, problems of community welfare councils, community organization and group process, law and social work, and psychiatric and medical information. In the following years, additional lecturers from the community included Clarice Platt, Maxine Virtue, Ruth Jennings, Rosemary Lippitt, Rilman Buckman, Theodore Hoffman, Roger Lind, and Robert Morrison.

During the 1951–52 academic year and the years following, a number of professors from the Schools of Medicine and Public Health and the College of Literature, Science, and the Arts (LS&A) taught courses at the school. These included physicians Solomon J. Axelrod, William H. Beierwaltes, Ronald Bishop, Ralph Brandt, Roscoe W. Cavell, Robert Coffer, Stuart Finch, John Gosling, William Hendrickson, Melvin M. Lipsett, William Oliver, George Richardson, Majorie Shaw, and Herbert T. Schmale. Additional lecturers were Richard Cutler, Wilma T. Donahue, Selma Fraiberg, David French, Julian Lasky, Robert Moore, and David Streeten. Courses taught by these lecturers were public health and medical care, medical information, psychiatric information, psychopathology, development of the individual, gerontology, and mental measurement.

The use of community professionals as lecturers declined during the first few years, and by 1955 few of these lecturers still taught at the school. At the same time, the school increased the number of lecturers from university units, such as Medicine, Psychiatry, Psychology, Public Health, institutes, and the Extension Service. During the period of 1951 to 1971, the following social workers at the University Hospital and the School of Public Health faculty held faculty appointments with the School of Social Work: Josephine Cannell, M.S.W., Katherine Cavell, M.S.S., Sylvia Goodman, M.S.S., William Hall, M.S.W., Ph.D., Ruth Locher, M.S.S.A., Katherine Post, M.S.S., Jules Schrager, M.S.W., and Elizabeth Watkins, M.S.S.A.

The Changing Faculty: 1952–53 to 1970–71

For each of the academic years for this period, additions and departures of faculty members are noted. A profile is provided for each of the new faculty members by year of appointment. The amount and nature of the information provided about faculty members varies depending on the availability of records. Information for profiles on many faculty members was obtained from the social work collections at the Bentley Historical Library. Dates for hiring and length of stay are taken from the *School Bulletins* and are, therefore, approximate time periods.

1952–53
New Faculty: Patricia Rabinovitz, Katherine Reebel, and Faye Portner
Departures: Leonore Van Vliet (Gottfried)

PATRICIA RABINOVITZ. Patricia Rabinovitz served the school as lecturer from 1944 to 1951. During this time, she was a psychiatric social worker and social welfare administrator with the Wayne County Bureau of Social Aid. She held B.A. and M.S.W. degrees from Wayne State University. In 1952 she joined the school full-time as assistant professor, retiring in 1968 as professor emeritus. She taught courses in social welfare administration and social services and provided leadership in these areas of the curriculum. She was actively engaged in community service, especially through presentation of institutes to public welfare departments and in participation in federal government commissions on health and welfare. In naming Rabinovitz professor emeritus, the regents said, "Throughout her tenure here, Mrs. Rabinovitz remained on call as a leader of workshops and institutes for the National Conference on Social Work and the American Public Welfare Administration. Professionally active from coast to coast, she continued also to exert leadership in programs of social welfare in the community and the state. In consequence of her good offices here, students in social work became notably better prepared than before for administrative posts in social welfare agencies. In courses prepared and taught for the School of Nursing and for the Sociology Department of the L.S. & A. College, she attractively presented her profession to students only obliquely concerned with it" (Board of Regents, 1968).

KATHERINE REEBEL. Katherine "Kay" Reebel joined the faculty as lecturer in social work, holding a B.A. degree from the Pennsylvania College for Women, an M.A. degree from the University of Pittsburgh, and an M.S.S. degree from Smith College School for Social Work. Reebel came to the university with practice experience in public welfare and medical social work. Her teaching experience prior to coming to the university included professorships at the University of British Columbia and Ohio State University. At the school, Reebel moved through the ranks to full professor, providing leadership in the development of a specialization in medical social work, contributing in large measure to the casework program, and teaching about practice methods, health and rehabilitation, alcoholism, and gerontology. She served as consultant to the School of Public Health. In 1974 the regents recognized her accomplishments at the school by appointing her professor emeritus, noting, "As a dedicated teacher she has been a source of inspiration, guidance and encouragement for her many students. Her colleagues attest to her high standards of quality and excellence in the practice of social work and her willingness to share her special areas of knowledge in a supportive and helpful way" (Board of Regents, 1974). Now age 100, Professor Emerita Reebel continues to live in her home in Ann Arbor.

FAYE PORTNER. Faye Portner came to the school from a position as assistant executive secretary of the Council of Social Agencies in Ann Arbor. She served as part-time lecturer in community organization and group process from 1949 to 1952 and as assistant professor before her departure in 1953.

1953–54
New Faculty: None
Departures: Faye Portner

1954–55
New Faculty: Robert D. Vinter

ROBERT D. VINTER. Robert D. Vinter came to the university after serving on the faculty at Springfield College in Massachusetts. Vinter held an A.B. degree from Trinity College and a master's in social work and a Ph.D. in social psychology from Columbia University. During his thirty-one years with the university, Vinter taught courses at the master's and doctoral degree levels, conducted research studies, and served in several administrative roles, including associate dean and acting dean. Upon his retirement in 1985, Vinter was cited by the regents of the university for distinction in social research, for his work in university affairs, and for "a long and distinguished career in the design of graduate-professional education programs" (Board of Regents, 1985). Among his many service activities at the national level, Vinter was a consultant to the President's Committee on Juvenile Delinquency, a member of National Institute of Mental Health committees and State of Michigan advisory boards, and a member of the Editorial Committee of the *Encyclopedia of Social Work* in 1965 and 1971.

Vinter's intellectual leadership and publications in social group work led to the creation of the premier group work program in the United States. His publications in social group work and social organizations gained wide use throughout the United States and the world. In naming Vinter professor emeritus, university regents recognized his work as "seminal in scope and widely acclaimed in the profession" (Board of Regents, 1985). In addition to social group work, Vinter established himself as an expert in administration and the juvenile justice system, teaching in areas of funding and fiscal management, agency administration, program design, and management. In recognition of his accomplishments at the school, the regents named Vinter the Arthur Durham Professor of Social Work.

1955–56
New Faculty: William Bechill and Wilbur J. Cohen

WILLIAM BECHILL. William Bechill joined the faculty as lecturer in social work, having received his M.S.W. degree from the University of Michigan in 1952. He had served as a rehabilitation consultant with the Kaiser-Frazer UAW-CIO Social Security Fund and as an administrator with the Michigan Rehabilitation Service. Bechill supervised students in the Michigan Office of Vocational Rehabilitation in Flint, Michigan, and taught courses in rehabilitation. Bechill left the school in 1960 for a position with the federal government.

WILBUR J. COHEN. Wilbur J. Cohen joined the faculty as professor of public welfare administration in January 1956. Cohen graduated from the University of Wisconsin-Madison with a bachelor's degree in philosophy. Cohen served on the staff of President Franklin D. Roosevelt's Cabinet Committee on Economic Security, which drafted the original Social Security Act. He served on the Social Security Board in Washington, D.C., from 1935 to the time of his coming to Ann Arbor in 1956. At the School of Social Work, Professor Cohen taught courses in social welfare administration and the social services at the master's level, as well as played a major role in teaching seminars and advising students in the doctoral program. On leave from the university, Professor Cohen was appointed by President John F. Kennedy as assistant secretary of the Department of Health, Education, and Welfare (HEW) in 1961, by President Lyndon B. Johnson as under secretary of HEW in 1965, and as secretary of HEW in 1968. Cohen returned to the university in 1969 to serve as dean of the School of Education, retiring as professor emeritus of education and public welfare administration in 1983.

The Wilbur J. Cohen Federal Building in Washington, D.C., was dedicated in April 1988. A book about Professor Cohen's life, *Mr. Social Security: The Life of Wilbur J. Cohen*, authored by E. D. Berkowitz, was published in 1995.

1956–57
New Faculty: Dorothy Robinson and Edwin J. Thomas
Departures: Helen Pinkus

DOROTHY ROBINSON. Dorothy Robinson was appointed as assistant professor of social work in 1956. Prior to her joining the faculty, Robinson had earned a B.A. degree at Wayne State University and an M.S.W. degree at Michigan and had served in a number of social work positions, including caseworker at Jewish Social Services and casework supervisor at University of Michigan Hospital and the Veteran's Readjustment Center. Robinson had attained the rank of professor prior to the time of her death in 1978. In a memorial statement, the regents noted, "Throughout her career Professor Robinson contributed a critical perspective gained through practice experience and a long-time interest in the clinical practice of social work and in mental health programs. She always treated her clients, her students, and her colleagues with great respect. She believed in students, in their ability to learn and to succeed. The brightness of her spirit and her concern for students was a dominant theme in her life at the School of Social Work" (Board of Regents, 1978).

EDWIN J. THOMAS. Edwin J. Thomas joined the faculty in 1956, holding a B.A. and an M.S.W. degree from Wayne State University and a Ph.D. degree in social psychology from the University of Michigan. Prior to his appointment at the school, Thomas was a research assistant at the U-M Research Center for Group Dynamics. Based on his research and writing, Professor Thomas became a leading scholar worldwide in the areas of behavior modification, intervention research, and alcoholism and unilateral family therapy. Thomas was a prime mover in the development of the Joint Doctoral Program in Social Work and Social Science, holding professorships in both social work and psychology. His students gained national reputations in social work education, a tribute to his excellence as a teacher, advisor, mentor, and scholar. He was a Senior Fulbright Scholar on two occasions—at the University of Bradford and at LaTrobe University. In naming Thomas professor emeritus of social work and professor emeritus of psychology in 1994, the regents noted, "He has published an impressive body of articles and books, many of which have been translated into foreign languages." During his tenure at the school as an "esteemed member of the faculty," Thomas received the university's Distinguished Faculty Achievement Award, was named to numerous Who's Who listings, and was named the Fedele F. Fauri Professor of Social Work (Board of Regents, 1994). In 2007 Professor Thomas was honored by the establishment of the Edwin J. Thomas Collegiate Professor of Social Work. Professor Emeritus Thomas currently resides in Ann Arbor.

1957–58
New Faculty: Henry J. Meyer

HENRY J. MEYER. Henry J. Meyer was recruited to the university to serve as head of the Joint Doctoral Program in Social Work and Social Science. At the time of his appointment, Meyer held a professorship at New York University, where he had demonstrated his interest in the relationship of social work to social science through his research and writing. Professor Meyer's educational background included bachelor's, master's, and doctoral degrees from the University of Michigan. For over a decade, Professor Meyer gave leadership to the development of the curriculum in the doctoral program and in linking the school to the social science departments of the university. Doctoral students became fondly attached to Professor Meyer due to his personal guidance in their education and careers. Following his directorship of the doctoral program, Meyer engaged in an interdisciplinary training program in family and population planning for students from developing nations around the world. In 1974 Meyer became the first School of Social Work educator to receive the university's Distinguished Faculty Achievement Award. After a distinguished career at the university, Meyer was named professor emeritus of social work in 1978. The Henry J. Meyer Fellowship Award and the Henry J. Meyer Collegiate Professor of Social Work are named in his honor. Regarding Meyer's development of the doctoral program, the Board of Regents noted, "A fine teacher and administrator, he led the way in expanding the program in a manner that made it a model for doctoral education in social work throughout the nation" (Board of Regents, 1978).

1958–59
New Faculty: Pauline Bushey and Paul Glasser

PAULINE BUSHEY. Pauline Bushey served the school as a field supervisor for an Aid to Dependent Children (ADC) study prior to her appointment in 1958 as assistant professor. Bushey was an experienced practitioner in the area of public assistance and was appointed to the faculty under a U.S. Vocational Rehabilitation grant, serving in this role through 1963.

PAUL GLASSER. Paul Glasser came to the university with extensive social work practice experience in psychiatric social work and social group work. He held a master's degree in social work from Columbia University and a doctoral degree in social science from the University of North Carolina. At Michigan he moved from assistant professor to professor of social work, teaching, writing, and providing leadership in the doctoral program and the group work program. Glasser became known internationally for his research and publications in social group work and the family. He served as editor for several social science journals and as senior editor of the *Encyclopedia of Social Work*. Glasser left the school in 1978 to become dean of the School of Social Work at the University of Texas–Arlington, hence to the deanship of the School of Social Work at Rutgers University.

1959–60
New Faculty: Mary E. Burns and Eugene Litwak

MARY E. BURNS. Mary E. Burns held faculty appointments at the University of Texas and the University of Chicago prior to coming to Michigan. She earned a B.A. and an M.S.W. degree from Michigan and a Ph.D. degree from the University of Chicago. Burns was appointed to the faculty as associate professor, departing in 1969 as professor to join the faculty at Western Michigan University School of Social Work. During her ten years at Michigan, Burns made significant contributions to the doctoral program and to the curriculum areas of social casework and human behavior and the social environment. At the national level she served as chair of the Advisory Committee on Advanced Education for the Council on Social Work Education.

EUGENE LITWAK. Eugene Litwak came to the school with research and teaching experience at Cornell University, the University of Chicago, and Columbia University. Litwak held a B.A. degree from Wayne State University and a Ph.D. in sociology from Columbia University. Prior to his appointment to the Michigan faculty as associate professor, Litwak held an appointment in the sociology department at Columbia. During his thirteen years on the faculty at Michigan, Litwak played a crucial role in the development of the Joint Doctoral Program in Social Work and

Social Science, in the introduction of social science content in the master's degree program, and in the conduct of research and writing on schools, family, neighborhoods, and social organizations. Known as an outstanding teacher, faculty adviser, and social researcher, Litwak was honored in 1967 with an appointment as a fellow at the Center for Advanced Study in the Behavioral Sciences at Stanford University. Litwak left Michigan in 1972 to join the faculty at Columbia University in the Department of Sociology and the School of Social Work.

1960–61
New Faculty: Rosemary Conzemius Sarri and William Turner
Departures: William Bechill

ROSEMARY C. SARRI. Rosemary Conzemius Sarri enrolled in the school's Joint Doctoral Program with B.A. and M.S.W. degrees from the University of Minnesota and extensive professional social work experience. She served as a lecturer during her doctoral studies, completing a Ph.D. degree in 1962, and became an assistant professor at that time, hence moving through the ranks to full professor. At the school she gained distinction through her research, teaching, and writing, as well as her contributions to international social welfare programs throughout the world. Among Sarri's teaching areas were gender studies, deviant behavior, executive leadership, social policy, and families and children in poverty. She served in several important administrative positions at the school, including head of the doctoral program, director of admissions, and head of the social welfare administration program. Honors to Sarri include a Fulbright Senior Scholarship, honorary degree D.H.L. from Western Maryland College, Significant Life-Time Achievement Award from the Council on Social Work Education, School of Social Work Distinguished Alumni Award, NASW Presidential Award for Research, and the University of Michigan Distinguished Faculty Achievement Award. Sarri was named professor emeritus of social work in 1993, at which time the Rosemary Sarri Scholarship was established. Professor Sarri resides in Ann Arbor and continues to carry out research as faculty associate and senior research professor emerita at the University of Michigan's Institute for Social Research.

WILLIAM TURNER. William Turner, M.S.W., was appointed lecturer in social work under a U.S. Vocational Rehabilitation grant. He remained on the faculty for six years, leaving to join the faculty at Wayne State University.

1961–62
New Faculty: Charles Wolfson

CHARLES WOLFSON. Charles Wolfson joined the faculty as lecturer under a U.S. Public Health Service grant, coming to the school with professional social work experience in the New York City Department of Welfare and a Jewish community center in New York. Wolfson held a B.A. degree from Long Island University and an M.S.W. degree from Wayne State University. At Michigan Wolfson moved through the ranks to professor of social work. His teaching expertise was in social group work, correctional systems, child welfare and juvenile justice, social welfare administration, and social policy. In his thirty years at the school, Wolfson consulted widely on the use of groups for prevention and treatment of delinquent behavior. For several years he was director of the school's Office of Agency and Community Relations. He published *Social Deviance and the Human Services* in 1984 and was named professor emeritus of social work in 1991. The regents of the university noted, "Professor Wolfson's expertise in the area of criminal justice programs in general, and juvenile justice programs in particular, earned him the respect of his colleagues, and of public and voluntary agencies throughout the state of Michigan" (Board of Regents, 1991).

1962–63
New Faculty: Philip Booth, George Bown, Jane Costabile, Merle Dinsmore, Herman Resnick, Jack Rothman, and Sheldon Siegel
Departures: Pauline Bushey

PHILIP BOOTH. Philip Booth was appointed as lecturer in social work and research associate in the School of Public Health in 1962. Booth had engaged in doctoral studies at the University of Chicago, completing all but the thesis requirement for a Ph.D. degree. In his career with the federal government, Booth was an economic analyst with the Social Security Board in Washington, D.C., prior to coming to Ann Arbor. He was chief of the program and legislative division of the U.S. Department of Labor. At Michigan he taught in the social services and policy area, advising students in both the master's and doctoral programs. He authored two books while at Michigan, *Social Security in America* (1973) and *California Farm Workers and Disability Insurance* (1967). In 1973 Booth was appointed associate professor emeritus of social work in recognition of "his invaluable contributions as a teacher, researcher, and prolific writer in his field" (Board of Regents, 1973). At this time, the regents noted, "Ironically, while Professor

Booth could never quite find the time to complete his own thesis for the doctorate, one of his most significant contributions as a teacher was the assistance he gave students while serving on their doctoral committees" (Board of Regents, 1973).

GEORGE BOWN. George Bown was appointed lecturer in social work on a U.S. Vocational Rehabilitation grant. He held an A.B. degree from Tufts University and an M.S.S. degree from Boston University. He had held administrative positions in the Lapeer State Home, the Detroit Consultation Center, and the Plymouth State Home and Training School. He developed and supervised field instruction learning and taught courses in the area of rehabilitation, departing from the university as assistant professor in 1966.

JANE COSTABILE. Jane Costabile was appointed to the faculty as lecturer in social work and the field director of a U.S. Children's Bureau-sponsored demonstration project of social group work with parents. Costabile held a B.A. degree from Alma College, an M.A. degree from McCormick Theological Seminary, and an M.S.W. degree from the University of Pittsburgh. Prior to coming to the school, Costabile had "excelled in the practice world in direct service and administrative positions in a variety of settings" (Board of Regents, 1979). She moved through the ranks to professor of social work, serving the school as director of the Office of Admissions and Financial Aid. She also served the state government as chair of the Advisory Committee on Child Placement for the Michigan Department of Social Services. At the local community level, Costabile served as president of Catholic Social Services of Washtenaw County. In 1979 the regents of the university saluted Costabile "for her seventeen years of service to the University and to the cause of social welfare of the citizens of the State of Michigan" by naming her professor emeritus.

MERLE DINSMORE. Merle Dinsmore joined the faculty as an assistant professor, holding B.A. and M.S.W. degrees from Michigan and previously working for a number of years as a social worker at the Children's Center of Wayne County. Dinsmore was appointed on a U.S. Vocational Rehabilitation grant, "with responsibility for classroom teaching and practice instruction in the field of vocational rehabilitation" (Regents' Proceedings, 1983). Dinsmore was recognized "as an outstanding practitioner and administrator by her professional colleagues." For several years, she served as director of the Office of Field Instruction. In naming Dinsmore professor emeritus in 1983, the regents noted "her special attention to students' practice experiences, and her regard for their educational goals and careers," earning her "the high esteem of students, faculty, and agency personnel."

HERMAN RESNICK. Herman Resnick served on the faculty for two years as an assistant professor under a U.S. Public Health Service grant. He developed and conducted field instruction in psychiatric social work, especially in social group work. Resnick left the faculty to pursue doctoral studies.

JACK ROTHMAN. Jack Rothman came to the school from a position as assistant professor of community work at the University of Pittsburgh, along with social work practice experience with the New York City Youth Board and B'nai B'rith Youth Organization. Rothman held a B.S.S. degree from City College of New York, an M.S.W. from Ohio State University, and a Ph.D. from Columbia University. At Michigan Rothman gave leadership to the development of the community organization program; produced numerous publications in professional journals; authored books on intergroup relations, social research and development, and intervention research; and was co-editor of a series of books with colleagues at Michigan. His teaching areas included utilization of research, organizational innovation, race and ethnic relations, and community practice. After twenty-two years at the school, Rothman left as professor of social work in 1984 to join the faculty at the University of California at Los Angeles.

SHELDON SIEGEL. Sheldon Siegel was appointed to the faculty as assistant professor on a federal aging grant. Siegel came to the faculty with a B.A. degree from Michigan, an M.S.W. from Wayne State University, considerable practice experience, and doctoral studies at Michigan, where he completed a dissertation entitled "Organizational Growth: Expansion and Diversity in Schools of Social Work." At Michigan Siegel served as director of the Office of Admissions and Financial Aid, taught in the areas of administration and aging, and was a faculty associate in the Institute of Gerontology. In 1979 Siegel left the university to become director of the School of Social Work at the University of Cincinnati, hence leaving to become dean of the School of Social Work at Indiana University.

1963–64
New Faculty: Frederick Cox, Maeda Galinsky, and Frank Maple
Departures: Arthur Dunham

FREDERICK COX. Fred Cox was appointed to the faculty as assistant professor, coming to the university with B.A. and M.S.W. degrees from UCLA, and hence completing a Ph.D. degree at the University of California at Berkeley. While at Michigan, Cox gave leadership to the community organization program, collaborating with his colleagues on a number of books on community organization and social policy. Cox served on the faculty for twelve years, leaving as associate professor in 1976 to become director of the School of Social Work at Michigan State University. He later moved from Michigan State to become dean of the School of Social Work at the University of Wisconsin–Milwaukee.

MAEDA J. GALINSKY. Maeda J. Galinsky completed her M.S.W. and Ph.D. degrees at the University of Michigan and then served for one year as lecturer in social work. She moved to the University of North Carolina at Chapel Hill, where she is now Kenan Professor of Social Work, teaching and writing extensively on group work practice.

FRANK F. MAPLE, JR. Frank F. Maple, Jr. was appointed to the faculty as assistant professor under a U.S. Public Health Service grant. Maple came to the school with B.A., M.A., and M.S.W. degrees from the University of Michigan and social work practice in the public schools. Maple taught group work practice for many years, as well as family treatment and school social work. Maple has published in the areas of group composition, school social work, problem solving through shared decision making, goal-focused interviewing, and creation of groups. Known as a superlative and innovative teacher, Maple has produced texts, videotapes, and computer software programs in the area of individual and family treatment and social groups. Maple was named professor emeritus of social work by the Board of Regents in 2003. Maple resides in Ann Arbor and continues to teach on a part-time basis at the school.

1964–65
New Faculty: Sydney Bernard, Harvey Bertcher, Sallie Churchill, Loraine Cook, Tom Croxton, Nathalie Drews, Jesse Gordon, and Lila Swell
Departures: Ralph Fletcher, Maeda Galinsky, Herman Resnick

SYDNEY BERNARD. Sydney Bernard came to the school as assistant professor with practice experience at the Washtenaw County Department of Social Welfare, A.B. and M.S.W. degrees from Michigan, and a Ph.D. degree from Brandeis University, where he completed a dissertation, "The

Economic and Social Adjustment of Low-Income Female-Headed Families." Bernard taught in the social welfare and social policy area, with special attention to public welfare systems. His publications include articles on the prevention and reduction of dependency, rehabilitation in a public assistance agency, fatherless families, and Medicaid. His teaching areas included the operation of public social services, families and social services, and administrative behavior. At Michigan Bernard "gained recognition as an expert on values and ethics issues in the social work profession, as well as issues related to dependency and public welfare," retiring as professor emeritus in 1991. At that time the regents noted, "Professor Bernard's retirement marks the departure of one of the most devoted members of the faculty of the School of Social Work" (Board of Regents, 1991). Professor Bernard continues to reside in Ann Arbor.

HARVEY BERTCHER. Harvey Bertcher came to the school as assistant professor after several years of professional practice and doctoral studies at the University of Southern California, where he earned a D.S.W. degree. He held a B.A. degree from Olivet College and an M.A. degree from Columbia. At Michigan Bertcher helped strengthen the social group work program, teaching and writing in regard to group formation, staff development, and self-instruction. In naming Bertcher professor emeritus of social work, the regents noted, "Professor Bertcher has a long record of national, university, and community service and has been recognized by the student body for his personal concern for students and their well-being. . . . Professor Bertcher has been a pioneer in the area of teleconferencing as a support system for a variety of persons, including homebound elderly persons, persons with illnesses such as multiple sclerosis, leukemia, hemophilia, as well as the caretakers of such persons" (Board of Regents, 1995). Professor Bertcher continues to reside in Ann Arbor.

SALLIE CHURCHILL. Sallie Churchill joined the faculty as assistant professor, having earned B.A. and M.S.W. degrees from the University of Minnesota and having worked as a psychiatric social group worker in a child guidance center and as a clinical instructor in child development at the University of Pittsburgh. In 1967 she left the school to pursue doctoral studies at the University of Chicago, completing her Ph.D. degree in 1970. At Michigan "she contributed enormously in the area of group work, specifically with children and adolescents, adoption, and the counseling of minors" (Board of Regents, 1996). Recognized as an outstanding teacher and mentor, Churchill was presented with the Distinguished Faculty Award by the School of Social Work Alumni Board of Governors in 1995. In naming Churchill professor emeritus, the regents noted that "Professor Churchill has also been one of the school's most beloved teachers, encouraging, inspiring, and supporting the students who have known her as a teacher, researcher, clinician, and humanitarian." Professor Churchill currently resides in Ann Arbor.

LORAINE COOK. Loraine Cook joined the faculty as an associate professor, giving leadership to the social casework program and the interpersonal practice division of the curriculum. Having obtained B.A. and M.S.W. degrees at Michigan, Cook completed her Ph.D. degree at the University of Chicago. Prior to coming to Michigan, Cook had been director of social services at Kalamazoo State Hospital and assistant professor of social work at State University of New York at Buffalo. Cook was promoted to full professor in 1969, retiring in 1986 after twenty-two years of service to the university. In naming her professor emeritus, the regents noted, "Professor Cook was known as one of the most distinguished teachers in the areas of interpersonal practice and human behavior and the social environment. She assumed a leadership role in the development of new courses, and was a leading member of the Curriculum Committee in the School of Social Work. . . . In her roles as divisional coordinator for interpersonal practice and head of the casework program, Professor Cook was an excellent advisor and liaison to social service agencies" (Board of Regents, 1987).

TOM CROXTON. Tom Croxton came to the school after obtaining his B.A. degree from Miami University and his J.D. and M.S.W. degrees at Michigan, and with professional practice experience as director of court services in a juvenile court in Marshall, Michigan. His appointment under a U.S. Children's Bureau grant recognized Croxton's expertise in law and social work related to children. His teaching and publications while at Michigan focused on these areas, including articles in the *Journal of Family Law, Child Welfare, Urban Crime and Urban Planning,* the *Journal of Juvenile Law,* the *Journal of Teaching in Social Work,* and *Social Work.* Croxton served in a number of administrative positions at the school, including acting associate dean and, for four years, director of the Office of Admissions and Financial Aid. While at the school, Croxton held the unique distinction of being the only faculty member on the nexus of social work and the law. In 2001 the Board of Regents named Croxton professor emeritus, saluting him as a "distinguished faculty member," with the faculty noting his "long history of being an absolute advocate for the students" and "his interest in the intersections between law and social work" (*Ongoing,* 2001). Professor Croxton currently resides in Ann Arbor.

NATHALIE DREWS. Nathalie Drews came to the school with A.B. and M.S.W degrees from Michigan and a strong practice background, including service with the American National Red Cross and the University of Michigan Hospitals. She was appointed as assistant professor on a U.S. Department of Rehabilitation grant, teaching social casework and providing field instruction for students at the League for the Handicapped in Detroit. While at Michigan, Drews was known as an outstanding teacher, pioneering instruction in the area of death and dying. She was a founding member of the Turner Geriatric Services Advisory Committee. She served as assistant dean for the Office of Student Services for a number of years. In naming Drews professor emeritus in 1993, the regents noted that "her retirement marks the departure of one of the most dedicated members of the faculty of the School of Social Work" (Board of Regents, 1993).

JESSE GORDON. Jesse Gordon joined the faculty as associate professor of social work and psychology, having been on the psychology faculty since 1959. Gordon held B.S. and M.A. degrees from New York University and a Ph.D. degree from Pennsylvania State University. His teaching areas included research methods in interpersonal practice, utilization of knowledge in direct practice, and comparative theories of personality. While at Michigan, Gordon carried out projects for the U.S. Department of Labor, focusing on the Youth Opportunity Program and on training materials for employment agency personnel. Gordon was named professor emeritus of social work and of psychology in 1993. At that time, the regents noted that "Professor Gordon played a major role in the integration of research and clinical practice." Prior to and during retirement, Gordon served the school as "overseer" in the completion and operation of the new School of Social Work building. Professor Gordon continues to reside in Ann Arbor.

LILA SWELL. Lila Swell served as lecturer in social work for one year on a U.S. Public Health Service grant. She held M.S.W. and Ed.D. degrees from Columbia University.

1965–66
New Faculty: Beryl Carter, John Erlich, Phillip Fellin, Charles Garvin, Martha Green, Stanley Kim, Mitchel Lazarus, Roger Lind, Sheldon Rose, Richard Stuart, John Tropman, and Darrel Vorwaller

BERYL CARTER. Beryl Carter (Rice) received her M.S. degree in social work from Columbia University and practiced social work at the Illinois State Psychiatric Institute in Chicago before coming to the university as assistant professor under a U.S. Public Health Service grant. She specialized in teaching courses on aging and social group work. She remained at the school until 1971, when she left for doctoral studies at Catholic University of America. She then served as professor at the University of the District of Columbia.

JOHN ERLICH. John Erlich, B.A., M.S., joined the faculty as assistant professor of social work under a U.S. Public Health Service grant. He was formerly director, Phoenix Project of Goddard-Riverside Community Center, New York City. During his six years at Michigan, Erlich was known as a dynamic teacher and field instructor, contributing to the literature in new areas of student power and youth movements. He collaborated with colleagues in publishing texts on *Changing Organizations and Community Programs, Promoting Innovation and Change in Organizations and Communities,* and *Tactics and Techniques of Community Intervention.* Erlich's collection of papers on campus protests is located in the Bentley Historical Library at the University of Michigan (1966–70). In 1971 Erlich departed to California State University at Sacramento, where he continued to teach and publish in the area of organizations, communities, and diverse societies.

PHILLIP FELLIN. Phillip Fellin received an A.B. degree from St. Benedict's College, an M.S.W. degree at St. Louis University, and a Ph.D. degree at Michigan. After four years of teaching at St. Louis University, in 1965 Fellin joined the Michigan faculty as associate professor and director of the Office of Field Instruction. Six years later he was appointed dean of the school, serving in this position from 1971 to 1981. After his deanship, Fellin continued on the faculty as professor of social work until his retirement in 1999. In naming Fellin professor emeritus and dean emeritus, the regents noted that "Professor Fellin attained national prominence as a social work educator and scholar, serving as chair of the Commission on Accreditation of the Council on Social Work Education, as First Vice-President of CSWE, and on numerous Council Commissions." He has been recognized in *Who's Who in America* and received the Doctor of Humane Letters from his college alma mater, Benedictine College, and the Alumni Merit Award from St. Louis University. Fellin authored and co-authored a number of widely used social work texts in the areas of research, community, and mental health. Professor Fellin continues to reside in Ann Arbor.

CHARLES GARVIN. Charles Garvin came to the school with B.A., A.M., and Ph.D. degrees from the University of Chicago, along with social work practice experience. He was appointed to the faculty as assistant professor, moving though the ranks to full professor in 1972. Garvin's teaching, writing, and research have been in the area of social group work, staff development, interpersonal practice, and social services. His teaching and writing in social group work added luster to this program and the school's reputation throughout the United States and abroad. His extensive journal and text publications, as sole author and in collaboration with colleagues, include books on the social services, group work, generalist practice, and interpersonal practice. Garvin served the school in administrative roles as head of the school's Curriculum Committee, as head of curricular areas, and as head of the Joint Doctoral Program. At the national level, he held positions of chair of the Group for the Advancement of Doctoral Education and the Association for the Advancement of Social Work with Groups, and he has served on editorial boards and as editor of professional journals. The regents saluted Garvin as a distinguished faculty member by naming him professor emeritus in 2001. Garvin continues to reside in Ann Arbor and to direct and participate in research projects at the school.

MARTHA GREEN. Martha Green was appointed to the faculty as assistant professor on a U.S. Vocational Rehabilitation grant. Formerly she had been a social work supervisor at Plymouth State Home and Training School. She served on the faculty for two years, teaching in the areas of social casework and field instruction.

STANLEY KIM. Stanley Kim was an assistant professor of social work at the University of Wisconsin–Milwaukee prior to coming to Michigan as assistant professor. Kim came to the school with an A.B. degree from the University of Hawaii and an M.S.W. and Ph.D. from Ohio State University. During his tenure at Michigan, Kim taught in the area of administration, corrections, and social welfare policy and services. He left Michigan in 1973 for a social work position in California.

MITCHEL LAZARUS. Mitchel Lazarus was employed in Minnesota with the Federation for Jewish Services and the Jewish Community Center prior to coming to the faculty as assistant professor under a U.S. Children's Bureau grant. He left the school in 1968 to become director of Westside Jewish Center in Los Angeles. While at Michigan, Lazarus was involved in the community and administration practice areas.

ROGER LIND. Roger Lind served on the faculty as a part-time lecturer for a number of years prior to his full-time appointment to the faculty. Before entering the Michigan doctoral program, Lind had been employed at the state level in the Department of Social Services. He completed his undergraduate degree at Yale University, an M.S.W. degree at Michigan in 1952, and a Ph.D. degree at Michigan in 1962, with a dissertation entitled "Organizational Structure and Social Workers' Performance." After ten years on the faculty at Michigan, teaching in the area of social administration and social services and policy, Lind departed from Michigan in 1975 to become professor of social work at the University of Wisconsin–Madison, serving also as director of the social work program there, then becoming director of the School of Social Work at the University of Louisville, and hence to New England.

SHELDON ROSE. Sheldon Rose was appointed to the faculty as assistant professor, having served as assistant professor at the University of Amsterdam, the Netherlands. Rose held a B.A. degree from the University of Missouri, an M.S.W. from Washington University, and a Ph.D. from the University of Rotterdam. While at Michigan, Rose published a number of articles on behavioral approaches to group work practice. Rose left Michigan in 1968 to become deputy director of the Peace Corps in Nepal, hence to the University of Wisconsin as professor of social work, where he continued to teach and write until his retirement from that university. Rose is the author of books on group therapy and children and adolescents.

RICHARD STUART. Richard Stuart came to the faculty from a teaching position at Rutgers, the State University of New Jersey. Stuart held a B.A. degree from New York University and M.S. and D.S.W. degrees from Columbia University. At the University of Michigan, he was a fellow with the Center for the Study of Human Growth and Development. While at Michigan he authored several articles and books, including *Trick or Treatment: How and When Psychotherapy Fails* (1970), and *Slim Chance in a Fat World: Behavioral Control of Obesity* (1972). Stuart left the university in 1975 to become a professor in social work at the University of British Columbia, then to the University of Utah, and hence to the University of Washington.

JOHN TROPMAN. John Tropman is presently on the faculty as professor of social work, and he is also professor in the Honors College, LS&A, and the Michigan School of Business. Tropman earned a B.A. degree at Oberlin College, an M.A. at the University of Chicago, and a Ph.D. from Michigan. His teaching areas include social policy, values, and attitudes toward welfare policies and disadvantaged groups; decision-making systems; and services and programs for the aged. Tropman has served in a number of administrative roles, including member of the University Grievance Board, head of the school's Joint Doctoral Program, chair of the Michigan Society of Fellows, coordinator of the M.S.W./M.B.A. program, and member of the Executive Committee of the Institute of Labor and Industrial Relations. He is currently a member of numerous university and school committees, as well as the advisor to numerous community social welfare agencies.

In 1986 Tropman received the Bernard Zell/Leonard W. Lurie Prize for the Teaching of Entrepreneurship from the university's School of Business. In 1988 he was awarded the Wilbur J. Cohen Award from the School of Education. As author of a number of books and journal articles, Tropman has received many honors, including Blackwell's Choice Outstanding Academic Book Title for 1996 (*The Catholic Ethic in American Society*) and mentions in *Dictionary of International Biography*, 25th Ed., *Who's Who in America, International Directory of Business and Management Scholars and Research* (published by Harvard Business School), and *Who's Who in American Education*. He currently is on a number of editorial boards. He served as interim dean of the school from September 2008 through December 2008. He has been appointed associate dean for faculty and academic affairs through December 2009.

DARREL VORWALLER. Darrel Vorwaller served on the faculty as instructor for two years following completion of the Michigan Joint Doctoral Program in Social Work and Social Science. His dissertation was entitled "Consequences of Social Mobility: An Analysis of Additive Effects of Social Class Statuses of Origin and Destination." He left the university to join the firm Woltz and Associates, Inc.

1966–67
New Faculty: Herman Borenzweig, Morton Casson, Alan Connor, David Cowley, Louis Ferman, Esther Goodman Sales, Edward Pawlak, Thomas Powell, John Riley, and Tony Tripodi
Departures: George Bowen, Lila Swell, William Turner, Darrel Vorwaller, Herman Borenzweig, Mort Casson, David Cowley, and Martha Green

HERMAN BORENZWEIG. Herman Borenzweig was appointed to the faculty as assistant professor on a U.S. Vocational Rehabilitation grant. He came to the university with an M.S.W. degree and the position of center director,

Manhattanville Community Center, New York City. At the school for one academic year, Borenzweig engaged in teaching of social group work and field instruction.

MORTON CASSON. Morton Casson was appointed lecturer in social work on a U.S. Public Health Service grant. He was on the faculty for one year.

ALAN CONNOR. Alan Connor came to the school as an assistant professor on a U.S. Children's Bureau grant, remaining on the faculty for several years. Prior to this appointment, Connor was community development field director, American Friends Service Committee, Zambia, Africa. Connor had completed the M.S.W. degree at Michigan and undertook doctoral studies in the School of Education while on the faculty, completing his Ph.D. with a dissertation entitled "Citizen Participation in the Community Development Block Grant Program." At Michigan Connor taught in a number of curricular areas, including child welfare, social group work, social casework, community organization, and field instruction.

DAVID COWLEY. David Cowley served on the faculty for one year as a lecturer in social work.

LOUIS FERMAN. Louis Ferman was on the faculty of the School of Social Work from 1966 to 1993, teaching courses in the human behavior and social environment sequence. He held a B.A. degree from Brown University, an M.A. from Boston University, and a Ph.D. from Cornell University. His teaching areas included unemployment, human resource organizations, mental health, and the economy. He was research director and research scientist at the U-M Institute of Labor and Industrial Relations from 1962 to 1993. "He was the author of more than fifty articles, chapters, monographs, and books on issues such as employment and unemployment, plant closings, job training for the hard-to-employ, poverty, and racial discrimination. Ferman was widely regarded as the 'father of informal economy research,' lecturing extensively in the U.S. and abroad on a wide range of industrial relations topics" (*Ongoing,* 1999).

ESTHER GOODMAN SALES. Esther Goodman Sales held an appointment as lecturer during the period of her doctoral studies at Michigan. She completed her M.S.W. at Michigan, as well as her Ph.D., with the dissertation, "Sex Differences in Responsiveness to Two Classes of Social Approval Stimuli." She collaborated with Professor Ed Thomas to publish *Socio-Behavioral Theory* *and Interpersonal Helping in Social Work: Lectures and Institute Proceedings*. She left Michigan in 1970 to join the faculty at the University of Pittsburgh School of Social Work.

EDWARD PAWLAK. Edward Pawlak held a faculty appointment for one academic year on a U.S. Public Health Service grant. He earned M.S.W. and Ph.D. degrees at Michigan, writing a dissertation, "The Administration of Juvenile Justice." He joined the faculty at Western Michigan University School of Social Work after teaching social group work at Michigan.

THOMAS POWELL. Thomas Powell came to the school as assistant professor, with A.B. and M.S.W. degrees from Boston College, and a D.S.W. degree from Smith College. His teaching areas include mental health policies and programs, interpersonal practice, and self-help organizations. Powell continues to serve on the faculty as a full professor. At Michigan he has been principal investigator of several mental health services research projects and was director of the Center for Self-Help Research and Knowledge Dissemination under the National Institute of Mental Health. Powell is the author of numerous journal articles and several books about understanding the self-help organization, working with self-help groups, and the relationship of self-help groups to professional practice. Powell is currently on the faculty and continues to publish in these areas, to serve as editorial reviewer for a number of professional journals, and to teach interpersonal practice and mental health courses.

JOHN RILEY. John Riley joined the faculty after completing a bachelor's degree at the University of Wisconsin, an M.S.W. degree from the University of California/Berkeley, and a Ph.D. from Brandeis University. He had been a fellow in community mental health at Harvard University. His initial appointment at Michigan was on a U.S. Public Health Service grant, with his focus on mental health administration. Riley gave leadership to the development of the school's specialization in social welfare administration. Author of numerous professional articles on mental health issues and on social welfare administration, Riley left the school in 1972 to become dean of the School of Social Work at Barry University.

TONY TRIPODI. Tony Tripodi joined the faculty in 1966, having earned A.B. and M.S.W. degrees at the University of California at Berkeley and a D.S.W. degree at Columbia University. Prior to coming to Michigan, Tripodi had been an assistant professor of social research and social welfare at the University of California at Berkeley. While at Michigan, Tripodi gave leadership to the research curriculum, served as associate dean of the school, and was the author of numerous professional journal articles and books, including three texts with his colleagues on social research and social program evaluation. In 1987 Tripodi moved to the University of Pittsburgh as associate dean in the School of Social Work, then to Florida International University, and hence became dean of the School of Social Work at Ohio State University.

1967–68
New Faculty: JoAnn Allen, Thomas Anton, Richard English, Irwin Epstein, Eileen Gambrill, Oliver Harris, Harry Lawrence, and Wayne Vasey
Departures: Edward Pawlak and Patricia Rabinovitz

JoAnn Allen. JoAnn Allen held an appointment on the faculty for 24 years, with her initial assignments related to a U.S. Vocational Rehabilitation grant. She came to the school in 1967 with a bachelor's degree from the University of Colorado, an M.S.W. from Michigan, doctoral studies, and considerable social work practice experience. At Michigan "Professor Allen became one of the school's outstanding teachers in interpersonal practice, as well as a leading authority on service programs for children and families. Her expertise on the behavior of children and families earned her the respect of her academic colleagues and professional practitioners. She was an inspirational teacher, advisor, and faculty liaison to social service agencies" (Board of Regents, 1991). In addition to teaching, Allen had a clinical practice at the Ann Arbor Center for the Family for some twenty years. In 1991 the regents of the university named Allen associate professor emeritus of social work, noting, "Professor Allen's retirement marks the departure of a leading clinician and dedicated teacher" (Board of Regents, 1991).

Thomas Anton. Thomas Anton came to the university as an associate professor of social work and political science. He held an A.B. degree from Clark University and M.A. and Ph.D. degrees from Princeton University. His appointment included a special assignment in the Michigan doctoral program for degrees in social work and political science. Anton's academic honors included a Guggenheim Fellow, Fulbright Fellow, and American Philosophical Society Fellow.

Richard English. Richard English earned his A.B. degree at Talladega College prior to coming to Michigan for doctoral studies. At Michigan he received M.A., M.S.W., and Ph.D. degrees, completing a dissertation, "Educational Aspirations of Black/White Youth" in 1970. While in doctoral studies, English served as lecturer in social work on a U.S. Vocational Rehabilitation grant. He was appointed assistant professor in 1971 and moved through the ranks to professor of social work. His teaching areas included families, ethnicity, and human service organizations. English had a distinguished teaching and administrative career at Michigan, serving as assistant dean of the School of Social Work from 1971 to 1974 and as associate vice president for academic services at the university from 1974 to 1981. He served as president of the Council on Social Work Education for a three-year term beginning in 1981. He held the Robert L. Sutherland chair in Mental Health and Social Policy at the University of Texas, Austin, from 1983 though 1985. He then left the University of Michigan to become dean of the School of Social Work at Howard University, hence becoming provost of this university. In 2005 English received the University of Michigan Alumni Association's Distinguished Service Award.

IRWIN EPSTEIN. Irwin Epstein held a B.A. degree from New York University and M.S.W. and Ph.D. degrees from Columbia University upon coming to the school. His prior experience in social work included group work in New York City, research assistant for Mobilization for Youth, Inc., and research consultant. While at Columbia, Epstein co-authored with Richard Cloward the classic article, "Private Social Welfare's Disengagement from the Poor" (1965). At Michigan Epstein was known as an extremely able instructor and researcher, collaborating with colleagues on research texts used widely throughout the United States. Epstein left Michigan to join the faculty at Hunter College in 1978.

EILEEN GAMBRILL. Eileen Gambrill came to Michigan holding a B.A. degree from the University of Pennsylvania and an M.S.S. from Bryn Mawr College. After completing her doctoral studies at Michigan, she was appointed as an assistant professor. Her dissertation was on "Effectiveness of Counterconditioning Procedure in Eliminating Avoidance Behavior." During her service at the school, Gambrill was regarded as an excellent teacher and social researcher. After four years on the faculty at Michigan, she accepted a faculty appointment at the University of California, Berkeley. Previously editor-in-chief of *Social Work Research and Abstracts,* Gambrill is current editor of the *Journal of Social Work Education.* She is the author of numerous articles in professional journals, as well as a number of books on behavior modification, casework, and critical thinking in clinical practice.

She received the School of Social Work Alumni Society's Distinguished Alumni Award in 2002. At the University of California at Berkeley, Gambrill was named Hutto Patterson Professor of Child and Family Studies in the School of Social Welfare.

OLIVER HARRIS. Oliver Harris was appointed to the faculty on a U.S. Public Health Service grant. He pursued doctoral studies at the University of Denver, completing a Ph.D. with his dissertation, "Day Care: A Study of Parents' Attitudes and Opinions Relative to Before and After School Care." He left Michigan in 1974 to take a faculty position at the University of Maryland. In 1980 at Maryland Harris co-edited the social work text, *Family Treatment in Social Work Practice*.

HARRY LAWRENCE. Harry Lawrence came to the school, having earned M.S.W. and D.S.W. degrees at the University of California at Berkeley. He was appointed assistant professor on a U.S. Public Health Service grant, teaching in the area of social group work. He left Michigan in 1978 for a faculty position at Arizona State University.

WAYNE VASEY. Wayne Vasey joined the faculty after serving as dean at the George Warren Brown School of Social Work at Washington University, St. Louis. Prior to this deanship, Vasey had been director of the School of Social Work at the University of Iowa. At Michigan Vasey was co-director of the Institute of Gerontology. Vasey loved to write, authoring articles for professional journals and two well-known books on social welfare, *Government and Social Welfare* and *Social Welfare and Human Rights*. In 1975 Vasey was named professor emeritus of social work by the regents, who called him "an outstanding social work administrator, writer and educator."

1968–69
New Faculty: Lawrence Gary, Armand Lauffer, William Neenan, Norma Radin, Martin Sundel, and Donald Warren
Departures: Mitchel Lazarus, Sheldon Rose, Eleanor Cranefield, and Lawrence Gary

LAWRENCE GARY. Lawrence Gary came to Michigan following his B.S. degree from Tuskegee Institute, hence receiving M.P.A., M.S.W., and Ph.D. degrees at Michigan. Gary served on the faculty as lecturer in social work for one year after completing his doctoral studies with his dissertation "Some Determinants of Welfare Policies in American States." Leaving for a faculty position at Howard University in 1969, Gary currently is a professor at the School of Social Work at Howard. At Howard Gary is a distinguished social work researcher and teacher and author of numerous journal articles and books, including *Mental Health: A Challenge to the Black Community* (1978) and *Black Men* (1981). At Howard he has held positions with the Institute for Urban Affairs and Research and the School of Social Work. He has held endowed chairs at Virginia Commonwealth University and Hunter College and has served as a distinguished visiting professor at a number of institutions. Gary has served on the Michigan School of Social Work's Visiting Committee and received the Michigan Alumni Association's Distinguished Alumni Service Award in 2002.

ARMAND LAUFFER. Armand Lauffer received a B.A. degree from Roosevelt University, an M.S.W. from Wayne State University, and a Ph.D. degree from Brandeis University. Following work as a research associate at Brandeis and curriculum specialist for the Council on Social Work Education, Lauffer joined the faculty as associate professor. At Michigan Lauffer was director of Continuing Education in the Human Services and director of Project StaR, Service Training and Research in Jewish Communal Development. His teaching areas included community and neighborhood organizations, neighborhood ethnography, staff and organizational development, and management of human resources. Lauffer held the Sol Drachler Endowed Chair in Jewish Communal Service at the school. He authored some two dozen texts on community organizing, social planning, staff and organizational development, and simulation gaming. He was series editor of the *Sage Human Service Guides* and series co-editor of *Sourcebooks for the Human Services*. He received the Career Achievement Award from the Association for Community Organization and Social Administration, CSWE. Lauffer was named professor emeritus by the regents in February 2002. Professor Lauffer currently resides in Israel.

WILLIAM NEENAN. William Neenan held joint appointments with Social Work and Economics at Michigan, departing for Boston College in 1980 to serve as dean of the College of Arts and Sciences. He later became vice president for academic affairs at Boston College. Neenan held A.B., M.A., and S.T.L. degrees from St. Louis University and a Ph.D. in economics from Michigan. At Michigan Neenan served as a liaison between the school's Joint Doctoral Program and the Economics Department. He advised students in the doctoral program and taught seminars in social work and economics, becoming known for his witty personality and engaging manner of teaching. In his early years at the school, Neenan authored two books: *A Normative Evaluation of a Public Health Program* (1967) and *Political Economy of Urban Areas* (1972).

NORMA RADIN. Norma Radin was appointed to the faculty as lecturer in social work at the close of her doctoral studies at Michigan, during which she earned M.S.W. and Ph.D. degrees. She held a B.A. degree from Brooklyn College and an M.A. degree in counseling and guidance from Columbia University. Her doctoral dissertation was "Childrearing Antecedents of Cognitive Development in Lower-Class Preschool Children." Radin was an expert in school social work, writing extensively on early childhood education interventions. Her academic research also focused on child development and parenting, the nontraditional family, and the influence of fathers and grandfathers on young children. The regents named Radin professor emeritus of social work in 1992, noting "the departure of an esteemed member of the faculty of the School of Social Work who was devoted to identifying influential factors in early childhood development." A collegiate professorship at the school was named in her honor, held by then Dean Paula Allen-Meares.

MARTIN SUNDEL. Martin Sundel came to the university for doctoral studies with a B.A. degree from St. Mary's University and an M.S.W. from Our Lady of the Lake College. He earned his M.A. and Ph.D. in social work and psychology from Michigan, with a dissertation, "Modification of Two Operants in Near-Mute Schizophrenics Using Reinforcement and Modeling Procedures." Sundel taught in the area of social group work and was a post-doctoral fellow at Harvard University in a community mental health program. Sundel co-edited with his colleagues Glasser, Sarri, and Vinter the book *Individual Change through Small Groups* (1985 edition). Sundel left the school in 1971 for a faculty position at the University of Texas at Arlington.

DONALD WARREN. Donald Warren, a sociologist, had a joint appointment with the Department of Sociology and was active in the doctoral program. In 1968 he was appointed to the school's faculty on a U.S. Public Health Service grant and served for five years at the school. His expertise in neighborhoods and the urban community was demonstrated in a number of books as well as articles in professional journals. His review "Neighborhoods in Urban Areas" appeared in the 1971 edition of the *Encyclopedia of Social Work*.

1969–70
New Faculty: Howard Brabson, Sheila Feld, Madison Foster, Harold John-
son, and Robert Segal
Departures: Mary Burns, Thomas Anton, Esther Sales, and Wilbur Cohen

HOWARD BRABSON. Howard Brabson joined the faculty after completing a
career in the U.S. Army, having worked as a caseworker and administrator
in vocational schools, and after service as administrator for VISTA. Brabson held a bachelor's degree from the College of the Ozarks, and M.S.W.
and D.S.W. degrees from the National Catholic School of Social Services, Catholic University. He founded the State of Michigan Association of
Black Social Workers and held leadership positions with the National Association of Black Social Workers, including the presidency of this organization. His honors include Outstanding Service Awards from NABSW,
Faculty Recognition Award at the University of Michigan, and School of
Social Work Alumni Society Award for Outstanding Teaching and Service
to Social Work. His teaching areas included community organization and
development, social planning, and personnel management. At Michigan
Brabson served on the university's Athletic Board, with the regents noting,
at the time of his appointment as associate professor emeritus of social
work in 1991, that he had "gained campus-wide respect as a devoted advisor
and mentor to minority students," particularly student athletes. Professor
Brabson currently resides in Ann Arbor.

SHEILA FELD. Sheila Feld received an A.B. degree from Brooklyn College and A.M. and Ph.D. degrees from the University of Michigan, joining the social work faculty as associate professor. During her tenure at
Michigan, Feld held posts of assistant dean from 1971 to 1981 and head
of the doctoral program from 1982 to 1989. Her teaching areas included
applications of social psychological theory/research to the delivery of social services, mental health, and marital and parental roles across the life
course. Her early research focused on social psychology theory, with her
co-authorship of *Americans View Their Mental Health* (1960), *Marriage
and Work in America* (1970), and *Social Psychology for Social Work and
the Mental Health Professions* (1982). She was recognized for her work
with the Senate Advisory Committee on University Affairs by receiving
the university's Distinguished Faculty Governance Award. Feld has been
co-director of a training grant on "Social Research Training on Applied
Issues on Aging" and was a fellow of the American Psychological Association. The regents named her professor emerita of social work in 2000,

and the faculty honored her by establishing the Sheila Feld Collegiate Professorship of Social Work. Robert Joseph Taylor was appointed to the professorship. Professor Feld currently participates in research on aging projects at the school.

MADISON FOSTER. Madison Foster came to the school as an assistant professor, having received a B.A. degree from Morehouse College, an M.S.W. from Michigan, and a Ph.D. from Bryn Mawr College. His dissertation at Bryn Mawr was entitled "Societal in Paradigms and Social Policy Theories: An Analysis of Urban Black Disruption Explanations, 1960–1970." His teaching areas included Black self-evaluation, Blacks and social policy, and social insurance in Western Europe. Illustrative publications while at Michigan include "Black Organizing: The Need for a Conceptual Model of the Ghetto" in *Catalyst*, "Minority Populations and Mental Health Manpower Development" (with L. Ferman), and "Black Blues and Black Revolutionary Workers" (with J. Erlich) in *Changes* (1971). He was honored as "Emergent Black Scholar" in 1975 by the Black Sociologists of the American Sociological Association. Foster left the school in 1984 to take a faculty position at Atlanta University.

HAROLD JOHNSON. Harold Johnson was appointed to the faculty as professor of social work, coming to the school with a B.A. degree from the University of Western Ontario and an M.S.W. degree from Wayne State University. Prior to joining the faculty, he had held leadership positions in a variety of public and voluntary social welfare agencies. Johnson was also professor of health behavior and health education in the School of Public Health. He gave leadership to the community practice curriculum at the school, and from 1975 to 1981 he was the director of the Institute of Gerontology. He was appointed dean of the school in 1981. He currently resides in Ann Arbor and Florida. A complete profile appears in chapter four, "The Johnson Years."

ROBERT SEGAL. Robert Segal came to the school from Brandeis University, where he completed his doctoral degree with a dissertation, "The Associations for Retarded Children: A Force for Social Change." He held a B.S. degree from the University of Wisconsin and an M.S.W. degree from the University of Pittsburgh. At Michigan he was an associate professor of social work and program director, Institute for the Study of Mental Retardation. He published in the field of mental retardation and remained on the faculty until 1979.

1970–71
New Faculty: Robert Carter, Yeheskel Hasenfeld, and David Himle

ROBERT CARTER. Robert Carter came to Michigan for doctoral studies, having completed his B.S. degree at Lynchburg College and his M.S.W. from the University of Tennessee. Completing his Ph.D. in the Joint Doctoral Program in 1969, he joined the faculty as assistant professor on a U.S. Public Health Service grant. His dissertation was entitled, "Gazing and Smiling and the Communication of Interpersonal Affect in a Quasi-Interview Situation." Carter developed teaching materials that utilized psychological and sociological theory and related this to professional practice. His interest and excellence in teaching led Carter to leave the university in 1978 for a faculty position in a liberal arts college.

YEHESKEL HASENFELD. Yeheskel Hasenfeld came to Michigan for doctoral studies with a bachelor's degree from Hebrew University and an M.S.W. degree from Rutgers. He served as instructor in social work during his doctoral studies at Michigan, completing a Ph.D. in 1970, when he was appointed assistant professor. His dissertation was entitled, "People Processing Organizations and Client Careers: A Study of Four Anti-Poverty Organizations." Hasenfeld's areas of teaching and research included sociology of the welfare state, client–organization relations, human service organizations, and social welfare administration. While at Michigan he rose to the rank of full professor of social work and sociology, was head of the Joint Doctoral Program, and served for five years as associate dean. He left the university to join the faculty at the University of California at Los Angeles in 1988.

DAVID HIMLE. David Himle came to the university for doctoral studies, having earned degrees in theology from the Lutheran ministry. He completed his M.S.W. and Ph.D. degrees at Michigan with a dissertation, "Effects of Instructions on Autonomic Response." His teaching areas included test and performance, anxiety stress management, marital conflict, interpersonal practice, and job satisfaction. Initially appointed as lecturer, he attained the rank of full professor prior to his death in 1993. In a memorial statement, the regents noted that "during his career, Professor Himle was a productive scholar, particularly in the areas of interdisciplinary studies on cognitive and behavioral theory and in interpersonal helping." At the time of his death, the regents recognized that "Professor Himle has left an enduring mark on his students and colleagues, both through his professional accomplishments and his qualities as a person. He was known to his students and colleagues as a creative and stimulating teacher with a flair for telling stories of things his mother used to say as a way of explaining rather complex ideas" (Board of Regents, 1993).

Summary

Faculty Members: 1970–71

Allen, JoAnn	Fellin, Phillip	Powell, Thomas
Bernard, Sydney	Ferman, Louis	Radin, Norma
Bertcher, Harvey	Foster, Madison	Reebel, Katherine
Booth, Philip	Freud, Clarice	Riley, John
Brabson, Howard	Gambrill, Eileen	Robinson, Dorothy
Carter, Beryl	Garvin, Charles	Rothman, Jack
Carter, Robert	Glasser, Paul	Sarri, Rosemary
Churchill, Sallie	Gordon, Jesse	Schroeder, Dorothy
Connor, Alan	Harris, Oliver	Segal, Robert
Cook, Loraine	Hasenfeld, Yeheskel	Siegel, Sheldon
Costabile, Jane	Himle, David	Stuart, Richard
Cox, Fred	Johnson, Harold	Sundel, Martin
Croxton, Tom	Kim, Stanley	Taylor, Mary
Dinsmore, Merle	Lauffer, Armand	Thomas, Edwin
Drews, Nathalie	Lawrence, Harry	Tripodi, Tony
English, Richard	Lind, Roger	Tropman, John
Epstein, Irwin	Litwak, Eugene	Vasey, Wayne
Erlich, John	Maple, Frank	Vinter, Robert
Fauri, Fedele	Meyer, Henry	Warren, Donald
Feld, Sheila	Neenan, William	Wolfson, Charles

Faculty Retiring/Departing: 1951–71

Anton, Thomas	Cranefield, Eleanor	Pinkus, Helen
Bechill, William	Dunham, Arthur	Portner, Faye
Borenzweig, Herman	Fletcher, Ralph	Rabinovitz, Patricia
Bown, George	Galinsky, Maeda	Resnick, Herman
Burns, Mary	Gary, Lawrence	Rose, Sheldon
Bushey, Pauline	Gottfried, Leanore	Sales, Esther
Casson, Morton	Green, Martha	Swell, Lila
Cohen, Wilbur	Lazarus, Mitchel	Turner, William
Cowley, David	Pawlak, Edward	Vorwaller, Darrel

PART FOUR   The School's Curriculum

Introduction

In creating the School of Social Work, the regents conveyed certain powers upon the governing faculty, including the provision of "the necessary
courses of instruction," commonly known as the curriculum, and "appropriate requirements for graduation" (Board of Regents, 1951). At the Institute of Social Work in Detroit, the total social work faculty served as a
curriculum committee, taking such actions as approving the courses offered, determining the courses from other academic units allowed toward
the degree, creating transfer of credit options, and determining the number
of credit hours necessary for the degree. The entire faculty continued to be
engaged in these curriculum activities in the new School of Social Work.

However, as the size of the faculty grew in the mid-1950s, a Curriculum Committee was formed to monitor and recommend changes in the
curriculum. Committee recommendations moved from this group to the
faculty as a whole for approval, following the old principle of *quod omnes
tangit ab omnibus approbetur*. In the early years the dean, and later a senior faculty member, chaired the Curriculum Committee. By 1964 one of
the major activities of the associate dean was curriculum development and
chairing of the Curriculum Committee. Under this arrangement, Associate
Dean Robert Vinter had a major influence on the direction and changes in
the school's curriculum in the 1960s.

This account of the curriculum in the School of Social Work from
1951 to 1971 draws mainly on information from *School Bulletins*. The curriculum is described in terms of its objectives and its basic framework of
course requirements and distribution of courses in the various curricular
areas. Major changes are cited with regard to the following:

- Conceptualizations of core curricular areas: practice methods or specializations, human growth and behavior/human behavior and the social environment, social welfare policies and social services, social research, and
  field instruction;
- Development of specific courses in these areas;
- Distribution of courses and total credit hours required for the M.S.W.
  degree.

Changes in curriculum organization and course offerings occurred
from year to year, with major revisions of the total curriculum, commonly
referred to in each instance as a "new" curriculum, occurring in 1958–59

and 1968–69. This discussion of changes in the curriculum is followed in the next section by attention to the faculty behind the curriculum, with the focus on individual faculty members who participated in a major way in teaching, research, scholarship, and service in the various curricular areas.

The School's Curriculum: 1951–52

In 1950–51 the total faculty of the Institute of Social Work met as a Curriculum Committee to prepare for changes in the curriculum for the 1951–52 academic year in the new School of Social Work. As a framework for curriculum revision, Professor Dunham, acting director of the institute, suggested five general aims for social work education: knowledge, professional attitudes, practice skills, research, and leadership. Based on the faculty's discussion of these aims, the 1951–52 *School Bulletin* states the school's objectives as follows:

> The School of Social Work seeks to provide professional education so that the student may equip himself to give the most effective possible service as a social worker. In making available social work education, this School seeks to help the student:
> 1. To acquire basic knowledge and understanding of social welfare needs; of the various methods of meeting these needs and of the effects of these methods upon the national economy; and of the nature, objectives, and methods of the profession of social work.
> 2. To develop professional attitudes and a professional philosophy; skill in practice in at least one area of social work; understanding of and ability to do research in reference to social work; and capacity for leadership in the field of social welfare.

The curriculum offered in the Institute of Social Work was changed for the School of Social Work in 1951–52 to include (1) Development of the Individual I and II, covering growth of the normal individual from the prenatal period through old age (replacing Mental Hygiene I and II); (2) Social Work and Social Backgrounds, covering the social, economic, political, and cultural components of social work theory, practice, and organization (replacing Introduction to Social Work and the Economic Basis of Social Work).

The curriculum for the 1951–52 year was a two-year program organized around basic course requirements and specializations. The *School Bulletin* indicated that "the basic requirements for all candidates for the degree are intended to ensure that all students have a common basis of knowledge and understanding for the practice of social work. In general, the programs of most students are fairly similar during the first year." Courses required for all candidates for the M.S.W. degree were Development of the Individual I and II, Social Work and Social Backgrounds, Community Organization for Social Work, Public Welfare, Social Case Work, Research Methods in Social Work, Thesis Seminar, and Field Work.

For the second year, the student selected a specialization, based on the view of the faculty that "professional education prepares students for practice within broad areas, and does not attempt to 'train' them merely for service in particular types of agencies or jobs." According to the *School Bulletin,* "The School seeks to emphasize the integration of the contributions of various specializations in the profession of social work." Specializations for the year 1951–52 were the following:

- Social Case Work (including opportunity for concentration on one or more of several areas of practice, including family case work, case work with children, medical social work, psychiatric social work, or school social work)
- Public Welfare Administration
- Community Organization
- Research in Social Work

At this time the school did not have a specialization in social group work, although basic courses were offered in this area. A limited number of students with experience in social work were accepted for a specialization in the area of executive management and leadership of voluntary social welfare agencies.

Course credit requirements for the M.S.W. degree were as follows:

Required courses	14 credit hours
Elective courses	12–16 credit hours
Fieldwork	12–16 credit hours
Thesis seminar	6 credit hours
Total hours for degree	48 credit hours

A thesis was required for all candidates for the degree. While a comprehensive oral exam was still required, after September 1951, "the student could be exempted from the oral exam if he completes the Social Work Seminar with a satisfactory grade (B or above)."

Fieldwork was defined as a controlled educational experience in social work practice, supervised by a qualified staff member in an established agency approved by the faculty, or supervised directly by a faculty member. The purpose of the fieldwork was to integrate actual practice with content gained in academic courses in the school. The fieldwork requirement was a minimum of 950 clock hours of fieldwork for 12 hours' credit. A maximum of four semester hours of additional credit in fieldwork could be taken as electives. Fieldwork normally extended through three semesters and included experience in at least two types of agencies, with emphasis upon the area of the student's specialization. In the 1951–52 academic year, forty-five social agencies and health organizations from both private and public service sectors participated in the fieldwork program, with seventy-seven supervisors providing instruction.

During the year of transition from Detroit to Ann Arbor, first-year courses were offered in both Ann Arbor and Detroit, with second-year courses offered only in Ann Arbor. Students could enter the school either in September or February. There was a provision for part-time students who carried fewer than ten hours of work in the school, but one or more semesters of full-time study was required for the degree. Ordinarily the program of a full-time student during one semester was 8 clock hours a week of class work (four courses), yielding 8 hours credit, and 20 clock hours a week of fieldwork, yielding 4 hours credit, or a total of 12 hours credit per term. The *School Bulletin* noted, "It is assumed that, on the average, two hours of class work will require four hours of preparation each week."

The *School Bulletin* of 1951–52 indicated that "the faculty has been making a careful study of problems of curriculum revision and planning, and it is expected that certain changes in the curriculum will be announced early in 1952 and will be put into effect in September, 1952." Changes planned for the curriculum for the 1952–53 year included (1) addition of a required course on Public Welfare II, to supplement Public Welfare I; and (2) addition of the elective courses Current Problems of Public Welfare Administration, Group Process in Social Work, Problems of Community Welfare Councils and Community Chests, Psychopathology for Social Workers, and Social Work Seminar. The addition of courses related to public welfare was made in keeping with the regents' direction when creating the school—that is, an emphasis on administration of public welfare services.

Grades
The *School Bulletin* of 1951–52 states that "a student is expected to attain at least an average of B in all of his work. In addition, his overall performance must be satisfactory in course work, in field work, and in his thesis study." An expanded reference to grades, with a definition of different levels of grades,

appeared for the first time in the *School Bulletin* of 1959–60. This definition of grades, which continued basically the same through the 1970–71 academic year, reads as follows:

> Letter grades from A through E are given for class and field instruction and students are expected to maintain at least a B average. When a student falls below this average, he may remain in school only with the approval of the Faculty Administrative Committee. Permission to remain in the School may be granted if there is reasonable likelihood that this grade average may be improved in a subsequent semester.
>
> B grades are given to students who do all the required work for the course satisfactorily. B plus and B minus reflect slight differences from this satisfactory level. A grades are given for exceptional individual performance and C grades are given when performance definitely falls below requirements for graduate work. D grades indicate unconditional failure, and E is given when a course is dropped after the end of the eighth week of a semester or the fourth week of a summer session.
>
> A student who is unable to meet minimum standards in his field placement may be dropped from field instruction at any time. In such instances an E grade is recorded on the student's record at the time he is withdrawn from the field agency, and the Faculty Administrative Committee will determine whether or not the student may remain in the School. I, for Incomplete, is used when illness or other compelling reason prevents completion of work and there is a definite plan in regard to when work will be completed.

The School's Curriculum: 1952–53 to 1958–59

During this time period, the development of the school's curriculum was guided by a curriculum policy statement adopted for accreditation purposes by the Council on Social Work Education in 1952. The policy statement called for a cohesive curriculum to "provide a framework of classroom and field courses and research within which the student may test and use theoretical knowledge, acquire professional skill, achieve a professional self-discipline, and develop a social philosophy rooted in an appreciation of the essential dignity of man." The policy allowed each school to design the specific courses but required coverage of three broad subject areas through classes, fieldwork, and research. The three areas were these: "the social services, their development, and their relation to the social order, to social change, and to community needs; knowledge and understanding of human behavior, needs and aspirations; and knowledge and understanding of social work practice" (Hollis & Taylor, 1951). "Responsibility for determining and organizing the appropriate combinations of courses to meet the requirements of the policy statement was left to the individual schools, with the proviso that the curriculum must ensure balance of subject matter and progression in learning" (Kendall, 2002).

The distribution of credit hours changed somewhat for the 1952–53 academic year, with a reduction of hours for the thesis seminar from 6 to 4. The total credit hours required for the degree remained at 48. A thesis continued to be required, along with an oral examination, which could be substituted by a seminar. Fieldwork continued to carry a range of between 12 and 16 credit hours. The *School Bulletin* stated: "Students having field placements in various cities throughout the state usually find it possible to arrange travel schedules without undue difficulty, sometimes through car pools. Some students live in the community where they are placed in field work, staying overnight in Ann Arbor or Detroit one night a week. Some overnight accommodations in Ann Arbor are available for $1.50. This arrangement is possible since three days each week are spent in field work, and all classes are offered on two successive days."

The "New" Curriculum of 1958–59
In 1957 the Board of Regents approved a plan submitted by the faculty to change the total hours required for the M.S.W. degree from 48 hours to 56 hours. This new requirement was established for students enrolling in the fall semester of 1958. The usual program for completing the program was two years of study, although acceleration of the program was possible through summer study. The 1958–59 *School Bulletin* restated the school's objectives as follows:

> The master's program seeks to help the student develop a professional philosophy and a capacity for leadership, and to acquire basic knowledge, skills, and attitudes in three major areas:
> 1. Social services and social welfare policies, and their interaction with social, cultural, and economic forces.
> 2. Human growth and behavior, including adaptations to group process and social organization.
> 3. Methods and processes utilized in social work practice.

These objectives were consistent with the guidelines provided in the curriculum policy statement of the Council on Social Work Education. The distribution of courses organized to meet these objectives was as follows:

Social Services and Social Policy   8 hours
  (Social Services I, II, III, Seminar)
Human Growth and Behavior   10 hours
  (Group Process and Social Organization I, Individual Growth and Be-
  havior I, II, Group Process III or Individual Growth and Behavior III)
Social Work Practice   18 hours
  (Introduction to Social Work Practice [casework and group work], So-
  cial Work Practice [casework or group work], Community Organization
  Practice, Research Methods, Administrative Aspects of Social Work, So-
  cial Work Practice III and IV)
Research Seminar I and II (thesis or participation in group research project)
Field Instruction   14 hours
Electives   6 hours
Total Credit Hours required for the degree: 56

A thesis continued to be a requirement for the degree, along with an option
of completing a group project, until the 1965–66 academic year. An oral
examination was no longer required.

Specializations were designed to provide the student with knowledge
and skill for the practice of social work in one of five major areas: social
casework, social group work, community organization, research in social
work, and social welfare administration. Within the social casework area,
further concentration was possible in family casework, public assistance,
medical social work, psychiatric social work, school social work (visiting
teacher), child welfare, or corrections. Within social group work, the student could concentrate further in leisure-time services or in treatment-
centered and institutional programs.

In this new curriculum, 14 hours of credit in field instruction were
required through field assignments in the two years of study. In the first year
of study, the student spent two days (16 hours) per week at a social agency
for 6 credit hours, usually one offering casework or group work services.
The second-year student gained 8 credit hours by spending twenty hours
per week in a social agency with a focus on the student's specialization.

Curriculum Policy and Reaccreditation
The curriculum at Michigan during the school's early years continued
to be guided by a 1952 CSWE curriculum policy statement. However, by
1962 the Council on Social Work Education produced a new curriculum
policy statement to guide schools of social work in curriculum development. The new policy statement differed from the previous one in several

respects, including the replacement of objectives that described what students should be taught by objectives about what the student was expected to learn. "The principles of continuity, sequence, and integration in the construction of the curriculum are made explicit in a section on learning experiences. . . . The 1962 policy retained the requirement of a concentration in a social work method, although not necessarily in a two-year sequence in the same method, as the best way to qualify as a professional practitioner" (Kendall, 2002). It was not until a new CSWE curriculum policy appeared in 1969 that schools gained "a high degree of freedom in curriculum development," that is, "schools were asked to define for themselves what they were trying to do and what they expected to achieve through their educational programs" (Kendall, 2002).

In 1962 the school prepared a report for reaccreditation by CSWE, with a site team visit to the school in the spring of 1963. The site team consisted of Professors Alfred J. Kahn, chair, Helen Harris Perlman, and Paul Simon. Following the site visit, the team's report began as follows: "The report by the faculty of the University of Michigan School of Social Work in connection with the reaccreditation process is relatively concise; yet it demonstrates a degree of alertness to basic problems, a spirit of experimentation, and a determination to move ahead which is throughout exciting and reassuring. This impression is reinforced by the team visit." The site team report commented on all areas of the curriculum, such as social services, human growth and behavior, research, and field instruction, with a major focus on the practice sequences of casework, group work, community organization, and administration.

The school was reaccredited, with the site team reporting: "The Dean is highly regarded by the University administration and colleagues in other departments and has assured strong leadership. The School has been provided with facilities, resources, personnel and support in a measure consistent with what has been possible for the University—and its steady growth and quality give evidence of the conviction that the University of Michigan needs and will support a strong School of Social Work. The faculty's capacity for self-study and for defining its own problems and priority tasks—as demonstrated in its reaccreditation report and its participation in the team visit—leave one with the conviction that future goals, when set, will be soundly conceived and vigorously pursued."

Curriculum: 1960–61 to 1970–71
In 1960–61 the *School Bulletin* began including information about the field of social work in relation to the school's educational objectives. Thus,

the bulletin announced: "A wide variety of opportunities for personally rewarding and socially valuable employment exists for men and women graduates of the School of Social Work. Specialists in human relations are needed in many fields to work constructively on the important social problems of our times. The demand for social workers far exceeds the supply. There are shortages in all areas of social work practice, in research, and in supervisory, policy-development, and administrative positions. Advancement is rapid for those with graduate training. Many positions in public agencies provide civil service status with protection of tenure, opportunities for promotion, and retirement plans."

The *School Bulletins* of 1961–62 through 1963–64 included a section, "Information on Social Work Methods and Settings." This section included definitions of social work methods and social services, as follows:

> There are two methods in social work that deal directly with people who need help: casework and group work. Both methods are used to help people of all ages achieve improved social and emotional adjustment. Caseworkers interview people individually and group workers guide participation in organized groups.
>
> There are three other methods of social work in which the professional provides leadership to staff and the lay community for the improvement in the quantity and quality of social services. These methods are community organization, administration, and research.

Students were advised that their choice for a practice method in the first year would be casework or group work, associated with a field placement in the chosen method. During the second year the student could (1) continue to learn practice skills in the same method with which he began at the school, (2) change from one direct method to the other, or (3) take fieldwork in one of the three other methods. Social welfare services were classified according to types of social problems and/or client groups. "Thus there are agencies which specialize in mental health problems, medical problems, income maintenance problems, services to children, leisure time and recreation services, services to juvenile delinquents or adult criminals (corrections). These agencies may be public or private, sectarian or non-sectarian, and they provide institution or non-institutional services or both."

By 1963–64 the *School Bulletin* included expanded definitions of social work practice methods, as follows:

Social work is a helping process aimed at solving social problems affecting individuals, groups, and communities. The objective is to achieve improved social and emotional adjustment of individuals of all ages and backgrounds and to strengthen the social environment in which they live. Caseworkers interview people individually, group workers guide participation in organized groups, and community organization workers serve planning committees made up of representatives of community groups. In each instance the general professional approach is similar—to guide individuals in a logical, orderly, objective process of problem solving. In addition to the practice methods of casework, group work, and community organization, social workers also engage in administration and social research. Administrators aid in the enactment of social policy into social services usually through a social welfare agency. They also contribute to the formulation of policy. Social researchers engage in fact finding and experimentation which provide a scientific basis for the development of practice method and of social policy.

Beginning in 1966–67 and continuing in 1967–68, the *School Bulletin* introduced new descriptions of practitioners of group work, community organization, and social welfare administration, as follows:

- Group workers serve individuals within and through small groups in order to achieve desired changes in client behavior, attitudes, and social relations.
- Community organization workers help to improve services for people in trouble and facilitate planning and action to prevent social ills. They foster team work among groups, gather information on social conditions, and work with citizens in social change efforts.
- Social welfare administrators in both top executive and beginning administrative assistant posts participate in operating and strengthening social welfare programs. In such positions as program or policy analyst or social legislation adviser, persons trained in this method also participate in shaping social policy relating to health and welfare concerns.

The "New Curriculum": 1968–69
Led by Associate Dean Robert Vinter in 1965 and the following years, and in collaboration with his colleagues, the faculty engaged in "a thorough revision of the master's curriculum" (Vinter & Sarri, 1997). In an article entitled "Social Work and Social Welfare," Professors Henry Meyer, Eugene Litwak, Edwin Thomas, and Robert Vinter (1967) described course development activities in both the doctoral and master's programs that influenced the

conceptual framework for the "new" 1968–69 M.S.W. curriculum. This framework "explicitly recognized the program's levels of social organization (interpersonal, group and family, organizational, community, and societal), particularly in the HBSE and practice methods areas, thereby providing the necessary foundation for the expanded ranges of practice specializations and fields of practice" (Vinter & Sarri, 1997). The objectives of the school's curriculum for 1968–69 were stated in *School Bulletins* as follows:

> The basic task of the School in the area of education is the preparation of qualified social work professionals through a two-year program of study leading to the degree of Master of Social Work. This program seeks to help the student develop a professional philosophy and a capacity for leadership as well as acquire basic knowledge, skills, and attitudes in three major areas:
> - Forces shaping public policy, social welfare organizations and the social services they provide;
> - Human growth and behavior, including relevant psychological, biological, and sociological knowledge;
> - Methods and processes comprising social work practice.

The framework for the new curriculum for 1968–69 was summarized by Fellin and Vinter (1969) in "Curriculum Development for Contemporary Social Work Education: University of Michigan," a chapter in the Tulane University volume *Modes of Professional Education* (1969).

> Our approach begins by reference to the level of intervention at which the professional practitioner must function, and seeks to prepare persons with appropriate competencies to assume entry positions at one of four levels. The level of intervention concept takes account of the "service units" toward which professional activity is directed (i.e., individuals, group, organizations, etc.) and the "service structures" through which such activity is conducted (i.e., the agencies and modes of "service delivery").
>
> Four major levels have been identified which now enjoy the exercise of social work skill and which are within the legitimate but not exclusive domain of this profession. These are the interpersonal, organizational, community, and societal levels. Each can be described with indications of the distinctive tasks and contemporary roles associated with it.
> (1) Social workers who function at the interpersonal level are concerned with modifying the behavior, or alleviating the difficulties experi-

enced by individuals and by small groups, such as families and gangs. These practitioners intervene directly in concrete human situations, and require various interpersonal skills to achieve modifications in these situations. Their efforts may be directed primarily at effecting change in persons, in their immediate social situations, or in both. Much of contemporary casework and group work practice is carried forward at this level.

(2) At the organizational level professionals are concerned with serving certain intra-agency tasks, effecting changes in agency arrangements, or in the agency's relations with its environment. . . . The ultimate purpose of such activities is to improve services for aggregations of clients. Staff training, program planning and analysis, supervision of subprofessionals, budgeting, and program evaluation are among the variety of roles recognized at this level.

(3) Professionals functioning at the community level of intervention deal with groups, organizations, governmental units, and population aggregates; they seek to alter and improve relations among these units to implement certain welfare goals. They may be attached to operating service organizations, and work out of these (e.g. district consultations or school-community agents), or they may serve within larger planning and coordinating organizations which do not deal directly with clientele.

(4) There are also professionals who perform tasks at the societal level, contributing to the development of social policy and health and social welfare programs at state, national, and international levels.

Each level of intervention calls for a somewhat distinctive pattern of skills, directs its efforts toward a different set of "targets," and, for the most part, attempts to solve a different set of problems—or differing dimensions of the same general problems. Each level of intervention affords avenues of advancement within a range of potential career lines in social work.

This new curriculum, grounded in a "levels of intervention" approach, included three broad divisions: social treatment, community practice, social welfare administration and policy development, with specializations within each division. Each specialization had a somewhat different pattern of required and elective study. The concept of social treatment is introduced for the first time in the curriculum as an umbrella category for the practice methods of social casework and social group work at an interpersonal intervention level.

Intervention Levels	Curricular Divisions	Practice Specializations
Interpersonal	Social Treatment	Social Treatment: Casework, Group Work, Social Treatment
Community	Community Service	Community Practice
Organizational Societal	Social Welfare Administration/Policy	Administration, Policy

Course content was distributed by credit hours as follows:

Course Areas	Social Treatment	Community Practice	Social Work Adm/Policy
Practice methods	10	10	10
H.B.S.E.	12	10	8
S.W. policy/services	4	4	4
Research	4	4	4
Practice skill	16	16	16
Total credit hours	56	56	56

Under this curriculum, field instruction was also referred to as practice skill instruction. Field instruction continued to be defined as "a controlled educational experience in social work practice supervised by a qualified professional in an established agency or supervised directly by a faculty member," with the "purpose of field instruction being to integrate actual practice with content gained in academic courses in the School." Sixteen hours of field instruction were required for the degree. The student was expected to spend the equivalent of two days a week for sixteen weeks with a minimum of 240 clock hours per term in an assigned agency (4 hours credit per term). Field instruction was taken in "a planned relationship to practice courses in the same specialization" (*School Bulletin*, 1968–69). The reconceptualization of the curriculum was accompanied by an expansion of the types of field instruction locales. By the year 1970–71 the school was using 170 field sites, compared to 45 agencies in 1951–52. Over 330 field instructors contributed their time and skills in supervising students in field instruction, compared with 77 instructors in 1951–52.

This new curriculum moved "toward more balanced instructional programs, toward inclusion of a broader range of social and behavioral sciences, toward training for competence in newer helping processes, and toward searching re-examination of the practice skill component of profes-sional education" (Fellin & Vinter, 1969). The revision effort involved re-view and changes in courses, development of new courses, and evaluation of the implementation of the effectiveness of the new curriculum. These efforts were directed by Associate Dean Robert Vinter and other senior faculty members in setting in motion "a foundation for continual efforts in the curriculum planning, evaluation, and renewal."

Course revision and development of new courses are exemplified in the course area of Human Behavior and Social Environment, a term used to replace Human Growth and Behavior. In keeping with the curriculum policy statement of CSWE, the title and orientation of this course area was changed to reflect a new focus on the social environment. New courses grounded in the behavioral and social sciences in this area included Per-sonality, Social Role and the Small Group, Theory of Interpersonal Change, Complex Organizations, Community Structure and Processes, Metropol-itan Problems and Urban Change, Societal Structure and Processes, In-novation and Change in Social Welfare Organizations, and Social Welfare Legislation and Change (*School Bulletin*, 1968–69).

The new curriculum gave attention to the inclusion of courses and course content on minority populations. For example, courses pertinent to the Black community were developed in keeping with a report by Lawrence Gary, doctoral student and later faculty member, "A Proposal for Relating Social Work Education to the Black Community." Courses in the area of Human Behavior and the Social Environment included Afro-American Culture and Life, Racism in American Society, and Politics and Economy of the Black Community (Gary, 1968).

The terminology for the specializations offered in 1970–71 changed slightly, but the basic structure of the curriculum remained the same as developed in 1968–69. In 1970–71 the name of the social treatment special-ization was changed to interpersonal practice. Three programs continued to be offered in this specialization: casework, group work, and social treat-ment. Specializations in community practice and in social welfare admin-istration and policy methods remained the same. Students interested in changing specializations or programs usually made the transfer between the first and second years of study.

Undergraduate Program in Social Work
During the period of 1951–71, the School of Social Work continued to par-ticipate in an undergraduate preprofessional program, which had the objec-tive of preparing "students for immediate entrance into semiprofessional

positions in social work and for more advanced study at the graduate level" (*School Bulletin*, 1958–59). This program included "courses in related social sciences and introductory courses with social welfare content." It was conducted by the Department of Sociology of the College of Literature, Science, and the Arts. The program was described as a "concentration" in social work, with most students completing a major in one of the social sciences. Professor Mary Taylor served as coordinator of this degree program.

Extension Service Programs in Social Work
The school continued its relationship with the university's Extension Service in 1951–52 and thereafter, providing courses in social work away from Ann Arbor. Each year through the auspices of the Extension Service, the faculty of the school, together with special lecturers, taught certain of the regular school courses in graduate study centers and other localities outside Ann Arbor and Detroit. The purpose of this program was to provide courses for groups of social work students on a graduate level who were unable because of their employment to come to Ann Arbor or Detroit for such courses.

Courses for the Adult Blind
A program of special studies initiated in 1945 under the sponsorship of the school continued in 1951–52 in co-operation with the Michigan State Normal College and the American Foundation for the Blind, with courses given at the Michigan State Normal College at Ypsilanti. This program was "designed as a special summer course of training for both blind and sighted persons, to fit them for such positions as case workers, public assistance visitors, and rehabilitation agents working with the blind" (*School Bulletin*, 1951–52).

U-M Fresh Air Camp
During the summer session program of 1953 at the School of Social Work, students were allowed to enroll for social work courses and fieldwork in casework or in group work at the U-M Fresh Air Camp on a lake twenty-five miles northwest of Ann Arbor. The *School Bulletin* noted that the camp provides "an integrated experience of theory and practice in dealing with childhood maladjustment. Students live at the camp for the period of the regular summer session, and board and lodging are provided." This program continued through the 1966–67 academic year.

Merrill-Palmer School
Co-operative arrangements with Merrill-Palmer School continued, "by which certain courses carried there are recognized after the manner of

cognates, and appropriate credit is allowed. The program is worked out with each student according to his course of study and his program of specialization" (*School Bulletin*, 1951–52).

Summer Institutes

A program of two-week institutes was offered during the 1952 summer session (regular session, 8 weeks) and for several years thereafter. These institutes provided an opportunity for brief, concentrated study and were primarily for persons currently employed in public and private social welfare agencies (*School Bulletin*, 1952–53). In March of 1953, the school, in collaboration with the Alumni Organization, began sponsoring an annual one-day educational institute for social work practitioners. These institutes featured nationally known persons in social work education and social welfare.

In 1954 an All-Upper-Peninsula Social Work Conference was offered by faculty members in Marquette, Michigan, in cooperation with Northern Michigan College of Education and the university's Extension Service. The following sessions were taught:

> Fedele F. Fauri: Evaluation and Impact of the "New" Social Security Law on Social Work
> Eleanor Cranefield: Community Planning for the Aged
> Patricia W. Rabinovitz: Impact of the "New" Social Security Measures on Public Assistance
> Clarice Freud: Social Services and Economic Security for Children

The 2nd All-Upper-Peninsula Social Work Institute was offered in 1956 in Marquette, Michigan, with the following sessions:

> Dorothy Schroeder: Interviewing and Recording for Diagnosis and Treatment
> Katherine R. Reebel: Interview and Recording for Medical Personnel
> Robert D. Vinter: Mental Hygiene in the School and in other Social Group Settings
> Patricia W. Rabinovitz: Personnel Policies and In-Service Training Program

Continuing Education Program

For the academic year 1970–71, the school placed institutes and extension courses under a Continuing Education Program, with Professor Armand

Lauffer as director. Expansion of continuing education efforts was made possible through a grant from the National Institute of Mental Health.

Review

In 1951–52 the two-year program leading to the M.S.W. degree required 48 credit hours. In 1958–59 a new curriculum changed the total credit hours required for the master's degree to 56. Major changes in this curriculum came about in 1968–69, still retaining the 56 credit hour requirement. This new curriculum moved "toward more balanced instructional programs, toward inclusion of a broader range of social and behavioral sciences, toward training for competence in newer helping processes, and toward searching re-examination of the practice skill component of professional education" (Fellin & Vinter, 1969). The school continued providing a preprofessional curriculum in social work at the undergraduate level. Significant in the school's activities was the provision of extension courses, summer institutes, and special arrangements for student learning at the university's Fresh Air Camp, the Merrill-Palmer School in Detroit, and the American Foundation for the Blind.

PART FIVE   The Faculty behind the Curriculum

Introduction

The major curricular areas and themes of the school's curriculum provide a framework for identifying faculty members associated with these parts of the curriculum.

Social Casework

Social casework was the dominant social work practice method taught at the school during the period from 1935 to 1951. Courses on casework practice were required of all students. By 1950 specializations in other practice areas had been established for the second year of study. Specialization options in the casework area were family casework, casework with children, medical social work, psychiatric social work, and school social work.

In 1951 a small group of women developed and taught courses in social casework. Five of these faculty members had attained their social work degrees from leading schools in casework as noted earlier: Eleanor Cranefield (University of Chicago), Clarice Freud (Western Reserve), Mary Taylor (Pennsylvania), Dorothy Schroeder (Smith College), and Helen Pinkus (Smith College). These individuals, along with Professor Kay Reebel

(Smith College) who joined the faculty in 1952, continued at the school until retirement, providing a strong core of faculty sometimes affectionately referred to as the "casework ladies," officed in "casework row." These faculty members taught the core social casework courses, Social Case Work I and II, as well as casework courses focused on specific fields of service.

Traditionally, teaching of social casework relied heavily on psychoanalytic theory, especially borrowed knowledge from Freudian theory. In many schools of social work, an emphasis on ego psychology as a theoretical base for casework practice emerged. The curriculum in social casework at Michigan in 1951 followed this national pattern. However, in the 1950s the Michigan curriculum increasingly focused on the application of knowledge from the social and behavioral science as well—for example, "role theory, small-group and social psychological theory. . . and learning theory and its application in behavior modification techniques" (Garvin & Glasser, 1971, 1974). From 1952 to 1971, a number of additional individuals were identified with the social casework area, including Professors Dorothy Robinson, Mary Burns, Merle Dinsmore, Loraine Cook, Nathalie Drews, Richard Stuart, Thomas Powell, JoAnn Allen, Eileen Gambrill, and David Himle.

Group Work

From 1951 to 1954 only a few courses in group work were offered at the school. For the academic year of 1951–52, Rachel Andresen, executive secretary, Ann Arbor Council of Churches, taught Group Work I and II. Faye Portner, assistant secretary, Council of Social Agencies, taught Group Process in Social Work.

Robert D. Vinter (1954–85) joined the faculty in 1954 and brought about a turning point in the development of a social group work program at Michigan. Vinter came to the school with practice experience in group work and as the first faculty member at the School of Social Work to have a combination of a master's degree in social work and a doctorate in a social science. Vinter taught a range of group work courses and provided the initial leadership in the development of what became known as the Michigan approach to social group work.

Paul Glasser (1958–78) added expertise to the group work program when he joined the faculty as assistant professor of social work. Glasser was head of the group work program at Michigan for many years, as well as a major participant in the development of social treatment as a specialization.

Rosemary C. Sarri (1960–93) was the third major appointment to the group work program. Sarri began teaching Group Work I in 1960, moving on to teaching Group Work II, III, and IV as well. Sarri played a significant role in the development of the group work program, as well as the program in social welfare administration.

In the following years, the following individuals with expertise in social group work joined the faculty:

Charles Wolfson (1961–91)
Jane Costabile (1962–79)
Frank Maple (1963–2003)
Harvey Bertcher (1964–95)
Sallie Churchill (1964–96)
Charles Garvin (1965–2001)
Sheldon Rose (1965–68)

Social Treatment

The use of the concept of social treatment was introduced into the new curriculum of 1968–69. The term was used to describe one of three major specializations, the other two being community practice and social welfare administration and policy. The *School Bulletin* (1968–69) stated: "Social treatment methods are aimed at modifying the behavior of the individual, his immediate social situation (family, gang) or both. By developing skills at this inter-personal level of intervention, students prepare for roles in restoring, sustaining, or improving the health and welfare of individual human beings in a variety of settings." The specialization in social treatment included three sequences:

- Casework sequence—prepares students for direct practice with and service to individual clients.
- Group treatment sequence—prepares students to treat individuals within and through groups.
- Social treatment sequence—by combining and integrating individual and group methods, prepares students to utilize techniques of direct service in a wide range of concrete human situations.

Community Organization

In 1951–52, Community Organization for Social Work I continued to be required of all candidates for the M.S.W. degree. The *School Bulletin* described this course as follows: "An introduction to community organization as one of the basic processes of social work. The community and social work. The nature, characteristics, and historical development of community organization. The community welfare council, community chest, and other agencies primarily concerned with this process. State-wide and national aspects of social welfare organization."

In 1951–52 community organization was one of the four specializations offered in the second year of study. In 1952–53 the Community Organization for Social Work title was changed to Community Organization for Social Welfare, taught by Professors Arthur Dunham and Faye Portner. From 1962 onwards, the school's program in community organization was strengthened through new faculty appointments. These included Professors Jack Rothman, Fred Cox, John Erlich, John Tropman, Al Connor, Harold Johnson, Irwin Epstein, Armand Lauffer, Donald Warren, Eugene Litwak, Howard Brabson, and Madison Foster.

Social Research
Social research as a practice specialization was offered in 1951. A research course in the new school curriculum continued to be required for all students. This course, Research Methods in Social Work I, was taught by Professor Ralph Fletcher. This course was described as follows: "The relation of research to social work practice. A survey of the methods of assembling, analyzing, and presenting data most commonly used in social work research." Research in social work was one of the four specializations offered in the second year of study.

Research continued to be a required course for the M.S.W. degree through 1971. In 1958–59 candidates for the M.S.W. degree were given the option of completing a thesis or group research project for 4 hours' credit. From 1965–66 onward there was no requirement for a thesis or group research project.

A number of faculty members taught social research courses and wrote about research methodology. Some of these faculty developed courses at the doctoral level, others at the master's level. Among faculty involved in the development of the research sequence at the master's level were Professors Ralph Fletcher, Robert Vinter, Edwin Thomas, Henry Meyer, Paul Glasser, Eugene Litwak, Rosemary Sarri, Jack Rothman, Jesse Gordon, Phillip Fellin, Tony Tripodi, and Irwin Epstein.

Social Welfare Administration
A major theme announced in the creation of the School of Social Work was that students be prepared for entry into public welfare work. The development of the school's curriculum reflected this objective in a number of areas, including the administration methods courses, as well as the social

services and social policy courses. In the early years of the School of Social Work, courses in administration were taught by Professors Arthur Dunham, Patricia Rabinovitz, Wilbur Cohen, and Fedele Fauri.

In 1960–61 the specialization was named social welfare administration, with the two principal courses renamed Administration I and II, continuing to be taught by Professors Dunham and Cohen. They were joined in this teaching in 1963–64 and ensuing years by Professors Patricia Rabinovitz, Robert Vinter, Rosemary Sarri, Roger Lind, Stanley Kim, Jack Riley, Sheldon Siegel, Wayne Vasey, and Yeheskel Hasenfield.

Several other faculty members contributed to the literature on social welfare administration, including Armand Lauffer (with others) in *Understanding Your Social Agency* (1977), *Volunteers* (1977), and *Grantsmanship* (1977); and Harvey Bertcher and Charles Garvin in *Staff Development in Human Service Organizations* (1988).

For the curriculum of 1968–69 a new specialization was created, named "social welfare administration and policy methods." This area included two sequences, social welfare administration and social welfare policy.

Social Services/Social Welfare Policy and Services

In 1951 the *School Bulletin* noted that courses in social welfare policy and services sought to help the student "to acquire basic knowledge and understanding of social welfare needs." The degree requirements at this time included only one of the policy/social services courses, Public Welfare I. Other courses in this area were required in relation to the student's specialization. In 1968–69, under a new curriculum structure, requirements in this area were reduced to only two courses (total of 4 hours' credit). The first course was Social Welfare Policy and Services I. The second was selected in relation to the student's specialization—Social Treatment, Community Practice, or Social Welfare Administration and Policy.

During the years from 1951 onward into 1960, Professors Arthur Dunham, Clarice Freud, Eleanor Cranefield, and Mary Taylor continued to teach these courses, along with new instructors, Dean Fedele Fauri and Professors Patricia Rabinovitz, Leanore Van Vliet, Helen Pinkus, Dorothy Schroeder, Katherine Reebel, Wilbur Cohen, and William Turner. Additional faculty began teaching the courses from 1961 to 1971: Charles Wolfson, Philip Booth, George Bown, Jane Costabile, Herman Resnick, Sheldon Siegel, Sydney Bernard, Sallie Churchill, Tom Croxton, Robert Vinter, Merle Dinsmore, Nathalie Drews, Roger Lind, Martha Green, Stanley Kim, John Riley, Jesse Gordon, Frank Maple, Robert Segal, Loraine Cook, Norma Radin, and Dorothy Robinson.

School Social Work

Courses related to the preparation of students for practice social work in the public schools have been offered under various forms: as a course in the casework methods sequence, as a course in human growth and behavior, and as a social services course. Initially, the term "visiting teacher" was used as a designation for social work practice in schools, followed by the term "school social workers" or "school social service." Traditionally at Michigan, school social work was offered as a concentration within the specialization of social casework.

School social work is first mentioned in the 1949–50 and 1950–51 bulletins of the Institute of Social Work, with a course offered entitled Case Work for School Social Workers. This course was taught by Professor Mary Taylor and described as follows: "Social case work methods as applied to problems of children in the public schools by social workers, by visiting teachers, and by other agencies working with children."

School social work was offered as an area of concentration within the social casework specialization in the school for 1951–52. Faculty involved in this area were Mary Taylor, Clarice Freud, Frank Maple, and Norma Radin.

Professors Robert Vinter and Rosemary Sarri engaged in research on group work in the public schools. Professors Henry Meyer and Eugene Litwak engaged in research centered on the problems arising in relations of families to schools. They conducted a Detroit Area Study in 1962–63 on family–school relationships in Detroit, publishing *School, Family, and Neighborhood: The Theory and Practice of School–Community Relations* (1974). Professors Rosemary Sarri and Frank Maple edited *The School in the Community* in 1972. The book represented one of the major goals of a national workshop in school social work in 1969, sponsored by the National Association of Social Workers and the National Institute of Mental Health "to stimulate innovation and change in school social work throughout the U.S."

Law and Social Work

Professor Robert Kelso, LL.B., first director of the Institute of the Health and Social Sciences in 1935, offered the first course on Law and Social Work. This course was required for the master of social work degree from 1935–36 until the close of the 1938–39 year, when it became an elective course. Professor Kelso continued to teach this course each year until his retirement in 1949–50. Throughout the time Professor Kelso taught the course, it was described in *School Bulletins* as "Survey of legal principles applicable to social welfare service." In 1950–51 the Institute of Social Work offered this course by a lecturer, Clare I. Toppin, Ph.B., LL.B., attorney at law, who continued to teach the course in 1951–52 and 1952–53 in the School of Social Work.

In 1953–54 the course Law and Social Work was replaced by Legal Aspects of Social Work and taught by Maxine B. Virtue, LL.B., director, Children's Study, James Foster Foundation. This course was described in the *School Bulletin* as "study of the basic concepts of jurisprudence and the function of the legal system as a part of the community. This course includes discussion of the common law system and the case precedent: structure and jurisdiction of courts; constitutional doctrines; domestic relations; criminal law. Certain procedural aspects of the law are included, such as pleading requirements encountered by social workers dealing with courts, and certain rules of evidence, such as those affecting the confidential nature of records or the admissibility of social case material." This course continued to be taught by Virtue through the academic year of 1960–61.

From 1954 to 1957–58, Virtue taught a second course in this area, Social Work and the Judicial Process, described as "a course designed for those currently employed by or working with courts and for others interested in analyzing methods for developing maximum co-operation between the fields of law and social work." From 1961–62 through 1967–68, Legal Aspects of Social Work was offered by a member of the Michigan Law School faculty, E. Donald Shapiro, director of the Institute of Continuing Legal Education.

Professor Tom Croxton (1964–2001), with M.S.W. and LL.B. degrees from the University of Michigan, began teaching Legal Aspects of Social Work in 1966–67. Croxton taught the course thereafter, renamed Law and Social Work in 1968–69, and published on this topic in professional journals.

Human Growth and Behavior/
Human Behavior and the Social Environment

The 1951–52 bulletin announced course requirements in the area of human growth and behavior to be Development of the Individual I and II (taught over the next few years by Professors Dorothy Schroeder, Helen Pinkus, James Cunningham, M.D., and Dorothy Robinson) and Social Work and Social Backgrounds (taught by Professors Mary Taylor and Ralph Fletcher).

The new curriculum introduced in 1958–59 used the title "human growth and behavior" for courses in this knowledge area. The objective of these courses was to help the student acquire basic knowledge, skills, and attitudes in human growth and behavior, including adaptations to group process and social organization. Required courses were:

- Group Process and Social Organization I (2 hours) (Professors Thomas, Vinter, and Glasser)
- Individual Growth and Behavior I (4 hours) (Professors Robinson, Schroeder, Reebel, and Burns)
- Individual Growth and Behavior II (2 hours) (Professors Robinson and Schroeder)
- Group Process and Social Organization II (2 hours) (Professors Meyer, Thomas, Vinter, and Litwak) or Individual Growth and Behavior III (2 hours) (Professors Schroeder, and Cook)

In 1968–69 a new curriculum renamed this area of knowledge "human behavior and social environment." Requirements were different for the three areas of specialization social treatment, community practice, and social welfare administration and policy. These requirements continued through 1971.

Social/Behavioral Science for Social Workers

The extension of social science knowledge and theory in the professional social work curriculum at Michigan came about through the addition of new faculty in the 1950s from the fields of psychology, social psychology, and sociology. As Vinter and Sarri (1997) note, "Early in this period the school recruited some faculty with both M.S.W. and social science Ph.D. degrees; they were called 'hybrids' and shared the dual orientations of the doctoral students. The first of these were Robert D. Vinter (1954) and Edwin J. Thomas (1956). Social scientists without the M.S.W. who were committed to collaboration between the sciences and the profession and to the aims of the joint program were soon also successfully recruited," including Henry J. Meyer and Eugene Litwak. These faculty members taught both doctoral and master's programs and engaged in research studies.

As Vinter and Sarri (1997) note: "During 1958–70 persons with doctorates explicitly appointed to contribute to the integration of social science within the curriculum, to conduct research, and to qualify for teaching in the doctoral program included, in order of appointment: Paul Glasser, Eugene Litwak, William Neenan (joint with Economics), Rosemary Sarri, Jack Rothman, Phillip Fellin, Charles Garvin, Sheldon Rose, Richard Stuart, John Tropman, Yeheskel Hasenfeld, Tony Tripodi,

Thomas Anton (joint with Political Science), Richard English, Eileen Gambrill, Irwin Epstein, Sheila Feld, Martin Sundel, David Himle, and Norma Radin."

In 1967 Professor Edwin Thomas edited *Behavioral Science for Social Workers*, in which all thirty-three contributions involved at least one faculty member at the University of Michigan School of Social Work. The foundation for this development of socio-behavioral theory for social work practice appears in Thomas's "Selecting Knowledge from Behavioral Science" in *Building Social Work Knowledge: Report of a Conference* (1964). The use of behavioral science in social work was exemplified in a volume edited by Professor Thomas and Esther Goodman entitled *Socio-Behavioral Theory and Interpersonal Helping in Social Work: Lectures and Institute Proceedings*.

Professor Thomas organized a set of presentations for the Annual Program Meeting of the Council on Social Work Education, to be published as *Socio-Behavioral Approach and Application to Social Work* (1967). Nine faculty members contributed to the following chapters of this publication:

1. "The Socio-Behavioral Approach: Illustrations and Analysis" (Thomas)
2. "Applications of Behavioral Treatment to Social Casework" (Stuart)
3. "A Behavioral Approach to Group Treatment of Children" (Rose)
4. "Applications of Socio-Behavioral Theory to Administrative Practice" (Lind)
5. "Implications of the Socio-Behavioral Approach for Community Organization Practice" (Fellin, Rothman, Meyer)
6. "Organizational Requisites for a Socio-Behavioral Technology" (Sarri, Vinter)

In 1971 Professor Thomas, along with Robert Carter and Claude Walter, published *Socio-Behavioral Techniques for Open Welfare Settings*, a progress report on research supported by the Social Rehabilitation Service of the U.S. Department of Health, Education, and Welfare. In 1974 Professor Thomas authored a book entitled *Behavioral Modification Procedure: A Sourcebook,* followed by numerous publications in this area.

Review

While the method of social casework provided the basic framework for study from 1935 to 1951, the teaching of this method was intermingled with content on the fields of social service that provided the context for social work practice. During this time, the student was always required to take a course in the practice method of community organization, but a methods specialization was offered only in social casework. By the 1949–50 academic year, specializations in other practice methods were offered for the second year of study, that is, community organization, research, and administration. These methods specializations were in place for the 1951–52 academic year in the new School of Social Work curriculum.

A number of impressions emerge in the presentation of faculty activities related to the curriculum. First, the early faculty members established a strong program in social casework, most often related to a range of fields of service. At the same time, the school always offered a course in community organization practice. While a strong social casework program continued, new faculty provided a teaching and knowledge resource for development of other practice methods. Thus, by the early 1950s a specialization in social group work was created, becoming a leading program in this area in the nation, as demonstrated by the scholarly publications of the faculty. During this period, the school's faculty developed a small but strong program in social welfare administration. By the early 1960s new faculty helped Michigan maintain a reputation for leadership in the area of community organization practice and gain a national reputation for programs in social research and social welfare administration. The school's faculty continued to provide strong programs in the areas of social services and social policy, such as medical and psychiatric social work, child welfare, and school social work. At the same time, the school continued its long tradition of providing courses in law and social work.

Perhaps the most dramatic change in the school's curriculum came with the addition of new faculty for the master's and doctoral programs, faculty with a social science and social work orientation. Separate courses in this knowledge content area were created and offered as theoretical foundations for the practice courses. Of particular note was the school's development of socio-behavioral theory as a foundation for interpersonal helping in social work. Faculty involved in teaching, research, and scholarly writing in general are identified in this section by time of arrival at the school and by illustrations of publications in the various curricular areas. By 1971 the school had amassed a large and highly talented faculty so that each part of the curriculum had not only excellent teaching but also scholarly writing and research that supported all areas of the total curriculum.

PART SIX   Summary of the Fauri Years

In summary, the following features about the School of Social Work during the period of 1951–71 moved the school into a position of national prominence in social work education.

The School's First Faculty
The school began with a small, dedicated, competent core of faculty members from the university's Institute of Social Work in Detroit, including Arthur Dunham, Eleanor G. Cranefield, Ralph C. Fletcher, Clarice Freud, Leanore Gottfried, and Mary Taylor. Joining these individuals in Ann Arbor were Fedele Fauri, Helen Pinkus, Kay Reebel, and Dorothy Schroeder.

The School's Deans
The first dean of the school, Fedele F. Fauri, was a lawyer experienced in social services and social welfare in the public sector at the local community, state, and federal levels of government. Fauri played the role of a "strong" dean for two decades, providing leadership within the school and the university, and in social work education and the field of health and social welfare at state and national levels. In 1964 Professor Robert Vinter was appointed by the regents to fill a new position of associate dean. In this capacity, Vinter gave leadership to curriculum development, course management, personnel appointments, and research and training grant development and administration. When Dean Fauri became vice president for state relations and planning at the university in 1970, Vinter became acting dean. In 1970 Professor Phillip Fellin was appointed assistant dean, serving in this position until his appointment as dean of the school in 1971.

The School's Location
The school first operated out of an old frame house on campus until 1957, when it moved across Washington Street to the Frieze Building. The Frieze Building provided the school with faculty and administrative offices, classrooms, conference rooms, and library in a central location.

The School's Student Enrollment/Graduates
The school's student enrollment increased dramatically during this twenty-year period, with the impetus for this growth coming from Dean Fauri and the faculty. The school began with a total enrollment of 187 students, 91 full-time and 96 part-time. By 1960 the total enrollment was 250 students, 152 full-time and 98 part-time. The school's total enrollment in 1970

was 769 students, 581 full-time and 188 part-time. For this year, the school ranked first of 70 schools of social work in full-time master's level enrollment. Through special recruitment efforts, the school's minority student population became 24 percent of the student population in 1970.

During the first ten years, the school graduated 550 students with the M.S.W. degree. In the next ten years, 1,790 students obtained an M.S.W., with a total of 2,340 M.S.W. degrees granted during the school's first twenty years.

The School's Tuition

At the opening of the school in 1951, the tuition for the full program in social work for each semester was $75 for residents, $200 for nonresidents. By 1960–61 tuition per semester had risen to $125 for residents, $300 for nonresidents. By the academic year 1970–71, tuition per semester was $270 for residents, $824 for nonresidents. (In contrast, tuition for a term in the year 2002–03 was $6,538 for residents, $11,958 for nonresidents.)

The School's Faculty

During the early years of the school, a small number of faculty members were joined by a large number of community professionals and faculty members from other schools and colleges at the university in the teaching of courses. The use of "outside" lecturers decreased as the size of the full-time faculty grew. The number of full-time faculty changed from nine in 1951 to twenty in 1960 to sixty in 1971. In this year, the school had the largest full-time faculty of all schools of social work in the nation. The school began with no minority members on the faculty and by 1970, through special recruitment efforts, had employed seven minority faculty members. In 1951 the faculty was composed of two-thirds women, but by 1970 women made up only 26 percent of the full-time faculty.

Faculty members recruited during the 1960s included people with social work practice experience in various fields of social service, many financed by federal government training grants. Individuals with doctorates in the social sciences were recruited for the doctoral and master's programs. In the 1960s, a large number of new faculty members came with an M.S.W. degree and a doctoral degree, many with an interest and experience in social research.

These twenty years were characterized by an increase in faculty members involved in social research projects, in federal social work training programs, in the publication of articles in professional journals and books, in presentations at state and national social work conferences, and in consulting services and board membership with social welfare organizations at all levels of government as well as the private sector of health and social services. During this period the school's faculty became nationally and internationally known for the publication of books on research findings, for textbooks in all social work practice areas, and for articles in social work and social science journals.

The School's Curriculum

The school's two-year master's program curriculum was strengthened year after year through changes in and additions to course offerings, with major changes introduced as "new curriculum" in 1958–59 and 1968–69. In 1951 course credit requirements for the M.S.W. degree totaled 48 hours, consisting of required courses, elective courses, fieldwork, and thesis seminar. The distribution of courses for the M.S.W. degree had requirements in the areas of social services and social policy, human growth and behavior, social work practice, research, field instruction, and electives.

The school's curriculum in 1951 had specializations in social casework, public welfare administration, community organization, and research. In the coming years, the curriculum was enhanced by the development of specializations in the full range of social work practice methods, gaining national prominence through faculty publications in these areas. The school's curriculum areas in health, mental health, child welfare, aging, and vocational rehabilitation were strengthened through state and federal funding for social work education.

A new curriculum in 1958 changed the total number of credit hours for the M.S.W. degree from 48 hours to 56 hours. During the 1950s there was an infusion of social science content into the curriculum. A thesis continued to be a requirement, with an option of a group project, until the 1965–66 academic year. Practice specializations were offered in casework, social group work, community organization, research, and social welfare administration.

The school's new curriculum in 1968–69 was characterized by a "levels of intervention" approach that included interpersonal, community, organizational, and societal levels. These were organized under curricular divisions of social treatment, community service, and social welfare administration and policy, as well as under practice specializations of casework, group work, community practice, administration, and policy. The curriculum became increasingly infused with social and behavioral science content, with faculty members gaining prominence nationally in this development.

The School's Service Programs

The school continued to provide course instruction at the undergraduate level in a preprofessional program within the Department of Sociology. The school continued to give courses in a number of Michigan and Ohio communities through the university's Extension Program, summer institutes, and a Continuing Education Program.

The School's Doctoral Program

The school introduced the first doctoral program in the nation in social work and social science, an interdisciplinary program in collaboration with social science departments of the university, with graduates taking faculty positions and deanships throughout the United States.

The doctoral program was created through the support of the university and the Russell Sage Foundation, the leadership of Dean Fedele Fauri and David French, and the participation of faculty members at the school and in professional schools and social and behavioral science departments of the university. Henry J. Meyer, a sociologist with ties to the profession and strong ties to Michigan—having taken bachelor's, master's, and doctoral degrees at this university—was recruited to head up the program, giving it outstanding and creative leadership from 1957 to 1970.

The School's Accreditation

The school continued to be accredited by the Council on Social Work Education during these two decades.

The Fellin Years

Chapter three, "The Fellin Years," covers the history of the school during the tenure of Dean Phillip Fellin.

An article printed in the university's student newspaper, *Michigan Daily*, on May 6, 1971, announced the school's appointment of a new dean.

Fellin Selected to Head School of Social Work
By Juanita Anderson

Assistant social work school Dean Phillip Fellin has been appointed the new dean of the school. Fellin will take office July l, succeeding Acting Dean Robert Vinter.

Fellin explained in an interview Tuesday that one of his first priorities will be to try to increase student and faculty participation in the school's governance.

"In every area students want increased involvement," said Fellin. "I think they should have it. The message I'm getting from students is that they are concerned about minority group content in the school and with working in the community," he added.

President Robben Fleming announced Fellin's appointment April 27. The Regents authorized Fleming to negotiate with Fellin at their April meeting.

In making the appointment Fleming said, "Dr. Fellin has made many contributions to the University since he first joined the faculty in 1965. He is known for developing innovative new ways to solve problems, and for stimulating creativity in others."

The method by which a new social work dean was to be selected was the subject of considerable debate within the social work school. Social Work Students Union had proposed that at least half the search committee's members be students, but the final compromise agreement resulted in a search committee composed of five professors, four students and a faculty chairman. Fellin said he does not feel the search committee dispute will hamper his effectiveness.

PART ONE   The School of Social Work: 1971–81

The School's Objectives and Programs: 1971
Social work education at Michigan at this time included four programs: the master of social work degree, the doctor of philosophy degree in social work and social science, the preprofessional program in the Department of Sociology, and the extension course and Continuing Education Program for social work professionals as well as for individuals interested in entering the master's program. The M.S.W. degree program's overall objective was described in the 1971–72 *School Bulletin* as follows:

> The basic task of the School was the preparation of qualified social work professionals through a four-term program of study leading to the degree Master of Social Work.
>
> This program seeks to help the student develop a professional philosophy and a capacity for leadership as well as acquire basic knowledge, skills, and attitudes in three major areas:
> - Forces shaping public policy, social welfare organizations and the social services they provide;
> - Human growth and behavior, including relevant psychological, biological, and sociological knowledge;
> - Methods and processes comprising social work practice.

The dean's annual report for 1972–73 to the university president noted the major goals of the School of Social Work as: "(1) providing programs of social work education based on knowledge and oriented toward service; (2) advancing basic and professional knowledge attuned to social work education and social welfare services; (3) cultivating and responding to opportunities for service to the social welfare field and the social work profession when such service facilitates education, research, and the application of knowledge." This report noted that "in pursuit of these objectives, the School's compelling commitment is to achieve excellence, to be sensitive to values of change and continuity, and to promote inclusiveness and diversity."

School Administration: 1971–81

Administrative personnel during the 1971–81 decade are listed here. Due to missing school records, a number of faculty members who served as program heads/committee chairs and as members of the Faculty Council are not identified.

Administrative Officers and Staff

Phillip Fellin, Dean (1971–81)
Richard English, Assistant Dean (1971–74)
Sheila Feld, Assistant Dean (1971–81)
Dee Morgan Kilpatrick, Assistant Dean (1974–81)
Tom Croxton, Acting Assistant Dean (1976–77), Director of Admissions (1978–81)
Sheldon Siegel, Director of Admissions (1971–?)
Charles Wolfson, Director of Practice Skill Instruction (1971–?)
Armand Lauffer, Coordinator of Continuing Education and Extension (1971–81)
Christina Neal, Director, School Librarian
Jane Costabile, Director, Student Services
Nathalie Drews, Director of Field Instruction

Directors of Doctoral Program

Rosemary Sarri (1970–77)
John Tropman (1972–73, 1978–79)
Yeheskel Hasenfeld (1979–80)
Norma Radin (1980–81)

M.S.W. Program Heads (1971)

Loraine Cook, Casework
Paul Glasser, Group Work
Harold Johnson, Community Organization
Jack Riley, Administration
Tony Tripodi, Research
Sydney Bernard, SWPS
Edwin Thomas, HBSE

M.S.W. Program Heads (1973–74)

JoAnn Allen, Casework
Harvey Bertcher, Group Work
Charles Garvin, Social Treatment

Harold Johnson, Community Organization
Tom Croxton, Administration
Tony Tripodi, Research
Edwin Thomas, HBSE
Sydney Bernard, John Tropman, SWPS

Program/Committee Heads (1980)
Sallie R. Churchill, Divisional Coordinator for Interpersonal Practice
Robert D. Vinter, Divisional Coordinator for Community, Administration, Policy, and Evaluation Practice
Charles Garvin, Sallie Churchill, Interpersonal Practice
Edwin Thomas, HBSE
Rosemary Sarri, SWPS
Tom Croxton, Jane Costabile, JoAnn Allen, Admissions, Financial Aid, Services
Ann Hartman, Curriculum Committee
Thomas Powell, Human Subjects Committee
Merle Dinsmore, Admissions, Financial Aid, Services Committee
Lawrence Berlin, Continuing Education
Howard Brabson, Merle Dinsmore, Practice Skill Instruction

Professional and Administrative Staff (1971–81)
Shirley Anderson, Special Assistant to the Dean
Roy W. Gaunt, Assistant to the Dean
Barbara Lardy, Executive Secretary to the Dean
Geraldine Flewelling, Barbara Hiebbner, Recorders
Winston Burt, Director of Admissions
Ann Smith, Research Associate
Ignacio Salazar, Assistant to the Director of Admissions and Financial Aid
Marvin Berman, Coordinator of Conferences and Extension Courses
Ted Y. Wilson, Editorial Associate
Rebecca Vaughan, Associate Director, Student Services
Marty McDaniel, Administrative Assistant, Secretary to the Dean
Barbara Hiebbner, School Registrar
Elizabeth Barlow, Administrative Associate
Joan Robinson, Administrative Assistant
Christine Sherman, Administrative Assistant
Joan Teifer, Administrative Assistant
Susan Finlayson, Executive Secretary

Sandra Rod, Student Services Assistant
Christina Neal, Librarian
Ann S. Fowler, Administrative Associate

The School's Faculty

At the beginning of the 1971–72 academic year, the faculty numbered fifty-five. These faculty members are listed in this document in "Part Two: The School's Faculty." By 1980–81 the size of the faculty had been reduced to fifty-one. During this decade a number of faculty members at the school held joint faculty appointments with other university units, including the Departments of Economics, Sociology, Psychology, Political Science, the Institute for the Study of Mental Retardation and Related Disabilities, the Institute of Labor and Industrial Relations, the Institute of Gerontology, the University Hospital, and the Center for Population Planning.

In 1974 the school established its first named professorship in honor of Professor Arthur Dunham. In 1935 Professor Dunham joined the faculty of the university's Institute of Health and Social Sciences in Detroit, which included the graduate social work program. From 1949 to 1951 Dunham served as acting director of the social work program, then called the Institute of Social Work, and continued as a faculty member in the School of Social Work until his retirement in 1963. Professor Robert Vinter was selected to hold the Arthur Dunham Professorship at the school.

In 1974 Professor Henry Meyer was honored by the university in receiving the university's Distinguished Faculty Achievement Award. Professor Meyer was head of the school's Joint Doctoral Program in Social Work and Social Science from the beginning of the program in 1957 to 1970. In 1971 he directed a program for the Agency for International Development at the Schools of Social Work and Public Health, with a focus on interdisciplinary training in family and population planning for students from developing nations around the world. Meyer retired from the school in 1978.

Faculty Policies and Guidelines

The school's *Manual of Policies and Procedures* included guidelines for faculty workload. A system of weighted units was used to help assess and balance assigned faculty responsibilities. This system attempted to take into account assigned responsibilities, which are of some duration, but it clearly did not encompass all academic and professional activities. Under this system a "normal" full-time faculty load was 10–12 units of assigned responsibilities, with 2 more units for discretionary activities. A typical full-time teaching load was assumed to be 6 units (three courses), unless other assigned duties required a reduction in teaching duties. The administrative responsibility for faculty assignment rested primarily in the Office of the Assistant Dean for Curriculum.

Guidelines for faculty promotion recommendations were developed by the dean in consultation with the Faculty Council. The dean reviewed candidates for promotion with the Faculty Council based on these guidelines. The criteria emphasized contributions to teaching, research, and service and allowed the dean to make the final decision on promotions to be recommended to the regents. The dean developed policies regarding salary with the Faculty Council and made final decisions regarding salary recommendations.

In 1975 the faculty approved a proposal that called for evaluation of the school's structure and organizational climate. Under this proposal, faculty members were surveyed each year regarding their opinions about the organizational structure and climate of the school on topics such as faculty workloads and opportunities for teaching, research, and service.

The Faculty Council/Executive Committee

Unlike most schools and colleges at the university, the School of Social Work did not have an executive committee until 1983. In the period from 1968 to 1983, the participation of the faculty in governance changed from a Faculty Advisory Council to a Faculty Council, hence to an Executive Committee. In May 1968 the school's faculty created an administrative group, called the Faculty Advisory Council, with functions somewhat similar to an executive committee but without administrative authority. This council consisted of seven elected members of the governing faculty, representing two members from each professorial rank and one elected at large. The dean appointed the chair of the council.

The members of the first Faculty Advisory Council consisted of Professors Eugene Litwak (chair), Wayne Vasey, Jesse Gordon, Tom Croxton, Jack Riley, Loraine Cook, and Phillip Fellin. Council members served as representatives of the governing faculty, "to advise the Dean on such matters as the Dean and the Faculty Council deem appropriate." As noted in a report to the Council on Social Work Education (CSWE, 1973), "The Council nominates members of all of the other committees at the School, advises the Dean, and makes recommendations to him on tenure, promotion, salaries, and termination. The Dean, in turn, makes recommendations on these matters to the University administration."

The school's governance structure was changed in 1973, with the Faculty Advisory Council becoming a Faculty Council. The nature and function of the new group changed somewhat, with the council composed of eight members, with two representatives from each rank and two at large. The functions of the new Faculty Council involved the following four major roles: "As the faculty's agent in the areas where the Dean is required to consult with the faculty on matters of policy; to initiate discussion with the Dean where appropriate; to appoint faculty members [to] selected School committees; to serve as the faculty for responsibility in reviewing procedures and initiating policy proposals with regard to School goals, educational programs other than the master's program, and to such areas as the faculty may determine (Fellin, 1972–73, *Annual Report*).

The faculty minutes of November 5, 1980, note that consideration was to be given to the creation of a faculty executive committee. Professor Tom Croxton "moved that the Dean, with the advice and consent of the Faculty Council, appoint an ad-hoc committee to study the positives and consequences of changing the governance of the School from a Faculty Advisory Council to a Faculty Executive structure and that this committee report their findings to the governing faculty at the January, 1981 meeting" (motion carried).

In the faculty meeting of March 25, 1981, "Professor Robert Vinter moved that the governing faculty resolve to propose to the Regents during 1981–82 that some form of Executive committee governance appropriate to this School be established, and that the resolution be communicated to the Executive Officers of the University, the Deanship Search Committee, and to active candidates for the deanship" (motion carried). In the faculty meeting of January 12, 1983, "Professor Tom Croxton presented a motion: I hereby move that the governing faculty of the School of Social Work of the University of Michigan adopt the bylaw changes attached hereto in order to establish an Executive Committee form of governance at the School and that these bylaw changes be forwarded to the Board of Regents for approval" (motion carried). The motion passed. The regents responded by approving the school's Executive Committee, to take office September 1, 1983.

School Committees
In 1971 the school continued to operate with a number of standing committees, as well as a number of committees on curriculum areas. The standing committees were the following:

> Admissions and Scholarships Committee
> Continuing Education and Extension Committee
> Curriculum Committee
> Faculty Search Committee
> Grievance Committee
> Minority Opportunities Committee

The Field Instructors Advisory Committee was established in 1971 as a way of involving field instructors, agency executives, and representative faculty members in the linking of classroom courses and field instruction. This committee began to explore the following issues:

- The role, rights, and responsibilities of field instructors and faculty serving as liaison to field agencies;
- Options for field instruction;
- The relations between casework, group work, and social treatment methods and between community practice, administration and policy methods;
- The frequency and nature of faculty liaison visits;
- The grading system for practice skill instruction;
- Participation by field instructors in the reaccreditation process of CSWE.

Members of the committee were Patrick Babcock, Danice Chisholm, Rod Fitch, Shirley Harrison, Mary Ellen Krauss, Rita Levine, Al Mendel, Francis Moynihan, Robert Myers, David Neal, Ralph Patterson, Ida Pettiford, John Reynolds, Cora Shoecraft, Marguerite Smith, Dale Swaisgood, Eugene Talsma, Samuel Tucker, Milt Weiner, and Robert Wright. Serving on the committee from the faculty were Nathalie Drews, Harvey Bertcher, Tom Croxton, Madison Foster, and Charles Wolfson.

The Fifty-Fifty Plus One Plan

In 1972 the faculty approved a plan, called fifty-fifty plus one, for participation of students in school committees. Under this plan, committees related to the educational programs of the school were allowed to have a membership of fifty percent faculty and fifty percent students, plus a chair designated by the dean. Faculty members of these committees were designated by the dean, while student members were chosen by the Student Union. The Human Subjects Review Committee and the Faculty Council did not include student membership. The Human Subjects Review Committee was designated by the university vice president for research to insure conformity with federal and university policies protecting the rights of human research subjects.

Community and University Services

An important component of the activities of faculty members has been the provision of service to the university community, as well as to boards and committees at local, state, national, and international levels. Service at the university by faculty included membership on university-wide committees such as the Committee on the Economic Status of the Faculty, the Senate Advisory Committee on University Affairs, the Board of Intercollegiate Athletics, the Long-Range Planning Committee, the University Council for Religious Affairs, the University Committee on Minority Recruitment, the Board for Student Publications, the Commission on Resource Allocation, the Civil Liberties Board, the Board of Directors of the Student Union, the University Student Relations Committee, and the Board for Student Publications.

Facilities

The school continued to operate in the Frieze Building. The Frieze Building included seven classrooms, a conference room, library, and an auditorium. Offices were provided, sometimes single, sometimes double, for all full-time faculty. Offices for administrative activities were provided in the building. Secretarial locations were provided in office suites and separate offices. A small lounge was created for use by secretarial and administrative staff. A student lounge and Student Union office were provided on the fourth floor of the Frieze Building. In 1979 the school traded office space in the north wing of the Frieze Building (facing Huron Street) for office space in the east wing and created a reading room above the library.

A Research and Service Center was established in 1971 at the Social Work Center Building at 1015 East Huron, two blocks from the Frieze Building, to provide for specific research and educational service activities of faculty, students, and staff. The center housed research projects and continuing education projects directed by faculty members of the school under grants from governmental departments, private foundations, and voluntary health and welfare agencies. The Continuing Education and Extension Program of the school was housed in the center.

Library

The Social Work Library at 1548 Frieze Building was one of the more than twenty divisional libraries in the University Library System. In 1971 the

Social Work Library contained approximately 14,000 volumes, received 223 periodicals, and maintained an extensive pamphlet file. The library provided limited reading space for students. By 1973 the library contained 19,219 monographs, 300 periodical titles, and 1,020 pieces of vertical file material. The library contained reference works such as encyclopedias, directories, statistical yearbooks, and periodical indexes. In 1973 the university gave an allocation for books and binding of periodical titles of $7,800 yearly, supplemented by $500 from the school's budget. In 1976 the Winkelman Foundation provided funding for refurbishing a room in the Frieze Building to serve as a library reading room. Christina W. Neal, B.S., A.M.L.S., served as librarian for the Social Work Library.

Long-Range Planning

In 1973 the school began a process for long-range planning, focused on social work education and the issues facing the social work profession in the next decade. These issues included such factors as the nature, quality, and length of social work education; the governance of the school; composition of the student body; funding of social work education; school–community roles and responsibilities; manpower needs; minority opportunities; and the school's environment. The faculty's self-study for CSWE reaccreditation in 1973 provided a foundation for this long-range planning process.

In 1973 the school participated in a university-wide Budget and Planning Office review of funding, program evaluation, and long-range planning. A university Program Planning and Evaluation Report was released in 1975–76, setting forth guidelines for school budgeting in the light of reduced state and federal funding for higher education. The school participated in the university's Evaluation and Planning Project, directed by Frank Rhodes, vice president for academic affairs. The task force in charge of the school's planning efforts was composed of Professors Robert Vinter, JoAnn Allen, Charles Garvin, Milan Dluhy, and Dean Phillip Fellin *(ex officio)*.

The evaluation efforts at the university level were particularly important for the long-range planning efforts at the School of Social Work. The school established a long-range planning committee to work with the dean so that the school could respond to change, new data, new ideas, and new alternatives in social work education. In this way the school sought to improve its ability to compete for resources, to use resources in a rational, planned manner, and to improve all areas of educational decision making (Fellin, 1974).

The School's Budget

In 1971–72 the school received federal funds for training projects supporting students and faculty from the Social Rehabilitation Service ($248,757)
and from the National Institute of Mental Health (NIMH; $542,378).
University funds for academic salaries in 1971 consisted of $945,374, with
$265,464 for student support, additional funds for the current account, and
a total general funds budget of $1,421,538. The school's budget in 1971 in-
cluded money for research projects as follows:

Law Enforcement Assistance Administration	$280,453
Department of Labor	$180,390
SRS	$46,939
AID	$99,258
NIMH	$99,528
Ford Foundation	$116,832

By 1981 a large part of the federal funding for instructional positions
had been eliminated. The university replaced some of this funding, but
the school was still included in budget reductions in salary and current
accounts from 1975 to 1981. These reductions in funding were relatively
small compared with other units of the university. For example, during
this period, funding for the School of Engineering was reduced by about
thirty percent (Duderstadt, 2003). In regard to funding from the university,
the school enjoyed the support of the Office of the Vice President for Academic Affairs, especially Vice Presidents Allan Smith, Frank Rhodes, and
Harold Shapiro. Consequently, a relatively strong instructional budget was
maintained, with only a slight decline in the number of full-time faculty
members.

Reaccreditation Report: 1973

An accreditation team from the Council on Social Work Education visited the campus in April 1973. The team consisted of Leon Ginsberg, chair,
Charles Guzzetta, Genevive Hill, and Juliette Ruiz. Sections of the reaccreditation report by this team are cited here.

> *The Dean's Role:* The Dean and the Vice-President for Academic Affairs
> told the team that the U-M operates under a "strong-dean system." There is
> some disagreement about the use of that term, however. What it appears to
> mean to the University administration and the Dean of the School of Social
> Work is that deans are given relatively wide latitude in making decisions

and operating their programs. It would appear that the Dean is "strong" in relation to the University Administration. However, it does not mean that the Dean is stronger than the faculty of the School of Social Work. . . . Major administrative and fiscal policy issues are decided by the Dean, with the advice of various appointed and elected groups. . . . The team did come to believe that while the Dean has ultimate authority in some areas, the faculty of the School has authority in others. . . . In every instance, it should be noted, the students and faculty expressed confidence in Dean Fellin and said that they were able to talk with him readily and to their satisfaction, even when the conversations dealt with matters that were in conflict. (*CSWE Report,* 1973)

External Review: 1979

In 1979 university President Shapiro noted in a presentation to the faculty that "the external review of the School will come as Dean Fellin reaches the end of his second five year appointment. The review is an important one and its recommendations will be taken seriously. He encouraged faculty participation in the process." Two committees, an internal one and an external one, were created to make this review. In May 1980 an outside team of social workers was invited to review the school's programs. The team was composed of June Hopps, Shanti Khinduka, William Reid, and Eleanor Sheldon. The team examined such topics as the mission of the school; the M.S.W., doctoral, and Continuing Education and Extension Programs of the school; the leadership and faculty of the school; the curriculum; and faculty research. Excerpts from the visiting team's report follow:

It should be said at the outset that the School of Social Work enjoys a well deserved eminence and prestige in the profession. The School has contributed significantly to the development of knowledge and to the education of social work practitioners. Its faculty and graduates have made outstanding contributions to the field. Its administrators, faculty, and alumni hold important leadership positions in the profession. . . .

Dean Fellin impressed us as an able and adroit administrator. The School seems to be efficiently and competently managed and administered. A substantial number of the faculty regard the administration as fair and responsive to faculty needs and concerns. . . .

Some faculty looked for more managerial strength and intellectual stimulation, while many faculty expressed the view that the Dean is a solid leader who has encouraged the faculty to be democratic in its deliberations. . . .

The School of Social Work is fortunate in having an array of very talented faculty. . . .

The Social Work-Social Science Ph.D. program can take legitimate credit for training some of the more productive researchers in social work in the United States. . . .

Perhaps the School has grown too big in size. It may prudent to trim the size of the master's program. . . .

The School's creative continuing education program has acquired a national reputation for the workshops and institutes held under its auspices, for the innovative projects it has launched, and especially, for the teaching materials generated by its faculty and administrators. (External Review, 1979)

Review: Challenges for the New Dean and the Faculty

In reflecting back to the decade of my deanship, I have identified six major challenges to the school in 1971. Responses to these challenges are elaborated upon in this chapter.

Challenge One: Student Participation

One of my first priorities, brought about by student activism, was to work with the faculty to increase student participation in school affairs. A plan to help meet this goal was called fifty-fifty plus one, adopted by the faculty in 1972. For the school's standing committees, membership became fifty percent students appointed by the Student Union and fifty percent faculty members, with a faculty chair. While students rarely filled their committee openings, student participation increased considerably, due in part by the offering of a 2-hour credit course related to committee membership and under the direction of a faculty member. Other changes related to student participation included the school's support of student organizations, particularly the organization of minority student groups. A School Grievance Committee was established, along with a Statement of Student Rights. By action of the faculty in 1972, six non-voting students selected by the Student Union were invited to represent the student body at faculty meetings.

Challenge Two: Diversity in Student Enrollment

An important challenge to the school was the goal of maintaining and increasing the number of minority students enrolled in the school. Efforts for reaching these goals included the appointment of a minority recruitment coordinator, faculty visits to in-state and out-of-state campuses, and increased publicity about the school's programs. The success of these efforts is reported in the section of this document on student enrollment, efforts which led to making Michigan a leader in minority student enrollment among schools of social work in the United States and among academic units at the University of Michigan.

Challenge Three: Faculty Composition

At the beginning of the 1970s approximately one-third of the school's faculty were supported by federal grants from public health, rehabilitation, child welfare, and aging services. These grants included stipends for students and involvement of grant faculty in regular faculty work assignments, classroom teaching, and field advising. This work assignment pattern served to assure "first class citizenship" for faculty members funded by outside grants. When the school was challenged by a significant decrease in federal funds for social work education, university funds were obtained to support most grant faculty members and move them on to the tenure track, assuring the continuance of a diverse and highly competent faculty. While the school's instructional budget, including federal and university funds, was reduced during this decade, there was a relatively small decline in the size of the faculty, from fifty-five to fifty-one, unlike most schools and colleges at the university.

The school was challenged by a need for minority and women faculty. In 1971–72 six of fifty-five (11%) faculty members were members of minority groups. In 1980–81 eight of fifty-one (16%) were members of minority groups. During this period the school recruited eight minority faculty members. However, for professional and personal reasons, three of these individuals left the school in the coming years for other opportunities, while four minority individuals on the faculty in 1970–71 also departed from the school prior to 1980–81. In 1971–72 the faculty of fifty-five was composed of fourteen women (25%). By 1980–81 the school had increased the number of women faculty members to twenty out of fifty-one faculty members (39%).

Challenge Four: Public Service through Continuing Education

During this decade the school continued its commitment to public service by emphasizing continuing education through interdisciplinary and social work training centers. These programs are described in "Part Three: The School's Curriculum." Examples of continuing education programs were:

- Child Welfare Learning Lab
- Mental Health Skills Lab
- Substance Abuse Project
- Training of State and Area Planners in the Field of Aging
- Project CRAFT (Curriculum Resources for Adoption and Foster Care Training)

- A Social Work Education and Population Planning Project, with the School of Public Health and the Department of Population Planning (Professors Henry Meyer, Paul Glasser, Charles Garvin, and colleagues)
- A Program for the Prevention of Child Abuse and Neglect, with the Law and Medical Schools (Professor Kathleen Faller and colleagues)

Three major social work training/study centers were established:

- A National Center for Child Welfare Training (Professor Ann Hartman and colleagues)
- A Region V Adoption Resource Center (Professor Dee M. Kilpatrick and colleagues)
- The National Assessment of Juvenile Justice Study (Professors Robert Vinter and Rosemary Sarri)

Challenge Five: Research
A limited number of faculty members were engaged in sponsored research projects at the beginning of this period. During this ten-year period the number increased significantly. Of special note were women's studies conducted by faculty members, including:

- Women's Drug Research Project (Professor Beth Reed)
- Research on Women, Alcoholism and the Workplace (Professor Edith Gomberg)
- Research on the Female Offender (Professor Rosemary Sarri)
- Research on Non-Traditional Child-Rearing Patterns (Professor Norma Radin)

Examples of additional research projects are:

- Decision-Making in the WIN Program (Professor Charles Garvin)
- Population/Family Planning for LDC Social Work Education (Professors Henry Meyer and Paul Glasser)
- Socio-Behavioral Techniques for Open Welfare Settings (Professor Edwin Thomas)
- National Assessment of Juvenile Justice Study (Professors Robert Vinter and Rosemary Sarri)
- Toward an Empirical Research Base for Community Organization Practice (Professor Jack Rothman)

- Observed Paternal Behavior with Preschool Children (Professor Norma Radin)
- Program in Manpower Studies (Professor Jesse Gordon)

Challenge Six: Budget Reductions

A major challenge emerged in the second half of the 1970s in regard to the school's budget. In an October 15, 1975, meeting of the faculty, I noted, "The University budget is in a critical condition. Further State reductions are expected in uncertain amounts." For the 1975–76 academic year, the university reduced the budgets of the several colleges and schools, and over the next years there was a reduction in federal funds to the school for social work training. Professor Harold Shapiro of the Department of Economics was named vice president for academic affairs in 1977 and developed plans for further reduction of the university's budget due to cuts from the state government. In his financial planning proposals, Shapiro emphasized that it would be possible for the university to become "smaller, but better." In the next few years, the reduction in school's general fund budget, as well as reduction in federal funds for faculty, did not permit the replacement of some faculty who retired or left for other positions. At the same time, the school maintained a "favored" position with the university's central administration, receiving smaller percentage reductions than most schools and colleges.

A Continuing Challenge

At the close of my deanship, in my final *Annual Report to the President* (1980–81), I noted that the overall continuing challenge to the school was to provide a balance in the areas of teaching, research, and service; to assure that these three goals of the university and the school reinforced each other; and to assure that the major function of the school continued to be the education of social workers, allowing for special functions of the doctoral program in relation to research and preparation of graduates for research and teaching roles.

Among the "firsts" during this decade were the following:

- Students were granted formal membership in the school's standing committees according to a fifty-fifty plus one plan, with fifty percent students and fifty percent faculty, plus a faculty chair.
- Faculty on federal grants for social work education were moved to university funding.
- A plan for evaluation of the school's structure and organizational climate was approved by the faculty.

- A Field Instructors Advisory Committee was established.
- A Research and Service Center was established to coordinate research projects and Continuing Education and Extension Programs.
- A long-range evaluation and planning plan was developed by the school.
- A plan was approved for admission of non-baccalaureate applicants.
- An advanced standing alternative for admission to the school was developed, permitting some students to complete the M.S.W. with 42 hours of credit.
- The position of curriculum coordinator for minority content was established.
- A minority relevant course requirement for all students was introduced.
- A statement on student rights and grievances was established by the faculty.
- An external review of the school's programs was carried out by an outside team of social work educators.
- The school was designated as the National Child Welfare Training Center, the Region V Adoption Resources Center, and the National Assessment of Juvenile Justice Study Center.
- The school joined the Medical School and the Law School in conducting an Interdisciplinary Program for the Prevention of Child Abuse and Neglect.
- The Leon and Josephine Winkelman Lecture Series was initiated.
- The school's first named professorship was established in honor of Professor Arthur Dunham.
- Professor Henry J. Meyer was the school's first recipient of the university's Distinguished Faculty Achievement Award.
- The school initiated its first quarterly newsletter to alumni, *Newsline*.

PART TWO   The School's Students

Admission to the School
In 1971 students were admitted to the school under the following classifications:

1. Regular admission. Granted to a student who is admitted unconditionally and who plans to work toward the Master of Social Work degree.
2. Lack of preparation. Granted when the student has not completed, with acceptable grades, 20 term hours in the social sciences.

3. Low record. Granted to students whose overall undergraduate grade average is below 2.70 (on a 4-point scale).
4. Nonaccredited institution. Granted to students whose baccalaureate degree was earned in a non-accredited institution.
5. Unclassified. Students admitted to specific courses, but not candidates for the M.S.W. degree.
6. Tentative. Granted when the records of the applicant are not sufficiently complete to warrant a permanent admission status.

In 1971–72 full-time and part-time students were defined as follows: "A full-time student in the School is one who is paying full program fees—eight hours or more credit in a regular term. Those paying reduced fees are regarded as part-time. The program of a full-time student during one term is usually composed of four or five classroom courses and two days of practice skill instruction. Two-hour credit courses meet for a single session, two hours in length, each week. It is assumed that each hour of class work will require at least two hours of preparation each week." In 1975–76 the following new categories were introduced: regular, tentative, and special. Regular and tentative covered the items 1–4 and 6, with special covering item 5, unclassified.

In 1976–77 a new category was introduced for students interested in part-time study for the M.S.W. degree. The *School Bulletin* noted: "Part-time applicants to the M.S.W. degree program are expected to meet the same admission requirements as any other applicant. Part-time status will be permitted only when personal circumstances preclude enrollment on a full-time basis, which is eight hours or more credit in a regular term. Students permitted to part-time status will remain part-time until they accumulate 14 hours of credit."

Admission Requirements 1971–72

According to the *School Bulletin, 1971–72,* an applicant for admission was expected to meet the following requirements for entry into the master's degree program:

1. He must have a baccalaureate degree from an accredited U.S. college or university. Applicants from unaccredited or foreign institutions may be admitted only on a provisional basis.
2. He should have completed, with acceptable grades, at least 20 hours in the various social sciences: sociology, psychology, political science, economics, history, and anthropology. A course in statistics is also desirable.
3. He must show probability of success in pursuing professional education for social work at the graduate level, based on his record in undergraduate

and any previous graduate work. Skill in oral and written communication is important.

4. He must possess personal qualifications considered essential to the successful practice of social work, such as sensitivity and responsiveness in relationships, concern for the needs of others, adaptability, good judgment, creativity, and integrity.

5. A personal interview with a representative of the School may be requested when the Admissions Committee requires further information before reaching a decision on an application.

6. Applicants are required to take the Miller Analogies Test. Other tests may be requested by the Admissions Committee.

7. Applicants from countries other than the United States whose native language is not English will need to know in advance whether or not their command of English is adequate for the program they wish to pursue. The University asks these applicants to take the English Proficiency Test for Foreign Students or the Test of English as a Foreign Language.

Non-Baccalaureate Admissions

A major change in admissions is stated in item eight of the 1973–74 *School Bulletin*:

> Admission is possible for a small number of non-baccalaureate applicants under the following criteria:
> a. All applicants must be 30 years of age or older.
> b. Preference will be given to residents of the state of Michigan.
> c. All applicants should have had at least two years of satisfactory collegiate studies at a university or junior college and/or the equivalent as measured by the College-level Examination program.
> d. Applicants must have demonstrated increasingly responsible achievements in a human service organization reflecting a variety of skills and capabilities.

In addition, the statement in this section includes the following statement: "Admission criteria are applied equally to all students without regard to race, creed, color, sex, or national origin."

In 1978–79 the *School Bulletin* expanded on the non-B.A. admissions clause as follows:

> Applications are evaluated by the following criteria:
> 1. Applicants must be 30 years of age or older.
> 2. Preference is given to Michigan residents.

3. Applicants must have at least two years of satisfactory college work, or three semesters of college work plus the equivalent of one semester as measured by the College Level Examination program.*

    If eligibility by College Level Examination is sought, the applicant must take subject examinations in the following areas: general Psychology (four hours of credit), Human Growth and Development (three hours of credit), Introduction to Sociology (four hours of credit), and Statistics (three hours of credit).

4. The experience of applicants must demonstrate that they have competence and ability for professional achievements in the performance of human service responsibilities. Applicants can demonstrate competence and ability in the achievements in human service responsibilities either in their (a) employment histories or in the history of their (b) volunteer activities, or a combination of both. The following statements describe minimum requirements for applicants to be considered eligible under this criterion:

    a. Employment—Applicants must have been employed in one or more human service positions, and must have demonstrated competence, growth, and increasing responsibility in direct service or planning of services. Applicants must have been so employed for a minimum of three years full-time, or the equivalent part-time.

    b. Volunteer Activities—Applicants must have held a series of responsible positions in established voluntary social service or community service organizations and have demonstrated increasing responsibility for planning or directing significant aspects of the organization's activities. If employment is not offered as a basis for the application, volunteer service should be substantial enough to be considered equivalent to three years of full-time employment. If a combination of (a) and (b) is offered, the total work and volunteer experience should be substantial enough to be considered equivalent to three years of full-time employment.

Advanced Standing

In 1977–78 the school introduced an advanced standing alternative for admission to the school. The plan was described as follows: "Applicants admitted to the School with a major in social work from an undergraduate program accredited by CSWE may be eligible for advanced standing of 14 credit hours, and may be eligible for the MSW degree after successfully completing

* "Two years" became defined as at least 60 semester hours of credit satisfactorily completed at an accredited institution. Three semesters meant at least 46 semester hours.

42 hours of graduate credit. Eligibility for advanced standing also requires a grade point average of 3.5 on a 4-point scale" (*School Bulletin,* 1977–78).

In 1979–80 the *School Bulletin* noted: "There are both advantages and disadvantages of being awarded advanced standing. The major advantage of advanced standing is that it may well shorten the time necessary to complete all requirements for the M.S.W. degree to three terms of full-time enrollment and thus there may be a savings of money. On the other hand, it is not always possible to complete all the requirements in three terms, and persons receiving advanced standing may not be able to make maximum use of the richness in course selections. Because of these and a number of related issues, it is recommended that eligible persons think carefully and discuss the issues fully with the appropriate Divisional Coordinator before deciding to apply for this option."

Student Enrollment: 1971–80

School records during this period report on full-time enrollment of M.S.W. and doctoral students, with part-time figures including those in a planned program, as well as nondegree students taking one or two courses. In some counts, students off-campus taking extension courses are included in part-time enrollment figures. Students from other departments of the university taking a course in the school are not included in the part-time enrollment figures.

M.S.W. and Ph.D. Student Enrollment: 1971–80

Year		Full-Time		Part-Time
	Total	M.S.W.	Ph.D.	M.S.W.
1971	593	558	35	237
1972	607	561	46	252
1973	661	610	51	316
1974	651	592	59	315
1975	558	509	49	293
1976	627	576	51	289
1977	579	540	39	281
1978	579	540	39	282
1979	503	469	34	309
1980	531	479	42	224

It is difficult to ascertain the reasons for the various fluctuations in full-time enrollment of M.S.W. students during this ten-year period, but the overall decline appears to be related to funding reductions and the university's mandate to contain enrollment. The highest enrollment came in the year of 1973, with the low year being 1979. The figures for 1977 and 1978 are identical, perhaps due to a printing mistake.

In 1973 the school ranked first among seventy-nine schools of social work in the number of applications received, total graduate enrollment, number of full-time students, and the number of M.S.W. graduates (Fellin, *Annual Report* 1973–74). In 1975–76 the dean's annual report noted that "societal trends [are] expected to bring about a continuation for expansion of social service manpower." In 1975–76 school had the largest number of full-time M.S.W. students and the largest number of M.S.W. graduates in the United States.

In 1980 the school responded to Vice President Rhodes' call for evaluation and planning with a Memorandum of Understanding. This document included a plan for the reduction and subsequent stabilization of the size of the student body, in keeping with the reduction of resources by the federal government and the State of Michigan.

Ethnicity in Enrollment
The range of cultural, ethnic, and racial backgrounds of the student body in 1971 reflected a policy approved by the governing faculty in 1965 to increase its enrollment of minority group students. This effort was expanded in 1967 with the employment of an assistant director of admissions and financial aid, whose primary responsibility was minority student recruitment. In 1971 this position was changed to the associate director of special services and admissions. Extensive contacts were developed with social work and social science faculty and placement personnel in many Black colleges and universities and other educational institutions having large Black, Chicano, and Puerto Rican enrollment. Recruiters (students and faculty) visited campuses in Michigan and in selected states in the Southwest and South and on the West Coast, leading to a dramatic increase in Hispanic student enrollment.

The school increased its minority enrollment so that by 1975–76, among schools of social work in the United States, Michigan was second in actual number of minority students of color, except for institutions that enrolled primarily minority students. The school was one of eight schools of social work in the nation with representation by all major minority groups of color in the student body. In 1975–76 the school led the university in percentage of minority students. By 1980–81 the school, with seventeen percent minority student enrollment of full-time M.S.W. students, continued to be a leader in minority enrollment, along with the Schools of Pharmacy and Education. Once again, in 1980, the school's faculty moved at a faculty meeting: "The School of Social Work should actively engage in efforts to increase the pool of minority applicants to the School. Attention should be paid to the recruitment of minority persons as specified by CSWE, especially within the State of Michigan, as well as from out of state" (*Faculty Minutes*, 1980).

Graduates of the School

During this period the school continued to be one of the leaders in the United States in the number of graduates with M.S.W. degrees. In 1974, under the direction of Professors Richard English and Norma Radin, a study was conducted to assess the effectiveness of graduates from 1968 to 1972. This follow-up study of graduates focused on collection of data on graduates' self-rating on specific social work skills and ratings by supervisors of these goals on the same skills. The findings of this study were reported in the school's alumni newsletter.

Number of M.S.W. Graduates
from 1971–72 to 1980–81

1971 (341)	1976 (352)
1972 (368)	1977 (305)
1973 (329)	1978 (356)
1974 (432)	1979 (286)
1975 (283)	1980 (322)

Admissions and Financial Aid

During the 1971–72 school year, the dean appointed a task force of faculty and staff to study the operations and organization of the Admissions and Financial Aid Office. The need for such a study was necessitated by several factors: (1) an increase in the volume of applications to the school; (2) a significant decrease in the availability of financial aid for students and an increasing number of applications for financial assistance; and (3) the responsibility of the office to implement the commitments that the school made to increase minority group enrollment.

Upon recommendations of the task force, several changes were made in the administration and staffing of the office. There was an increase in the professional staff and a reorganization of staff duties. The office became staffed by a director and two associate directors, one for admissions and financial aid and the other for admissions and special services. An admissions representative had special responsibility for Chicano student recruitment. There were two full-time secretaries and one half-time secretary. The administrative responsibility of the office was under the assistant dean. Guiding the office in application processing and decision making was the *Office of Admissions and Financial Aid Manual of Policies and Procedures*.

Year-Round Operation
The year-round operation of the school for enrollment, which began in 1965, continued as follows: "Full-time enrollment is permitted twice each year and applicants may choose between two time-span plans depending upon whether a program of study is begun in the winter or in the fall term. Students are not admitted to begin a program of full-time study during the spring-summer term" (*School Bulletin*, 1972–73).

Tuition
In the school's presentation of tuition, residence is defined in the 1971 *School Bulletin* as follows: "Residence is usually established by living in the state as a non-student for six months prior to enrollment. However, there are exceptions relating to age, marital status, employment, and relationship to University personnel which the student will find in the General Information bulletin of the University. When question is raised about a student's residency status it is the student's responsibility to clarify the matter with the Director of Student Certification." The 1973–74 *School Bulletin* presented a more detailed explanation of the residency rules as found in the university's Office of Student Certification.

1971–72 Full Program Term Tuition
Michigan residents $270
Non-Michigan residents $824

1980–81 Full Program Term Tuition
Michigan residents $934
Non-Michigan residents $2044

The school provided a variety of fellowships, scholarships, and student aid for the master's degree program, including agency scholarships, graduate assistantships, and university scholarships. A number of stipends were available from government departments in Michigan and from other states in such fields as child welfare, corrections, mental health, public assistance, medicine, and school social work. Most of these plans were offered to persons who agreed to work in the sponsoring department upon completion of their studies.

A number of traineeships were awarded to students from U.S. governmental agencies, including the U.S. Children's Bureau, the U.S. Public Health Service, the U.S. Rehabilitation Services Administration, and the Administration on Aging. By 1980–81 traineeships were available to students from the U.S. Department of Health, Education, and Welfare, particularly the National Institute of Mental Health; the U.S. Department of Justice, particularly the Law Enforcement Education Program; and the U.S. Bureau of Indian Affairs. At the university level, scholarships were available from the Center for Continuing Education for Women. Barbour scholarships were available for women enrolled in the school from Asian countries. Loan funds were available to social work students under the National Defense Education Act, the Guaranteed Student Loan Program, and the Michigan Department of Education Direct Loan Program.

Student Services and University Resources

The Office of Student Services at the university provided services and served as a coordinating agency for facilitating the educational development of students. Social work students had the benefit of the services of a number of university organizations during the period from 1971 to 1981, as well as services provided at the school through the Offices of Admissions, Financial Aid, and Student Services. The university's Office of Student Services included six units: Career Planning and Placement, Counseling Services, Health Service, Housing, Community Services, and Student Programs. Immediate help for a wide range of programs and questions was available through a 24-hour telephone counseling information and referral service under the auspices of Counseling Services. The university also had services provided through the International Center, Disabled Student Services, Minority Student Services, Veterans Services, Center for the Continuing Education of Women, the Coalition for the Use of Learning Skills, and the Reading and Learning Skills Center.

The School of Social Work maintained a file in the Social Work Library of current employment opportunities in social work. Faculty advisers were available for consultation with regard to employment opportunities.

Student Relationships/Student Organizations

In 1972 the faculty of the school formalized student participation in the school's affairs by approving an arrangement of fifty percent student-to-faculty ratio of membership on school standing committees, with one faculty serving as chairperson. The Faculty Council, the Governing Faculty, and the Human Subjects Review committee were not included in this arrangement.

A statement on student rights and grievances was first noted in the 1973–74 *School Bulletin* as follows: "The School of Social Work Grievance Committee is authorized to consider and take appropriate action on any school matter properly submitted to it by a student in the School of Social Work or by a member of the faculty of the School of Social Work." The committee was composed of three students and three faculty members with equal voting rights among the members. "These six members then elect a seventh person (from the faculty) to serve as chairman."

In accordance with the recommendations of the Council on Social Work Education, the School of Social Work developed and approved the following statement of student rights:

1. The right of protection with all due process of the law against prejudiced or capricious academic evaluations, improper disclosure of students' views, beliefs, and political associations, and limitations upon freedom of expression.
2. The right of students to organize in their own interests as students.
3. The right to have representation and participation on standing committees of the School.
4. The right of students, individually or in association with other individuals, to engage freely in off-campus activities, exercising their rights as citizens of community, state and nation. Students shall not claim to formally represent the School of Social Work or the University unless authorization has been obtained.
5. The right to establish and issue publications free of any censorship or other pressure aimed at controlling editorial policy, with the free selection and removal of editorial staff reserved solely to the organizations sponsoring those publications. Such publications shall not claim to represent the School of Social Work or the University unless authorization has been obtained.
6. The right of students and recognized student organizations to use School of Social Work meeting facilities provided the meeting facilities are used for the purpose contracted, subject only to such regulations as are required for scheduling meeting times and places.
7. The right of students and recognized student organizations to invite and hear speakers of their choice on subjects of their choice.
8. The right to petition proper channels for changes in curriculum, practice field instruction, faculty adviser, grades, and to petition proper channels in cases of grievance.

9. The right of students, who are participating in research or scholarly endeavors under faculty direction as a part of their formal academic program, to receive appropriate recognition for their contribution to the process.
10. The right of equal opportunity to enjoy these rights without regard to race, color, sex, national origin, religious creed, or political beliefs.
11. Enumeration of certain rights herein shall not be construed as to nullify or limit any other rights possessed by students; on the other hand exercise of these rights falls within more general University-wide regental policies.

Student organizations in 1971 included the Association of Black Social Work Students, Los Trabajadores de la Raza, Social Work Student Union, and Conciencia Boricua.

The faculty minutes of February 2, 1977, noted: "Dean Fellin reported that representatives of the Student Union had reported inconclusively on student attitudes regarding the removal of the cigarette machine from the School's lounge. They promised to return to the Dean with a more conclusive report." In April 1977 Dean Fellin reported that the students had voted on the question of removing the cigarette machine as follows: Take machine out: 78 yes, 83 no; allow smoking in classrooms: 52 yes, 130 no; allow smoking in library: 39 yes, 146 no. In response, the machine was left in the lounge.

The Blue Book

In an effort to provide information about the school to students, as well as to facilitate communication between students, faculty, and administration, an informational Blue Book was introduced in 1980. In an introduction to students, Dean Fellin noted: "This is your Blue Book. It won't help you buy or sell a used car, but I hope it helps you in other ways as you find your way through the School of Social Work." The Blue Book included information about the school in the following areas: organizational chart, faculty roles, practice skill instruction, library, media lab, division coordinators, responsibilities of the deans, the governing faculty, university resources and services, student organizations, committees of the school, and the Grievance Committee.

PART THREE The School's Faculty

Introduction

In the fall term of the 1971–72 academic year, the School of Social Work faculty was composed of fifty-five members. There was considerable turnover of faculty during the coming decade, with twenty-seven new members hired, twenty-four departing from the university for other positions, and several retirements. By 1980–81 the faculty consisted of fifty members, with the decrease over the decade due to the impact of funding reductions from the university and the federal government in curtailing replacements. Faculty members hired during this period held doctoral degrees from a wide-range of fields and universities, including five individuals from the school's Joint Doctoral Program in Social Work and Social Science, four from the University of Chicago, and one each from the university's Departments of Sociology and Political Science, the School of Education, and the School of Public Health. New faculty also came from Case Western University, Johns Hopkins University, the University of Cincinnati, Yale University, Bryn Mawr College, Washington University, the University of Oregon, and the University of Minnesota.

The School's Faculty: 1971–72
The following faculty members held regular tenure-track appointments in the school at the opening of the fall term, 1971: Jo Ann Allen, Sydney Bernard, Harvey Bertcher, Philip Booth, Howard Brabson, Robert Carter, Sallie Churchill, Alan Connor, Loraine Cook, Jane Costabile, Fred Cox, Tom Croxton, Merle Dinsmore, Nathalie Drews, Richard English, Irwin Epstein, Sheila Feld, Phillip Fellin, Louis Ferman, Madison Foster, Clarice Freud, Charles Garvin, Paul Glasser, Jesse Gordon, Oliver Harris, Yeheskel Hasenfeld, David Himle, Harold Johnson, Stanley Kim, Armand Lauffer, Harry Lawrence, Roger Lind, Eugene Litwak, Frank Maple, Henry Meyer, William Neenan, Thomas Powell, Norma Radin, Katherine Reebel, Jack Riley, Dorothy Robinson, Jack Rothman, Rosemary Sarri, Dorothy Schroeder, Robert Segal, Sheldon Siegel, Richard Stuart, Mary Taylor, Edwin Thomas, Tony Tripodi, John Tropman, Wayne Vasey, Robert Vinter, Donald Warren, Charles Wolfson.

The following twenty-six individuals joined the faculty between 1971–72 and 1980–81: Joyce Beckett (1975–85), William Birdsall (1973–2001), Milan Dluhy (1972–87), Richard Douglass (1975–77), John Ford (1972–74), Martha Gizynski (1974–86), Gerald Goff (1979–83), Edith Gomberg (1974–98), Murray Gruber (1972–80), Ann Hartman (1974–86), Alfreda Iglehart (1978–85), Srinika Jayaratne (1979–2009), Charles Jones (1971–79), Dee M. Kilpatrick (1972–83), Lenore Kroman (1974–81), William Lawrence (1977–86), Elizabeth Mutschler (1979–97), Eliseo Navarro (1972–79), Lorraine Perry (1971–83), Beth Reed (1973–present), Lawrence Root (1978–present), Brett Seabury (1975–present), Kristine Siefert (1979–present), David Street (1973–76), Helen Weingarten (1981–2000), Mayer Zald (1977–2001).

The following twenty-four faculty members departed for other positions during this period, listed in the order of departure, and including years of service: Eileen Gambrill (1967–72), Eugene Litwak (1959–72), John Riley (1966–72), Stanley Kim (1965–73), Donald Warren (1968–74), Richard English (1967–74), Oliver Harris (1967–74), John Ford (1972–75), Roger Lind (1965–75), Richard Stuart (1965–75), Fred Cox (1963–76), David Street (1973–77), Robert Carter (1970–78), Richard Douglass (1975–78), Irwin Epstein (1967–78), Paul Glasser (1958–78), Harry Lawrence (1967–78), Dorothy Robinson (1956–78), Eliseo Navarro (1972–78), Charles Jones (1971–79), Robert Segal (1969–79), Sheldon Siegel (1962–79), Murray Gruber (1972–80), William Neenan (1967–80).

The following nine faculty members retired as professors emeriti during this period: Philip Booth, Dorothy Schroeder, Fedele Fauri, Clarice Freud, Katherine Reebel, Wayne Vasey, Henry Meyer, Mary Taylor, and Jane Costabile.

A number of individuals served on the faculty as lecturers, instructors, or professors, either part-time or with major appointments at other units of the university. A partial list includes the following: Dorothy Herberg, Mary Elizabeth Johnson, Shulamit Reinharz, Joseph Teresa, Rebecca Vaughan, Claude Walter, Josephine Cannell, Jules Schrager, Raymond Snowden, Robert Bykowski, Marjorie Ziefert, Mary Corcoran, Winston Burt.

Gender and Minority Group Status

Changes in the composition of the faculty over this ten-year period showed a considerable increase in female faculty but only a small increase in the number of minority faculty. Special efforts to attract female and minority group faculty were successful, but several minority faculty members left the school for personal and professional reasons.

For the 1971–72 academic year, the faculty comprised fourteen women (25%) and forty-one men (75% men), and in 1980–81, twenty women (39%) and thirty-one men (61%). In the article "Women in Social Work," Suzan Alexander and Terri Torkko (2001) noted:

> Emeriti Deans Fedele Fauri and Phillip Fellin were regarded as progressive in their thinking regarding gender. It was during their tenures that the doors were opened wide to women faculty.
>
> Some of these new faculty had strong backgrounds in research, which added a new dimension to the program as many of them were interested in researching gender issues. Once hired, these women were supported and encouraged, and they flourished in their positions.

A battle of the sexes may have been raging in the streets in the '70s, but, in large part thanks to Fellin's leadership, it was a relative oasis of calm inside the walls of the School.

Professor Emerita Sheila Feld, who joined the faculty in 1969 and was named the first women Assistant Dean of the School in 1971, applauds the efforts of both deans.

"By the '70s, the School had become much more research and scholarship oriented. It was a good place to be as a woman because we were given the support needed to develop a career."

Professor Ann Hartman, who left Ann Arbor in 1986 after 12 years at the School to become Dean of the Smith College School of Social Work, agrees wholeheartedly with Feld's assessment. "Phil Fellin was amazingly unsexist and was extremely supportive of women on faculty. He believed the School should be a marketplace of ideas."

All of these women proved to be valuable additions to the faculty who influenced the social work profession enormously.

Profiles of New Faculty Members: 1971–81
Additions and departures of faculty members are noted for each of the academic years of this decade. A brief profile is provided for each of the new faculty members, by year of appointment.

1971–72
New Faculty: Lorraine Perry and Charles Jones

LORRAINE PERRY. Lorraine Perry came to the school as assistant professor, having received B.A. and M.S.W. degrees from Wayne State University and a Ph.D. from the School of Social Service Administration, University of Chicago. Her teaching and scholarly activities were in the areas of administration and policy methods, complex organizations, staff development and supervision, community organization practice, political economy of the Black community, and the practice of professionals in minority communities. She was engaged in research related to mental retardation, the criminal justice system, and Black community organizations. She was the recipient of a Rockefeller Foundation award for study in the Stanford/Sloan Program in Business Administration. While at Michigan, Perry was promoted to associate professor. She left the school in 1983 to move to Japan.

CHARLES JONES. Charles Jones joined the faculty following his appointment as professor and associate director of the Social Work Program at

Antioch College. Jones held a B.A. degree from the College of the Ozarks and an M.S.W. from Fordham University. While at Michigan, he earned a Ph.D. in education and community development. His dissertation was titled "Social and Psychological Variables Affecting Professional Continuing Education Learning Groups" (1977). His social work practice before coming to Michigan included work with the Office of Economic Opportunity, U.S. Government, the NYC Housing Authority, and the NYC Department of Public Welfare. At Michigan Jones taught courses in community organization practice methods, human behavior and the social environment, and social welfare policy and services. Jones left the school in 1979 to become associate professor and program director of the Social Work Program at University of Texas at Arlington. Hence he joined the faculty of the University of Michigan–Flint, where he directed the Social Work Program.

1972–73
New Faculty: Milan Dluhy, John Ford, Murray Gruber, Dee M. Kilpatrick, and Eliseo Navarro
Departures: Eugene Litwak and John Riley

MILAN DLUHY. Milan Dluhy joined the faculty with a B.A. from the University of Illinois, an M.A. from Southern Illinois University, and a Ph.D. in political science from the University of Michigan. Prior to coming to the school, Dluhy was a lecturer in political science at the University of Michigan–Flint and at Eastern Michigan University. Dluhy's teaching areas included social welfare policy and services, social welfare administration, urban social policy, and housing policy. Dluhy served the school in a number of administrative roles, including director of Continuing Education in the Human Services, head of the Social Policy curriculum area, and project director of the CRAFT project on adoption and foster care. Dluhy was author, coauthor, and co-editor of a number of books and articles on social policy, political advocacy, interdisciplinary planning, and community development. Dluhy left the school as associate professor in August 1987 to become professor of social work and acting dean of the School of Public Affairs and Services at Florida International University.

JOHN FORD. John Ford served on the faculty for two academic years. He earned M.S.W., M.P.H., and Ph.D. degrees from the University of Michigan. He was a graduate of the school's Joint Doctoral Program in Social Work and Social Science, with a dissertation in 1976 entitled "Labeling the Alcoholic: Some Predisposing Factors and Treatment Consequences." Ford left the university to take a position at Cornell University, directing the social work program there and serving as dean of studies at Cornell, hence departing for an appointment as vice president at Emory University.

MURRAY GRUBER. Murray Gruber joined the faculty as associate professor, previously holding an appointment at the School of Applied Social Sciences at Case Western Reserve University. Gruber held a B.A. degree from Brooklyn College and M.S.S.A. and D.S.W. degrees from Case Western Reserve. Gruber's teaching areas included administration and mental health, problems of children and youth, social movements, social planning, and organizational theory. At Michigan Gruber was a productive scholar, publishing articles in the *Journal of Education for Social Work, Social Work, Journal of Psychiatric Nursing, Viewpoints,* and *Administration in Social Work.* Gruber was the school's representative to the Michigan Department of Social Services and was a consultant to numerous community human service organizations. Gruber left the school in 1980 for a position at the School of Social Work, Loyola University of Chicago.

DEE M. KILPATRICK. Dee Kilpatrick came to the school from a faculty position at School of Social Work at Denver University. He held a B.A. from Le Moyne College, Memphis, an M.S.W. from the University of California at Berkeley, and a Ph.D. from the School of Social Service Administration at the University of Chicago. Kilpatrick's teaching and scholarly work focused on social research, family and children's programs, and complex organizations. He was appointed assistant dean in 1974, serving in this position until 1981. His major administrative responsibilities in this position included the overseeing of admissions, financial aid, and special supportive student services, and recruitment of faculty.

Kilpatrick was director of the Region V Adoption Resource Center at the school and participated in the school's National Child Welfare Training Center. He was the school's liaison to the university's Interdisciplinary Program on Child Abuse and Neglect. In 1975 Kilpatrick was a member of the Crime and Delinquency Review Committee of the U.S. Department of Health, Education, and Welfare. From 1976 to 1979 he served on the board of the National Conference on Social Welfare. He participated in and chaired countless site visit accreditation teams of CSWE and served as a member of North Central Accreditation teams. Kilpatrick spent a 1982–83 sabbatical year at the Jane Addams School of Social Work, University of Illinois at Chicago, hence joining the faculty there in 1983.

ELISEO NAVARRO. Eliseo Navarro came to the school after completing a Ph.D. in the School of Social Service Administration at the University of Chicago. He had served as director of a mental health agency and had other practice experience in social work. He held an M.S.W. degree from Our Lady of the Lake College, Worden School of Social Work, in San Antonio, Texas. Before coming to Michigan, Navarro had served as assistant professor at the University of Texas–Austin and at Loyola University School of Social Work at Chicago. His teaching was in the areas of social welfare policy and services, particularly related to the Chicano community. He was associate professor at the school until he left in 1978 for a social work service position in San Antonio, Texas.

1973–74
New Faculty: William Birdsall, Beth Reed, and David Street
Departures: Philip Booth, Stanley Kim, Dorothy Schroeder, and Donald Warren

WILLIAM BIRDSALL. William Birdsall received an A.B. degree and Ph.L. degree from St. Louis University, hence earning a Ph.D. degree in economics from Johns Hopkins University, and B.D. and S.T.L. degrees in theology at Woodstock College. Prior to coming to Michigan, Birdsall was a visiting professor of economics at McMaster University. Prior to that, he served for five years as an economist in the Division of Economics and Long Range Studies, Office of Social Security Administration, Washington, D.C. He joined the faculty as an associate professor of social work, providing a link between the school and the Department of Economics, particularly in relation to the school's doctoral program. His teaching and research interests were in the area of policy analysis, program evaluation, prevention and treatment of women's drug abuse, social securing and welfare programs, measurement of poverty and inequality, and mental health client outcome studies. Birdsall was a principal investigator on several major projects, including the Detroit Area Study and studies under federal research grants. He served as consultant to numerous local, state, and national social welfare organizations. He was a member of the school's Executive Committee. At the university level, Birdsall served as chair of the Budget Priorities Committee and as president of the university's chapter of the American Association of University Professors. Birdsall was faculty associate at the Institute of Gerontology and the Institute for Social Research. Upon retirement in 2001, Birdsall was appointed associate professor emeritus of social work by the university regents.

BETH REED. Beth Reed joined the faculty after serving as coordinator of NIMH training programs at the Drug Dependence Institute, Yale University. She held a B.A. degree from the University of Rochester and M.A. and Ph.D. degrees from the University of Cincinnati. She is currently professor of social work, teaching courses in the school in women's studies and psychology. Reed has been a visiting scholar, Phillips Institute of Technology, Victoria, Australia. At the University of Michigan she holds a joint appointment with the Women's Studies Program. She served as chair of the Faculty Senate in 1988–89. Her current research includes a study of services for women experiencing problems with alcohol and other drugs, a follow-up study of young people who were once in treatment for AOD problems, and program evaluations on dual diagnosis, homelessness. Other areas of research interest include gender, race, social systems, community organization, social planning, and interpersonal violence. Reed's funded research has included projects on Women in Drug Abuse Treatment (NIDA) and W.O.M.A.N. Center Evaluation Project (NIDA). Reed has received numerous faculty recognition awards.

DAVID STREET. David Street, a sociologist, held an appointment with the university's Department of Sociology when he was appointed professor of social work. Street held a B.S.Ed. degree and M.A. and Ph.D. degrees in sociology from the University of Michigan. He provided a link between the Department of Sociology and the school's Joint Doctoral Program in Social Work and Social Science. He collaborated with other members of the school's faculty and the Department of Sociology in his research and publications on juvenile corrections and human service organizations. He left the school in 1976 to join the faculty at the University of Illinois at Chicago.

1974–75
New Faculty: Martha Gizynski, Edith Gomberg, Ann Hartman, and Lenore Kroman
Departures: Richard English, Clarice Freud, Katherine Reebel, and John Ford

MARTHA GIZYNSKI. Martha Gizynski became a lecturer at the school in 1969 while working in the university's Institute of Human Adjustment and was appointed as assistant professor of social work in 1974. She obtained an A.B. degree from Radcliffe College and M.S.W. and Ph.D. degrees from the University of Michigan. Her doctorate was from the school's Joint Doctoral Program in Social Work and Social Science. Upon retirement in 1986 the university's Board of Regents noted: "Professor Gizynski became one of the School's outstanding teachers of interpersonal practice and theory. Her teaching was informed by her research in the areas of family and children's services and ego psychology, and by her on-going commitment to the clinical practice of social work. Her publications reflect the scope of her interests, ranging in subject from adolescents, post-surgery trauma, supervisory relationships, maternal depression, and coping mechanisms of the elderly." As the regents saluted Gizynski as professor emeritus of social work, they noted: "Her retirement marks the departure of one of the most accomplished teachers and clinicians on the School of Social Work faculty" (Board of Regents, 1986). Gizynski held an appointment at the Institute for Human Adjustment, Rackham Graduate School, and at the university's Psychological Clinic.

EDITH GOMBERG. Edith Gomberg joined the faculty of the School of Social Work following appointments at Yale University in the Departments of Psychology and Sociology and the School of Public Health, and as associate professor of psychology at the University of Puerto Rico. She held degrees from Brooklyn College (B.A.), Columbia University (M.A.), and Yale University (Ph.D.). At Michigan she served on the School of Social Work faculty and was research scientist in the Institute of Gerontology, faculty associate in the Institute for Social Research, and professor of psychology in the Department of Psychiatry. Her teaching and scholarly interests included alcohol and drug studies, gender and deviant behavior, adaptation of the elderly, and ethnicity and race issues.

In naming Gomberg professor emerita in 1998, the university's Board of Regents noted: "Professor Gomberg's research has focused on alcohol use and problems in women and the elderly, and her work both defined and set a standard for the field." The regents went on to state, "Professor Gomberg played a key role in the establishment of the University of Michigan Alcohol Research Center. She is the author of more than 50 peer-reviewed publications, a number of book chapters, and has edited 6 books, serving on the editorial boards of numerous journals." Gomberg was regarded as "an internationally respected scholar, lecturer, and consultant" (Board of Regents, 1998). After leaving the school, Gomberg continued her appointments with the Alcohol Research Center and the Department of Psychiatry. As director of the Clinical Research Training in Alcoholism, she was honored at the time of her departure with a Festschrift. During her career, Gomberg was listed in *American Men and Women of Science; Who's Who of American Women; Who's Who in America;* and *Who's Who in Science and*

Engineering. The Edith S. Gomberg Collegiate Professor of Social Work is named in her honor.

ANN HARTMAN. Ann Hartman came to the University of Michigan from a position of associate professor in the Graduate School of Social Service at Fordham University. She held a B.A. from Wellesley College, an M.S.W. from Smith College School for Social Work, and a D.S.W. from Columbia University School of Social Work. Prior to joining the faculty at Fordham, Hartman held a number of casework and administrative positions in New York. At Michigan Hartman served as divisional coordinator of the Interpersonal Practice Division and served on the school's executive, doctoral, curriculum, and search committees. At the university level, she served on the University Council, the Board in Control of Intercollegiate Athletics, the Executive Committee of the Center for the Continuing Education of Women, and the Civil Liberties Committee. She directed Project CRAFT, which was funded by the Clark Foundation and the Children's Bureau and related to foster care and adoption agencies. She also was faculty director of the school's National Children Welfare Training Center funded by the U.S. Children's Bureau.

Hartman's excellence in teaching at Michigan was recognized and highly regarded by students and colleagues, as she demonstrated an unusual ability to meld theoretical knowledge into the teaching of social work practice. At Michigan Hartman became known nationally for her publications in social casework, child welfare, and family treatment. Hartman was co-founder and staff member of the Ann Arbor Center for the Family. Hartman left the school to become dean of the Smith College School of Social Work. She served on the editorial board of *Social Work*, hence becoming editor-in-chief.

LENORE KROMAN. Lenore Kroman joined the faculty with a rich social work practice experience in the mental health area. She was appointed on a National Institute of Mental Health-funded training program to teach and advise students in field instruction in mental health agencies and hospitals. Kroman came to the school as an associate professor of social work, holding B.A. and M.S.S.A. degrees from Michigan, and continued on the faculty until her death during the 1981–82 academic year. While at Michigan, Kroman was the principal investigator of a field testing project for a program evaluation instrument for evaluating community mental health services. She was a consultant to the Southwest Detroit Community Mental Health Center, Adult Care Services of Detroit, and Michigan Council on Children and Youth.

1975–76
New Faculty: Joyce Beckett, Richard Douglass, and Brett Seabury
Departures: Oliver Harris, Roger Lind, Richard Stuart, and Wayne Vasey

JOYCE BECKETT. Joyce Beckett joined the faculty with experience as a clinical social worker and as lecturer in casework at Bryn Mawr, and with degrees from Temple (B.A.) and Bryn Mawr (M.S.S., Ph.D.). As an assistant professor at Michigan, Beckett taught in the areas of ego psychology, casework, and family therapy. Her research focused on married women and work. At the school, she chaired the Minority Opportunity Committee and she served on the university's Student Relations Committee. Her publications included articles on Black families, women and work, race and women, and Black mothers and employment. Beckett departed in 1985 for a position at Virginia Commonwealth University School of Social Work.

RICHARD DOUGLASS. Richard Douglass joined the faculty as an assistant professor with a background in public health and a specialty in alcoholism. Prior to coming to the school, Douglass was research associate at the university's Highway Safety Research Institute. He was appointed to the faculty on a federal grant from the Center for Prevention and Control of Alcoholism. He provided a link between the school and public health. Douglass held three degrees from Michigan—a B.S., M.P.H., and Ph.D. He taught courses related to alcoholism and program evaluation. Douglass left the school for another position in 1977.

BRETT SEABURY. Brett Seabury joined the faculty with degrees from Wesleyan University (B.A.), Simmons College School of Social Work (M.S.), and Columbia University (D.S.W.). His dissertation was entitled "A Systems Model of Case Services" (1976). He came to the school from a position as assistant professor, University of Maryland School of Social Work and Community Planning. At Maryland, Seabury was a member of the clinical concentration, teaching graduate and undergraduate clinical methods courses. At Michigan Seabury was associate professor, teaching courses on environmental interventions, ethnic sensitive interpersonal practice, integrated methods, organizational change, social work with groups, working with involuntary clients, generalist foundation skills, primary associations, institutional racism, social oppression, indigenous healing systems, human communication theory, and poverty. Seabury's courses have received enthusiastic acclaim from students for his engaging teaching style and innovative creation of course content.

Throughout his career Seabury has participated, along with students, in numerous "movements" for social and economic justice. Seabury's community and educational service has included consultations with many health and social welfare agencies, along with presentations at over 150 workshops and conferences in Europe, Canada, and the United States, on such topics as advocacy, case management, contracting, crisis intervention, group treatment, indigenous healing systems, interactive video simulations, metaphors in social work practice, planned short-term treatment, reading emotions on the face, resistance, and task-centered casework.

1976–77
New Faculty: None
Departures: Fred Cox and David Street

1977–78
New Faculty: William Lawrence and Mayer Zald
Departures: Robert Carter and Richard Douglass

WILLIAM LAWRENCE. William Lawrence came to the school with experience in a number of administrative roles, including assistant administrator for the Human Resources Administration of New York City, an appointment in the Office of Economic Opportunity in Washington, D.C., and chief of the Office of Research and Program Evaluation in Washington, D.C. Lawrence received an A.B. degree from Whitman College and an M.S.W. from Columbia University, and he engaged in graduate studies in sociology and social research at Columbia University and New York University. An expert in the fields of social welfare administration, personnel and fiscal management, and program development, Lawrence taught and participated in the development of curriculum in these areas. He directed a national in-service planning and management training program for personnel of Area Agencies on Aging, holding an appointment with the Institute of Gerontology. In naming Lawrence associate professor emeritus of social work in 1986, the regents noted about Lawrence, "He also played a key role in working with agencies to develop the professional practicum for students in social welfare administration. Professor Lawrence was active in the school's continuing education program and conducted many workshops and seminars for social work practitioners" (Board of Regents, 1986).

MAYER ZALD. Mayer Zald received a joint appointment on arriving at the university as professor of social work and professor of sociology, later also becoming professor of business administration. He held a B.A. degree from Michigan, an M.A. degree from the University of Hawaii, and a Ph.D. from the University of Michigan. Before coming to Michigan, Zald served on the faculties of the University of Chicago and Vanderbilt University. Professor Zald provided a link between the Joint Doctoral Program in Social Work and Social Science and the Sociology Department, where he served for two terms as chair of the department.

In naming Zald professor emeritus of sociology, social work, and business administration in 2001, the regents noted, "A superb and highly original researcher, Professor Zald is the author or editor of some 20 books and edited collections and nearly 80 articles, book chapters, and review essays. His work spans the fields of organizational studies, collective behavior, and social theory, and he has made lasting and distinguished contributions in each area. His research accomplishments have garnered numerous awards and prizes, including election to the American Academy of Arts and Sciences and his selection as Distinguished Senior Faculty Lecturer in the College of Literature, Science, and the Arts. Professor Zald is renowned and revered for his generosity in contributing to the work of students, other scholars, and the wider intellectual communities of which he remains such a vital part" (Board of Regents, 2001).

1978–79
New Faculty: Lawrence Root
Departures: Robert Carter, Irwin Epstein, Paul Glasser, Charles Jones, Harry Lawrence, Henry Meyer, Dorothy Robinson, and Mary Taylor

LAWRENCE ROOT. Lawrence Root joined the school's faculty with degrees from Haverford College (A.B.), Bryn Mawr College (M.S.S.), and the School of Social Service Administration, the University of Chicago (Ph.D.). Root came to the school from the University of Chicago, where he was lecturer and assistant to the dean, as well as staff director of the university's Washington Center for the Study of Welfare Policy. He is currently professor of social work, and from 1993 to 2008 he directed of the Institute of Labor and Industrial Relations at the University of Michigan. From 1990 to 1994 he was director of the UAW-GM Educational Development Counseling Program; from 1988 to 1990, co-director of the UAW-Ford Life/Education Planning Program; and from 1981 to 1984, director of the National Older Workers Information System with the Institute of Gerontology. Since coming to Michigan, Root has been principal investigator of numerous sponsored research projects and has served on several university-wide and school committees. Root's teaching and research interests include employment and social welfare, employment-based services, poverty and income maintenance, aging, and work. He is author of numerous articles in journals such as *Federal Probation, Social Development Issues, Social Service Review, the Annals, Journal of Higher Education, Monthly Labor Review,* and *Administration in Social Work,* as well as chapters in edited books. Root is the author of *Fringe Benefits: Social Insurance in the Steel Industry* (1982).

1979–80
New Faculty: Elizabeth Mutschler, Gerald Goff, Alfreda Iglehart, Srinika Jayaratne, and Kristine Siefert
Departures: Eliseo Navarro, Jane Costabile, Murray Gruber, and Sheldon Siegel

ELIZABETH MUTSCHLER. Elizabeth Mutschler received a diploma in social work from the School of Social Work in Ludwigsburg, Germany, and M.S.W. and Ph.D. degrees from Washington University in St. Louis. From 1975 to 1978 she served on the faculty of the University of Maryland–Baltimore. She joined the Michigan faculty as assistant professor and was hence promoted to associate professor in 1984.

Professor Mutschler's scholarly contributions were in three areas: analysis of treatment procedures and therapists' behaviors that facilitate client change, evaluation of empirical procedures in clinical practice, and technology-based decision objectives and monitor outcomes. She served on the university's Research Priorities Committee and on the university's Senate Assembly. She assisted with management information systems development at area hospitals and conducted workshops on technology for faculty and students. She was director of a training and evaluation project funded by NIMH, and chaired the Human Subjects Review Committee of the school. She was a visiting professor at the Hebrew University of Jerusalem and Tel Aviv University, as well as at the School of Social Work, Freiburg. In 1997 Mutschler was named associate professor emerita of social work by the regents of the university, who noted: "Professor Mutschler is truly a pioneer, having forged significant new paths of learning and having worked tirelessly to assist social workers around the world in achieving the best possible modes of practice."

GERALD GOFF. Gerald Goff was appointed to the faculty as assistant professor and project director for social work in the Institute for the Study of Mental Retardation and Related Disabilities. His teaching included courses on principles of behavior modification and on mental health and disabilities. He held a B.S. degree from Western Michigan University, an M.S.W. from Wayne State University, and a Ph.D. from the University of Oregon. Goff left the school's faculty when the Institute for the Study of Mental Retardation and Related Disabilities closed.

ALFREDA IGLEHART. Prior to her appointment as assistant professor, Alfreda Iglehart served as lecturer in the school, research assistant in the Center for Afro-American and African Studies, and teaching assistant in the Women's Studies program at the University of Michigan. She held degrees from St. Mary's University (B.A.), Worden School of Social Service, Our Lady of the Lake University (M.S.W.), and the University of Michigan (Ph.D.). Iglehart's teaching and research interests included social change and family, program planning for female offenders, and program evaluation. While at the school, she served on the Curriculum Committee, the Doctoral Committee, and the Faculty Council. Her community service included membership on the advisory boards of the National Urban League Research Department and the Criminal Justice Institute, Atlanta University. She collaborated with Professor Rosemary Sarri and Josefina McDonough in studies sponsored by the National Institute of Corrections. Her journal publications included articles on wives and work, women in prison, and social change. In 1979 she authored *Married Women and Work.* Iglehart left the school in 1985 for a faculty position at the University of California–Los Angeles.

SRINIKA JAYARATNE. Srinika "Siri" Jayaratne joined the faculty with a B.A. degree from the University of California–Riverside, and an M.S.W. and a Ph.D. in social work and psychology from the University of Michigan. Jayaratne came to Michigan following teaching positions at the University of Oklahoma and Washington State University. He taught courses on social research and on behavior modification, among others. His administrative roles at the school included assistant dean for research and associate dean for faculty and academic affairs. He has been a visiting professor at Wilfrid Laurier University and completed a sabbatical at the University of Melbourne School of Social Work in 2003. Jayaratne's research has included studies of work stress on health and well-being of mental health practitioners, national surveys of social workers, and ethics and social work. He has served on the editorial boards of *Social Work, Social Work Research and Abstracts,* and the *Social Work Dictionary,* and he acted as consulting editor for *Social Service Review, Advances in Social Work,* the *Journal of Social Service Research,* the *Gerontologist,* and the *Journal of Social Education.* He is author (with R. L. Levy) of *Empirical Clinical Practice* (1979). He is author of over seventy-five journal articles and book chapters and has presented papers at over fifty professional conferences. He was awarded a Fulbright Fellowship for 2008. He is a recipient of the school's Distinguished Faculty Achievement Award.

KRISTINE SIEFERT. Kristine Siefert joined the faculty with two degrees from Michigan (A.B. and M.S.W.) and two degrees from the University of Minnesota (M.P.H. and Ph.D.). She came to the school with teaching experience in the area of health services and interpersonal practice, and with practice experience as a medical social worker. At Michigan Siefert has held several administrative roles, including assistant dean for research; coordinator, M.S.W./M.P.H. dual degree program in social work and child and family health; interim director, Center for the Study of Youth Policy; associate director, NIMH Center on Poverty, Risk, and Mental Health; and associate dean for faculty and academic affairs. Known among students as a superb teacher, Siefert has teaching and research interests in social work in health care, family and child health, preventive intervention, and maternal and infant mortality. Siefert is highly regarded for her involvement in doctoral thesis supervision at the university and the school.

Siefert has published over fifty articles and reviews in the leading social work and health journals and has given over forty conference presentations. She has been principal and co-principal investigator and primary faculty member of over twenty research and training grants. Her service activities have been numerous, including consulting editor, editorial board member, editorial reviewer for professional journals, member of advisory committees of national organizations, and member of school and university committees. In 2000 Siefert received the Harold R. Johnson Diversity Service Award from the University of Michigan. She currently has the honor of serving on the faculty as the Edith S. Gomberg Collegiate Professor of Social Work.

1980–81
New Faculty: Helen Weingarten
Departures: William Neenan

HELEN WEINGARTEN. Helen Weingarten earned a B.S. degree in human ecology from Cornell University, an M.S.W. degree from the University of Missouri, and a Ph.D. in social psychology and social work from the

University of Michigan. She joined the faculty as assistant professor and was promoted to associate professor in 1987. Weingarten's research focused on conflict management. In the 1988–89 academic year, she was a visiting professor at Hebrew University in Jerusalem. From 1989 to 1991 she directed the Interdisciplinary Program in Conflict Management Alternatives through the Center of Research on Social Organization in the College of LS&A. She was a founding member of Fairteach (Faculty and Staff Against Racism). She served as a faculty mentor with athletes associated with the Michigan Athletic Department. Her publications included work on divorce among the elderly and interpersonal models of conflict resolution. She delivered a paper to the Dalai Lama at the University of Michigan in 1994. In 2000 the regents named Weingarten associate professor emerita of social work.

Summary of Faculty Size: 1971–81

1971–72 (55)	1976–77 (56)
1972–73 (60)	1977–78 (57)
1973–74 (59)	1978–79 (51)
1974–75 (59)	1979–80 (52)
1975–76 (58)	1980–81 (50)

Faculty Members: 1980–81

Jo Ann Allen, Joyce Beckett, Sydney Bernard, Harvey Bertcher, William Birdsall, Howard Brabson, Sallie Churchill, Alan Connor, Loraine Cook, Jane Costabile, Tom Croxton, Merle Dinsmore, Milan Dluhy, Nathalie Drews, Sheila Feld, Phillip Fellin, Louis Ferman, Madison Foster, Charles Garvin, Martha Gizynski, Gerald Goff, Edith Gomberg, Jesse Gordon, Ann Hartman, Yeheskel Hasenfeld, David Himle, Alfreda Iglehart, Srinika Jayaratne, Harold Johnson, Dee M. Kilpatrick, Lenore Kroman, Armand Lauffer, William Lawrence, Frank Maple, Elizabeth Mutschler, Lorraine Perry, Thomas Powell, Norma Radin, Beth Reed, Lawrence Root, Jack Rothman, Rosemary Sarri, Brett Seabury, Kristine Siefert, Edwin Thomas, Tony Tripodi, John Tropman, Robert Vinter, Helen Weingarten, Charles Wolfson, Mayer Zald.

PART FOUR   The School's Curriculum

Introduction

The structure and major components of the school's 1971 curriculum were established in a major curriculum revision in 1968–69. The conceptual framework for the curriculum created at that time focused on several levels of social organization and intervention (i.e., interpersonal, group and family, organizational, community, and societal). These levels were viewed as calling for "a somewhat distinctive pattern of skills and dealing with different sets of problems" (Fellin & Vinter, 1969).

This curriculum included three broad divisions: social treatment (casework, group work, social treatment), community practice, and social welfare administration and policy development, with social work practice specializations within each division. Each specialization had a somewhat different pattern of required and elective study, with a common course requirement of 56 credit hours for the M.S.W. degree. All students were required to take courses in the knowledge areas of practice methods, practice skill training, human behavior and social environment, social welfare policy and services, and research.

Curriculum Model

Intervention Levels	Curricular Divisions	Practice Specializations/ Sequences
Interpersonal	Social Treatment	Social Treatment Casework, Group Work, Social Treatment
Community	Community Service	Community Practice
Organizational/ Societal	Social Welfare Administration/ Policy	Administration/Policy Social Work Administration, Social Work Policy

Administrative Leadership
Professor Sheila Feld served with distinction as assistant dean for curriculum during this ten-year period. The responsibilities of the assistant dean included the chairing of the curriculum committee, coordinating the work of the curriculum subcommittees, developing the course schedule, assigning faculty to courses, and relating to students in regard to degree requirements and academic difficulty. Faculty members chaired the major curriculum areas (i.e., Social Work Practice Specializations, Human Behavior and the Social Environment, Social Welfare Policy and Services, Research, and Practice Skill Instruction).

During these years, Professors Ann Hartman, Charles Garvin, and Sallie Churchill each served in the position of divisional coordinator for interpersonal practice. At various times Professors Jack Rothman, Sheldon

Siegel, Robert Vinter, Rosemary Sarri, John Tropman and Harold Johnson served as divisional coordinator for community, administration, policy, and evaluation practice. Within each division, faculty members provided curriculum leadership as chairs of the specific practice specializations. Serving as heads of the Joint Doctoral Program during this decade were Professors Rosemary Sarri, Yeheskel Hasenfeld, John Tropman, and Norma Radin, all graduates of the school's Joint Doctoral Program in Social Work and Social Science.

Requirements for the Master of Social Work Degree

In 1971 the requirements for the M.S.W. degree were stated in the *School Bulletin* as follows:

1. A minimum of three terms must be spent in full-time residence, except that a student who transfers one year of credit from an accredited school of social work shall be required to spend two terms in full-time residence.
2. The student must achieve a grade average of B, and over-all performance must be satisfactory in course work and in practice skill instruction.
3. Work for the degree must be completed within six years of the student's first enrollment in the School.
4. Graduating students are expected to attend commencement exercises.
5. Credit and course requirements. A student is required to complete 56 hours of credit for the Master of Social Work degree. The distribution of required courses varies according to specialization.

In 1971 the curriculum structure described above provided the framework for the student's election of a specialization and a method of practice sequence. The student had an opportunity, through electives and course options, to tailor "his educational experience to fit his own particular professional interests" (*School Bulletin*, 1971–72). The *School Bulletin* noted that "None of the specializations seeks merely to train students for service to a particular age group or in a particular type of agency; rather, each is designed to prepare students for competent beginnings in social work practice in any of several professional roles." The practice specializations and methods sequences were described as follows:

1. Specialization in Interpersonal Practice

Interpersonal practice methods are aimed at modifying the behavior of the individual, his immediate social situation (family, gang) or both. By developing skills at this interpersonal level of intervention, students prepare for roles in restoring, sustaining, or improving the health and welfare of individual human beings in a variety of settings.

Programs in this specialization include:

Casework—prepares students for direct practice with and service to individual clients.

Group Work—prepares students to treat individuals within and through groups.

Social Treatment—by combining and integrating individual and group methods, prepares students to utilize techniques of competent interpersonal service to individuals, families, and other groups in all practice settings.

2. Specialization in Community Practice

Community practice methods are aimed toward the planning and implementation of change programs and improving relationships among components of the community—groups, organizations, public and private agencies, schools, governmental units—in order to accomplish certain social welfare and community goals. Community intervention methods prepare students for roles in urban affairs, educational, manpower, housing, race relations, law enforcement, or health programs and projects.

3. Specialization in Social Welfare Administration and Policy Methods

Social welfare administration and policy development are aimed toward the organization and advancement of social services and social policy. Two programs in this specialization are:

Social Welfare Administration—prepares students for administrative responsibilities—such as staff development and training, program planning and analysis, budgeting, supervision, information systems design, and program evaluation—in social welfare organizations.

Social Welfare Policy—prepares students for responsibilities in the formulation, implementation, evaluation, and modification of social welfare policies and programs on state, regional, and national levels, within planning units of governmental or voluntary welfare organizations, or in such roles as legislative assistant or technical consultant.

Knowledge Areas of the Curriculum

Credit and course requirements varied according to specialization, but all students completed courses in practice methods, practice skill instruction, human behavior and social environment, social welfare policy and services, research, and electives. Course areas and specific courses offered in each area were identified but not defined in the 1971–72 *School Bulletin*. These areas were defined in the 1973–74 *School Bulletin* as follows:

Courses in Practice Methods

All students take at least one course in a practice method each term. The specific courses taken depend on the student's Program of specialization. Students in any of the Programs comprising the Interpersonal Practice Division take the same introductory practice methods course; subsequent courses are taken in casework, group work, or social treatment practice methods, depending on the Program of specialization. All students in the community practice division take two common practice methods courses and then choose further courses in social action or social planning practice methods. All students in the Social Welfare Administration and Policy Division take two common practice methods courses, choose further courses in administration or policy practice methods, depending on their Program of specialization, and also take one course in interpersonal or community practice methods.

Courses in Practice Skill Instruction

Practice skill instruction courses are offered every full term with four such courses required of all candidates for the degree (16 credit hours). The student spent the equivalent of two days a week for sixteen weeks with a minimum of 240 clock hours per term in an assigned agency. The credit acquired for practice skill instruction was four hours per term. The student elected social treatment, casework, group work, community practice, social welfare administration, or social policy development as a preferred method of practice for the first year of practice skill instruction. For the second year, the study could continue in the same method as that of his first year, or could change to another practice method.

Courses in Human Behavior and Social Environment

Courses in the area of Human Behavior and Social Environment are designed with the goal of including social and behavioral science knowledge within the basic social work curriculum. All students are currently required to take four to six of the 22 courses regularly offered in this area. These cover a wide range of social science knowledge.

Courses in Social Welfare Policy and Services

Courses in the area of Social Welfare Policy and Services focus on particular types of social welfare programs pertinent to various student interests. All students take at least two courses: one basic course designed to provide the tools to analyze contemporary welfare policies and programs and one specialized course. Separate courses cover a full range of social welfare programs including courses in the areas of corrections, family and children, income maintenance, mental health, health and rehabilitation, public assistance, housing, human resources, and race and ethnic relations.

Courses in Research
To help critically evaluate the theory and knowledge available from the social and behavioral sciences and to foster the interpretation of research findings for application to social welfare problems, all students take two courses in research. The first basic course is common to students in all practice methods. The second course is specialized and focuses on research issues relevant either to interpersonal influence, community problems, complex organizations, or policy development.

Elective Courses in Social Work and Cognate Areas
All students have a minimum of six elective courses, and may take electives from graduate departments or other professional schools at the University.

With regard to the school's curriculum and teaching patterns, the individualization of instruction was enhanced by the mechanism of "special studies" courses. By this means courses in newly developing areas in social welfare were added to the school's curriculum for the year 1972–1973. Examples included Advanced Ego Psychology, International Social Work, Population Planning and Social Control, and seminars in Drugs, Black Family, Chicano Culture, and Youth and Social Policy.

Curriculum Changes
In 1977 the curriculum was reorganized to include two major divisions: (1) interpersonal practice and (2) community, administrative, and policy practice (CAPP). The division of interpersonal practice still included casework, group work, and social treatment specialization, with the CAPP division changed to include community practice, social welfare administration, social policy and planning, and social program evaluation. New descriptions were provided for the programs in the two practice divisions, as follows:

Community Practice/Social Welfare Administration/Social Policy-Planning/Social Program Evaluation Division
Community Organization is that method of social work practice oriented to social action and change at the community level, and with the development

of cohesion and integrity among community groups and members.

Social Welfare Administration is that method of social work practice concerned with the management and direction of organizational behavior so that goal outcomes are achieved as efficiently and effectively as possible within the framework of social work values.

Social Policy and Planning are those methods of social work practice concerned with the analysis, development and implementation of social policy into operational plans for achieving social goals.

Social Program Evaluation is that method of social work practice concerned with the utilization of scientific methodologies for the assessment of the performance of human service organizations, policies, and programs.

Interpersonal Practice Division

The division of interpersonal practice was described as methods aimed at the restoration, maintenance, and enhancement of social functioning and included change objectives relating to the individual, family, or small group, their immediate social environment, and the transactional relationship between person(s) and environment. First-year courses focused on the "generic" aspects of interpersonal practice. In the second year, students choose from a variety of options for concentration. The concentrations were interpersonal practice with children and youth, with families, with groups, in community mental health, in health settings, in schools, from a behavioral framework, and from a clinical casework framework.

Minority Relevant Content

In 1972–73 the school's faculty approved a plan for giving special attention to minority content in the curriculum. The Curriculum Committee reviewed courses in terms of integration of minority group content, revision of course objectives, and bibliography, supporting the development of library, audiovisual, and bibliographic resources pertinent to minority content.

The systematic use of student course evaluations regarding course content permitted the faculty to monitor course content, including minority content, in the courses offered. The evaluations informed faculty members, students, and the curriculum committee with regard to course content, instructor's presentation, course organization, and instructor–student relations. A computer program provided for rapid analysis and reporting of results to faculty and students. In addition, the results of an alumni survey administrated to graduates of the past five years were used for curriculum review and development.

In 1975 a position of curriculum coordinator for minority content was established, in order "to strengthen the efforts to incorporate minority content through the assessment of specific responsibilities. The position involves resource development, assistance to faculty members, knowledge development, and course development" (*CSWE Report,* 1983). Initially the coordinator's activities were directed to minority groups of color. However, the focus changed in the following years to include gender and other special populations affected by bias and/or oppression. For example, a course on Gay Issues in Social Work was offered as an elective special study course (*CSWE Report,* 1983).

In 1978 the faculty established a minority relevant course requirement. "The School requires a Minority Relevant Course Requirement for all students. Students can meet this requirement by taking a course within either the School or the University-at-large. . . .This requirement states that ALL students must take at least one course from a designated list of minority relevant courses" (*CSWE Report,* 1983).

The 1979–80 *School Bulletin* included a special section entitled "Minority Relevant Course Requirement." This section stated that "the Governing Faculty of the School recently reaffirmed its commitment to continue to initiate, support, and develop mechanism and procedures designed to integrate minority content into all elements of the curriculum to ensure that future graduates have knowledge in this area." The bulletin further noted: "In defining what is meant by minority content, two dimensions have been identified for focus. The first focus is upon specified, identifiable target groups with special socio-cultural heritage and experience; at present four primary target groups have been specified: Black, Hispanic, Asian American, and Native American. The second focus is on certain social processes that are critical to practice with minority populations. These processes concern various forms of discrimination and oppression (for example, racism, sexism, ageism) that occur across the four target populations identified above, as well as involving many other groups."

During the 1978–79 year, the faculty approved an exemplary list of courses within the school and the university that would serve to meet this requirement. The 1980 *School Bulletin* noted that "the courses that qualify as meeting this requirement must devote a substantial portion (50% or more) of planned course matters (class sessions, readings, student assignments, etc.) to minority relevant content." In the report to CSWE in 1983, the school indicated that a focus was also placed on oppressed population's such as women, the elderly, as well as racial and cultural minorities. To meet the requirement, at least fifty percent or more of planned course material must focus on one or both of the dimensions of minority relevant content (*CSWE Report*, 1983).

Grades

The description of the school's grading policies and procedures in 1971 remained the same as those established in 1959. The *School Bulletin* of 1971–72 stated:

> Letter grades from A through E are given for class and practice skill instruction, and students are expected to maintain at least a B average. When a student falls below this average, he may remain in school only with the approval of the Faculty Advisory Committee. B grades are given to students who do all the required work for the course satisfactorily, B plus and B minus reflect slight differences from this satisfactory level. A grades are given for exceptional individuals' performance and C grades are given when performance definitely falls below requirements for graduate work. D grades indicate unconditional failure, and E is given when a course is dropped after the end of the fourth week of a term or the second week of a half-term. I, for Incomplete, is used when illness or other compelling reasons prevent completion of work and there is a definite plan in regard to when work will be completed.

In 1972 the faculty made a minor modification in grading policies with regard to incomplete courses. The 1972–73 *School Bulletin* indicates that "any student who accrues more than four hours of Incompletes will receive a letter from the Associate Dean indicating that fact immediately after the end of the term. The student will be required to consult with his or her adviser regarding a plan for making up such Incompletes, and will be required to submit this plan in writing within two weeks to the Associate Dean." If a student failed to meet this expectation, the associate dean would consult with the Faculty Council regarding further action. In 1973 the grading policies were modified to state: "When I is used, it is accompanied by a letter grade in parentheses, used to indicate the student's grade position prior to completion of work. Any grade I remaining on a student's record twelve months after the conclusion of the term in which the grade was awarded reverts to E."

In December 1972 the faculty voted to change the grading system for the field instruction course from an A to E scale to include an optional satisfactory/marginal/unsatisfactory plan for a two-year period. In 1974 the faculty moved to continue for two more years this optional grading system. Effective with the winter 1975 term, the satisfactory/marginal/unsatisfactory plan became permanent for all students. These grades carried no honor points and could not be averaged with grades for academic courses. Students had the option of determining (in consultation with faculty liaison and field instructor, if they chose) the application of the new grading system or of the A through E grading system to each term's practice skill instruction requirement. However, once the student selected one system or another, he or she could not change the preference until the following term.

The grading system for practice skill instruction included the following definitions:

> *Satisfactory* means that the qualify of performance for practice skill instruction is acceptable and credit is granted for the course. Students who perform at a level which would bring a letter grade of B or above are given a Satisfactory grade.
>
> *Marginal* means that performance in practice skill instruction is less than satisfactory but short of failing. Students who perform at a level of B minus to C minus letter grade are given a grade of Marginal.
>
> *Unsatisfactory* means that the quality of performance is inadequate and no credit is granted. Any student performing below a C minus letter grade in practice skill instruction is given an Unsatisfactory grade.

In 1976 the policy regarding incompletes was changed from the incomplete grade reverting to an E to the following: "Any grade I remaining on a student's record more than two terms after the conclusion of the term in which the grade was awarded reverts to a permanent Incomplete, and credit can be earned only by retaking the course." Further modifications were made in regard to Incompletes, including the restriction that "in no case shall a student with more than six hours of Incompletes be allowed to register for a full program of courses" (*School Bulletin*, 1977).

In 1978 the modification was made that "any student who comes before the Faculty Council because he or she has accrued more than four hours of Incompletes in each of two successive terms of enrollment will not be allowed to register for a full program of courses" (*School Bulletin*, 1978). This policy would prevail even though incompletes accrued from the first semester were made up.

In 1979–80 the faculty introduced a new section of the *School Bulletin* entitled "Academic Difficulty." This statement read as follows:

At the end of each term a subcommittee of the Faculty Council reviews the records of students in academic difficulty. Students include those who are not achieving at a level required for the Master's degree—a grade average of B, and overall performance that is satisfactory in coursework and practice skill instruction; have more than four hours of Incomplete grades in any one term; have been dropped from practice skill instruction because they have been unable to meet minimum standards to practice skill instruction, or receive a marginal or Unsatisfactory grades in practice skill instruction in conjunction with a grade-point average of B or lower.

The subcommittee of the Council may recommend a variety of actions, including, but not limited to, the following: reduced credit hour enrollment, enrollment in remedial coursework, discontinuance of enrollment for the forthcoming term until Incomplete grades are removed, demonstration of competency in a given area prior to future enrollment in particular courses or practice skill instruction, and withdrawal of admission to the School.

If the disposition under consideration is to withdraw the student's admission, and the only method of returning to the School is reapplication, at the student's request the entire Faculty Council meets to consider the case and the student and his or her faculty adviser is permitted to appear before the full Faculty Council on the student's behalf.

The rules regarding Incompletes previously established are once again listed in this statement on academic difficulty.

Interdepartmental Programs

School Bulletins continued to note: "The School co-operates with the other schools and departments of the University in helping students to work out programs of study in special cases where the student's interests lie partly in the field of social welfare and partly in some closely adjoining field. In cooperation with the School of Education a limited number of experienced teachers are accepted for a part-time program in school social work. The program meets the minimum employment requirements for this position in Michigan school districts. The School participates with the University's Institute of Labor and Industrial Relations, with the Institute of Gerontology and Public Health, and with the School of Public Health in permitting students to choose a core group of electives in these and related areas. Students may take special studies through arrangements with other units of the University, such as the Survey Research Center, the Population Studies Center, and the Detroit Area Study."

Continuing Education, Extension Courses, Special Institutes
The school's Continuing Education Program was developed in order to bridge the gap between the discovery of new knowledge and technology and application in practice. With initial support from the National Institute of Mental Health, the program became one of the largest and most varied social work programs of this nature in the United States. In 1972 over 1,400 practitioners and administrators received training in short-term workshops, institutes, and symposia. The program received support from the Social and Rehabilitation Service, the Rehabilitation Services Administration, the Administration on Aging, the Law Enforcement Assistance Administration, the Department of Labor, and a number of state and local agencies for continuing education activities. The program had collaborative relationships with the Schools of Public Health, Education, and Natural Resources; the Institute of Gerontology; Labor and Industrial Relations; and Public Policy Studies. The program carried out special projects with the Michigan Civil Rights Commission, the Office of Youth Services, the Department of Social Services, and the Department of Mental Health, and it worked closely with community mental health centers and mental health boards in a number of communities to develop workshops.

Workshops were established in a spring/summer symposium for training of educators and staff development specialists. An example was the gaming workshops developed by Professor Lauffer and conducted at the Annual Forum of the National Conference on Social Welfare in 1972 and at regional, state, and National Association of Social Workers' meetings. The program presented "mini courses" for administrators and practitioners, drawing over 700 people. Workshops in 1976 dealing with feminist concerns are another example of the spring/summer symposium. This symposium included Assertive Training for Women, Feminist Psychotherapy: A Workshop for Women Practitioners, and Leadership Techniques for Women.

During the decade of 1970–80, the school became the national leader in the area of continuing education, due largely to the leadership of Professor Armand Lauffer and faculty members at the school. Professor Armand Lauffer became recognized as the leading authority in the area of continuing education and social work, and his books on this subject gained national and international attention. Based on Lauffer's conception of continuing education, programs in extension, spring/summer symposium, consultation, and special projects brought educators, researchers, policymakers, practitioners, and administrators together on campus, in communities, and in the state to bridge the gap between new knowledge and the changing needs of practice.

During 1971 and 1972, the Continuing Education Program conducted a national public policy dialogue on the separation of services from income maintenance and public welfare, a state-wide dialogue on the politics of narcotics programs, a regional dialogue on public policy and the family, a training conference for juvenile court judges, and a national conference on the utilization of research for operations personnel in work incentive programs (*CSWE Report*, 1973). Led by Professor Henry J. Meyer, the Social Work Education and Population Planning Project was funded by a five-year grant from the Agency for International Development in cooperation with the School of Public Health and the Department of Population Planning at the university. Professors Charles Garvin and Paul Glasser were involved in training faculty members from developing counties, in presenting workshops for social workers from developing countries, and in preparing teaching materials. Other programs developed by the Continuing Education Program included the following:

- A Child Welfare Learning Lab, supported by the Social and Rehabilitation Services of the Department of Health, Education, and Welfare (HEW), in collaboration with the Michigan Department of Social Services.
- A Mental Health Skills Lab, supported by the National Institute of Mental Health (NIMH).
- A Substance Abuse Project with the Michigan Department of Public Health.
- Training of state and area planners in the field of aging in collaboration with the Institute of Gerontology and funded by the Administration on Aging.

Project CRAFT, Curriculum Resources for Adoption and Foster Care Training, was conceived by Professor Lauffer and Mr. Peter Forsythe and funded by the Edna McConnell Clark Foundation. The project was designed to provide leadership training for adoption and foster care workers, and to develop special training materials for child placement. During CRAFT's first three years, monographs were produced that reflected not only the best current thinking in child development but sound, effective child care practice. The monographs included *Finding Families*, by Ann Hartman; *No Child Is Unadoptable*, by Sallie Churchill and Lynn Nybell; and *Resources for Child Placement and Other Human Services*, by Armand Lauffer. In its fourth year, CRAFT was combined with a new project funded by the Children's Bureau of HEW. Activities in these projects set the stage for a proposal by the school to become a National Child Welfare Training Center.

In keeping with the school's commitment to improving child welfare services in the state and nation through its educational programs, in 1976 the school developed a collaboration with the Medical School and the Law School in an Interdisciplinary Program for the Prevention of Child Abuse and Neglect. The program was funded under a grant from the Harry A. and Margaret D. Towsley Foundation of Ann Arbor. Social Work personnel involved in the project were Professors Paul Glasser and Kathleen Faller, along with Ms. Leora Bowden of the Social Services Department of University Hospital. The program offered an opportunity for increasing interaction among Social Work, Law, and Medicine in regard to teaching, research, and continuing education programs with a special focus on child advocacy.

The school conducted a training project in child and family services, funded by the Department of Health, Education, and Welfare (HEW), under the direction of Professor Sheldon Siegel. The project focus was on improving the competencies of Social Work graduates in the design and implementation of programs in child and family services. Under this program a special seminar was offered by Sally Brown and Pearl Axelrod of the School of Education.

In 1979 the school was designated as the National Child Welfare Training Center, with funding from the Office of Human Development and HEW. Professor Ann Hartman acted as director, assisted by Professor JoAnn Allen. The administrative director was Sylvia Sims Gray. The center was part of a major five-year initiative on the part of the federal government to enhance services to children and families by expanding the availability of child welfare education and training materials. In its first year of operation, the center convened meetings in Harper's Ferry, Ann Arbor, and Denver to coordinate the work of regional staff, Children's Bureau project officers, and the national Advisory Committee. The center also sponsored a seminar in Washington, D.C., at the Hubert H. Humphrey Building. The seminar dealt with the "Status of Adoption and Foster Care in the United States" and brought together national leaders concerned with child welfare education and practice as well as the public policy area. Following the seminar, participants and guests were honored at a White House reception hosted by first lady Rosalynn Carter.

In 1979 the school was designated Region V Adoption Resources Center, established to facilitate efforts to eliminate barriers to adoption and to promote permanent placement for children in the region. The center was funded by the U.S. Children's Bureau, one of the ten centers in the United States. The center was directed by Professor and Assistant Dean Dee Morgan Kilpatrick. Activities of the center included provision of technical assistance grants to the six states in Region V to sponsor training workshops and conferences, to hire specialized consultants, and to sponsor recruitment campaigns to find parents for special needs and minority children.

Extension Courses

The school offered credit courses through its Extension Program to individuals interested in advancing their knowledge, in accumulating undergraduate and graduate credits, and in possible eventual entry into the school's M.S.W. program. Classes were held in various continuing education centers operated by the university's Extension Service throughout Michigan.

Winkelman Lecture Series

The Leon and Josephine Winkelman Lecture Series was initiated in 1978, established with funds from the Leon and Josephine Winkelman Foundation by the Winkelman brothers, Stanley, John, Frederick, and Henry. The lecture series is a memorial to the parents of the Winkelman brothers. The principal focus of the annual lecture series is on the field of gerontology. Within this context, the series is interdisciplinary in nature, emphasizing the presentation and discussion of emerging knowledge from the social and biological sciences and the helping professions. The activities of the lecture series involved a public lecture by a distinguished scholar and seminar sessions with students and faculty of the university over a two-day period. The first three lectures were:

1978: "Aging, Social Class, and Ethnicity," Professor Zena Smith Blau, University of Houston.

1979: "Principles of Hospice Care," Daniel C. Hadlock, M.D., Medical Director, Hospice Orlando.

1980: "The Ethnic Factor in the Delivery of Social and Health Services to the Elderly," Professor Barbara Solomon, University of Southern California.

Welfare Reform Symposium

This symposium was offered in 1977–78, jointly sponsored with the School of Education, focusing on welfare reform. Dean Wilbur Cohen of the School of Education, long-time faculty member of the school, chaired the one-day meeting on national and state welfare reform legislation. Participants were Deputy Assistant Dr. Michael Barth, secretary for Income Security Policy at the Department of Health, Education, and Welfare; Dr. Wendal Primus, senior staff economist for the U.S. House Committee on Ways and Means; and Dr. John Dempsey, director of the Michigan Department of Social Services. Professor Milan Dluhy, director of continuing education at the school, developed the program for the symposium.

Symposia: 1979–80
The school joined the Bush Program in Child Development and Social Policy and the Psychology Department in sponsoring a lecture series by Dr. John Bowlby of the Tavistock Institute. Professor Larry Berlin, director of the Continuing Education Program, organized a workshop on "The Black Experience," bringing to campus leading Black scholars in social work and social science to discuss such topics as Black family life and lifestyles, social work in the Black community, and physical and mental health among Blacks. A fall conference on training in the human services included presentations over a three-day period by leaders in continuing education throughout the United States. Outstanding social work educators who visited the school to present lectures and seminars were:

> Professor Gisela Knopka of the University of Minnesota: "Adolescence: A Time of Great Strength, Potential, and Vulnerability."
> Professor Jona Rosenfeld of the Paul Baerwald School of Social Work, Jerusalem: "Service to the Individual or Collective . . . Lessons from the Wars of Israel."
> Professor Naomi Gottlieb of the University of Washington: "Education of Social Workers for Clinical Evaluation."
> Professor Shirley Cooper of Mount Zion Hospital, San Francisco: "Field Teaching: Acculturation and Education for Clinical Social Work Practice," in memory of Professor Dorothy Robinson.

Review
The reorganization of the curriculum in 1968–69 provided the conceptual framework and the course requirement arrangements for the curriculum in 1971. This curriculum was organized around intervention levels, curricular divisions, and social work practice specializations. Some minor adjustments were made in the curriculum from year to year, with a major review coming in 1977–78, the addition of a social program evaluation specialization, and the creation of new options for concentration in interpersonal practice methods.

Throughout this decade the faculty continued to give special attention to the inclusion of minority-relevant content in the curriculum. By 1978 the faculty had established a minority-relevant course requirement for all students, as well as made efforts to integrate minority content into all elements of the curriculum.

The grading system of the school remained essentially the same over this ten-year period except for a change in grading for practice skill instruction. In 1972 the faculty changed the grading system for field instruction to include an optional plan of satisfactory/marginal/unsatisfactory grades, becoming a permanent plan for all students in 1975.

The school's Continuing Education Program instituted a number of arrangements to present parts of the curriculum to social workers not enrolled in the school. This program included workshops, institutes, symposia, and extension courses. Many of these programs were carried out in collaboration with other academic units at the university as well as social welfare agencies in the community and the state. Of special note was the designation of the school as a National Child Welfare Training Center and Region V Adoption Resources Center.

In 1978 the Leon and Josephine Winkelman Lecture series was initiated through the support of the Winkelman family. A special symposium chaired by Dean Wilbur Cohen of the School of Education focused on welfare reform. A Conference on Training in the Human Services was offered by the school through presentations by visits of prominent professors in social work education.

PART FIVE   Summary of 1971–81

Dean's Annual Reports

During this decade I had the pleasure of serving as dean under President Robben W. Fleming, Interim President Allan Smith, and President Harold Shapiro. These individuals were extremely helpful and supportive, as well as the vice presidents I worked closely with—Carolyn Davis, Billy Frye, James Lesch, Frank Rhodes, John Romani, Allan Smith, Charles Overberger, Alfred Sussman—and especially Charles Allmand, assistant to the vice president for academic affairs. Excerpts from the dean's *Annual Reports to the President* of the university appear below in order to provide a flavor of the accomplishments of faculty at the school and some of the changes that occurred during this decade.

1971–72 Annual Report to President Robben W. Fleming

During the past year the School initiated a comprehensive self-study of its programs and operations, directed toward a scheduled review of accreditation status by the Council on Social Work Education.

This review process offers the School an excellent opportunity to reassess its objectives, operations, and total program. It is expected to stimulate the School to evaluation, improvement, and new approaches to social work education.

On a personal note, the year has been an eventful one for Assistant Deans Richard English, Sheila Feld, and myself. We have sought to create an atmosphere of open communication by keeping the faculty, students, and staff as fully informed as possible. We have sought increased participation on their part in the affairs of the School. During our first year we have enjoyed the support of members of the School, the University, and the community. This has facilitated our efforts to maintain and improve the quality of the School's programs and to assure the School's leadership role in social work education. We look forward to the coming years with a little less apprehension, and considerable optimism.

1972–73 Annual Report to President Robben W. Fleming

After somewhat exhaustive deliberations over a period of two years, the School has approved a new governance for faculty–administration relations. The structure builds on the previous governing system, with changes mainly in the nature and functions of the School's Faculty Council. Implementation of the new structure begins in Fall 1973. The School's new statement of governance more clearly identifies the jurisdiction of the faculty and the Dean in terms of areas of authority, and increases faculty participation in the decision-making process. Under the new structure, the Faculty Council will be composed of eight members of the faculty elected by the Governing Faculty, with two representatives from each professorial rank and two at large. The Council will be chaired by the Dean.

1973–74 Annual Report to President Robben W. Fleming

This year the School of Social Work continues to rank first among the 79 Schools of Social Work in the United States in total number of applications received, total graduate enrollment, the number of full-time students, and the number of M.S.W. degrees granted.

In a survey conducted by Columbia University's Comparative Organizational Research Program, the School of Social Work at Michigan was ranked as one of the top five graduate schools of social work, and was the only public institution in this top-ranked group.

The School established a named professorship in honor of Professor Emeritus Arthur Dunham. Professor Robert D. Vinter was named by the Regents of the University to hold this professorship.

1974–75 Annual Report to President Robben W. Fleming

This year marks the fortieth anniversary of the master's degree program in social work at the University of Michigan. By 1951 the number of master's degrees awarded was 321. In this 40th anniversary year the . . . number of M.S.W. degrees awarded totaled 4153.

A review of the annual reports for social work over the past 40 years reveals several themes:

- a constant effort to meet the manpower needs of the State of Michigan and the nation in the area of social work and social welfare;
- a high priority on the needs of the State of Michigan for professional social workers, through degree offerings and extension offerings;
- a high priority on education of individuals for social work in the public services.

A number of factors stand out as significant in assisting the School toward these goals:

- the leadership of Dean Fauri and the faculty;
- the impetus provided by a 1965 report of the Michigan Citizens Committee on Higher Education, which called for an increase in the facilities and faculties of the Schools of Social Work in Michigan, to meet the increased demand for professional social workers in the coming ten years;
- the full utilization of opportunities offered by the University's year-round operation of the School;
- the infusion of increased University funds to the success of the School, under the leadership of Deans Fauri and Vinter, in attracting federal funds and support for social work education.

As a result of the relatively recent constraints from state and federal funding sources, the School has entered a period of stabilized enrollment. At the same time the application rate continues to rise, making it necessary to reject a large number of qualified applicants for admission.

In addition to the master's program, the School has, since 1957, administered a joint social work and social science doctoral program. There have been 63 Ph.D. degrees awarded under this program by the Rackham School of Graduate Studies. Graduates of the program now teach in social work programs in over 40 universities, with some graduates employed in social science departments and in social work research.

The School's goals of increasing the knowledge for professional practitioners carried out through the scholarly and research activities of the faculty cover a wide range of social programs and social work practice topics.

This year the School's Faculty Council completed a written set of guidelines for promotion.

The most crucial issue for the School in the coming year is related to its funding. The School's programs have traditionally benefited from the strong University support, federal funding to students and faculty, and from private support. The School's ability to maintain a superior and diverse faculty and student body depends on continuation of adequate funding. Many recent fiscal decisions at the state and federal level threaten the maintenance of quality programs in social work at the University of Michigan.

At the same time the faculty and staff of the School will attempt, with resolve and determination, to maintain the School's leadership position in social work education.

1975–76 Annual Report to President Robben W. Fleming

The 1975–76 academic year has been a most active and productive one for the faculty and staff of the School of Social Work. Already engaged in a major task of curriculum revision, the faculty combined these efforts with activities specifically related to consideration of issues raised in President Fleming's annual State of the University address, and the call from Vice President Rhodes for completion of an Evaluation and Planning report.

While both the M.S.W. and doctoral program continue to receive a high number of applications, we have sought to stabilize the enrollment in both programs in keeping with budget reductions from University and federal funds. Still, due in part to the year-round program, Michigan enrolled the largest number of full-time M.S.W. students of any school in 1975, and had the highest number of graduates for the year. Out of a total of 34 doctoral programs, Michigan is one of four (the others being Brandeis, California/Berkeley, and Columbia) which had over 45 students last year.

Michigan was one of only eight schools which had all major minority groups (Black, Chicano, Asian American, Native American, and Puerto Rican) represented in their social work student bodies in 1975.

The University continues to provide significant financial aid support for students in need, but the School faces serious problems in maintaining its goal of a diversified student body. Federal funds for social work education have been cut drastically over the past few years, with a severe adverse effect on the School's capacity to provide financial aid for students in need. Although the University makes a significant investment in financial aid for our students, highlighted by the fact that approximately 65% of financial aid grants to our student are from School/University funds, such funds still are not sufficient to meet the great need of poor and minority students. Slightly less than one-half of the students enrolled in the School in 1975–76 received financial aid from funds administered through the School. Unless additional financial aid resources are obtained, the School's student composition will change markedly and the proportion of minority students will decrease.

Recognizing the considerable strength of the faculty, we also see major problems in this area which the School faces for the coming five years. Due to decreases in federal funding for faculty support, and to decreases in general funds support for faculty, the School has been unable to replace members who have retired or have taken positions elsewhere. The current faculty is more limited than is desirable in representation of women and minorities.

Special Projects have been conducted by faculty members of the School over the past five years. I want to make special note of these projects, as they have contributed in large measure to the School's programs and to its stature. Under the direction of Professor Henry J. Meyer, a Social Work Education and Population Planning Project was established in 1971, funded through a five-year grant from the Agency for International Development. Professors Paul Glasser and Charles Garvin joined Professor Meyer in contributing to the study programs for social workers from developing countries and the projection of teaching materials in the social work/family planning area.

The National Assessment of Juvenile Corrections project was established in 1971, sponsored by the Law Enforcement Assistance Administration and lodged in the Institute for Continuing Legal Education and the School of Social Work. The co-directors of this project were Professors Rosemary Sarri and Robert Vinter. The project involved a national study of the relative effectiveness of alternative correctional programs for different types of juvenile offenders. During the project period numerous doctoral students at the University, both from our joint program and from other University units, have participated in the research activity, as have a number of faculty members from within the University community. Publications of the project deal with the nature and effectiveness of existing juvenile programs and provide policy recommendations for change in the correctional system.

Consistent with the School's high priority on education of individuals for social work in the public services, several special collaborative efforts have been made with the Michigan Department of Social Services, particularly through the School's Continuing Education and Extension Program. Of special note was the establishment of a Child Welfare Learning Laboratory designed to assist the Department of Social Services in building its internal capacity for training child and family services personnel. The project was funded by the Social and Rehabilitation Service of the Department of Health, Education, and Welfare.

1976–77 Annual Report to President Robben W. Fleming

The School continues to survey the employment patterns of the School's graduates. Responses from the May 1976 graduates indicate a bright employment picture, as only five individuals of more than 200 graduates reported that they were involuntarily unemployed six months after graduation. Graduates from the joint social work–social science doctoral program had no difficulty in locating teaching positions, filling positions at such universities as the University of Wisconsin, Michigan State, Western Michigan, the University of California, the University of Delaware, Washington University, and the University of Chicago. Since the initiation of the doctoral program 20 years ago, 88 doctoral degrees have been granted through the Horace H. Rackham School of Graduate Studies. Over 50 universities now have graduates from the Michigan doctoral program teaching in their schools of social work.

The School has continued to collaborate in a number of ways with the Michigan Department of Social Services, with our arrangements and involvement fully supported by the director of the department, Dr. John T. Dempsey. A staff/faculty exchange resulted in contributions of MDSS staff to the School and in special projects by faculty members.

Of special note were Professor Sydney Bernard's participation in the work of the department's Management Action Team in Wayne County; Mr. Roy Gaunt's work with personnel in the Bureau of Management and Staff Development in Lansing; and Mr. Robert Little's contributions to the School's teaching and continuing education programs. These projects are in keeping with one of our major objectives of preparing social workers for the public social services.

I have briefly described a number of activities at the School which are funded from "outside" sources, both private and public. The School has traditionally sought support of this nature in order to enhance the substantial educational efforts provided for by the state's budget allocation to the University. As we note in the section on special projects, there is often an emphasis on interdisciplinary collaboration and on emerging areas of social service and research.

Reductions in funding, particularly in federal support for social work education, and enforced reductions at the University over the past few years, threaten to remove the School's Vital margin which has contributed to its national and international reputation. A number of educational activities, such as course offerings, liaison to field agencies, faculty research, and University and community service, have been reduced to accommodate budget constraints.

We face problems in maintaining the quality and diversity of our faculty, in supporting our highly regarded continuing education and extension program[s], and in maintaining faculty workloads which allow time for research and field service activities. We are making every effort to generate economies and effectively use our existing resources to maintain a quality program. Faculty and staff have been most responsive in this regard.

1977–78 Annual Report to President Robben W. Fleming

If there is any one term that best characterizes the School of Social Work, it would be the word "active." It seems that no year is ever "normal" at the School; there are always changes in student interests and "demands" in faculty activities, in curriculum development, and there is always unfinished business.

By all accounts, the Social Work end of the Frieze Building is an active place. The entrance bustles with social work students, users of the fourth floor student lounge overflow into the halls, the classrooms turn into lunch rooms at noon, the old Carnegie library is always jammed, and posters everywhere vie for attention.

Despite the outward appearance of a "Times Square" atmosphere, the high level of energy and excitement within the School also truly marks it as a marketplace of ideas. Students and faculty constantly struggle to relate the knowledge of academics to the practice of social work in the real world.

So it is, in any given year, difficult to capture and describe anywhere near the total range of activities at the School. Yet, each year I take pride in highlighting a few characteristics which seem to convey the quality of the School and its leadership role in social work education.

1978–79 Annual Report to Interim President Allan F. Smith

The 1978–79 academic year has been a most difficult one for the School of Social Work.

For many of us it seemed like our misfortunes were endless. In the early part of the year our colleague, Dorothy Robinson, met with an untimely death. Throughout the year there followed a number of illnesses which required faculty members to be absent from the classroom. Faculty members and social workers from the community were most responsive in taking on extra responsibilities in order to maintain our course offerings. Students accepted these disruptions and changes with good grace. These strains took their toll on us, but as we reflect back over the year, there are a number of accomplishments that deserve recognition.

1979–80 Annual Report to President Harold T. Shapiro

This year marks the completion of 45 years of professional social work education at the University of Michigan. During this period some 5781 students have obtained the Master of Social Work degree. Graduates of the School are distributed throughout the United States, and in many parts of the world . . . particularly in Australia, India, Japan, Korea, the Philippines, Israel, Canada, and Great Britain. Although younger than many of its sister schools, Michigan has emerged as the top-ranked school at a public university, and is ranked second only to Columbia among all the United States Schools of Social Work.

The strengths of the school are difficult to capture in words, but they surely come from the aggressiveness, competitiveness, and drive for excellence of the faculty and student body, and the School's success in integrating the goals of professional education, knowledge, and public service. This annual report seeks to highlight some of the activities of the 1979–80 year which have contributed to the attainment of these goals.

Even with the constraints of reduced fiscal resources, the School seeks to maintain and improve the quality of its programs and to assure its leadership role in social work education. Given our history, we have ample reason to view the Eighties with considerable optimism.

An outside review of the School came at the call of the Office of the Vice President of Academic Affairs, a review related to the intent of Dean Fellin to leave the deanship upon completion of his second five-year term in the summer of 1981. The Vice President noted, "It seems appropriate at this time to commence a thoughtful review of the school's accomplishments during the decade of Dean Fellin's leadership, and to assess appropriate directions and strategies for the School in the coming decade." The report of the review noted: "It should be stated at the outset that the School of Social Work enjoys a well deserved eminence and prestige in the profession. The School has contributed significantly to the development of knowledge and to the education of social work practitioners. Its faculty and graduates have made outstanding contributions to the field. Its administrators, faculty, and alumni hold important leadership positions in the profession."

The External Review report was followed up with deliberations on the part of the faculty to create a "Statement of the Future Direction of the School of Social Work."

1980–81 Annual Report to President Harold T. Shapiro

During this year the School's faculty devoted special efforts to the preparation of documents in response to Vice President Rhodes' call for evaluation and planning, terminating in the development of a Memorandum of Understanding. The documents dealt with the mission of the School, trends in society affecting the social work profession and social work education, the educational objectives of the master's program and the joint doctoral program in social work and social science, student enrollment and placement, research, service, inter-unit relations, faculty composition and activities, and facilities.

An objective stated in the School's Memorandum of Understanding was the development of a more systematic and comprehensive job placement program. This has been achieved, largely due to the special efforts of Assistant Dean Dee Kilpatrick, Professor Joyce Beckett, doctoral student Kathy Pottick, and Kay Paul. Our survey of 1980 graduates conducted by Ann Fowler shows that the overall picture of employment remains positive. Only seven percent of our respondents were still seeking employment in social welfare positions six months after graduation. Sixty percent were working in social service organizations under public auspices. Sixty-five percent of the graduates had starting salaries of $15,000 or more (compared to fifty percent in 1979), and 33 percent began employment at $17,000 or over. A large number of respondents had noted that they had used the School's Employment Service office for assistance in job-finding. Alumni were also given credit for assisting graduates in the search for first employment.

Over the past decade the School's faculty has emerged as a leader in the publication of scholarly works. A review of publications during the history of the School reveals a dramatic increase in authorship of articles and books by the faculty in the decade 1970–1980. It was during this period that major text books were authored by Michigan faculty, books which are used in social work education in this country and abroad. A number of these texts have been translated into foreign languages.

It was my pleasure to accept the appointment as Dean of the School of Social Work in 1971, at a time when the school had been moved to national prominence through the leadership of Dean Fedele F. Fauri and Associate Dean Robert Vinter, and a highly qualified faculty and student body. As I leave the deanship, I am confident that the School will continue its leadership in social work education. During this past decade the faculty and the University administration have demonstrated an unusually high degree of support and commitment to excellence in social work education, and to the efforts of the deans of the School to enhance this excellence.

I am particularly grateful to Assistant Dean Sheila Feld and Assistant Dean Dee Kilpatrick for their service during these years to assure a quality education for our students and a satisfying work experience for our faculty; to the faculty members for their constant cooperation, and especially to those who sought to divert me from my return to teaching; and to the countless number of students who shared with me their desire to study at Michigan, their appreciation for our efforts to assist them with special needs while at the School, and their high regard for the quality of education they received at Michigan.

School of Social Work Building. Photo: Philip T. Dattilo.

Fedele F. Fauri, Dean of the School of Social Work, 1951–70. Photo: School of Social Work collection.

Robert D. Vinter, Acting Dean of the School of Social Work, 1970–71. Photo: School of Social Work collection.

Phillip A. Fellin, Dean of the School of Social Work, 1971–81. Photo: School of Social Work collection.

Harold R. Johnson, Dean of the School of Social Work, 1981–93. Photo: School of Social Work collection.

Paula Allen-Meares, Dean of the School of Social, 1993–2008. Photo: Philip T. Dattilo.

John E. Tropman, Acting Dean of the School of Social Work, 2008. Photo: U-M Photo Services: Martin Vloet.

Laura Lein, Dean of the School of Social Work, 2009– . Photo: U-M Photo Services: Martin Vloet.

Dean Emeritus Phillip Fellin lectures on the history of the School of Social Work during the 2008 reunion weekend. Photo: Tanya C. Hart Emley.

Sheila Feld, Assistant Dean 1971–81 and head of the doctoral program 1982–89.
Photo: Collection of Phillip Fellin.

Dean Harold R. Johnson (right) thanks alumnus Paul M. Gezon, MSW '57, for his
service to the School and the Alumni Society. Photo: Collection of Phillip Fellin.

Professors Tom Croxton and Kay Reebel. Photo: Collection of Phillip Fellin.

Professor Merle Dinsmore (second from left). Photo: Collection of Phillip Fellin.

Emeritus faculty luncheon, 1997. Photo: Collection of Phillip Fellin.

Emeritus faculty luncheon, 2003. Photo: U-M Photo Services: Martin Vloet.

Professors Henry Meyer, James Mandiberg, Charles Garvin, and Dean Paula Allen-Meares, spring 1995. Photo: U-M Photo Services: D. C. Goings.

Professor Richard English (center) receives the U-M Alumni Association's Distinguished Service Award, 2005, pictured with Professors Phillip Fellin (left) and Siri Jayaratne. Photo: U-M Photo Services: Lin Jones.

Dean Fedele Fauri (left) and Dean Phillip Fellin. Photo: Collection of Phillip Fellin.

Professor Dee M. Kilpatrick (left) and Dean Phillip Fellin. Photo: Collection of Phillip Fellin.

The Johnson Years

Chapter four, "The Johnson Years," covers the history of the school during the tenure of Dean Harold Johnson from his appointment as dean on July 1, 1981, through the close of his deanship at the beginning of the winter term 1993.

PART ONE   The School of Social Work: 1981–93

Profile of the Dean

Following nearly twenty years of experience in the trade unions and in community service organizations in Canada and the United States, Harold Johnson joined the University of Michigan faculty in 1969 as professor of social work and director of the community practice program. From 1975 to 1981 he was co-director of the University of Michigan–Wayne State University Institute of Gerontology. He was appointed dean of the School of Social Work in 1981. He also held an appointment in the School of Public Health as professor of health behavior and health education. He served as national president of the Association for Gerontology in Higher Education, as a consultant to the National Institute of Mental Health and the National Institute on Aging, and as a member of the Commission on the Legal Problems of the Elderly of the American Bar Association (SSW, *Self-Study*, 1991).

During his deanship, Johnson gave leadership to international projects at the school, directing Health Care of the Elderly: A Cross-Cultural Perspective from 1981 to 1988. In 1984 Dean Johnson was recognized with an honorary doctor of philosophy degree from Yeungnam University in Gyongsan, Korea. He has been listed in *Who's Who in America, Who's Who Among Black Americans, Who's Who Among Human Services Professionals,* and *Who's Who in the Midwest.* At the close of his deanship in December of 1992, Johnson served as special counsel to the university president and interim secretary of the university. In 1993 Johnson was recipient of the Dreamkeeper Award in recognition of his exceptional contributions to the University's commitment to cultural diversity. A professorship at the school, the Harold R. Johnson Endowed Chair in Gerontology, and the Harold R. Johnson Diversity Service Award at the university are named in Johnson's honor. In December of 1995, the university's Board of Regents named Johnson professor emeritus of social work, professor emeritus of health behavior and health education, and dean emeritus. In awarding Johnson emeritus status, the regents noted: "He is widely respected for the dynamic and thoughtful leadership he brought to the University and the School of Social Work and for his personal attributes of fairness, tolerance, and good humor" (Board of Regents, 1995).

Administrative Personnel of the School
Administrative personnel of the school during the 1981–93 period are listed below.

> Harold R. Johnson, Dean
> Yeheskel Hasenfeld, Associate Dean
> Ruth E. Dunkle, Associate Dean
> Sheila Feld, Associate Dean
> Diane Vinokur, Assistant Dean for Research and Development
> Srinika Jayaratne, Assistant Dean for Research and Development
> Nathalie Drews, Assistant Dean of Student Services
> Edith Lewis, Assistant Dean of Student Services
> Dee M. Kilpatrick, Affirmative Action Coordinator
> Shirley Anderson, Assistant to the Dean
> Elizabeth Barlow, Administrative Associate
> Larry Coppard, Director, Community Relations, and Professional Development
> Susan Finlayson, Executive Secretary
> Ann Fowler, Administrative Associate
> Roy Gaunt, Assistant to the Dean
> Barbara Hiebbner, School Registrar
> Lillian Jarman-Rohde, Director of Professional Practicum
> Christina W. Neal, Librarian
> Darlene Nichols, Librarian
> Kathy Okun, Office of Alumni Relations and Development
> Joan Robinson, Administrative Assistant
> Sandra Rod, Student Services Assistant

The School's Faculty

The functions and rights of the faculty were specified in the report of the site visit team for the accreditation of the school in 1991 as follows: "The School's faculty is clearly responsible for admission of students, establishing the curriculum, determining the students' course of study, and recommending degree candidates. Faculty are involved in the development of policies related to hiring, retention, promotion and tenure, and in the process of recruiting and recommending candidates for faculty appointments. They are involved in promotion and tenure through an elected body, the Executive Committee, although appointments to the committee are made by the Provost. The by-laws of the Board of Regents of the University and the School's Faculty Handbook specify policies and practices related to faculty rights and responsibilities. Formal guidance procedures are outlined in the Faculty Handbook" (SSW, *Self-Study,* 1991). The governing faculty of the school consists of those members of the school who are professors, associate professors, and assistant professors.

Guidelines for the annual review of the faculty were developed prior to 1983 and appeared in the school's 1983 CSWE *Self-Study.* Included in these guidelines were:

- Procedures for rating performance of teaching, knowledge development, and service.
- Criteria for annual review.
- Translation of total performance into salary increments.
- Information for faculty prior to executive committee reviews.
- Information for faculty after executive committee review.
- Preamble to criteria for teaching, knowledge development, and service.

The Michigan Mandate

Recruitment of new faculty members from 1981 to 1993 was guided by the faculty's policies and efforts to have a diverse faculty. In 1988 the school followed the direction of the Michigan Mandate instituted by university President James Duderstadt. The mandate was a commitment on the part of the university based on the following proposition stated by President Duderstadt: "We believe that the University has a mandate to build a model of a pluralistic, multicultural community for our nation, an environment which is supportive of all individuals, regardless of race, creed, national origin, gender or sexual orientation, which values and respects and, indeed, draws its intellectual strength from the rich diversities of people of different races, cultures, religions, nationalities, and beliefs" (State of the University

Address, October 1988). A related action by President Duderstadt in 1989 was his creation of a President's Advisory Commission on Women's Issues, with a number of challenges directed toward increasing the presence of women in areas where they were underrepresented, including the challenge to increase the number of female faculty at the university.

The School's Policies on Nondiscrimination
The school followed the university's policies on nondiscrimination, including its affirmative action statement:

> The University of Michigan, as an equal opportunity, affirmative action employer, complies with applicable federal and state laws prohibiting discrimination, including Title IX of the Educational Amendments of 1972 and Section 504 of the Rehabilitation Act of 1973. It is the policy of the University of Michigan that no person, on the basis of race, sex, color, religion, national origin or ancestry, age, marital status, handicap or Vietnam-Era Veteran status, shall be discriminated against in employment, educational programs and activities or admissions.
>
> The School follows the policies of the University as an Equal Employment–Affirmative Action Employer, and, as an academic unit of the University shares the commitment to the principles of equal opportunity and affirmative action, as evidenced by the policy as stated in the EEO/Affirmative Action Policy of the University of Michigan which is adhered to in all hiring practices.

The School of Social Work adheres to the university's Policy Statement on Sexual Orientation (1984): "The University of Michigan believes that educational and employment decisions should be based on individuals' abilities and qualifications and should not be based on irrelevant factors or personal characteristics which have no connection with academic abilities or job performance. Among the traditional factors which are generally 'irrelevant' are race, sex, religion, and national origin. It is the policy of The University of Michigan that an individual's sexual orientation be treated in the same manner. Such a policy ensures that only relevant factors are considered and that equitable and consistent standards of conduct and performance are applied" (SSW, *Self-Study*, 1991).

The School of Social Work followed the university's policy regarding students with disabilities. The *School Bulletin* (1992) stated: "The University of Michigan complies with federal and state laws which affect qualified persons with disabilities. It is the policy and practice of the School of

Social Work to provide equitable educational opportunities for students with documented disabilities in all programs and activities, including internships or field placements."

The Executive Committee
The school's Executive Committee operated within the policies of the university's Board of Regents, as follows:

> The Executive Committee, in addition to managing selected administrative functions, is charged with the duties of investigating and formulating educational policies for consideration by the faculty and shall act for the faculty in matters of budgets, promotions and appointments. (Sec. 5.06, Regents' By-Laws)
>
> The Executive Committee consists of the Dean of the School and six members of the Governing Faculty. The six appointed members of the Governing Faculty consist of one from each professorial rank, and three members at large. The Dean of the School serves as chairperson of the Executive Committee. (SSW, *Self-Study,* 1991)

School Committees
The CSWE *Self-Study* (1991) also stated,

> All committees, except the Doctoral, Human Subjects Review, Search, and Executive Committees, may be composed of 50% faculty, 50% students, plus a faculty member as chair. Students on School committees are assigned by the Social Work Student Union. Faculty members and chairpersons of School committees are appointed by the Dean with the concurrence of the Executive Committee. Standing Committees of the School include:
> - Admissions, Financial Aid, and Student Services
> - Curriculum
> - Faculty Search
> - Minority and Gender Affairs
> - Student Grievance
> - Extramural Committees: Committees for which the jurisdiction and authority lies outside the School, including: Human Subjects Review, Supervising Committee for the Doctoral Program.

Over the years faculty members of the School have served in key leadership positions in university-wide governance, including appointments such as the following:

Beth Reed, Chair of Senate Advisory Committee on University Affairs (SACUA)
William Birdsall, Chair of Budget Priorities Committee
Harvey Bertcher, Chair of Student Services Committee
Edith Gomberg, Chair of Research Policies Committee
Lawrence Root, Chair of Committee on the Economic Status of the Faculty

Alumni Society

The University of Michigan School of Social Work Alumni Society was formed in 1982, with Dean Johnson and Professor John Tropman giving direction to this development. The purposes of the society were to:

- Encourage a continued flow of outstanding student candidates for the school.
- Familiarize alumni with problems and progress of the school so that they may assist the advancing of its programs.
- Infuse professional practice and social service ideas, perspectives, and needs into the school.
- Facilitate opportunities for continuing education for social work graduates.
- Provide financial support for the school and the university.
- Develop a wider fellowship between faculty, alumni, and students so that they may mutually benefit from each other's advice, help, and experience.

At the time of the founding of the Alumni Society, board members were Jesse Bernstein, Laura Williams, David Krehbiel, Lori Hansen Riegle, James Martin, Mary Ann Daane, Ernstine Moore, Marilyn Robey, Carla Overberger, Stephen Thomas, Michael Pfaff, and Vern Dahlquist. Faculty representatives were Professors Alfreda Iglehart, Vivian Shapiro, and John Tropman.

An annual meeting of the Alumni Society was held each fall. The organization was directed by a board of governors elected by the society's members. Membership was available to all alumni who have received degrees or certificates from the School of Social Work, faculty members of the school, and others who have demonstrated a vital interest in the School of Social Work (*School Bulletin,* 1992–94).

A newsletter to alumni, called *Newsline,* established in 1971, was renamed *Ongoing* in 1981. The newsletter provided a mechanism for communication to alumni and included a letter from the dean, along with news items about faculty and alumni. Copies of these newsletters are available in the social work collections at the Bentley Historical Library. Selective "tidbits" from *Ongoing* about faculty and staff of the school are included in Part Three: The School's Faculty. Excerpts from *Ongoing,* in the form of comments from the dean, are included in Part Five: Summary.

Winkelman Lecture Series

The Leon and Josephine Winkelman Lecture Series was initiated in 1978, established with funds from the Winkelman Foundation by the Winkelman brothers, Stanley, John, Frederick, and Henry. The lecture series was created as a memorial to the parents of the Winkelman brothers. The principal focus of the series is on the field of gerontology. The lectures for the period of 1981 through 1992 are as follows:

1981 Bernice C. Neugarten, Northwestern University, "New Perspectives on Aging and Social Policy"
1982 Bent Rold Andersen, Commission on the Elderly in Denmark, "Creating Coherent Public Policy for the Elderly in a Welfare State"
1983 Matilda White Riley, National Institute on Aging, "Aging and Society: Notes on the Development of New Understandings"
1984 Gabe J. Maletta, Geriatric Research, Education and Clinical Center, Minneapolis, "Diagnosis and Management of Dementias in the Geriatric Patient"
1986 Mildred Seltzer, "A New View of Older Women in America"
1987 Theodore Goldberg, "Health Care of the Elderly: The Canadian Experience"
1988 Gary Andrews, "Contradictions and Innovations in Health Care of the Elderly: A Doctor's Dilemma"
1989 John Pickering, "Death and the Law"
1990 Olivia Maynard, Director, Office of Services to the Aging, State of Michigan, "Gerontic Imperatives: Danger and Opportunity"
1992 Gene Cohen, "Understanding Creative Potential in Later Life: Impact on Research, Practice, and Policy"

The Fedele F. and Iris M. Fauri Memorial Lecture in Child Welfare

This lecture series was established in 1984 through gifts from alumni, faculty, friends, and members of the Fauri family. The series is presented annually in recognition of former University of Michigan Dean of the School of Social Work Fedele F. Fauri and his wife, Iris. The lecture series provides a forum for the discussion of ideas and proposals to enhance the well-being of young people. The lectures for the period of 1984–92 were the following:

1984 Winifred Bell, "The Struggle for a Coherent Child Welfare Policy"
1985 Peter Forsythe, "The Future of Child Welfare: How Will Current Issues and Trends Affect the Decade Ahead?"
1986 Alvin Poussaint, "Black Children: Coping in a Racist Society"
1987 Justice Rosemary Barkett, "Children and the Courts: Salvation or Damnation"
1990 Jonathan Kozol, "America's Children: The Homeless, Hungry, and Poor"
1990 Ruth Massinga, "Beyond the Rhetoric: To Enhanced Child Well-Being"
1992 Congressman Sander Levin, "Children in Poverty and the Welfare Crisis: What Can Be Done?"

Facilities

The school continued to be housed in the Frieze Building during this decade, with research and training projects located in the Social Work Center Building on Huron Street and in several commercial buildings near the school. The Social Work Library, located in the Frieze Building, was originally a Carnegie Library for the city of Ann Arbor. In 1991 the school's library housed approximately 40,000 volumes, received more than 500 periodicals, and maintained an extensive pamphlet and reprint file. The school also maintained a computer teaching facility in the Frieze Building, as well as a media lab. The report of the 1991 site visit reaccreditation team from the Council on Social Work Education noted: "Plans are underway for a state-of-the-art facility for the School. The current facility, the Frieze Building—a remodeled school house—is well maintained but by no means adequate for the School's enterprise" (CSWE report, 1991). The reference to the Frieze Building as a "remodeled school house" pertains to the fact that the Frieze, built in 1907, was Ann Arbor High School until purchased by the university in 1956, with the School of Social Work moving in 1957.

Plans for a new School of Social Work building were presented in a 1988 document, *Prospectus for a New Building for the School of Social Work*, by Dean Harold Johnson. He was assisted by Professor Jesse Gordon, coordinator, and an advisory committee of Professors Kathleen Faller, Sheila Feld, Thomas Powell, and Lawrence Root. The school moved out of the Frieze Building to its new location in 1998. In October 2004 the university announced that the Frieze Building would be demolished, except for the original Carnegie Library facade, to make room for a dorm and academic space.

The School's Reaccreditation: 1983
A site visit team from the Council on Social Work Education visited the school from October 25 to 28, 1983, for purpose of the reaccreditation of the master's program. The team was composed of Maurice Hamovitch, professor, School of Social Work, University of Southern California (chair); Patricia Ewalt, dean, School of Social Work, University of Kansas; Grace Harris, dean, School of Social Work, Virginia Commonwealth University; Robert Stewart, Timberlawn Psychiatric Center.

The site visit team report of December 6, 1983, stated in summary, "Overall, this is a very good School of Social Work, with an excellent faculty and administration, dedicated to the principles contained in the accreditation standards. The faculty has just completed a massive revision of its curriculum, based on several years of self-study. The new curriculum shows promise of providing an excellent educational program. The administration of the School has been reorganized within the first two years, with full faculty involvement, and the procedures in place . . . including key committees such as the Executive Committee, the Curriculum Committee, the Search Committee, should assure continuous self-study and monitoring to keep abreast of the changing demands of the profession and the University."

The following are excerpts from the Reaccreditation Report:

Administration of the School: "The Dean of the School of Social Work, who reports to the Vice President for Academic Affairs, has held this position for two years. In meetings with the Vice President it is clear that the dean is held in high esteem by the Vice President and that the Vice President has a positive opinion regarding the changes instituted by the dean, principally the increased emphasis upon scholarly endeavors and research on the part of the social work faculty and the curriculum changes."

Faculty: "The faculty of this School have well-deserved, excellent reputations as scholars and contributors to social work knowledge."

Students: The Reaccreditation Report reported that student rights were protected by a statement of student rights. Two major concerns were raised: (1) "Some students believe that there is an over emphasis in the courses on the research interests of the faculty at the expense of the needs of the students for learning practical skills in dealing with their clients." (2) In regard to the issue of minority and gender content in courses, "There is an unevenness among faculty members in the extent of attention paid to these issues in different courses."

The Commission on Accreditation of CSWE reported to University of Michigan President Harold Shapiro as follows: "At its meeting on January 16–20, 1984, the Commission on Accreditation reviewed the application submitted by the school of social work of the University of Michigan for reaffirmation of accredited status of its master's degree social work program. It is with regret that I inform you of the Commission's action to place the program in probationary status because of the School's failure to meet accreditation standards to the extent necessary to warrant the retention of accredited status." The following reasons were given:

- "Non-compliance due to characteristics of the Non-BA program."
- "Outcome objectives of the curriculum not included in school self-study."
- "Major specializations need definition."
- "Clarification of the Extended Degree program needed."

In this letter the school was invited to show cause in regard to standards for probationary accreditation. The school provided "show cause" materials to the commission, and the chair of the commission responded in June 1984 to President Shapiro: "At the May 21–25 Commission on Accreditation meeting the Commission evaluated the show cause materials submitted by the School, stating: 'After a review of these materials the Commission determined that the program had shown cause and voted to rescind its prior action.' I am pleased to advise you that the Commission reaffirmed the accredited status of the master's degree program to June 1990."

The School's Reaccreditation: 1991
The faculty of the school engaged in a self-study of the school's programs during 1990, which led to a report to the Commission on Accreditation of CSWE. A visiting team came to the school for a site visit in March 1991. The team was composed of Dean June Gary Hopps of Boston College (chair), Professor Julia Norlin of the University of Oklahoma, Dean Emeritus Bernard Ross of Portland State University, and Dean Roosevelt Wright, Jr., of the University of Texas–Arlington.

The site visit team's *Report to the Commission* included the following summary and conclusion:

The Team found the University of Michigan School of Social Work to be an outstanding, dynamic and successful program. Major strengths include:

- The gestalt of the School as a part of and player in a first rate, pre-eminent research University.
- A long history of commitment to social work education, with an emphasis on knowledge development in keeping with the mission of the University. Several research institutes and centers provide opportunity for students and faculty to be at the cutting edge of research and scholarship on pressing social problems.
- A faculty of excellent caliber, sufficient size, and diversity in talent, background and interest who provide stimulation for knowledge development and innovative teaching.
- The capacity to share abundantly in the University's resources: in fiscal allocations, in library support, in access to administrative resources throughout the structures of the University, and most important, in the freedom and autonomy to direct its enterprise.
- A research enterprise that is at the forefront among schools of social work.
- A doctoral program that is nationally and internationally renowned; that contributes faculty to many schools, informs policy development and practice regionally, nationally and internationally; and, more relevant to this report, informs the MSW program.
- An MSW program with strong dual degree options and variety of courses, a number of which are laudable for their depth and level of scholarship.
- Research centers and projects that forge linkages to students, alumni/ae, practitioners, and communities.
- Students—the people the School admits and graduates. The admissions process and continued support of students is outstanding. The particular attention and assistance given minority students is exemplary.
- Strong alumni-ae and the way they are organized to make contributions to the welfare of the School. The alumni are invested in the School, a well-organized group, giving focus and support to the campaign for the new building and development of practicum opportunities. They also provide opportunities for research.
- The President's leadership in strategic planning for the University for the next decade and the Dean's participation in that process, both of which bode well for the future of the University and the School.
- A Dean highly respected as a visionary leader. He has brought and encouraged innovative programs, attracted and supported outstanding

faculty, is committee to diversity and supports faculty/staff development. He has expanded the School's resources and is working effectively to get a new school built. The Dean follows in the tradition of strong leaders, one of whom is involved in the faculty and offers leadership nationally.

For all of its excellence and strengths, there are areas that may need ongoing attention.

- For the future, the School must be aware that the commitment to research, with all of its great virtues, may have tended to eclipse contributions to service and this is particularly evident in the level of support of students through liaison and advising functions.
- Similarly, sequential curriculum design, planning and monitoring may also have suffered. Although there is great depth at the course level in many instances, it is not universal and this might well account for vagueness in the explication of the foundation curriculum.
- There may also be some inattention to the professional practicum and how that course of study relates to the educational foundation and advanced curriculum.
- Current space occupied by the School in scattered sites interferes with interaction of faculty and students.

In sum, the School, its administration, its faculty and their creativity and dedication are impressive. With full attention to the last enumerated items, all aspects of the program will reflect equal excellence.

Despite this summary by the site visit team, at its meeting in October 1991, the Commission on Accreditation deferred action pending receipt of further information on curriculum and educational outcomes. The commission noted that the site visit came at a time when the curriculum was in transition and that reviewing two sets of curriculum documents created some confusion. The school responded to the Commission on Accreditation with additional materials, and at its February 1992 meeting, the Commission reaccredited the master's degree program through October 1999, the full eight-year cycle.

PART TWO   The School's Students

Admission to the School

The *School Bulletin* for 1981–83 announced that "the School of Social Work seeks to enroll well-qualified students with diverse backgrounds consistent with its goals, curriculum, and commitments. The University of Michigan, as an Equal Opportunity/Affirmative Action employer, complies with applicable federal and state laws prohibiting discrimination, including Title IX of the Education Amendments of 1972 and Section 504 of the Rehabilitation Act of 1973. It is the policy of The University of Michigan that no person, on the basis of race, sex, color, religion, national origin or ancestry, age, marital status, handicap, or Vietnam-era veteran status, shall be discriminated against in employment, educational programs and activities, or admissions." The 1983–85 *School Bulletin* included sexual orientation and financial need in its anti-discrimination statement. This bulletin also stated that "in pursuit of its goal of a diverse student body, the School of Social Work encourages applications from minorities, non-residents, international students, and those who are seeking a career change or further training."

Criteria for Admission

Applicants for admission are expected to meet the following requirements:
1. The applicant must have a baccalaureate degree from an accredited college or university.
2. Applicants should have completed, with competitive grades, an undergraduate program in social work or a major in one of the social sciences, including sociology, psychology, political science, economics, history, and anthropology. Applicants who have other majors and a minimum of 20 semester hours in some combination of social science courses are also encouraged to apply.
3. Applicants are expected to show probability of success in pursuing professional education for graduate social work. This determination shall be based primarily on an evaluation of the records of undergraduate and all previous graduate education and of employment experience in the human services.
4. Applicants must possess personal qualifications considered essential to the successful practice of social work, such as sensitivity and responsiveness in relationships, concern for the needs of others, adaptability, good judgment, creativity, integrity, and skill in communication. (*School Bulletin*, 1983–85)

Provisions for Non-Baccalaureate Degree Applicants

The 1981–83 *School Bulletin* notes: "Admission is possible for a limited number of persons who do not hold baccalaureate degrees. The goal of this provision is to recruit a limited number of individuals who are currently active as employees or volunteers in human service organizations, yet lack both the MSW and the BA (and otherwise would have little opportunity for completing both)." Specific requirements were identified, such as at least two years of collegiate study and a minimum amount of volunteer work and/or employment in human service organizations, as well as some of the usual requirements for admissions listed above.

Advanced Standing

During this decade, the school continued its policy on advanced standing introduced in 1977–78. Under this policy "applicants admitted to the School with a major in social work from an undergraduate program accredited by CSWE may be eligible for advanced standing of 14 credit hours and may be eligible for the M.S.W. degree after successfully completing 42 hours of graduate credit. Eligibility for advanced standing requires an overall grade-point average of 3.5 on a 4-point scale" (*School Bulletin*, 1981–83).

Student Enrollment

Full-time students enrolled in the M.S.W. program ranged in number from 489 in 1980 to 481 in 1990. Doctoral program enrollees increased during this period from forty-two to sixty. The M.S.W. minority enrollment moved from 17 percent in 1980 to 16 percent in 1990. In 1980 enrollment by gender was 27 percent male, 73 percent female; in 1990, 19 percent male, 81 percent female.

Full-Time Students

Year	Total	M.S.W.	Doctoral
1980	531	489	42
1985	501	456	45
1990	541	481	60

MSW Full-Time Student Enrollment by Ethnicity

Year	Total	Asian-Am.	Black	Chicano	Native Am.	Puerto Rican	White	Other	Foreign
1980	489	6	64	10	1	0	389	6	12
1985	456	6	58	6	2	1	376	2	5
1990	481	10	55	6	3	4	383	2	8

M.S.W. Full-Time Student
Enrollment by Gender

Year	Total	Male	Female
1980	489	134	355
1985	456	75	381
1990	481	89	392

M.S.W. Full-Time Student Enrollment
by Student's Major, Fall 1990

Interpersonal Practice	81%
Administration	10%
Policy	4%
Community Organization	3%
Research	2%

M.S.W. Graduates:
1981–82 to 1991–92

1981–82 (280)
1982–83 (264)
1983–84 (212)
1984–85 (249)
1985–86 (282)
1986–87 (269)
1987–88 (276)
1988–89 (282)
1989–90 (266)
1990–91 (281)
1991–92 (276)

Financial Aid

The school provided a range of financial aid awards to students on the basis of demonstrated financial need as determined by a careful review of the student's budget and resources. These awards included tuition scholarships, social agency scholarships, traineeships, and long- and short-term loans. Financial aid was also available through the university's Office of Financial Aid, through university scholarships, Minority Merit Awards, the College Work-Study Program, National Direct Student Loans, Alumni Scholarships, and Continuing Education of Women Scholarships. Among other sources of scholarships were the U.S. Department of Health and Human Services, the U.S. Bureau of Indian Affairs, Michigan Commission on Indian Affairs, scholarships for students from other countries, and emergency loan funds.

Tuition/Fees
Tuition/fees for students enrolled in the school were established by the university, with a differentiation between Michigan residents and non-Michigan residents. The university's Office of the Registrar administered the classification of students in terms of residence, following regulations published in school bulletins.

> *1981–82 Full Program Term (Semester) Tuition:*
> Michigan residents $1,266
> Non-Michigan residents $2,746
>
> *1991–92 Full Program Term Tuition:*
> Michigan residents $3,037
> Non-Michigan residents $6,352

Student Services and University Resources
Student services were available to students in the School of Social Work through the university's Office of Student Services and through the school's Office of Admissions, Financial Aid, and Student Services, later named the Office of Student Services. Examples of university services included housing, health, International Center, Disabled Student Services, Minority Student Services, Veterans, Center for the Continuing Education of Women, Coalition for the Use of Learning Skills, and Career Planning and Placement Office. School services included orientation of new students, faculty advising, academic and nonacademic counseling, student information, job referral, and job placement services.

Student Relationships /Student Organizations
School bulletins during this period continued to publish the school's statement of student rights and grievances established in 1972, as noted in the 1991–93 *School Bulletin*. The activities of several student organizations served students at the school, including the Association of Black Social Work Students, Coalition of Asian Social Workers, Doctoral Student Association, Los Trabajadores de la Raza, Social Work Student Union, Women's Caucus, and Alliance of Lesbian and Gay Men Social Workers. Since 1969

students continued to participate in school committees as part of the fifty-fifty plus one plan.

PART THREE The School's Faculty

Introduction

In the fall term 1981, the faculty consisted of forty-nine members, with the same number at the close of the fall term 1992. There was considerable turnover of faculty members in this decade. Eighteen members left the school for other positions and eleven members retired. Replacing these members were twenty-nine new hires. The composition of the faculty in 1981 was thirty males (61%) and nineteen females (39%). There were eight members of minority groups (16%). By the fall of 1992 the faculty consisted of twenty-seven males (55%) and twenty-two females (45%), with twelve members of minority groups (24%).

Changes in the composition of the faculty reflected the school's objectives, as stated in the school's 1991 reaccreditation self-study report. This report noted:

> The School's objectives with regard to faculty composition flow from overall School goals of providing instruction in broad areas of social work practice and social welfare, of infusing the curriculum with empirically based knowledge, and of generating and disseminating new knowledge to promote the social welfare of the state and the nation. Objectives relative to faculty include:
> 1. To maintain a faculty of sufficient size and breadth to provide education for the range of social work roles identified in the curriculum.
> 2. To fulfill curriculum objectives by assuring that competence in practice methods, fields of service, human behavior and the social environment, and research, is adequately represented among faculty.
> 3. To maintain and increase the representation of ethnic minority and women faculty members.
> 4. To promote the centrality of the School of Social Work within the larger University.

Faculty 1981–82

Forty-nine individuals made up the governing faculty of the school for the 1981–82 academic year: JoAnn Allen, Joyce Beckett, Sydney Bernard, Harvey Bertcher, William Birdsall, Howard Brabson, Sallie Churchill, Loraine Cook,

Tom Croxton, Merle Dinsmore, Milan Dluhy, Nathalie Drews, Kathleen Faller, Sheila Feld, Phillip Fellin, Louis Ferman, Madison Foster, Charles Garvin, Martha Gizynski, Gerald Goff, Edith Gomberg, Jesse Gordon, Ann Hartman, Yeheskel Hasenfeld, David Himle, Alfreda Iglehart, Srinika Jayaratne, Harold Johnson, Dee M. Kilpatrick, Armand Lauffer, William Lawrence, Frank Maple, Elizabeth Mutschler, Lorraine Perry, Thomas Powell, Norma Radin, Beth Reed, Lawrence Root, Jack Rothman, Rosemary Sarri, Brett Seabury, Kristine Siefert, Edwin Thomas, Tony Tripodi, John Tropman, Robert Vinter, Helen Weingarten, Charles Wolfson, and Mayer Zald.

Changes in Faculty Composition
1981–82
New Faculty: Kathleen Faller
Departures: None

KATHLEEN FALLER. Kathleen Coulborn Faller is currently the Marion Elizabeth Blue Professor of Social Work. She is a graduate of Oberlin College and earned M.S.W. and Ph.D. degrees from the University of Michigan. Faller is principal investigator on the Training Program on Recruitment and Retention of Child Welfare Workers, funded by the Department of Health and Human Services, and principal investigator of the Hasbro Early Assessment Project, projects that involve collaboration with the U-M Law School and the U-M Medical School. She is director of the Family Assessment Clinic at the university.

Faller is involved in research, clinical work, teaching, training, and writing in the area of child welfare. Her research involves the use of multidisciplinary assessments with first-time substantiated child protection cases, successful criminal prosecution of sexual abuse, allegations of abuse in cases involving divorce, and descriptive studies of subcategories of sexual abuse cases. She is the author of eight books, as well as over seventy research and clinical articles, and a number of book chapters, encyclopedia entries, and book reviews. She received the Outstanding Service Award from the American Professional Society on the Abuse of Children (U-M SSW *Faculty Research and Publications*, 2007).

1982–83
New Faculty: Barry Checkoway
Departures: Merle Dinsmore (retired), Gerald Goff, Dee M. Kilpatrick, and Loraine Perry

BARRY CHECKOWAY. Barry Checkoway is currently professor of social work and urban planning. Checkoway holds a B.A. degree in government from Wesleyan University and M.A. and Ph.D. degrees in history and urban affairs from the University of Pennsylvania. Before coming to the school, Checkoway was assistant professor of urban and regional planning at the University of Illinois–Urbana. In 1989 he was visiting scholar at the London School of Economics and Political Science and in 1990 he was the Arnulf Pins Professor of Social Work at the Hebrew University of Jerusalem. Checkoway's research interests focus on social change at the community level, with research projects funded by numerous national and international organizations.

Checkoway is founding director of the Edward Ginsberg Center for Community Service and Learning and has directed the Michigan Neighborhood AmeriCorps Program involving graduate students and community-based organizations in Detroit neighborhoods. Checkoway presently directs a number of projects concerned with youth participation in community planning and public policy, with youth empowerment solutions for peaceful communities and youth participation in community philanthropy. Checkoway is widely published in over forty journals. He is the author of books on health care, social planning, and the metropolitan community, as well as a number of professional guides related to youth, evaluation, community change, mental health, and community leadership.

1983–84
New Faculty: Betty Blythe
Departures: Madison Foster and Jack Rothman

BETTY BLYTHE. Betty Blythe joined the faculty as an assistant professor of social work, having been an instructor at the University of Washington School of Social Work. Blythe held a B.A. degree from Seattle University, and M.S.W. and Ph.D. degrees from the University of Washington. Her fields of interest were child welfare, prevention, practice evaluation, and group methods. Her publications include numerous journal articles and a number of books. She left the school in 1987 to join the faculty of the University of Pittsburgh School of Social Work.

1984–85
New Faculty: Oscar Barbarin, Rose Gibson, Catalina Herrerias, Edith Lewis, and Diane Vinokur
Departures: Joyce Beckett, Afreda Iglehart, and Robert Vinter (retired)

OSCAR BARBARIN. The following is excerpted from his retirement memoir (Board of Regents, June 2001).

> Oscar Barbarin III, Ph.D., professor of social work, School of Social Work, and professor of psychology, College of Literature, Science, and the Arts, retired from active faculty status on May 31, 2001.
>
> Professor Barbarin received his A.B. degree from St. Joseph's Seminary College in 1968, his M.A. degree from New York University in 1971, and his M.S. and Ph.D. degrees from Rutgers University in 1973 and 1975 respectively. He joined the University of Michigan faculty in 1979 as assistant professor of psychology. He was named assistant professor of social work in 1984, associate professor in 1985, and professor in 1991. He was appointed adjunct associate professor of psychology in 1986 and professor of psychology in 1992.
>
> Professor Barbarin's research focused on the development of culturally-sensitive assessments of psychological disorders in African-American and Latino children. He worked with the Detroit Department of Human Services' Head Start program to design and implement a program of universal preventive screening of psychological and social risks. In South Africa and Uganda, he pursued projects related to culture and children's mental health, and many of his papers examine the interplay of the social, emotional, and academic development of African-American children.
>
> A productive researcher and scholar, Professor Barbarin collaborated on several books and published numerous articles in professional journals on childhood cancer. The Regents named him professor emeritus of social work and professor emeritus of psychology.

ROSE GIBSON. The following is excerpted from her retirement memoir (Board of Regents, January 1997).

> Rose C. Gibson, professor of social work in the School of Social Work, faculty associate in the Research Center for Group Dynamics, Institute for Social Research, and faculty associate in the Institute of Gerontology, retired from active faculty status on December 31, 1996.
>
> Professor Gibson received her B.A. degree in 1946 from Wayne State University and her M.A. and Ph.D. degrees, in 1968 and 1977, respectively, from the University of Michigan. She joined the Institute of Gerontology as a research investigator in 1979. She was promoted to assistant research scientist in 1982 and associate research scientist in 1984. She joined the faculty of the School of Social Work in 1985 as an associate professor. She was

granted tenure in 1988 and was promoted to professor in 1992. She has been a faculty associate in the Institute for Social Research since 1987.

A nationally and internationally recognized scholar on the subject of race and aging, Professor Gibson is known for her empirical models of race differences in the aging process. She was the first to identify a black–white morbidity crossover in national data and to identify race differences in the meaning and measurement of self-reported health in national surveys. She has published numerous articles and book chapters, as well as several books, including *Different Worlds: Inequality in the Aging Experience*, *Blacks in an Aging Society*, *Health in Black America*, and *Aging and the Life Course*. Her textbooks on inequality in aging are widely used in undergraduate sociology courses.

Professor Gibson is editor-in-chief of *The Gerontologist*, the largest multidisciplinary peer-reviewed research journal on aging. She chaired the Governor's Task Force on New Work and Retirement Arrangements for the Older Worker and was vice chair of the Governor's Task Force on Employment Opportunities for Older Citizens. Her awards include the Wilber J. Cohen Award for outstanding contributions to aging research and the Ida I. Beam Distinguished Professorship. Her groundbreaking work on racial differences in mortality rates, retirement, and health status has brought her international acclaim and has brought distinction to the School of Social Work and the University of Michigan.

The Regents now salute this distinguished faculty member by naming Rose C. Gibson professor emerita of social work.

CATALINA HERRERIAS. Catalina Herrerias came to the school as assistant professor of social work, holding B.A., M.S.W., and Ph.D. degrees. Her teaching interests included ethnic minority populations, families and children, child welfare, women's issues, human sexuality, and self-concept of noncustodial mothers. Herrerias left the school in 1987 for a position at another educational institution.

EDITH LEWIS. Edith Lewis came to the school with B.A. and M.S.W. degrees from the University of Minnesota and a Ph.D. in social welfare from the University of Wisconsin–Madison. Prior to coming to the school, Lewis was lecturer at the School of Social Work at the University of Wisconsin. Lewis is currently associate professor of social work and adjunct professor in the U-M Women's Studies Program. Her research interests include methods used by women of color to offset personal, familial, community, and role strain. Lewis has been involved in the development of the Network

Utilization Project intervention to systematically address individual, family, and community concerns. She teaches in the areas of culturally competent social work methods, group process, family relationships, behavioral theory and interventions, community social system methods, and feminist practice. She has made presentations at numerous professional conferences and has published in a number of professional journals.

Lewis has authored and co-authored over twenty chapters for books and other publications. She is the co-author, with Professor Lorraine Gutierrez, of *Empowering Practice with Women of Color* (1999), and co-editor of *Multicultural Teaching in the University* (1993). She has been honored with a Fulbright Research and Teaching Fellowship, University of Ghana; Woman of the Year in Leadership, U-M Women of Color Task Force; Faculty of the Year Award, School of Social Work students; Outstanding Instructor Award, Michigan Student Assembly; and an Outstanding Teaching Award, Association of Black Student Social Workers. Lewis continues on the faculty.

DIANE KAPLAN VINOKUR. Diane Vinokur, currently associate professor of social work, holds a B.A. degree from Oberlin College, and three degrees from the University of Michigan: M.S.W., M.A. in sociology, and Ph.D. in sociology and social work. She joined the faculty after serving as research coordinator at the National Child Welfare Training Center at the school. She has served as assistant dean for research and development at the school. She has scholarly interests in the application of social psychological and organizational theories to human service organizations and their personnel. She studies the implications of such findings for social work education and training and for nonprofit management. She has been involved in research on interdisciplinary teams and total quality management in medical and psychiatric settings. Vinokur is co-director of the U-M Nonprofit and Public Management Center, a collaboration of the Schools of Social Work and Public Policy. Her publications appear in a variety of social work and social science journals.

1985–86
New Faculty: Ruth Dunkle, Marilyn Flynn, Sharon Keigher, Sherrie Kossoudji, and Paul Wilson
Departures: Loraine Cook (retired), Martha Gizynski (retired), Ann Hartman, Yeheskel Hasenfeld, and William Lawrence (retired)

RUTH DUNKLE. Ruth Dunkle came to the school from Case Western Reserve University, where she held positions in the School of Nursing and the School of Applied Social Sciences. Dunkle completed a "hat trick" at Syracuse University, earning a B.S. degree in human development, an M.S.W., and a Ph.D. in social science. At Michigan Dunkle served as associate dean from 1987 to 1991 and head of the Joint Doctoral Program in Social Work and Social Science from 1996 to 2001. She is currently the Wilbur J. Cohen Collegiate Professor of Social Work and co-directs a National Institute on Aging training program, Social Research Training on Applied Issues of Aging.

Dunkle's areas of research and teaching include service delivery to impaired elders, clinical gerontology, and decision-making in long-term care. She has served as co-director of the Hartford Foundation planning grant, Strengthening Geriatric Social Work. Her research has included a number of funded projects by the University of Michigan, NIA, and NIMH. Dunkle is widely published in professional journals and has co-authored and co-edited seven books on older adults, aging, and health care. Dunkle has been the recipient of a Distinguished Faculty Achievement Award.

MARILYN FLYNN. Marilyn Flynn joined the school's faculty as associate professor, holding an A.B. degree from Roosevelt University and M.S.W. and Ph.D. degrees from the University of Illinois–Urbana. She came to the school following an appointment as associate professor at the School of Social Work, University of Illinois–Urbana. While at Michigan she was the director of the Children and Youth Initiative of Detroit/Wayne County. She left the school in 1991 to take a position as professor in the College of Urban, Labor, and Metropolitan Affairs at Wayne State University. She then moved to Michigan State University, becoming the director of the School of Social Work and professor of social work. Hence, Flynn became dean at the School of Social Work, University of Southern California.

SHARON KEIGHER. Sharon Keigher joined the faculty as assistant professor of social work, holding a Ph.D. from the University of Chicago. Her teaching interests included social development, public policy, management, organizational behavior, health care policy, mental health and aging, and institutional and community-based services. She left the school in 1992 for a position at the School of Social Work, University of Wisconsin–Milwaukee, where she became director of the social work program.

SHERRIE KOSSOUDJI. Sherrie Kossoudji came the school as an assistant professor in social work and assistant professor of economics, having earned a B.A. degree at Miami University and a Ph.D. in economics from the University of Michigan. She is presently an associate professor of social work and an adjunct associate professor in the Department of Economics, and faculty associate, U-M Institute of Labor and Industrial Relations. Her research and teaching interests include immigrant work lives, labor market inequalities, migrant worker opportunities, gender economics, and labor and social welfare policy.

Kossoudji has directed a number of funded research projects and is currently engaged in research on the economics of welfare cutbacks and on undocumented migrants, immigrants, and workers. Her service activities at the university have included membership on the Senate Assembly and on the Committee on the Economic Status of the Faculty. In 1998 she was a Rackham Summer Institute Faculty Fellow.

PAUL WILSON. Paul Wilson joined the faculty as associate professor of social work and associate research scientist, School of Public Health. At the time of his appointment, Wilson held a B.A. from Acadia University, an M.Div. from Union Seminary, and M.S.W. and Ph.D. degrees from Washington University. Prior to coming to Michigan, Wilson was associate professor of social work at the University of Illinois–Urbana. Wilson's research and teaching interests included effective service delivery systems, such as organizational and administrative aspects of service delivery, and relationship between informal social networks and formal service systems. Wilson left the school in 1991 for a position at Boston College School of Social Work.

1986–87
New Faculty: Larry Gant, Robert Ortega, and Mary Van Hook
Departures: Milan Dluhy, Tony Tripodi, Betty Blythe, and Catalina Herrerias

LARRY GANT. Larry Gant holds an A.B. degree from the University of Notre Dame and M.S.W., M.A., and Ph.D. degrees from the University of Michigan. Associate Professor Larry Gant's research focuses on program evaluation of small and moderate-size human service and social action organizations in urban communities; and the creation, implementation, and evaluation of community-based health promotion initiatives in the areas of early childhood development, substance abuse prevention, sexually transmitted diseases, and HIV/AIDS. Gant has also developed and implemented computer labs in urban schools and foster care facilities in Detroit. His research has been supported by numerous state, national, and international organizations. His teaching areas include community organization and social planning; alcohol, tobacco, and other drugs; and AIDS. He is the recipient of the Harold R. Johnson Diversity Service Award.

Gant has written extensively on stress/burnout in human service agencies, AIDS, program evaluation, and multiculturalism and diversity. He has co-edited books on HIV/AIDS. Gant has served as research consultant and program evaluator for numerous health and social welfare organizations in the state of Michigan. Gant continues on the faculty.

ROBERT ORTEGA. Robert Ortega is currently associate professor of social work. He completed the "hat trick plus one" at the University of Michigan, earning a B.A. in psychology, an M.S.W., an M.A. in psychology, and a Ph.D. in social work and psychology. His teaching and research interests are in the areas of human behavior and the social environment, marriage and the family, severe mental illness, juvenile justice and child welfare, ethnic- and gender-sensitive practice, interpersonal practice with families and groups, juvenile justice and child welfare policy and practice, research methods, and treatment intervention design and development. Ortega has presented papers and written on these topics with a special focus on multiculturalism in research and practice. His current research interests focus on Latinos, child welfare, and mental health help-seeking behaviors. Ortega directs a number of research projects that examine the underutilization of mental health and child welfare services by the Latino population. He is co-founder of the Latino Community Outreach Project, which provides research, student training, and evaluations of programs serving Latino communities throughout Michigan. Ortega's writings have appeared in a number of professional books and professional journals. He has been the recipient of a number of awards and honors, including the Faculty Award, U-M Latino/a Task Force; American Association of State Social Work Boards Service Award; U-M Harold R. Johnson Diversity Service Award; and Michigan Outstanding Hispanic Educator of the Year.

MARY VAN HOOK. Mary Van Hook served on the faculty as assistant professor until her departure to the University of Central Florida in 1995, where she became director of the social work program. Van Hook received an A.B. degree from Calvin College, an M.S. degree from Columbia University, and a Ph.D. from Rutgers University. Prior to coming to Michigan, Van Hook served on the faculty at the University of Iowa. Her teaching interests included mental health services for rural populations and interpersonal practice.

1987–88
New Faculty: Sandra Danziger, Kris Kissman, Shirley Lockery, Ira Schwartz, and Zulema Suarez
Departures: None

SANDRA DANZIGER. Sandra Danziger completed a "hat trick" at Boston University, earning A.B., M.S., and Ph.D. degrees in sociology. Before coming to the school, Danziger was affiliated with the Institute for Research on Poverty, University of Wisconsin–Madison. Danziger is currently professor of social work. She has directed the Michigan Program on Poverty and Social Welfare Policy, a joint program of the Schools of Social Work, Public Policy, and Law. Her primary research interests are the impact of public programs on the well-being of families and the causes and consequences of adolescent pregnancy and parenthood. She has been the principal investigator on the Women's Employment Survey and the Implementing Welfare to Work Programs in Michigan study. Danziger has been a visiting research scientist with the U.S. Department of Health and Human Services. She has served as the associate editor of the *Journal of Family Issues*, editor of a special issue of *Children and Youth Services Review*, issue editorial advisor for *The Future of Children*, and reviewer of manuscripts for numerous professional journals. She has been a member of the United States General Accounting Office Welfare Reform Advisory Committee and a member of the NASW Blue Ribbon Panel on Economic Security. She received the Society for Social Work Research Excellence in Research Award in 2006. Her publications have appeared in a wide range of professional journals and books.

KRIS KISSMAN. Kris Kissman came to the school from a teaching position at the University of Arkansas at Little Rock. She received a B.S.W. from Wichita State University, an M.S.W. from the University of Kansas, and a Ph.D. from the University of Texas at Arlington. At Michigan Kissman directed the school's Teen Parent Child Abuse Prevention/Intervention Project. Her teaching areas included women's issues, family systems, and behavioral modification.

SHIRLEY LOCKERY. The following comes from her retirement memoir (Board of Regents, May 2003):

> Shirley A. Lockery, Ph.D., associate professor of social work in the School of Social Work, will retire from active faculty status on May 31, 2003.
> Professor Lockery received her B.A. degree (1971) from California State University–Los Angeles, and M.S.W. (1974), M.P.A. (1974), and Ph.D. (1982) degrees from the University of Southern California–Los Angeles. From 1983–90 she was a faculty member at San Diego State University. She joined the University of Michigan faculty in 1990 as an assistant professor and was promoted to associate professor in 1998.

As a social gerontologist, Professor Lockery has worked extensively on health issues surrounding ethnic and racial minorities. Her primary interests are in ethnogerontology, aging policy and services, and health policy and services. In recognition of her outstanding leadership in the National Institutes on Minority Aging, she received an award of appreciation. She is a fellow of the Gerontological Society of America and is a member of the Academy of Certified Social Workers.

Professor Lockery received numerous training grants and research awards, including a National Institute on Aging minority investigator award with the Health and Retirement Study. She has authored and co-authored numerous refereed journal articles, book chapters, monographs, and book/film reviews. Professor Lockery served on the editorial board of *Gerontology and Geriatrics Education* and as consulting editor of *Health and Social Work*, associate editor of the *American Journal of Health Promotion* (special populations section), and reviewer for *The Gerontologist, Social Work Education Journal* and the *Social Work and Health Care Journal*. She is also the author of "Impact of Dementia Within Minority Groups," a chapter in *Losing a Million Minds: Confronting the Tragedy of Alzheimer's Disease and Other Dementias*, published by U.S. Congress' Office of Technology Assessment.

The Regents now salute this distinguished faculty member by naming Shirley A. Lockery associate professor emerita of social work.

IRA SCHWARTZ. Ira Schwartz came to the school after serving as senior fellow and director of the H.H. Humphrey Institute of Public Affairs at the University of Minnesota. He held a B.S. degree from the University of Washington and an M.S.W. from the University of Minnesota. At Michigan Schwarz was the director of the Center for the Study of Youth Policy. His publications appeared in journals such as *Behavioral Science and the Law; Journal of Law, Ethics, and Public Policy;* and *Journal of Adolescent Health Care*. He authored *(In) Justice for Juveniles: Rethinking the Best Interest of the Child* (1989). His teaching and research interests were juvenile justice and child welfare policy research. He left the faculty in 1994 to take the position of dean of the School of Social Work at the University of Pennsylvania.

ZULEMA SUAREZ. Zulema Suarez joined the faculty after serving on a postdoctoral research training grant under Professor Sheldon Danziger. Suarez held a B.A. degree from the Herbert H. Lehman College, CUNY, an M.S.W. from New York University, and a Ph.D. from the School of Social Service Administration, University of Chicago. Her teaching interests included sociocultural and help-seeking characteristics of low-income minority populations, health, and social service programs and policies. Suarez left the school in 1995 to join the faculty at Wayne State University, hence moving to New York.

1988–89
New Faculty: Sheldon Danziger, Robert Taylor, and Mary Lou Davis-Sacks
Departures: None

SHELDON DANZIGER. Sheldon Danziger holds a B.A. degree in economics from Columbia University and a Ph.D. in economics from Massachusetts Institute of Technology. Prior to coming to Michigan, Danziger was director of the Institute for Research on Poverty and professor of social work at the University of Wisconsin–Madison. At Michigan he has directed the Social Work Research Development Center on Poverty, Risk, and Mental Health. Danziger is the Henry J. Meyer Distinguished University Professor of Public Policy, Gerald R. Ford School of Public Policy, and senior research scientist, Population Studies, Institute for Social Research. He has been director of the Research and Training Program on Poverty, the Underclass, and Public Policy, and he is currently co-director of the National Poverty Center at the Ford School. He has served as visiting scholar at the Russell Sage Foundation, the U.S. Department of Health and Human Services, and the U-M Institute of Public Policy Studies. Danziger's research includes studies of trends in poverty and inequality and the effects of economic and demographic changes and government social programs on disadvantaged groups.

Danziger's publications include over twelve books and over one hundred professional journal articles. He is a Fellow of the American Academy of Arts and Sciences and has been honored with the Flynn Millennium Year Prize for Applying Social Work Concepts to Research on Social Well-Being, University of Southern California; the U-M Rackham Society of Fellows; and the U-M Presidential Initiatives Fund Award. Danziger was named a Guggenheim Fellow in 2008.

ROBERT JOSEPH TAYLOR. Robert Taylor holds a B.A. degree from Northwestern University, as well as an M.S.W., an M.A. in sociology, and a Ph.D. in social work and sociology from the University of Michigan. He is currently associate dean for research at the school and is the Sheila Feld Collegiate Professor of Social Work. He is faculty associate at the Institute for

Social Research and at the Center for Afro-American and African Studies at Michigan. Taylor served as a faculty member at the Graduate School of Social Work at Boston College prior to joining the Michigan faculty.

Taylor conducts extensive research on informal social support networks of adult and elderly Black Americans. He has been principal investigator for grants from the National Institute on Aging, which focus on the role of religion in the lives of Black and White elderly adults. Other research interests include racial identity, marital relationships, and the use of social services among Black Americans. He is currently co-investigator of an NIMH grant on African American Mental Health Research Program. Taylor is co-editor of two books, *Family Life in Black America* (1997) and *Aging in Black America* (1993). His writings have appeared in a large number of professional journals and in chapters of over thirty-five books. Taylor is the recipient of a University of Michigan Distinguished Faculty Achievement Award.

MARY LOU DAVIS-SACKS. Mary Lou Davis-Sacks came to the school having completed a "hat trick" at the University of Michigan, earning a B.G.S., an M.S.W., and a Ph.D. in social work and psychology. Before coming to the faculty, Davis-Sacks served as a research associate at the U-M Survey Research Center. At Michigan her teaching interests included survey research, management, and complex organizations. Davis-Sacks left the school in 1991.

1989–90
New Faculty: None
Departures: Edith Gomberg (retired)

1990–91
New Faculty: Daniel Saunders and David Tucker
Departures: Sydney Bernard (retired), Howard Brabson (retired), Norma Radin (retired), Charles Wolfson (retired), Marilyn Flynn, Mary Lou Davis-Sacks, and Paul Wilson

DANIEL SAUNDERS. Daniel Saunders holds a B.A. from St. John's University, and an M.S.S.W. and Ph.D. in counseling and guidance from the University of Wisconsin–Madison. Prior to coming to the school, Saunders was associate scientist, Department of Psychiatry, University of Wisconsin–Madison. At Madison Saunders was principal investigator for research projects on Preventing Injuries from Marital Violence, funded by the Centers for Disease Control, and the Traumatic Aftermath of Violence Against Wives, funded by the National Institute of Mental Health. At Michigan Saunders is currently associate professor and the co-director of the university's Interdisciplinary Research Program on Violence Across the Lifespan. He is also co-director of a project on Interdisciplinary Training on Violence and Mental Health funded by NIMH. He has been principal investigator for numerous research projects on treatments for men who batter, professional training on domestic violence, and post-traumatic stress in battered women. Saunders' teaching interests include family and group interventions, domestic violence, interpersonal skills, and research methods. Saunders' writings appear in over sixty journals and book chapters.

DAVID TUCKER. David Tucker holds an M.S.W. from McGill University and a Ph.D. in inter-organizational relations and social policy from the University of Toronto. Tucker's scholarly areas of interest include the formation, growth, and death of organizations; the structural analysis of inter-organizational service delivery systems; and the application of macro organizational theory to the analysis of selected social policy issues. At Michigan Tucker has served as head of the school's Joint Doctoral Program in Social Work and Social Science. Prior to coming to Michigan, Tucker served on the faculty at McMaster University, Hamilton, Ontario, Canada.

Professor Tucker is widely published in scholarly journals such as *Human Services in Complex Organizations, Social Service Review, Evolutionary Dynamics of Organizations, Journal of Marriage and the Family,* and *Journal of Sociology and Social Welfare.* He is co-editor, with Professors Charles Garvin and Rosemary Sarri, of *Integrating Knowledge and Practice* (1997). Tucker continues on the faculty.

1991–92
New Faculty: Betty Brown-Chappell, Valire Carr Copeland, and Berit Ingersoll-Dayton
Departures: Jo Ann Allen (retired), Nathalie Drews (retired), and Sharon Keigher

BETTY BROWN-CHAPPELL. Betty Brown-Chappell joined the faculty as assistant professor of social work, holding B.A., M.A., M.S.W., and Ph.D. degrees. Her teaching and research interests included social welfare policy and executive leadership in large urban settings, community organization, and administration and policy methodologies. She left the school in 1996 for a faculty position at Eastern Michigan University.

VALIRE CARR COPELAND. Valire Copeland joined the faculty as an assistant professor, leaving after four years to take a position at the School of Social Work, University of Pittsburgh. Prior to coming to the school, Copeland served as a post-doctoral fellow at the University of Michigan School of Public Health. She held a B.S.W. from Livingstone College and M.S.W. , M.P.H., and Ph.D. degrees from the University of Pittsburgh.

BERIT INGERSOLL-DAYTON. Berit Ingersoll-Dayton holds a B.A. degree from Oberlin College as well as an M.S.W. , M.A., and Ph.D. in social work and psychology from the University of Michigan. Prior to joining the school's faculty, Ingersoll-Dayton was associate professor in the Graduate School of Social Work and the Department of Psychology at Portland State University. Ingersoll-Dayton's interests include the area of social support and clinical research with respect to families in later life. She has focused on positive and negative aspects of support, gender differences, issues of equity and reciprocity, and cross-cultural differences in marital and inter-generational relationships. In relation to clinical research, she has assessed various group interventions with the elderly, intergenerational family therapy approaches, and methods of assisting employed caregivers of the elderly. She is a Fellow of the Gerontological Society of America. Ingersoll-Dayton is currently professor of social work at the school, co-principal investigator of a project funded by the National Institute on Aging, "Social Research Training on Applied Issues of Aging," and project director of a number of research projects on issues of aging. Ingersoll-Dayton's writings have appeared in numerous professional journals and in several chapters of edited books.

1992 (Fall)
New Faculty: Susan McDonough
Departures: None

SUSAN MCDONOUGH. Susan McDonough came to the school as assistant professor of social work after serving as assistant clinical professor at Brown University. She holds a B.S. degree from Northern Illinois University, an M.A. from Northeastern Illinois University, an M.S.W. from Smith College School for Social Work, and a Ph.D. from the University of Illinois at Urbana–Champaign. McDonough currently serves as associate research scientist in the School of Social Work. While at Michigan she has served as research scientist at the U-M Center for Human Growth and Development and has coordinated the school's post-master's Infant Mental Health

Certificate Program. Her teaching at the school has included research seminars on mental health of children, courses on infant and child behavior and development, interpersonal practice with families and with children and youth, human development, and ego psychology. She has taught courses in the post-graduate Infant Mental Health Certificate Program and the Medical School Residency training program. Her scholarly interests include clinical work with families of young children and children's mental health. She has directed NIMH-funded research in these areas.

Professor McDonough's writings have appeared in a wide range of health, psychology, and social work journals, edited works, and technical reports and training manuals. She was co-editor of a special issue of the *Infant Mental Health Journal*. McDonough is a frequent presenter at national and international conferences, and she consults widely in the field of infant and early childhood development. In the year 2000 she was scientific program chair of the 7th International Congress, World Association for Infant Mental Health.

Part-Time and Adjunct Professors

Faculty members who held their major appointments in other units of the university or had part-time faculty or adjunct appointments with the school include the following:

> C. Patrick Babcock, adjunct assistant professor of social work.
> Candyce Berger, associate professor of social work, associate dean of hospital social work services, University Hospital.
> Wilbur Cohen, professor of public welfare administration, dean, U-M School of Education.
> Larry Coppard, adjunct associate professor of social work and adjunct instructor in family practice, U-M School of Medicine.
> Mary Corcoran, professor of social work. Corcoran currently holds appointments in social work, political science, and the Institute of Social Research.
> Douglas D. Davies, adjunct assistant professor of social work.
> Don Duquette, adjunct professor of social work and of law.
> Richard English, professor of social work, associate vice president for academic services, University of Michigan.
> Laura Nitzberg, University Hospital.
> Vivian Shapiro, associate professor of social work, associate professor emerita of social work (1987).
> Bennie Stovall, adjunct assistant professor of social work.

Research and Training Projects

The school's faculty participated in a large number of social work training programs for students and social welfare and education personnel during this decade. Several of these programs were international in scope, especially those sponsored by the Kellogg Foundation. Faculty members gave direction to research projects, many interdisciplinary in nature and often funded by federal and state research funds as well as by foundations. Complete records are not available for all of these projects, but a number are listed as examples of the wide range of topics and the number of faculty engaged in research during this decade.

In 1982 the school established a research office, headed by an assistant dean of research "responsible for fostering faculty research, initiating and facilitating grants, and in general, creating a supportive research environment within the School of Social Work." Professor Diane Vinokur held this office, followed by Professor Siri Jayaratne, and currently directed by Professor Robert Taylor. This office published a report on faculty research in 1988–90 and 1990–92. Introducing these reports from the research office, Dean Harold Johnson noted: "Research is the lifeblood of higher education in general, and graduate professional education in particular. It expands and enhances our knowledge base—it informs and enriches our curriculum—and, it leads to improvements in the quality of professional services. Thus, the School of Social Work at the University of Michigan is extremely proud of the leadership role it has played, and continues to play, in social work research and scholarship" (School of Social Work, 1988). In listing the names of faculty engaged in research and the titles of their projects, the report notes that "several factors have contributed to this noteworthy record": a large, highly qualified, research-oriented faculty; a faculty truly interdisciplinary in composition; and a unique interdisciplinary Ph.D. program in social work and social science. Trends in research expenditures at the school from 1980 to 1991 are noted in the first report, showing a movement from under two million dollars during the period of 1980–88 to five million in 1989, six million in 1990, and over seven million in 1991.

Illustrative research and social work training projects of faculty during the period of 1981–92 include the following:

- *Oscar Barbarin*: Sibling adjustment to childhood cancer; reducing risks of AIDS among African American families with hemophilia; illness, family life, and development of Black children.
- *Barry Checkoway*: Community initiatives to improve health of the

elderly; involving young people in community change; community
initiatives to promote health of older people in Latin America.
- *Sallie Churchill*: Counseling minors without parental consent.
- *Tom Croxton*: Counseling minors without parental consent; social
work standards of practice; the juvenile justice system.
- *Sandra Danziger*: The impact of terminating general assistance; adolescent pregnancy and parenthood; women's employment survey;
implementing welfare to work programs.
- *Sheldon Danziger*: Poverty, the underclass, and public policy; multidisciplinary training on minority poverty and the underclass; racial
and spatial inequalities in employment and housing; welfare effects
on mental health and child development.
- *Ruth Dunkle*: National Institute on Aging training in social research
on applied issues on aging; strengthening geriatric social work.
- *Kathleen Faller*: Teaching and training in child sexual abuse; child
welfare; interpersonal violence.
- *Sheila Feld*: National Institute on Aging training in social research on
applied issues on aging.
- *Phillip Fellin*: NIMH Project on Depression, Awareness, Recognition, and Treatment; counseling minors without parental consent.
- *Larry Gant*: Impact of terminating general assistance; program evaluation of human service organizations; community-based health
initiatives: HIV/AIDS.
- *Charles Garvin*: Group therapy; social work with groups; ameliora-
tion of conflicts among youth groups; interdisciplinary project on
child abuse and neglect; task-centered group work; treatment of du-
ally diagnosed clients; participation of clients in AA groups.
- *Ruth Gibson*: Health, physical functioning, and informal support of
the Black elderly.
- *Martha Gizynski*: Role of the family in psychosocial outcomes of
children with cancer.
- *Edith Gomberg*: Alcoholic women in treatment.
- *David Himle*: Burnout and job satisfaction.
- *Srinika Jayaratne*: Job satisfaction; developing a research-based pre-
ventive intervention curriculum.
- *Harold Johnson*: Public policy issues in an aging society; health care
of the elderly: a cross-cultural perspective.
- *Sharon Keigher*: Homelessness among the elderly.
- *Sherrie Kossoudji*: Impact of terminating general assistance.
- *Armand Lauffer*: Professional training for Jewish communal service;

community self-help in Israel; the future of Jewish leadership: a Delphi study in Israel and the Diaspora.

- *Edith Lewis*: The network utilization project.
- *Frank Maple*: Computers, laser discs, software, and teaching practice.
- *Elizabeth Mutschler*: Information systems for health care providers in ambulatory care; computer-assisted decision support in human service agencies.
- *Robert Ortega*: Self-help and the Latino community; infant mortality in Michigan's child welfare system; mental health help-seeking behaviors.
- *Thomas Powell*: Center for self-help research and knowledge dissemination; evaluation of state service systems; improved mental health services for older adults.
- *Norma Radin*: Primary caregiving fathers; at-risk/disabled infants and toddlers and their families.
- *Beth Reed*: Treatment of drug abusers; services to women with problems of alcohol and other drugs; program evaluations of dual diagnosis, homelessness.
- *Larry Root*: The well-being of the elderly; employment and social welfare services; union management programs.
- *Rosemary Sarri*: Impact on working welfare women and their families of the reduction in AFDC outlays; evaluations: Michigan Human Services Adolescent Shelter, planning for youth services for juvenile offenders in Wayne County; career pattern and status of Michigan children in out-of-home placement; children at risk for out-of-home placement; educational programs for prisoners.
- *Daniel Saunders*: Long-term evaluation of treatments for domestic violence; differential assessment of domestic violence victims; risk factors for severe domestic assault.
- *Ira Schwartz*: (In) justice for juveniles; Center for the Study of Youth Policy; infant mortality in Michigan's child welfare system.
- *Brett Seabury*: Computers, discs, software, teaching practice; time-limited practice; indigenous healing systems; use of the Internet for teaching social work practice skills.
- *Vivian Shapiro*: Role of the family in psychosocial outcomes of children with cancer; prevention research and children's mental health.
- *Kristine Siefert*: Infant mortality in Michigan's child welfare system; role of the family in psychosocial outcomes of children with cancer; prevention research and children's mental health; maternal mortality and race.

- *Robert Taylor*: Research in aging Black populations; social integration among aging Blacks; religious life of Black Americans.
- *Edwin J. Thomas*: Unilateral family therapy for alcohol abuse; marital communication; methodologies of intervention design; intervention research and training.
- *John Tropman*: American values and social welfare; National Institute on Aging training in social research on applied issues on aging; entrepreneurship.
- *David Tucker*: Organizational change.
- *Mary Van Hook*: Promoting integrated services in rural America.
- *Diane Vinokur*: Job satisfaction patterns of social support, Michigan Department of Mental Health project.
- *Robert Vinter*: Juvenile delinquency and youth crime; juvenile justice system.
- *Helen Weingarten*: Later life divorce.
- *Additional Projects*: Additional faculty engaged in research and training projects were William Birdsall, Armand Lauffer, Berit Ingersoll-Dayton, Jack Rothman, and Yeheskel Hasenfeld. Faculty members were involved in number of international programs, such as projects directed by Dean Harold Johnson, assisted by Larry Coppard through the Kellogg International Program on Health and Aging. Several faculty members directed centers involved in research and training: Professors Edwin Thomas, Robert Vinter, Rosemary Sarri, Charles Garvin, Thomas Powell, Ira Schwartz, Oscar Barbarin, Kathleen Faller, Beth Reed, Armand Lauffer, Larry Root, Barry Checkoway, Sheldon Danziger, Ann Hartman, and Dee M. Kilpatrick.

Members of the Faculty in the Fall Term, 1992

Oscar Barbarin, Harvey Bertcher, William Birdsall, Betty Brown-Chappell, Barry Checkoway, Sallie Churchill, Valire Carr Copeland, Tom Croxton, Sandra Danziger, Sheldon Danziger, Ruth Dunkle, Kathleen Faller, Sheila Feld, Phillip Fellin, Louis Ferman, Lawrence Gant, Charles Garvin, Rose Gibson, Jesse Gordon, David Himle, Berit Ingersoll-Dayton, Srinika Jayaratne, Harold Johnson, Kris Kissman, Sherrie Kossoudji, Armand Lauffer, Edith Lewis, Shirley Lockery, Frank Maple, Susan McDonough, Elizabeth Mutschler, Robert Ortega, Thomas Powell, Beth Reed, Lawrence Root, Rosemary Sarri, Daniel Saunders, Ira Schwartz, Brett Seabury, Kristine Siefert, Zulema Suarez, Robert Taylor, Edwin Thomas, John Tropman, David Tucker, Mary Van Hook, Diane Vinokur, Helen Weingarten, and Mayer Zald.

Summary of Faculty Size: 1992

1981–82 (49)	1985–86 (47)	1989–90 (53)
1982–83 (46)	1986–87 (46)	1990–91 (48)
1983–84 (45)	1987–88 (51)	1991–92 (48)
1984–85 (47)	1988–89 (54)	1992 (F) (49)

Faculty Retirements
Faculty members retiring during this period were Professors Jo Ann Allen, Sydney E. Bernard, Howard V. Brabson, Loraine M. Cook, Merle L. Dinsmore, Nathalie A. Drews, Martha Gizynski, Edith Gomberg, William C. Lawrence, Norma L. Radin, Robert D. Vinter, and Charles S. Wolfson.

PART FOUR   The School's Curriculum

Introduction
The basic curriculum structure for the M.S.W. degree offered by the school in 1981 was established in 1977, with two major divisions and several practice specializations within each division. The Interpersonal Practice Division consisted of specializations of casework, group work, and social treatment. The Division of Community Practice/Social Welfare Administration/Social Policy-Planning/Social Program Evaluation included four specializations cited in the division title. Students in both practice divisions took courses in Practice Methods, Practice Skill Instruction, Human Behavior and Social Environment, Social Welfare Policy and Services, Research, and elective courses. Each specialization had a somewhat different pattern of required and elective study in these areas.

The Master of Social Work Degree Requirements
The general curricular policies for the M.S.W. for 1981 were noted in the 1981–83 *School Bulletin* as follows:

> The degree of Master of Social Work (M.S.W.) will be granted to those who fulfill the following requirements:
> 1. A minimum of three terms must be spent in full-time residence, except that a student who transfers one year of credit from an accredited school of social work shall be required to spend two terms in full-time residence.
> 2. The student must achieve a grade average of B, and overall performance must be satisfactory in coursework and in practice skill instruction.

3. Work for the degree must be completed within six years of the student's first enrollment in the School.

4. Credit and course requirements. A student is required to complete 56 hours of credit for the Master of Social Work degree, unless advanced standing has been granted, in which case credits may be reduced in some instances to 42 hours. The distribution of required courses varies according to program of specialization.

The 1981 Curriculum Model
Interpersonal Practice Division

This division was based on a definition of interpersonal practice methods as those aimed at the restoration, maintenance, and enhancement of social functioning. It included change objectives relating to the individual, family, or small group, their immediate social environment, and the transactional relationship between person(s) and environment. In the first year, students in this division took courses grounded in this definition of interpersonal practice. In the second year, students chose from a variety of options for a concentration. Concentrations were interpersonal practice with children and youth, families, and groups; in child welfare; in community mental health; in criminal justice; in health settings; in schools; from a behavioral framework; and from a clinical casework framework with adults. Each second-year concentration was defined as a package of required and recommended courses in interpersonal methods, human behavior and social environment, social welfare policy and services, research, and practice skill instruction (*School Bulletin*, 1981–83). Students in this division typically took four courses in practice skill instruction, one each term, spending the equivalent of two days a week in an assigned agency.

Community, Administration, Policy, Evaluation Practice Division

The practice methods in this division were aimed at improving social welfare by work with communities, social welfare organizations, or policymakers. Four programs of specialization were included in this division: community organization, social welfare administration, social policy and planning, social program evaluation.

Community organization was defined as that method of social work practice oriented to change at the community level—that is, to the development of cohesion among community groups and members to neighborhood work, intergroup work, social action, and community planning.

Social welfare administration was defined as a method of social work practice concerned with the management and direction of organizational behavior. This practice involves management of environmental relations, program planning and development, fiscal management, personnel management and staff development, information systems, program assessment and evaluation, and organizational development.

Social policy and planning was defined as method of social work practice concerned with the analysis, development, and implementation of social policy into operational plans for achieving social goals.

Social program evaluation was defined as a method of social work practice concerned with the use of scientific methodologies for the assessment of the performance of human service organizations, policies, and programs. It involves assessment design, specification of program goals and means, data collection and processing, quantitative and qualitative data analysis, report writing, and results interpretation.

Each of these specializations contained a common core of courses in the first term, with students in social policy and planning and in social program evaluation taking a common core in the second term as well. After taking the core courses, students were able to elect a number of optional methods and elective courses, including the option of taking a "minor" set of courses in a related area. In community organization, students typically took a two-day-per-week field placement for four terms. In social welfare administration and social policy and planning, students took a Practice Skill Instruction Lab and a two-day-per-week placement in the second term, followed by a third term block, five-day-per-week placement. Social program evaluation students followed a variety of plans, including one- and two-day-per-week placements in the first year as well as block placements in the third term of study. Accompanying these practice oriented courses and field instruction were requirements for courses in human behavior and social environment, social welfare policy and services, research, and elective courses.

Minority Relevant Course Requirement /Gender Content
The school's planning in this area was built on an effort of the faculty that began giving special attention to minority content in the curriculum in 1972. The Curriculum Committee reviewed courses in terms of integration of minority group content, revision of course objectives, and bibliography; and it supported the development of library, audio-visual, and bibliographic resources pertinent to minority content. The systematic use of student course evaluations regarding course content permitted the faculty to monitor minority content in the courses offered.

Beginning in the fall term of 1979, the faculty established a minority relevant course requirement for all students. To qualify as meeting this requirement, at least fifty percent or more of planned course matters (class sessions, readings, student assignments, etc.) must focus on one or both of the following dimensions of minority relevant content: (1) specified, identifiable target groups with special socio-cultural heritage and experience—Black, Hispanic, Asian American, and Native American; (2) social processes that are critical to practice with minority populations. These processes concern various forms of discrimination and oppression that occur across the four target populations, as well as involving many other groups.

In 1981 the school's faculty reaffirmed its commitment to continue to initiate, support, and develop mechanisms and procedures designed to integrate minority content into all elements of the curriculum. In this year the faculty also instructed the Curriculum Committee of the school to develop a plan for curriculum review and revision that recognized the importance of integrating appropriate content concerning gender into the curriculum.

The 1983–92 Curriculum Model

The faculty re-conceptualized the curriculum for the 1983 academic year by changing the terminology in some instances, by reorganizing specializations to include both practice and a field of service, and by changing course credit hours from 2 hours to 3 hours. Students in these specializations continued to take relevant required courses in the areas of human behavior and the social environment and research, as well as elective courses.

Under the new curriculum plan, students chose major and minor specializations in methods of practice and a substantive field of service specialization. The practice methods divisions were specified as interpersonal practice (with individuals, families, and groups), macro practice (community organization, social policy and planning, and administration), and research/evaluation. These constituted a practice major. Students in interpersonal practice also chose a minor specialization in a macro practice area. Similarly, those majoring in a macro practice area or in research/evaluation chose a minor from one of the other two areas. Students took three courses in their major methods area and two in the minor. One research course appropriate to the major methods area was required.

Students were able to select a field of service specialization from five alternatives: families, children and primary groups; human resources and economic support; criminal and civil justice; physical and mental health; basic and continuing education. The field of service specialization involved

(1) enrollment in two courses in a chosen field of service, (2) completion of a professional practicum related to the field of service, and (3) enrollment in an integrative seminar that focused on the use of practice skills in the chosen field of service. The seminar provided an opportunity for students and faculty to discuss the application of different practice methods to that field of service.

A variety of field instruction alternatives were available to students, depending in part on their methods specialization. In most cases, students began their first practicum in their second term on a two-day-per-week basis and continued at the same agency four days per week during their third term. In their fourth term, students returned to two days per week in the field. Students received 14 credit hours for a total of 960 hours spent in professional practicum.

The distribution of the 56 credit hours required for the M.S.W. degree was as follows:

Major practice method	3 courses	9 credits
Minor practice method	2 courses	6 credits
Field of practice	2 courses	6 credits
Professional practicum	3 terms	14 credits
Human behavior and the social environment	3 courses	9 credits
Research	1 course	3 credits
Integrative seminar	1 course	3 credits
Electives	2 courses	6 credits

The curriculum described above continued, with minor modifications, through 1992. Changes included elimination of the integrative seminar (3 credits), increase in electives to 7 credit hours, and increase in professional practicum credit hours to 16, with the total hours required for the M.S.W. remaining at 56. Curriculum changes in 1991 included a reconceptualization of the first and second years of study, the professional foundation and advanced practice specializations. Professional foundation content was provided for all students in their first year of study. Most of the foundation content was provided in the first term. The requirement that all students complete a foundation methods course in interpersonal practice and one in macro practice assured that all students would have a "generalist" practice perspective, as defined by CSWE's curriculum policy statement.

A new required foundation course, Theories of Individual, Family, and Social Environment, was created in the human behavior and social environment area, with a "person in environment" focus that assured knowledge in the human biological, social, psychological, and cultural systems. A new foundation course was introduced for the area of social welfare policy and services in order to separate foundation content from advanced content. In the second term, students took some advanced content courses and began a methods specialization that carried over into the second year of study as an advanced practice specialization. A specialization in a field of service was also required.

In the research area, the required course was expanded to 4 credit hours, with a course offered for students specializing in interpersonal practice and a different one for students specializing in macro practice. A new curricular arrangement was introduced for interpersonal practice students, who were required to complete 6 hours of advanced practice credit, with these courses including 2 hours of human behavior and social environment content. Choices for advanced practice methods courses were Interpersonal Practice with Individuals, Cognitive/Behavioral Practice, Interpersonal Practice with Families, and Interpersonal Practice with Groups.

Grades

The grading system for the year 1981 and thereafter is stated in *School Bulletins* as follows:

> Letter grades from A through E are given for class and practice skill instruction. A grades are given for exceptional individual performance, B grades are given to students who do all the required work for the course satisfactorily, B+ and B- reflect slight variations from this satisfactory level. C grades are given when performance definitely falls below requirements for graduate work. D grades indicate unconditional failure, and E is given when a course is dropped after the end of the third week of a term or the second week of a half term. Credits toward degree requirements are not earned for courses in which D or E grades are obtained. I for Incomplete is used when illness or other compelling reasons prevent completion of work and there is a definite plan in regard to when work will be completed.
>
> Students may elect a grading system of Satisfactory, Marginal, or Unsatisfactory for practice skill instruction. These grades carry no honor points and cannot be averaged with grades for academic courses. Any students who receive Marginal or Unsatisfactory grades in conjunction with

a grade point average of B or lower will be referred to the Faculty Council for review of their academic status. This grading system for practice skill instruction is defined as follows:

Satisfactory means that the quality of performance for practice skill instruction is acceptable and credit is granted for the course. Students who perform at a level which would bring a letter grade of B or above are given a Satisfactory grade.

Marginal means that performance in practice skill instruction is less than satisfactory but short of failing. Students who perform at a level of B- to C- letter grade are given a grade of Marginal.

Unsatisfactory means that the quality of performance is inadequate and no credit is granted. Any student performing below a C- level letter grade in practice skill instruction is given an unsatisfactory grade.

Academic Difficulty

At the end of each term, a subcommittee of the Faculty Council reviewed the records of students in academic difficulty. The *School Bulletin* (1981–83) noted: "Such students include those who (1) are not achieving at a level required for the master's degree—a grade average of B and overall performance that is satisfactory in coursework and practice skill instruction, (2) have more than four hours of Incomplete grades in any one term, (3) have been dropped from practice skill instruction because they have been unable to meet minimum standards to practice skill instruction in conjunction with a grade-point average of B or lower."

The subcommittee of the council could recommend a variety of actions, including, but not limited to, the following: reduced credit hour enrollment, enrollment in remedial coursework, discontinuance of enrollment for the forthcoming term until Incomplete grades are removed, demonstration of competency in a given area prior to future enrollment in particular courses or practice skill instruction, and withdrawal of admission to the school (*School Bulletin*, 1981–83).

Bulletins for 1983–85, 1986–87, and 1988–90 do not include information on grading or definitions of grades. These topics are included in the 1991–93 *School Bulletin*. The definitions of grades are the same as those introduced in 1981. However, the grading system for practice skill instruction was established for all students as consisting of "S" (satisfactory), "M" (marginal), and "U" (unsatisfactory).

School Bulletins for 1986–87, 1988–90, and 1991–93 include sections on academic standing and discipline. The 1991–93 *School Bulletin* states:

To maintain good academic standing, a student must a) have a cumulative graduate grade point average of "B" or better for all graduate courses taken for credit and applied toward the social work degree; b) maintain a passing grade in the Professional Practicum, with no grades of "U" (unsatisfactory) or "E" or no grades of marginal for 1 or more credit hours; and c) not accumulate nine (9) or more credit hours of Incomplete grades.

A student who fails to maintain good academic standing will be placed on academic probation for the following term. The student, in consultation with the faculty advisor, will be required to devise a plan to remove the probationary status, and it is forwarded to the Associate Dean for approval. If approved, the plan will be placed in the student's record. Otherwise, the student's situation is subject to review by the Committee on Academic Difficulty.

Enrollment Options
Year-Round Operation
Full-time enrollment was permitted twice each year under two plans, fall-term plan and winter-term plan. A full spring-summer term of courses was available to students.

Fall-Term Plans
Students had two choices for following this plan: (1) The first program covered a time period of two academic years and applied only to students who were admitted to begin study in interpersonal practice or community organization in the fall term. Students enrolled in the fall term, completed the following winter term, took a spring-summer recess, and then completed a fall and winter term. (2) The second program applied to students admitted for a program of study in social welfare administration, social policy and planning, or social program evaluation. Students enrolled the fall, winter, spring-summer, and fall terms, completing study in December, having taken sixteen continuous months to complete degree requirements.

Winter-Term Plan
This program applied to all students who began any program of study in the winter term. Students completed the winter, spring-summer, fall, and winter terms, completing degree requirements within a time period of sixteen continuous months.

The time periods for study for all other students were referred to as the 16-months curriculum schedule and the 20-months curriculum schedule. Beginning in 1986–87, admission to the M.S.W. program was limited to the fall term, except for students who were admitted under "advanced standing" or with transfer or extension credits equivalent to one term. These students were admitted in the winter term and completed the degree in a time period of three terms. This admission policy continued through the 1991–92 period.

Part-Time and Off-Campus Programs
Extended Degree Program
The 1983–85 *School Bulletin* announced an Extended Degree Program that enables students to complete the M.S.W. degree requirements through a combination of part-time and full-time enrollment, taking courses both on- and off-campus. Classes at off-campus sites were taught by regular School of Social Work faculty and scheduled to facilitate participation of those who were employed. Students admitted to this program had to meet the admission criteria for all students admitted to the M.S.W. program. Extended degree students were permitted to earn up to 28 credit hours in approved part-time course work prior to assuming full-time, on-campus status. Students in this program were required to complete two terms in residence on-campus.

Post-M.S.W. Management Certificate Program
A Certificate in Management was made available to experienced social workers who had an M.S.W. degree. These individuals could take courses with content on organization analysis, program design, implementation, management, funding and fiscal management, personnel management and development, management information systems, program evaluation, and executive leadership. To earn the certificate, the individual completed 9 hours of credit at the graduate level.

Part-Time Non-Degree Program
Students not enrolled in a school degree or certificate program were able to take off-campus courses in social work. Part-time non-degree students could receive graduate credits or continuing education units through the U-M Extension Service. Up to 14 hours of credit in this program could be applied toward the M.S.W. degree.

Dual Degree Programs
By 1988 the school had established requirements for dual degrees through the School of Business Administration (MSW/MBA) and School of Public Health (MSW/MPH). By 1991 the school also provided for a dual degree through the School of Architecture and Urban Planning (MSW/MUP).

School Social Work
The school's curriculum provided for completion of courses necessary for approval as a school social worker in the State of Michigan (*School Bulletin,* 1981–83).

Certificates
The school participated with the university's Institute of Labor and Industrial Relations and with the Institute of Gerontology in permitting students to choose a core group of electives that led to certificates of specialization in those areas, the Specialist of Aging Certificate and Certificate in Industrial Relations.

Continuing Education
An annual spring/summer symposium was offered by the school for practitioners interested in learning about new developments and skills in social work practice and social welfare. The Continuing Education Program provided technical assistance to public and voluntary agencies in the form of workshops, training, and information sharing.

Extension Program
The school offered a number of courses in communities outside Ann Arbor through the Extension Division of the university. Students accepted to the M.S.W. program could apply a total of 14 hours credit toward the degree.

PART FIVE   Summary of the Johnson Years

Dean's Annual Reports
By way of review, excerpts from Dean Harold Johnson to the university president for the period of 1981–87 are quoted here. The dean's annual reports were discontinued after 1987. Excerpts from *Ongoing*, the alumni newsletter, are included for the period 1988–92. The text of the full annual reports and *Ongoing* cited here are available in the Social Work Collections at the Bentley Historical Library.

1981–82

> **The Instructional Program.** The revision of the School's curriculum was the major objective in 1981–82. It was prompted by a growing awareness that, across the nation, schools of social work are being pressed to prepare

professional social workers who are better able to design, organize, and deliver high quality services with diminished resources.

The MSW curriculum was completely revised to provide students with multiple practice skills, expertise in a field of service, and the capacity to assess and evaluate professional practice.

A major emphasis has been placed on enhancing the relationship between faculty, students, and cooperating public and private agencies. Fewer agencies are being selected for placement of students, with preference given to innovative agencies which have demonstrated their interest in education and research.

With social service agencies beginning to upgrade their management information systems, increasing educational emphasis is being placed on computer literacy for social work students.

Among other significant changes in the curriculum was the shift to a "constant run" model, allowing students to complete the two year program in 16 months, and moving to a three credit hour format for all courses.

Extended Degree Program. In 1981–82 the School approved an Extended Degree Program, allowing students to earn a Master's in Social Work through a combination of on and off-campus coursework.

Research Development. Top priority in the School of Social Work has been given to faculty research initiatives.

Research development is viewed as an opportunity to inform the curriculum, that is, to keep it current and strengthen our instructional knowledge base.

A plan was developed to organize an Office of Research Services to assist faculty in the conceptualization, implementation, and evaluation of research and evaluation projects.

Office of Agency and Community Relations. A plan was established to organize an Office of Agency and Community Relations to strengthen the relationship between the School and the social service agencies and other organizations at which students are placed for their professional practicum.

Governance of the School. Considerable effort in 1981–82 was spent planning the reorganization of the School to increase faculty participation in the governance process . . . to the review and revision of policies and procedures to permit the organization of an Executive Committee to work with the Dean on educational and fiscal matters.

Introduction. The 1982–83 academic year saw the completion of two full years under the leadership of Dean Harold Johnson. In that time, the School has undergone a number of changes achieving more effective programs with fewer resources. Central among these has been the revision of the curriculum at the MSW level, and the increased emphasis on the development of external resources for both research and program enrichment. Faculty and staff have extended themselves in each of these areas, increasing productivity in both quantitative terms.

While it has meant great hardship, budget reductions have forced the School into a period of reexamination and renewal. More efficient use of resources has prompted the reorganization of the School's structure, educational programs, and supportive services.

Reaccreditation and Self-Study. In tandem with its own self-study, the School faces in the upcoming year its 10-year reaccreditation review by the Council on Social Work Education. The School has used the opportunity to assess every aspect of life at the School.

Office of Alumni Relations and Development. This past year, the School moved aggressively into the development arena, seeking gifts from graduates and friends to offset declines in the budget. The Office of Alumni Relations and Development, under the direction of *Dr. Kathy Okun*, has been engaged in communicating with alumni and friends of the Schools. Primary among these communications has been the improvement of ONGOING, the School of Social Work newsletter, which is now published quarterly.

Doctoral Program in Social Work and Social Science. Since its review by the graduate school during the 1981–82 academic year, the Doctoral Program, under the leadership of Professor *Sheila Feld*, has striven to achieve the recommendations outlined in the review committee's report. Primary among these have been the extension of the Program's interdisciplinary research focus, the involvement of supervising faculty in the development of Program policy development and implementation, and assurances that incoming students are cognizant of and adhere to the Program's commitment to research.

Facilities. Space concerns continue to plague the School. Faculty are spread across campus, including three central campus buildings, which confounds their ability to interact easily. The library system, with its outstanding collection, remains cramped in a facility half again too small.

1983–84

Faculty. The many accomplishments of our faculty continue to be reflected in their research, publications, and professional leadership and service. The contribution of one of our outstanding faculty members, Professor *Rosemary Sarri*, was recognized by the University which presented her with a Distinguished Achievement Award, noting her outstanding contributions to social work and social welfare.

Furthermore, many of the faculty have recently enriched their own professional expertise through collaboration with professional colleagues abroad. Faculty have received Fulbright awards or spent sabbaticals studying in Australia, Norway, England, Israel, and Japan, and the Dean is a key investigator of international gerontology projects in Asia and provides continuing leadership to a Kellogg grant for cross-cultural study of health care of the elderly in Europe and North America.

The Joint Doctoral Program in Social Work and Social Science. The Joint Doctoral Program initiated post-doctoral training this year, with the successful competitive award of an NIMH training grant on Intervention Research Training, prepared by Professor *Edwin J. Thomas*.

To further this direction, a large pre and post doctoral training program proposal was prepared this year for submission to the National Institute on Aging entitled "Social Research Training on Applied Issues of Aging" (subsequently awarded).

Task forces in each disciplinary area have been meeting in response to the recent Rackham review of the program in order to continue to improve the curriculum and relationships with the participating social science departments.

Alumni Relations and Development. The First Annual Meeting of the Alumni Society was held in September, 1983, representing the first time that alumni returned to the School from across the country. They participated in a 2-day session of workshops and social activities. The evening banquet's keynote speaker was Dr. Agnes M. Mansour, the Michigan Director of Social Services.

Facilities. Recognizing the burgeoning importance of computers in our society as well as in professional work, the School has established a social work computer facility in the Frieze building.

1984–85

Introduction. The 1984–85 academic year continued to reflect the progress of the School of Social Work in advancing professional education, research, and services in social welfare, giving it national recognition as one of the foremost leaders in the field. Among the significant accomplishments of the School were: a major increase in training funds, including a $1.24 million pre and post doctoral instructional grant in aging, dramatic increases in the number and amount of alumni donations, the addition of several promising faculty members, and continued innovation in the educational programs of the School, both at the master's and doctoral levels. Under the leadership of *Dean Harold Johnson*, the School is developing a firm foundation to enhance its continued leadership and excellence.

Research. [The academic year] 1984–85 saw the continued growth of faculty involvement in developing research and training programs in the School, generating $156,493 in research funds and $1,953,889 in training funds.

Poverty Conference. The School received funding to organize the World Feminization of Poverty Conference.

Curriculum. In 1984–85 the School continued to strengthen its curriculum by creating an ongoing evaluation system for curriculum review and renewal.

Alumni Relations. The School established two new awards, with the Distinguished Alumni Award given to Nancy Amidei and the Community Service Award to Stanley J. Winkelman.

1985–87

Major Challenges Facing the School:
- How do we "retool" our academic and professional programs and curriculum to articulate with the current and developing needs of the rapidly-changing society and profession?

- How do we recruit and maintain a diversified faculty that can be responsive to these needs?
- How do we recruit and maintain a diversified student body that can be responsive to these needs?
- How do we encourage and support research that will inform practice today and tomorrow, based upon scientific theory and empirically-based inquiry?
- How can the School benefit from the interdisciplinary and interprofessional expertise on campus to strengthen its own programs?
- How can the above questions be best answered given the limited financial resources available to support the School's programs?

Excerpts from Ongoing: 1988–91
1988

From the Dean. I am pleased to report to you that the School of Social Work is in the forefront of the struggle to improve race relations at this University. Approximately one year ago . . . I appointed a Task Force on Race and Gender to examine every facet of the School's programs to identify problems related to race and gender. The Task Force recently released a preliminary report including a number of recommendations focused on personnel, curriculum, and student recruitment and retention.

From the Dean. Dear Alumni and Friends, In the process of going to press with this issue, an exciting development has taken place at our School. The Regents of the University of Michigan have authorized the School of Social Work to proceed with the planning of a new building to be situated on the southwest corner of South University and East University streets. I know you join me in the rush of enthusiasm and sheer delight that accompanies this important announcement.

1989

From the Dean. A presentation about the new building for the School of Social Work was made at the annual meeting of the Alumni Society, including:
- The Dean's Vision: Dean Harold Johnson
- The Architect's Vision: Howard Sims, President, Sims-Varner, Inc.
- An Alumnus' Vision: Edward S. Egnatios, Chair, Building Committee

1991

From the Dean. I want to take this opportunity to reflect on one of the most enjoyable aspects of my tenure as dean: the organization of the School of Social Work Alumni Society. The Society was launched in 1982. The primary reason the Society was formed was to provide a vehicle for the School to secure the advice of its graduates. This advice and support is absolutely essential for the School to remain one of the leading schools of social work in the world.

October 4, 1991 represents a milestone in the growth and development of the School of Social Work at the University of Michigan. This day marks the first meeting of the School's newly appointed Visiting Committee. The Committee, made up of five of our graduates, one cognate faculty member, and two members at large, included: George Downs (Princeton University), Eileen Gambrill (University of California/Berkeley), Lawrence Gary (Howard University), John Longres (University of Wisconsin/Madison), Jeanne Marsh (University of Chicago), Elizabeth Douvan (University of Michigan), Hon. Avern Cohn, U.S. District Judge, Hon. John Conyers, Jr., U.S. Representative, 1st District, Michigan.

Summary: 1987–92

Brief summary statements regarding the period of 1987–92 appear below, drawn from various sections of the *Ongoing* newsletter.

The School's Faculty

The school continued to make special efforts to recruit minority and female faculty members so that by the fall of 1992 the faculty consisted of forty-nine members, the same number as in 1981. The school continued to make special efforts to recruit minority and female faculty members so that by 1992 there were fifty-five percent male, forty-five percent female members, and twenty-four percent members of minority groups, compared with thirty-nine percent female and sixteen percent minority members in 1981. An increasing number of part-time and adjunct professors participated in teaching at the school and in carrying out liaison functions.

Faculty members retiring and gaining emeritus status during the period 1981–92 were Merle Dinsmore, Robert Vinter, Loraine Cook, Martha Gizynski, William Lawrence, Edith Gomberg, JoAnn Allen, and Nathalie Drews.

Curriculum

Curriculum changes in 1991 included a reconceptualization of the first and second years of study, the professional foundation and advanced practice specializations. All courses in the curriculum included objectives and content related to gender and women's issues and ethnic minorities. The school continued operating under a year-round arrangement, with full-time enrollment permitted under fall-term and winter-term plans. The course requirement for the M.S.W. degree remained at 56 hours credit. A number of part-time and off campus programs continued to be offered.

Research and Training Programs

A dramatic increase in funding for research and training occurred from 1988 onwards, with expenditures in research moving from approximately 1 million dollars to over 7 million dollars. A number of international programs, especially in the areas of aging and mental health, were conducted through the school.

Facilities

Under the leadership of Dean Johnson and a faculty committee, in 1988 the school developed a *Prospectus for a New Building for the School of Social Work*.

Student Enrollment

The number of full time M.S.W. students ranged from 489 in 1980 to 481 in 1990. The percent of minority students in the school ranged from seventeen percent in 1980 to sixteen percent in 1990. Full-time enrollment by gender was seventy-three percent female, twenty-seven percent male in 1980; eighty-one percent female, nineteen percent male in 1990.

Tuition

Tuition for one term increased from $1,266 for Michigan residents, $2,746 for non-residents in 1981–82 to $3,037 for Michigan residents, $6,352 for non-residents in 1991–92.

Reaccreditation

The school prepared self-study reports for site visit teams from the Council on Social Work Education in 1983 and 1991, leading to reaccreditation of the school by the Commission on Accreditation of CSWE.

CHAPTER FIVE

The Allen-Meares Years

This chapter describes characteristics of the School of Social Work during the deanship of Paula Allen-Meares. The chapter includes five parts: The School of Social Work, 1993–2008; The School's Students; The School's Faculty; The School's Curriculum; and Summary.

PART ONE   The School of Social Work: 1993–2008

Profile of the Dean of the School

Paula Allen-Meares was appointed dean of the school at the beginning of the winter term, 1993. In a letter to the faculty in November 2007, the dean wrote, "It is with bittersweet feelings that I write to you today to announce that I will step down from the deanship of the School of Social Work at the end of this academic year. I am concluding my third term as dean, and it is time for me to refresh and renew." She concluded her letter by noting, "As I prepare to step down from the deanship and become a member of its esteemed faculty, I am confident that Michigan's School of Social Work is strong, productive, and well-prepared for the future."

Dean Allen-Meares was Norma Radin Collegiate Professor of Social Work and professor of education. Her research interests include the tasks and functions of social workers employed in educational settings; psychopathology in children, adolescents, and families; adolescent sexuality; premature parenthood; and various aspects of social work practice. She was principal investigator of the school's Global Program on Youth and a co-investigator on an NIMH research grant. She remains principal investigator of a Skillman Foundation Good Neighborhoods grant.

Dean Allen-Meares has served on a number of editorial boards and has served as editor-in-chief of many important journals. Additionally, she has been a member of many national professional and scientific committees promoting the intellectual and empirical advancement of the profession. She has served as a member of the Advancement of Social Work Research, treasurer of the Council on Social Work Education, chair of the Publication Committee of NASW, and vice president of the National Association of Deans and Directors of Social Work. She serves as a member of the Board of Trustees of the William T. Grant Foundation and has served as president of the Society for Social Work and Research and as a University of Michigan Senior Fellow. She is presently chair of the New York Academy of Medicine's national advisory panel and a member of the Institute of Medicine of the National Academies. Dean Allen-Meares has served on a number of committees at the University of Michigan that promote interdisciplinary research and instruction, fundraising, and diversity, including serving as past chair of the University of Michigan's Health Sciences Council (U-M Faculty Research and Publications, 2007). Dean Allen-Meares is the recipient of the 2008 Harold R. Johnson Diversity Award.

On June 12, 2008, Dean Allen-Meares sent a message to the faculty noting:

> It has been a deep pleasure to work with each and every one of you during my 15 years of service as Dean and faculty at the UM-SSW. As I reflect upon what we have accomplished together, I am sincerely moved and very proud. I just wanted to let you know that I have accepted a position as Chancellor of the University of Illinois Chicago campus effective January 2009. With warmest regards and best wishes to you and the new dean, Paula.

Interim Dean

John E. Tropman was appointed by the Board of Regents to serve as interim dean of the school for the period of September 1 through December 31, 2008. Tropman is professor of social work, as well as a visiting and adjunct professor in management organizations in the Ross School of Business, faculty associate in the Program in American Culture and the Michigan Journalism Fellows Program, and assistant to the dean for external relations in the School of Social Work. On September 1, 2008, he also began his tenure as associate dean for faculty affairs. Teresa A. Sullivan, provost and executive vice president for academic affairs, noted: "Professor Tropman has given distinguished service in numerous administrative roles during his career at Michigan. He was head of the doctoral program in social work and social science, acting director of the Institute of Gerontology, chair of the Michigan Society of Fellows, a member of the Institute of Labor and

Industrial Relations Executive Committee, a member of the UM Grievance Board, among other positions." A complete profile for Tropman appears in the chapter of this volume entitled "The Fauri Years."

New Dean

Professor Laura Lein was appointed dean of the School of Social Work, beginning January 1, 2009. Dean Lein received a B.A. degree in sociology/anthropology from Swarthmore College and M.A. and Ph.D. degrees in social anthropology from Harvard University. Lein came to Michigan from the University of Texas at Austin, where she served on the faculty since 1985. As principal investigator and research scientist at the School of Social Work at Texas, Lein developed research programs on women, work, poverty, and family. Her publications include nine books and edited volumes, as well as over fifty articles and book chapters. In making this appointment, Teresa Sullivan, provost and executive vice president of the University of Michigan, noted: "President Coleman and I are extremely pleased that Professor Laura Lein is assuming the leadership of the School of Social Work. She is recognized as a dedicated teacher, mentor and scholar whose commitment to social justice and the use of evidence-based research to shape social policy is genuine. We are confident of her ability to articulate a vision for the School of Social Work that will position it as a truly interdisciplinary leader among our other schools and colleges and a national leader in the ongoing debates over social work practice and education" (U-M memo, Teresa Sullivan, August 4, 2008).

Past Deans and Directors (1921–2009)

> Arthur E. Wood, 1921–35, director of Curriculum in Social Work
> Robert W. Kelso, 1935–50, director of Institute of Health and Social Sciences, Institute of Public and Social Administration
> Arthur Dunham, 1950–51, acting director of Institute of Public and Social Administration
> Fedele F. Fauri, 1951–70, dean of the School of Social Work
> Robert Vinter, 1970–71, acting dean of the School of Social Work
> Phillip Fellin, 1971–81, dean of the School of Social Work
> Harold R. Johnson, 1981–93, dean of the School of Social Work
> Paula Allen-Meares, 1993–2008, dean of the School of Social Work
> John E. Tropman, 2008, interim dean of the School of Social Work
> Laura Lein, 2009–present, dean of the School of Social Work

Associate and Assistant Deans: 1983–2008
The associate dean for educational programs has overall responsibility for educational programs and provides guidance and direction in all matters related to students. Richard Tolman served in this position from September 2002 through August 2006. Professor Mary Ruffolo was appointed to this position for the period September 2006 to December 2009.

The associate dean for faculty and academic affairs has overall responsibility for a broad range of activities related to faculty and administrative functions both within the school and the broader university community. Professor Srinika Jayaratne served in this position from September 1990 to January 2003, followed by Kristine Siefert for a one-year period, hence followed by Jayaratne from January 2004 to August 2008 and by John Tropman from September 2008 to December 2009.

The associate dean for research works with the faculty and others in developing research proposals and training grants. In addition, the associate dean coordinates the submission of research proposals, acts as the school's liaison with the university's Division of Research Development and Administration, and performs such other functions as may be assigned by the dean. Professor Robert Taylor currently serves in this position, having been appointed in September 2003. Prior to this time, the position was held by Kris Siefert, Carol Mowbray, Ken Lutterman, and Leonard Eron.

The assistant dean for student services acts on student applications for admission and financial aid. The assistant dean has primary responsibility for student recruitment, the development of financial aid resources, information and referral programs, and employment services. Tim Colenback, appointed in 2000, currently serves in this position. He succeeded Clarita Mays, who served from July 1992 to 1999. In 2007 this office expanded to career services for M.S.W. students, particularly in regard to the job search process and the job market. Michelle Woods is the director of this program.

The assistant dean for hospital social work services is the liaison between the school and university hospitals. Kathleen Wade has served in this position since October 2001, preceded by Candyce Berger.

The Joint Doctoral Program in Social Work and Social Science is currently directed by Professor Lorraine Gutiérrez, preceded in this time period by Professors Charles Garvin, Ruth Dunkle, and David Tucker.

The School's Policies on Nondiscrimination
All policies and procedures related to nondiscrimination with regard to faculty and staff are contained in the *University of Michigan Standard Practice Guide*. The school's policies and procedures are reproduced in the

Social Work Faculty Handbook, including sections on sexual harassment, nondiscrimination based on sexual orientation, and discriminatory harassment, as well as appendices detailing instructional and research staff grievance procedures and rules and procedures for academic misconduct.

The school's *Student Guide* contains the university affirmative action statement, policy statement on sexual orientation, and policy statement on students with disabilities. The *Student Guide* also contains specification of student rights and responsibilities, the University of Michigan code of student conduct, and policies related to drugs and alcohol, sexual assault, sexual harassment, and freedom of speech. The guide includes the student code of academic and professional conduct.

School Administrative Committees

The school's Executive Committee was created by the regents to assist the dean. The Executive Committee, in addition to assisting the Dean, is charged with the duties of investigating and formulating educational and instructional policies for consideration by the faculty and acts for the faculty in matters of budgets, promotions, and appointments. The Executive Committee has the power to initiate, review, and consult with the Dean on any policy matter affecting the operation of the School. The Executive Committee consists of the Dean of the School, and five tenured faculty serving three-year terms, and one untenured faculty serving a two-year term. The Dean of the School serves as Chairperson. Only those members of the School who are professors, associate professors, or assistant professors who hold appointments of one-half time or more are eligible to vote for members or to hold office on the Executive Committee. Clinical faculty, research scientists, and adjunct faculty are ineligible to vote for members or hold office on the Executive Committee. The associate deans and assistant deans are not eligible for election. (*Faculty Handbook,* 2004)

Executive Committee membership (2008): Paula Allen-Meares (chair), Sandra Danziger, Jorge Delva, Larry Gant, Sherrie Kossoudji, Kris Siefert, Sean Joe, Robert Taylor (ex-officio), and Siri Jayaratne (ex-officio).

All school committees—with the exception of the Human Subjects Committee, Executive Committee, Doctoral Committee, and the Search Committee—may be composed of fifty percent faculty and fifty percent students, plus a faculty member as chair.

In addition to the executive committee, other standing committees of the school include:

Academic Concerns Committee
Curriculum Committee
Doctoral Committee
Instructional Technology and Continuing Education Committee
Lecturer Advisory and Review Committee
Multicultural and Gender Affairs Committee
Office of Global Affairs Advisory Committee
Recruitment, Admissions and Financial Aid Committee
Search Committee
Student Services and Graduation Committee
Student Grievance Committee
Field Advisory Committee

Committees external to the school include the Human Subjects Committee and the Supervising Committee for the Doctoral Committee. Ad hoc committees may be formed from time to time at the discretion of the dean and Executive Committee (CSWE, 1999).

The School's Budget
The school's *CSWE Self-Study* (1999) notes:

> The schools and colleges within the University of Michigan have been granted extensive autonomy with regard to the development and administration of their respective general funds budget. Each unit has the autonomy to use its funds in a flexible manner consistent with the goals and priorities of the individual unit.
>
> Budget development begins within the School and is conducted by the Dean in consultation with the School's Executive Committee, Faculty, and the administration group. Faculty members are made aware of budget priorities prior to formal discussion with the Provost. A budget conference is scheduled each fiscal year with the Provost/Executive Vice President, staff members, and representatives of the University Budget Priorities Committee. A final budget allocation is provided the dean in late summer.
>
> The School of Social Work depends primarily on internal funding (general funds) to cover the costs of its educational programs and attendant support services. Similarly, the School depends primarily on external funds (grants and contracts) to cover the costs of its research and post-doctoral training activities. Financial aid funds for students come primarily from internal funds, but are augmented by external funds and gifts.

The school's budget for the 2006–07 year was $15,644,650 (*Report to CSWE,* 2007).

Facilities

The School of Social Work Building is located at the corner of East University and South University, 1080 South University Avenue. The School of Social Work occupies 69,000 square feet of the building, with about one-third of the building occupied by the International Institute. The building houses 152 individual offices for faculty, graduate students researchers, visiting scholars, and emeriti professors. Terry Bennett served as facilities manager until July 2008, when he was succeeded by Jerome Rork.

The Social Work Library is a hub of the building, with over 40,000 volumes, seating space for 170 persons, four group study rooms, three classrooms, and eighty computer workstations. The library is staffed by one full-time and two part-time librarians, and one full-time and two part-time information resources specialists. The school building has four large classrooms, all with connections for laptops, and has remote video and computer capacity, a number of seminar rooms, a clinical suite, a computer classroom, and a videoconferencing studio.

The Vivian A. and James L. Curtis School of Social Work Research and Training Center is located next to the library.

The lobby of the building—McGregor Commons—serves as a large informal lounge with an outdoor adjoining courtyard.

Alumni Society

The University of Michigan School of Social Work Alumni Society was formed in 1983. The purposes of the society are stated in the *School Bulletin* as follows:

> To encourage a continued flow of outstanding student candidates for the School; familiarize alumni with problems and progress of the school, so that they may assist the advancing of its programs; infuse professional practice and social service ideas, perspectives and needs into the School; facilitate opportunities for continuing education for Social Work graduates; provide financial support for the School and the University; develop a wider fellowship between faculty, alumni and students so that they may mutually benefit from each other's advice, help and experience.
>
> Members are alumni who have received degrees or certificates from the School of Social Work, faculty members of the School and others who have demonstrated a vital interest in the School of Social Work. The organization

is directed by a Board of Governors elected by the Society's members. The Board of Governors works closely with the Alumni Officer of the School to plan and promote alumni activities. (*School Bulletin*, 1983–84)

Alumni Society Board of Governors (2005)
Carol Wasserman (president), Amy Ellwood (vice president), Judy Garza (secretary), Clarita Mays, Sally Schmall, Tammy Burgess, Susan Leahy, Elizabeth Sawyer Danowski, and Jane Dewey.
Faculty: Diane Kaplan Vinokur, Robert Ortega, and Laura Nitzberg.
Ex-officio: Dean Paula Allen-Meares, Deborah Cherrin, and Lindsey Rossow-Rood.

Alumni Society Board of Governors (2007)
Sally Schmall (president), Jane Dewey (vice president), Elizabeth Danowski, Laurel Capobianco, Sean de Four, Amy Ellwood, Judy Garza, Clarita Mays, Jose Reyes, Carol Wasserman, Blanca Almanza, Dana Bright, Bill Cabin, and Jerilyn Church.
Ex-officio: Dean Paula Allen-Meares, Lindsey Rossow-Rood, and Laurie Bueche.

Alumni Society Board of Governors (2008)
Laurel Capobianco (president), Sean de Four (vice president), Jane Dewey (secretary), Blanca Almanza, Dana Bright, Bill Cabin, Jerilyn Church, Clarita Mays, Sally Schmall, and Carol Wasserman.
Faculty Representatives: Joe Himle, Berit Ingersoll-Dayton, and Diane Kaplan Vinokur.
Ex-officio: Paula Allen-Meares, Lindsey Rossow-Rood, and Laurie Bueche.

Visiting Committee
The school has a Visiting Committee that meets periodically at the school. The committee is composed of members from other universities, the University of Michigan, and the Alumni Society.

Committee Membership (2004–05)
Greg Duncan (2002–05), Institute for Policy Research, Northwestern University
Lawrence Gary (1991–2005), School of Social Work, Howard University

Virginia Hodgkinson (2002–05), Georgetown Public Policy Institute, Georgetown University

F. Ellen Netting (2003–06), Virginia Commonwealth University

Andrew Scharlack (2003–06), School of Social Welfare, University of California/Berkeley

Fernando Torres-Gil (2005–08), School of Public Policy and Social Research, UCLA

Carol Wasserman (2004–05), Alumni Society Board of Governors' Liaison

Committee Membership (2007–08)

Barbara Berkman (2006–09), School of Social Work, Columbia University

Mark Courtney (2005–08), University of Washington

Larry Davis (2006–09), School of Social Work, University of Pittsburgh

James S. House (2006–09), Institute for Social Research, University of Michigan

Cecelia Munoz (2005–08), National Council of LaRaza

Mark R. Rank (2006–09), Geroge Warren Brown School of Social Work, Washington University

David Takeuchi (2005–08), School of Social Work, University of Washington

Laurel Capobianco (2007–09), Alumni Society Board of Governors' Liaison

Winkelman Lecture Series

The Leon and Josephine Winkelman Lecture series, initiated in 1978, continues to be offered at the school. This lecture series was established with funds from the Leon and Josephine Winkelman Foundation by the Winkelman brothers, Stanley, John, Frederick, and Henry Winkelman. The lecture series is a memorial to the parents of the Winkelman brothers. The principal focus of the series is on the field of gerontology.

Lectures for the period from 1993 to 2008 were:

Ronald J. Angel, "The Acute and Long-Term Care of Minority Elderly: Implications of Health Care Financing Reform" (1994)

Herbert A. Rosefield, "Geriatric Prisoners" (1995)

Martha Ozawa, "The Economic Well-Being of the Elderly in a Changing Society" (1996)

W. Andrew Achenbaum, "Social Security: Yesterday and Today" (1996)

Brant E. Fries, "The National Nursing Home Resident Assessment Instrument: What Do You Do with 6 Million Assessments?" (1998)

William Meezan, "Translating Rhetoric to Reality: The Future of Family and Children's Services" (1999)

Edward Gramlich, "Social Security in the 21st Century" (2000)

K. Sue O'Shea, "Embryonic Stem Cells: Basic Science and Clinical Applications" (2002)

Robert L. Kahn, "Successful Aging: Myth or Reality" (2004)

Robert P. Kelch, "A Socially Responsible Health Care System in the Era of Longevity Genes" (2006)

Jeffrey B. Halter, "Diabetes in the Heterogeneous Geriatric Population: Challenges and Opportunities" (2008)

Fedele F. and Iris M. Fauri Memorial Lecture Series

The Fedele F. and Iris M. Fauri Memorial Lecture in Child Welfare was established in 1985 through gifts from alumni, faculty, friends, and members of the Fauri family. This lecture is presented annually in recognition of former University of Michigan Dean and Vice President Fedele F. Fauri and his wife, Iris M. Fauri. The lecture series is intended to serve as a forum for the discussion of ideas and proposals to enhance the well-being of young people. Lectures for the period from 1993 to 2008 were as follows:

James K. Whittaker, "Reframing the Practice Task in Child Welfare: Challenges and Opportunities" (1994)

Sheila B. Kamerman, "The Triumph of History and Politics over Demography and Social Change" (1994)

Donna Shalala, "On Behalf of the Children" (1997)

A. Sidney Johnson, "Child Welfare: Challenges and Opportunities" (1997)

Joanne M. Csete, "Challenges to Children's Well-Being in a Globalizing World: A UNICEF Perspective" (1999)

David Liederman, "The State of Children in America: Are We Y2K Ready?" (1999)

Sara Rosenbaum, "Child Health Policy and the Next American Presidency" (2000)

Richard P. Barth, "What Is the Goal of Child Welfare Services: Permanency or Self-Sufficiency?"

Michael Sherraden, "Assets, Poverty, and Children" (2002)

Ruth McRoy, "Improving Outcomes for Children and Families: An Intersystemic Approach to Child Welfare Service Delivery" (2003)

Jonathan Rauch, "Should the Government Approve Same-Sex Marriage?" (2004)

Marianne Udow, "Child Welfare and Michigan: What Do We Know, Where Do We Go? A Public Health Perspective on Child Welfare" (2005)

Joycelyn Elders, "Against Health? How Ideologies of Health and Healthcare Can Stand in the Way of Good Living" (2006)

Howard Markel, "A Historically Based Thought Experiment: Meeting New Challenges for Children's Health and Well-Being in the 21st Century" (2007)

Gary Freed, "The Impact of the 'Aging of America' on Children's Health" (2008)

The School's Reaccreditation

The school submitted a self-study report to the Commission on Accreditation of the Council on Social Work Education in February 1999. A site visit report for the M.S.W. program was received following the visit by the accreditation team, with a response by the school in June 1999. The Commission on Accreditation reviewed the self-study documents, the site team report, and the school's response at its October 1999 meeting and reaccredited the M.S.W. program for the full eight-year cycle ending October 2007.

The school's mission and goals were articulated in the self-study report to the Council on Social Work Education (CSWE) in 1999 in terms of social work's purposes, values, and ethics.

> Throughout its history the School of Social Work has been dedicated to the pursuit of excellence in social work education. Its administration and faculty believe that the profession of social work can best be advanced through an educational program of the highest quality dedicated to the education of social workers to act in influential ways in social work and social welfare institutions; a high priority on research, knowledge development and dissemination; a commitment to serve the society and its social welfare institutions, as well as the profession, to assist in the profession's endeavors to improve the well-being of citizens, and to achieve a more just and equal society.

The mission of the School of Social Work is grounded in the profession of social work and the University of Michigan. The School draws from the profession's tradition of seeking to enhance the ways in which individuals, singly and collectively, seek to meet their needs in the social environment and the ways in which the social environment responds to the needs of individuals. The actions of social workers may be aimed at individuals, families, groups, communities, or organizations as well as the interactions among them. As such, the School seeks to prepare social workers to help prevent, reduce, or resolve problems that grow out of individual–environment transactions as well as strengthen the potential of people to lead creative and satisfying lives in their social environments.

The School seeks to enhance the social work competencies of its students, in order to assist in developing a social and physical environment in the society which sustains and enhances overall well-being, and to promote social and economic justice and empowerment and eliminate oppressive social conditions.

The educational program for the master's degree in social work is designed to prepare students for advanced social work practice. Thus, the mission of the school, adopted by the faculty in 2004, is as follows:

Educate graduates for advanced social work practice and lifelong professional growth and development; prepare graduates to serve society at the local, state, national and international levels; promote social and economic justice and empowerment and eliminate oppressive social conditions; create and disseminate, through research and knowledge building, social innovations using interdisciplinary problem-solving effort. (*Report to the Commission on Accreditation*, CSWE, 2007)

In 2005 the school's faculty began preparation for the process for reaccreditation review. The CSWE Commission on Accreditation provided the school with an alternative to the traditional reaffirmation process, a process

designed for programs that have well articulated and stable curricula and would like to commit some of the resources they would normally use in the self-study process to different program improvement activities. The Commission on Accreditation (COA) provides programs such an opportunity through an accreditation compliance audit and a special project. This option involves two independent activities:

- the completion of a reaffirmation compliance audit to demonstrate program compliance with accreditation standards and,
- a special project which addresses a subject of significance to the social work profession or the social work program (and which is related to the program's mission, goals, and objectives). (SSW materials, 2005)

A site visit on accreditation occurred at the school in December 2007. A compliance audit entitled "Report to the Commission on Accreditation, CSWE" (August, 2007) was prepared for the visit.

In regard to the reaccreditation process, Dean Allen-Meares noted: "As part of our CSWE reaffirmation efforts for the MSW program, we hosted Dr. Barbara White, dean of the School of Social Work, University of Texas–Austin, for a site visit on December 11. She gave most positive observations about the School, including a notation on our faculty, who have 'exceptional qualifications through credentials, experience, and productivity. They demonstrate the ability to design curricula, develop and implement effective pedagogy, and contribute to knowledge through their prolific scholarly work.' Similarly, Dr. White praised our commitment to diversity and nondiscrimination as evidenced by both PODS [privilege, oppression, diversity, and social justice] and our alternative affirmation, highlighted our excellent library resources, and praised our evaluation of and continuous work on relevant curriculum" (*Ongoing*, Winter/Spring 2008). Final action of the Commission on Accreditation came to the school in 2008, with the commission reaffirming the school's accreditation for eight years, until June 2015.

PART TWO   The School's Students

Admission to the School
The school's admissions policies and procedures remained essentially the same during the period 1993–2008. *School Bulletin* announcements include criteria for admissions, application dates, the components of the application, and special groups, including extended degree program, transfer, international, and non-baccalaureate degree applicants. Information about admissions is cited from the *School Bulletin*, 2006–07, and in the *Report to the Commission on Accreditation, CSWE* (August, 2007).

Affirmative Action
The School adheres to the University's Affirmative Action Policy and welcomes applications from all persons regardless of race, sex, color, religion,

creed, national origin or ancestry, disability, age, marital status, sexual orientation, disability, or Vietnam-era Veteran status. In pursuit of its goal of a diverse student body, the school encourages applications from students of color, members of the LGBT community, disabled persons, nonresidents, international students, and those who are seeking a career change or further training.

Criteria for Admission

Admission to the Master of Social Work Program as a degree-seeking student is limited to the Fall Term only. Each fall approximately 330 new students enter the MSW program. Admission to the School is competitive. The selection process includes an evaluation of each applicant's demonstrated and potential abilities as a student, practitioner and leader in the social work field.

Admission decisions are based primarily on an evaluation of previous undergraduate and graduate work, recommendations, experience in the human services, and the applicant's written supplementary statement.

Applicants for admission to the MSW program are expected to meet the following criteria:

1. Completion of a U.S. bachelor's degree or its equivalent, with competitive grades, from an accredited institution. (Prospective students applying to the non-baccalaureate degree program do not have to meet this requirement).

2. Prior academic record must reflect a liberal arts perspective including twenty academic semester credits in psychology, sociology, anthropology, economics, history, political science, government and/or languages. Students must have knowledge about social, psychological and biological determinants of human behavior, and of diverse cultures, social conditions and social problems. Student who have not acquired 20 semester credit hours in a combination of these content areas prior to submission of their application may be admitted on the condition that these requirements are met prior to enrollment in the MSW program.

3. Intellectual and personal qualities likely to lead to roles and careers that have centrality in the social welfare system. This includes a commitment to engage in social work roles that involve social welfare institutions and systems most likely to have an effect on major social problems and that serve the most economically and socially disadvantaged groups in our society.

4. Personal qualifications considered essential to the successful practice of

social work, such as sensitivity and responsiveness in relationships, concern for the needs of others, adaptability, good judgment, critical thinking, creativity, integrity and skill in oral and written communication.

Student Enrollment

The following tables include information about student enrollment. As can be noted in Table 1, there was a dramatic increase in full-time student enrollment, from 481 in 1990 to 606 in 2006. Table 2 shows enrollment by ethnicity, with minority student enrollment increasing from 16.6% in 1990 to 26.6% in 2006. Student enrollment by gender is presented in Table 3, with over 80% female students for each of the years cited. Table 4 indicates that in 2004 64% of the students were enrolled in the direct practice/clinical method of study, 17% in community organization and planning, 8% in administration/management, and 11% with other method combinations. Table 5 shows the number of MSW graduates for the academic years 1990–91, 1995–96, 2000–01, 2003–04, 2004–05, 2005–06, and 2006–07, ranging from 281 to 360.

Table 1: Full-Time MSW Students

1990 (481)	1996 (567)	2000 (554)	2004 (634)	2005 (589)	2006 (606)	2007 (604)

Table 2: MSW Full-Time Enrollment by Ethnicity

Year	Total	AA	AI	ASA	MA	PR	W	OM	F	O*
1990	481	55	3	10	6	4	383	2	8	0
1996	567	85	2	29	19	3	403	0	16	0
2000	554	63	3	27	9	2	382	15	21	32
2004	634	89	11	36	20	3	414	16	21	24
2005	589	72	9	37	17	3	401	15	16	19
2006	606	72	8	38	22	7	405	14	17	23
2007	604	73	9	41	16	2	406	12	0	45

*AA:African American/Black; AI: American Indian/Native American; ASA: Asian American; MA: Mexican American; PR: Puerto Rican American; W: White; OM: Other Minority; F: Foreign; O: Other

Percent Minority/Non-Foreign Students

1990 (16.6%)	1996 (24.3%)	2000 (21.4%)	2004 (27.6%)	2005 (25.9%)	2006 (26.6%)	2007 (25%)

Table 3:
Full-Time MSW Enrollment by Gender

Year	Total	Male	Female
1990	481	89 (18.5%)	392 (81.5%)
1996	567	86 (15%)	481 (85%)
2000	554	68 (12%)	486 (88%)
2004	634	84 (13%)	550 (87%)
2005	589	71 (12%)	518 (88%)
2006	606	71 (12%)	535 (88%)
2007	604	74 (12%)	530 (88%)

Table 4:
Full-Time MSW Student Enrollment by Student's Major

Methods of Practice	2004	2005	2006
Direct Practice/Clinical	64%	61%	61%
Community Organizing & Planning	17%	19%	16%
Administrative/Management	8%	10%	11%
Other	11%	10%	12%

Table 5: Graduates

1990–91 (281)	1995–96 (325)	2000–01 (326)	2003–04 (310)	2004–05 (360)	2005–06 (298)	2006–07 (303)

Fees, Expenses, and Financial Aid

Full Program Tuition for 2005–06 (nine credit hours or more)
Michigan resident tuition $8,146 per semester
Non-Michigan resident tuition $13,874 per semester

Full Program Tuition for 2006–07
Michigan resident tuition $8,726 per semester
Non-Michigan resident tuition $14,481 per semester

Full Program Tuition for 2007–08
Michigan resident tuition $9,215 per semester
Non-Michigan resident tuition $15,144 per semester

Financial aid for students comes from two basic sources: the School of Social Work for departmental grants and scholarships and the University Office of Financial Aid for federal loans and work-study. Among the school's scholarships, fellowships, and honors in 2005 were the following:

Alumni Society Fellowship in Children and Families Program
Ara C. Cary Fellowship in the Child and Family Program
Arthur L. Johnson Endowed Scholarship
Child Welfare Fellowship
Clarice Ullman Freud Fellowship
Eleanor Cranefield Scholarship
Frankel Fellowship in Jewish Communal Service
Gus Harrison Scholarship in Social Work and Public Administration
Howard and Judith Sims Endowed Fellowship in Child and Family
    Program
Kenneth G. Lutterman Memorial Scholarship
Mandell L. Berman Award
McGregor Fellowship in Geriatric Social Work
Olivia P. Maynard Children and Family Fellowship
Rainbow Network MSW Scholarship
Rosemary Sarri Endowed Scholarship
School of Social Work Scholarships
Selena Brown Memorial Scholarship
UAW-GM Fellowship in the Child and Family Program
Wheeler Family Memorial Scholarship

Additional scholarships for 2006–08 included the Agency Paid Field Instruction, Andrea Foote and Jack Erfurt Scholarship, Bruce Allen Schaffer Memorial Award, Clara P. Davis and Larry E. Davis Award, Dean's Scholarships, Drachler Program Fellowships, Geriatric Scholarship, Harold T. and Vivian B. Shapiro Prize, Michigan Scholarships, Opportunity Grants, and University of Michigan Office of Financial Aid Resources.

A few recent scholarships include the following.

Irene and William Gambrill Fellowship
In 2008 Eileen Gambrill (Ph.D. '65) established the Irene and William Gambrill Fellowship, named after her parents, who in Eileen's words "provided an example of caring for the fate of others, thinking critically about issues and discussing them in an atmosphere of inquiry in which

disagreements were never taken personnaly." Gambrill also noted: "I hope that this fellowship will nourish those who have an interest in attending to ethical obligations that are such an important part of the profession of social work and that should be a guidepost in research, practice, and policy." The Gambrill Fellowship supports doctoral students whose research focuses on integrating practice, research, and ethical issues.

Mervin and Helen S. Pregulman Endowed Scholarship Fund
Mervin (AB '44) and Helen (AB '49) Pregulman named the School of Social Work as the beneficiary of additional funds to enhance the Mervin and Helen S. Pregulman Endowed Scholarship Fund, established in 1997 to provide for students working within the field of Jewish communal service. In regard to this recent gift to the school, Mervin noted: "Helen and I have always been interested in the success of the School of Social Work, especially in the Sol Drachler Program" (*Ongoing*, 2008).

Edwin J. Thomas Trust
In 2008 Professor Emeritus of Social Work and Professor Emeritus of Psychology Edwin J. Thomas established a trust for the benefit of the School of Social Work. The trust establishes the Edwin J. Thomas Endowed Faculty Research Award, which will support research conducted by outstanding doctoral faculty members at the school.

Student Organizations
Several organizations are active each year and serve students at the school. These organizations include:

> Adventure Therapy Group
> Association of Black Social Work Students
> Christians in Social Work Association
> Coalition of Asian and Pacific Islander Social Workers
> Doctoral Student Organization
> Rainbow Network
> School Social Workers
> Sigma Phi Omega (Gerontological Honor Society)
> Social Welfare Action Alliance
> Social Work International Students in Action
> Social Work Student Union
> Student Organization of Latina/o Social Workers
> Students Organizing for Social Justice

PART THREE The School's Faculty

Introduction

During the academic year 1993–94 the faculty consisted of forty-four members with tenure or on the tenure track. Members of the faculty at this time were the following: Paula Allen-Meares, Oscar Barbarin, Harvey Bertcher, William Birdsall, Betty Brown-Chappell, Barry Checkoway, Sallie Churchill, Valire Carr Copeland, Tom Croxton, Sandra Danziger, Sheldon Danziger, Ruth Dunkle, Kathleen Faller, Sheila Feld, Phillip Fellin, Lawrence Gant, Charles Garvin, Rose Gibson, Berit Ingersoll-Dayton, Srinika Jayaratne, Harold Johnson, Sherrie Kossoudji, Armand Lauffer, Edith Lewis, Shirley Lockery, Frank Maple, Susan McDonough, Elizabeth Mutschler, Robert Ortega, Thomas Powell, Beth Reed, Lawrence Root, Daniel Saunders, Brett Seabury, Kristine Siefert, Zulema Suarez, Robert Taylor, John Tropman, David Tucker, Mary Van Hook, Diane Vinokur, Helen Weingarten, and Mayer Zald. Represented in this group of forty-four members were 53% male, 47% female; 27% minority, 73% White; 55% professors, 20% associate professors, and 25% assistant professors.

For the academic year 2007–08, the faculty consisted of forty-six members with tenure or on the tenure track. The school's document *Faculty Research and Publications* (U-M SSW, Fall 2007) includes profiles for tenure track and research professor faculty and the eight clinical and research scientist faculty. Of the tenure track faculty, 46% were male, 54% female; 37% minority, 63% White; 43% professors, 34% associate professors, and 22% assistant professors.

Summary of Faculty Size: 1993–July 2007

1993–94 (44)	1998–99 (47)	2003–04 (46)
1994–95 (45)	1999–00 (50)	2004–05 (49)
1995–96 (44)	2000–01 (44)	2005–06 (45)
1996–97 (46)	2001–02 (44)	2006–07 (44)
1997–98 (45)	2002–03 (44)	2007–08 (46)

Tenure Track and Research Faculty 2007–08

Allen-Meares, Paula, Dean and Norma Radin Collegiate Professor of Social Work, Professor of Education

Chadiha, Letha, Associate Professor of Social Work

Chatters, Linda, Professor of Social Work, Professor of Public Health

Checkoway, Barry, Professsor of Social Work

Danziger, Sandra, Professor of Social Work

Delva, Jorge, Professor of Social Work

Dunkle, Ruth, Wilbur J. Cohen Collegiate Professor of Social Work

Faller, Kathleen, Marion Elizabeth Blue Collegiate Professor of Social Work

Fitch, Dale, Assistant Professor of Social Work

Ford, Briggett, Assistant Professor of Social Work

Gant, Lawrence, Associate Professor of Social Work

Gershoff, Elizabeth, Associate Professor of Social Work

Grogan-Kaylor, Andrew, Associate Professor of Social Work

Gutiérrez, Lorraine, Professor of Social Work, Professor of Psychology

Himle, Joseph, Assistant Professor of Social Work, Assistant Professor of Psychiatry

Hollingsworth, Leslie, Associate Professor of Social Work

Ingersoll-Dayton, Berit, Professor of Social Work

Jayaratne, Srinika, Professor of Social Work, Associate Dean

Joe, Sean, Assistant Professor of Social Work, Assistant Professor of Psychiatry

Kieffer, Edith, Associate Professor of Social Work

Kossoudji, Sherrie, Associate Professor of Social Work

Lewis, Edith, Associate Professor of Social Work

Li, Lydia, Associate Professor of Social Work

McDonough, Susan, Associate Research Professor of Social Work

Ortega, Robert, Associate Professor of Social Work

Oyserman, Daphna, Edwin J. Thomas Collegiate Professor of Social Work, Professor of Psychology

Paley, Julia, Assistant Professor of Social Work, Assistant Professor of Anthropology

Perron, Brian, Assistant Professor of Social Work

Powell, Thomas, Professor of Social Work

Reed, Beth, Associate Professor of Social Work, Associate Professor of Women's Studies

Reisch, Michael, Professor of Social Work

Root, Lawrence, Professor of Social Work

Ruffolo, Mary, Associate Professor of Social Work, Associate Dean

Saunders, Daniel, Professor of Social Work

Seabury, Brett, Associate Professor of Social Work

Shanks, Trina, Assistant Professor of Social Work

Siefert, Kristine, Edith Gomberg Collegiate Professor of Social Work

Spencer, Michael, Associate Professor of Social Work

Staller, Karen, Associate Professor of Social Work

Taylor, Robert, Sheila Feld Collegiate Professor of Social Work, Associate Dean

Tolman, Richard, Professor of Social Work

Tropman, John, Professor of Social Work

Tucker, David, Professor of Social Work

Vinokur, Diane, Associate Professor of Social Work

Woodford, Michael, Assistant Professor of Social Work

Yoshihama, Mieko, Associate Professor of Social Work

Clinical and Research Scientist Faculty

Paul, Janice, Assistant Professor of Social Work and of Art

Ribaudo, Julie, Clinical Assistant Professor of Social Work

Richards-Schuster, Katherine, Assistant Research Scientist

Sherman, Beth, Clinical Assistant Professor of Social Work

Tapia Granados, Jose, Assistant Research Scientist

Voshel, Elizabeth, Clinical Assistant Professor of Social Work, Director of Field Instruction

Wade, Kathleen, Research Assistant Professor of Social Work, Assistant Dean of Hospital Social Work

Zinn, Frank, Research Assistant Professor of Social Work, Director of Global Activities

Emeritus Faculty

Oscar Barbarin, Sydney E. Bernard, Harvey J. Bertcher, William Birdsall, Howard V. Brabson, Sallie R. Churchill, Tom A. Croxton, Sheila C. Feld, Phillip A. Fellin, Charles D. Garvin, Rose Gibson, Martha N. Gizynski, Jesse E. Gordon, Harold Johnson, Armand A. Lauffer, William C. Lawrence, Shirley A. Lockery, Elizabeth Mutschler, Katherine R. Reebel, Rosemary C. Sarri, Vivian Shapiro, Edwin J. Thomas, Robert D. Vinter, Helen R. Weingarten, Charles S. Wolfson, and Mayer N. Zald

Faculty Awards

Some faculty members recognized by the school and the university with distinction include the following, with a more complete listing of awards from outside the university to be found in faculty profiles.

Collegiate Professorships

Norma Radin Collegiate Professor of Social Work
Paula Allen-Meares
Wilbur J. Cohen Collegiate Professor of Social Work
Ruth Dunkle
Edwin J. Thomas Collegiate Professor of Social Work
Daphna Oyserman
Edith S. Gomberg Collegiate Professor of Social Work
Kristine Siefert
Sheila Feld Collegiate Professor of Social Work
Robert J. Taylor
Henry J. Meyer Collegiate Professor of Social Work and Public Policy
Sheldon Danziger
Fedele F. Fauri Professor of Social Work
Edwin J. Thomas
Arthur Dunham Professor of Social Work
Robert D. Vinter
Arthur P. Thurnau Professor
Lorraine M. Gutiérrez

Endowed Chairs

Marion Elizabeth Blue Professor of Social Work
Kathleen Coulborn Faller
Harold R. Johnson Professor of Social Work
Louis Burgio
Sol Drachler Chair in Jewish Communal Leadership
Karla Goldman

Awards

U-M Distinguished Faculty Achievement Award
Siri Jayaratne, Howard Brabson, Beth Reed, Ruth Dunkle, Robert Taylor, Rosemary Sarri, Edwin J. Thomas, Henry J. Meyer
U-M Distinguished Faculty Governance Award
Beth Reed, Sheila Feld
U-M LS&A Excellence in Education Award
Lorraine Gutiérrez

U-M Faculty Career Development Award
Ruth Dunkle, Michael Spencer, Edith C. Kieffer
U-M Career Development for Women Faculty Award
Kristine Siefert, Lorraine Gutiérrez
U-M Faculty Recognition Award
Beth Reed
U-M Regents Public Service Award
Beth Reed
U-M Academic Women's Caucus Award
Rosemary Sarri, Beth Reed
U-M Women of Color Award
Edith Lewis
U-M Latino Leadership Award
Robert M. Ortega, Lorraine M. Gutiérrez
U-M Circle Award for Exemplary Service
Robert M. Ortega
U-M DreamKeeper Award
Harold R. Johnson, Beth Reed
U-M Department of Psychiatry Teacher of the Year Award
Joseph Himle
U-M Regents' Public Service Award
Beth Reed
U-M Faculty Career Development Award
Michael Spencer
U-M Regents' Medal
Lawrence Root
U-M School of Social Work Alumni Distinguished Faculty Award
Sallie Churchill, Howard Brabson
U-M Distinguished Alumni Service Award
Richard English, Rosemary Sarri
U-M Graduate School Student Mentor Award
Rosemary Sarri
U-M Michigan Society of Fellows Senior Fellow
John E. Tropman
Michigan Student Assembly Outstanding Instructor Award
Edith Lewis
Michigan Campus Compact Faculty Award
Lorraine Gutiérrez
Association of Black Social Workers Outstanding Teaching Award
Edith Lewis, Trina R. Shanks

Bernard Zell/Leonard W. Lurie Prize, U-M School of Business
John Tropman
Wilbur J. Cohen Award, U-M School of Education
John Tropman
Rosalie Ginsberg Award for Community Service and Social Action
Beth Reed, Lorraine Gutiérrez, Larry Gant
Sarah Goddard Power Award
Beth Reed
Harold R. Johnson Diversity Service Award
Robert Ortega, Larry Gant, Mieko Yoshihama, Kristine Siefert, Beth Reed, Lorraine Gutiérrez, Michael Spencer, Janice Paul, Paula Allen-Meares

Calendar of Arrivals/Departures: 1993–2007
See school website (www.ssw.umich.edu) and *Faculty Research and Publications* (U-M SSW, Fall 2007) for extensive profiles for current faculty members.

1993–94
Arrivals: Paula Allen-Meares and Ronald Astor
Departures: Louis Ferman, Jesse Gordon, David Himle, Kris Kissman, Rosemary Sarri, Ira Schwartz, and Edwin Thomas

PAULA ALLEN-MEARES, B.S., State University of New York/Buffalo; M.S.W., Ph.D., University of Illinois–Urbana. Research interests: Schools, adolescents, parenting.

RON ASTOR, B.A., California State University; M.S.W., University of Southern California; M.A., Hebrew Union College; Ph.D., University of California, Berkeley. Research interests: Children, family violence, school-based violence prevention programs, school social work, and ecological interventions.

1994–95
Arrivals: Lorraine Gutiérrez, Carol Mowbray, Richard Tolman, and John Wallace
Departures: Harvey Bertcher, Zulema Suarez, and Mary Van Hook

LORRAINE GUTIÉRREZ, A.B., Stanford; A.M., University of Chicago; A.M., Ph.D., University of Michigan. Research interests: Empowerment-oppressed groups, mental health, Latinos.

CAROL MOWBRAY, B.S., M.S., Tufts University; Ph.D., University of Michigan. Research interests: Psychosocial rehabilitation, women's mental health, program evaluation, consumerism in mental health programs.

RICHARD TOLMAN, B.S., Northwestern University; M.S.W., University of Michigan; Ph.D., University of Wisconsin–Madison. Research interests: Group work and family violence, interpersonal practice.

JOHN WALLACE, JR., Ph.D., University of Michigan. Epidemiology, etiology, and prevention of a variety of adolescent problem behaviors.

1995–96
Arrivals: David Burton, Leslie Hollingsworth, and Sharon Stephens
Departures: Betty Brown-Chappell, Sallie Churchill, Valire Copeland, and Harold Johnson

DAVID BURTON, B.S., M.S.W., University of Houston; Ph.D., University of Washington. Research interests: Sexual aggression by youth and children.

LESLIE HOLLINGSWORTH, B.A., Bennett College; M.S.W., Syracuse University; Ph.D., Purdue University. Research interests: African American families, child welfare, adoption, foster care.

SHARON STEPHENS, B.A., M.A., Ph.D., University of Chicago. Research interests: Cultural anthropology, cultural transformation in Sami (Lapp) history.

1996–97
Arrivals: Michael Spencer and Mieko Yoshihama
Departures: Rose Gibson

MICHAEL SPENCER, B.A., University of Hawaii; M.S.S.W., University of Texas; Ph.D., University of Washington. Research interests: Race, poverty, mental health, children and families.

MIEKO YOSHIHAMA, B.A., Sophia University, Tokyo; M.S.W., Ph.D., University of California, Los Angeles. Research interests: Violence against women/immigrants, race, culture, class, mental health.

1997–98
Arrivals: Mark Holter
Departures: Elizabeth Mutschler and Sharon Stephens

MARK HOLTER, B.A., M.S.S.W., and Ph.D., Columbia University. Research interests: Psychosocial rehabilitation, mental health services research, homelessness, program evaluation.

1998–99
Arrivals: Andrea Hunter and Mary Ruffolo
Departures: None

ANDREA HUNTER, B.A., Spelman College; M.S., Ph.D., Cornell University. Research interests: Linkages between the life course, families, and social structure, with a specific focus on Black Americans.

MARY RUFFOLO, B.S., University of Dayton; M.S.W., University of Illinois–Urbana; Ph.D., Ohio State University. Research interests: Intersection of mental health interventions with children, adolescents and their families.

1999–2000
Arrivals: Janet Finn, Briggett Ford, William Meezan, Daphna Oyserman, Michael Reisch, and Deborah Schild
Departures: Sheila Feld and Phillip Fellin

JANET FINN, B.A., University of Montana; M.S.W., Eastern Washington University; M.A., Ph.D., University of Michigan. Research interests: Cultural constructions of adolescence, pathology, and social work intervention.

BRIGGETT FORD, B.A., M.S.W., University of Michigan; M.P.H., Ph.D., University of Pittsburgh. Research interests: African American families, mental health, violence, DSM-IV.

WILLIAM MEEZAN, B.A., University of Vermont; M.S.W., Smith College for Social Work; Ph.D., University of Illinois–Urbana. Research interests: Evaluation of children, youth and family programs.

DAPHNA OYSERMAN, B.S.W., M.S.S.W., Hebrew University of Jerusalem; M.A., Ph.D., University of Michigan. Research interests: Interface between context, culture, identity, and basic psychological processes.

MICHAEL REISCH, B.A., New York University; M.A., Ph.D., State University of New York at Binghamton; M.S.W., Hunter College. Research interests: Social policy, community organization, history and philosophy of social welfare.

DEBORAH SCHILD, B.A., San Jose State University; M.S.W., California State University, Sacramento; M.P.H., Ph.D., University of California, Berkeley. Research interests: Maternal and child health, infant mortality reduction, pregnancy intervention and attitudes, genetics policy and services, primary care policy.

2000–01
Arrivals: Lydia Li
Departures: Oscar Barbarin, Tom Croxton, Charles Garvin, Andrea Hunter, Susan McDonough, Helen Weingarten, and Mayer Zald

LYDIA LI, Hon. Diploma, Hong Kong Baptist College; M.S.W., University of Hong Kong; Ph.D., University of Wisconsin–Madison. Research interests: Caregiving, social support, race differences in health and disability, formal and informal care.

2001–02
Arrivals: Dale Fitch, Deborah Gioia, Andrew Grogan-Kaylor, and Karen Staller
Departures: Ronald Astor, William Birdsall, Janet Finn, and Armand Lauffer

DALE FITCH, B.A., Oklahoma Baptist University; M.S.S.W., Ph.D., University of Texas at Arlington. Research interests: Mental health, child abuse, information technology, systems theory, community practice and administration and policy.

DEBORAH GIOIA, B.A., Northeastern University; M.S.S.W., Columbia University; Ph.D. University of Southern California. Research interests: Functional outcomes (e.g., vocational) of young adults diagnosed with schizophrenia, neurocognitive aspects of schizophrenia.

ANDREW GROGAN-KAYLOR, B.A., M.S.S.W., Ph.D., University of Wisconsin–Madison; M.A., Union Theological Seminary. Research interests: Poverty and child well-being, foster care, child maltreatment.

KAREN STALLER, B.A., J.D., Cornell University; M.Phil., Ph.D., Columbia University. Research interests: Runaway and homeless youth, law, social problem construction, history of social welfare, qualitative research methods.

2002–03
Arrivals: Letha Chadiha and Jorge Delva
Departures: Shirley Lockery and John Wallace

LETHA CHADIHA, B.S., Tuskegee Institute; M.A., Washington State University; M.S.W., Ph.D., University of Michigan. Research interests: Family caregiving involving older African Americans.

JORGE DELVA, B.S.W., M.S.W., Ph.D., University of Hawaii. Research interests: Prevention and treatment of chemical dependency, drug epidemiology, program evaluation, survey research, cross-cultural and cross-national research.

2003–04
Arrivals: Linda Chatters, Joseph Himle, Trina Shanks, and Michael Woolley
Departures: David Burton and Frank Maple

LINDA CHATTERS, A.B., University of California, Berkeley; Ph.D., University of Michigan. Research interests: Religious involvement and well-being, social support networks of adult/elderly African Americans, intergenerational family relations, families and health.

JOSEPH HIMLE, M.S.W., Ph.D., University of Michigan. Research interests: Mental health, anxiety, depression, psychosocial interventions, cognitive-behavioral therapy, interface between neurobiology and psychosocial interventions in mental health.

TRINA SHANKS, B.S., Olin School of Business; M.Ph., University of Oxford; Ph.D., Washington University. Research interests: Poverty, wealth and child well-being, intergenerational economic inequality, family policies and programs.

MICHAEL WOOLLEY, B.S., M.S.W., Virginia Commonwealth University; Ph.D., University of North Carolina. Research interests: School social work, interpersonal practice with children and families, development of assessment instruments for practice, and the cognitive processes of instrument item response.

2004–05
Arrivals: Elizabeth Gershoff, Matthew Howard, Sean Joe, and Julia Paley
Departures: Sheldon Danziger

ELIZABETH GERSHOFF, B.A., University of Virginia; M.A., Ph.D., University of Texas at Austin. Research interests: Child poverty, community violence, youth violence, neighborhood violence prevention, parenting impacts on child behavior.

MATTHEW HOWARD, B.A., M.S., Western Washington University; M.S.W., Ph.D., University of Washington. Research interests: Substance abuse, abuse, and dependence; juvenile delinquency; youth violence; antisocial behavior in youth.

SEAN JOE, B.A., M.S.W., State University of New York/Stony Brook; Ph.D., University of Illinois–Urbana. Research interests: Self-destructive behaviors, including suicidal behavior, community organizing, and positive youth developments.

JULIA PALEY, B.A., University of Pennsylvania; M.A., Ph.D., Harvard University. Research interests: Political anthropology, urban studies, urban neighborhoods, ethnicity, and ethnographic methodology.

2005–06
Arrivals: None
Departures: William Meezan, Deborah Gioia, Mark Holter, and Deborah Schild

2006–07
Arrivals: Michael Woodford and Brian Perron
Departures: Michael Woolley and Matthew Howard

MICHAEL WOODFORD, B.S.W., M.S.W., Memorial University of Newfoundland, Canada; Ph.D., University of Toronto, Ontario, Canada. Research interests: Community participation in policy making, HIV/AIDS prevention, LGBT-related oppression, qualitative methodology.

Brian Perron, B.A., The College of St. Scholastica; M.S.W. University of Wisconsin–Madison; Ph.D., Washington University–St. Louis. Research interests: Services for persons with serious mental illnesses and substance use disorders, and comorbidities.

2007–08
Arrivals: None
Departures: Michael Reisch

2008–09
Arrivals: Louis Burgio, Karla Goldman, Sandra Momper, H. Luke Shaefer, and Bradley Zebrack
Departures: Julia Paley, Jose Tapia Granados

Lou Burgio, B.A., Canisius College; M.A., Ph.D., University of Notre Dame. Research interests: Applied gerontology, translational resources, clinical trials.

Karla Goldman, B.A., Yale University; M.A., Ph.D, Harvard University. Research interests: American Judaism, history of Jewish women, Black–Jewish relations, urban Jewish communities.

Sandra Momper, B.S., University of Slippery Rock; M.S.W., Ph.D., University of Pittsburgh. Research interests: Gambling, substance abuse, mental health and health disparities among rural urban American Indians.

H. Luke Shaefer, B.A. Oberlin College; M.A., Ph.D., University of Chicago. Research interests: Disadvantaged working families and U.S. social policy, nonprofit management, human service organization in public policy.

Bradley Zebrack, B.A., University of California, Los Angeles; M.S.W., Ph.D., University of Michigan.Research interests: Psychosocial oncology research and practice, program development, health disparities, patient advocacy.

2009
Arrivals: Laura Lein

Laura Lein, B.A., Swarthmore College; M.A., Ph.D., Harvard University. Research interests: Households in persistent poverty, NGOs and human services, women's employment, child care, interdisciplinary approaches and the combination of quantitative and qualitative data.

Retirement Memoirs
Retirement memoirs for the following faculty members who retired during the time period 1993–2008 are located in the Administration, Finance, and Operations Office: Louis A. Ferman (1993), Jesse E. Gordon (1993), Rosemary Sarri (1993), Edwin J. Thomas (1993), Harvey J. Bertcher (1995), Harold R. Johnson (1995), Sallie R. Churchill (1996), Rose C. Gibson (1996), Elizabeth Mutschler (1997), Phillip A. Fellin (1999), Sheila C. Feld (2000), Helen R. Weingarten (2000), Oscar A. Barbarin (2001), William C. Birdsall (2001), Tom A. Croxton (2001), Charles D. Garvin (2001), Armand A. Lauffer (2001), Mayer N. Zald (2001), Frank F. Maple, Jr. (2003), and Shirley A. Lockery (2003).

Faculty Research
In 1982 the school established a Research Administration Services office ("Research Office"), headed by an assistant/associate dean of research. Professor Diane Vinokur served as administrator for the office, followed by Professors Siri Jayaratne, Kris Siefert, Carol Mowbray, and Robert J. Taylor. In 2004 Professor Taylor initiated a School of Social Work Research Administration Newsletter, which focuses on faculty research spotlights, research activity reports, and special articles on foundation guidelines, human subjects review, and so forth. Volume 1 of the newsletter lists thirty-three research projects being carried out by faculty members in 2003. Volume 2 lists fifty-eight research projects (new and ongoing) for 2004. Additional listings of research projects of the faculty appear in *Ongoing*, the school's alumni magazine, and in a document produced by the Research Office, *Faculty Research and Publications* (U-M SSW, Fall 2007). This document lists publications by tenure track and research professors from January 2002 to May 2007. A complete listing of research activities of the faculty is available in the Research Office.

Ongoing Grants of Social Work Faculty
The following faculty research is reported on in *Faculty Research and Publications* (Fall 2007).

During fiscal year 2007 the school had 102 ongoing research grants—thirty-three from federal agencies, twenty-three from foundations, fourteen from state and other external sources, and thirty-two from internal university sources. The following faculty members directed these research projects:

Federal Grants. Letha Chadiha, Barry Checkoway, Jorge Delva, Dale Fitch, Ruth Dunkle, Berit Ingersoll-Dayton, Kathleen Faller, Robert Ortega, John Tropman, Mieko Yoshihama, Briggett Ford, Robert Joseph Taylor, Larry Gant, Elizabeth Gershoff, Joseph Himle, Sean Joe, Edith Kieffer, Michael Spencer, Beth Reed, Susan McDonough, Daphna Oyserman, Kristine Siefert, Richard Tolman, Michael Woolley, Larry Gant, Leslie Hollingsworth, Trina Shanks, Ruth Dunkle, Barry Checkoway, Jorge Delva, Letha Chadiha, Sean Joe, Charles Garvin, Kristine Siefert, David Tucker, Michael Spencer, John Wallace, and Mieko Yoshihama.

Foundation Grants. Paula Allen-Meares, Larry Gant, Leslie Hollingsworth, Trina Shanks, Ruth Dunkle, Barry Checkoway, Jorge Delva, Letha Chadiha, Sean Joe, Charles Garvin, Kristine Siefert, David Tucker, Michael Spencer, Edith Kieffer, John Wallace, and Mieko Yoshihama.

State-Funded Grants. Kathleen Faller, Charles Garvin, Sherrie Kossoudji, Mary Ruffolo, and Daniel Saunders.

Internal U-M Grants. Letha Chadiha, Barry Checkoway, Larry Gant, Lorraine Gutiérrez, Ruth Dunkle, Berit Ingersoll-Dayton, Lydia Li, Kathleen Faller, Dale Fitch, Charles Garvin, Elizabeth Gershoff, Michael Spencer, Leslie Hollingsworth, Sean Joe, Sherrie Kossoudji, Robert Ortega, Daphna Oyserman, Michael Spencer, Karen Staller, Richard Tolman, Michael Woolley, and Mieko Yoshihama.

Gift Grants. Larry Gant, Lorraine Gutiérrez, and Mieko Yoshihama.

Proposals funded July 2007–March 2008. Paula Allen-Meares, Larry Gant, Barry Checkoway, Jorge Delva, Kristine Siefert, Ruth Dunkle, Dale Fitch, Charles Garvin, Michael Spencer, Elizabeth Gershoff, Joseph Himle, Sean Joe, Edith Kieffer, Sherrie Kossoudji, Lydia Li, Sandra Momper, Trina Shanks, John Tropman, Susan McDonough, Brian Perron, Daniel Saunders, Kathleen Faller, Richard Tolman, Karen Staller, Robert Joseph Taylor, Letha Chadiha, John Tropman, and Mieko Yoshihama.

Training and Research Grants
The School of Social Work received a five-year grant from the Children's Bureau entitled Recruitment & Retention of Child Welfare Professionals Program. The purpose of this program is to develop a training curriculum designed to sustain a reliable workforce, along with research related to the

program. Principal investigators of the program are Kathleen Coulborn Faller, Frank Vandervort, Robert M. Ortega, and John Tropman. Products in 2008 from this program are as follows:

> "African American and White Child Welfare Workers' Attitudes Towards Policies Involving Race and Sexual Orientation," by S. Jayaratne, K. Faller, R. M. Ortega, and F. Vandervort.
>
> "Exit Interviews with Departed Child Welfare Workers," by R. P. Gonzalez, K. Faller, R. M. Ortega, and J. Tropman.
>
> "Legal Ethics and High Child Welfare Worker Turnover: An Unexplored Connection," by F. Vandervort, R. P. Gonzales, and K. Faller.
>
> "Descriptive Statistics on New Child Welfare Workers," by J. Tropman, K. Faller, M. Grabarek, C. Grinnell-Davis.
>
> "Public and Private Foster Care Workers: A Comparison of Degrees of Commitment to Child Welfare," by S. Jayaratne and K. Faller.
>
> "Race Matching In-Service Delivery: Is there an Elephant in the Living Room?" by S. Jayaratne, R. M. Ortega, K. Faller, and F. Vandervort.
>
> "Training Child Welfare Workers from a Cultural Humility Perspective," by R. M. Ortega and K. Faller.

Skillman Foundation

As noted in *Ongoing* (Winter/Spring 2008), "Detroit-based Skillman foundation teamed with the School of Social Work to cultivate the Good Neighborhoods initiative, which works with city residents to develop child-friendly communities where children can grow up healthy, well-educated, safe, and prepared for adulthood." The foundation awarded the first grant to the school in October 2005 and a second grant of $900,000 in 2007. Dean Emerita Paula Allen-Meares is principal investigator, Professor Larry Gant is co-principal investigator, and Associate Professor Leslie Hollingsworth and Assistant Professor Trina Shanks are co-investigators of the program.

PART FOUR   The School's Curriculum

Introduction

This description of the school's curriculum for the master's degree in social work is adapted from the 2006–07 *School Bulletin* and the *Report to CSWE* (2007). Changes in the curriculum have continued to be generated through committees on content areas and the Curriculum Committee, with final approval by the governing faculty. The school's curriculum over time has reflected changes in the guidelines provided by the Curriculum Policy Statement of the Council on Social Work Education and its Commission on Accreditation. The school's faculty has examined the curriculum on a continuous basis, periodically restating the school's specific curriculum objectives, developing and modifying courses, and changing the organization of content areas and course credit requirements for each area and for the M.S.W. degree.

The school continues a program that recognizes advanced standing for qualified B.S.W. graduates, a reduced curriculum that covers three terms of study. Dual degree programs continued to be offered by the school in conjunction with other units of the university. The first programs included social work and business administration, social work and public health, social work and urban and regional planning, and social work and public policy, followed in later years by social work and law, and social work and information. Since 1957 the school has had a doctoral program in social work and social science.

Curricular Objectives

The *School Bulletin* of 2006–07 states the curricular objectives of the master's program, noting that the governing faculty has mandated that all courses and field instruction should address four themes: (1) multiculturalism and diversity, (2) social justice and social change, (3) promotion, prevention, treatment, and rehabilitation, and (4) a knowledge base of behavioral and social science research.

The NASW professional code of ethics provides a foundation for identifying the responsibilities the school and its graduates have for clients, client systems, employing organizations, the profession, and society. Each course in the curriculum and field instruction addresses relevant ethical issues.

The school's curricular objectives reflect the faculty's conviction that the school must innovate and enter into emerging arenas for social work practice, foster social change through research and knowledge development, expand and improve collaboration with other instructional and research units and social welfare agencies, and consolidate resources to enhance educational quality.

Specific curricular objectives include the following:

- Provide students with analytical skills and knowledge essential to effective practice and to assess the effectiveness of current social work methods.

- Develop students' knowledge of service fields and ways of formulating and evaluating effective practice methods.
- Equip students to integrate various practice methods at different levels of intervention (e.g., individual, family, community organization, societal) to improve service quality.
- Provide students with knowledge and understanding of social and behavioral science and research applicable to social work practice so that they will be able to update and improve skills.
- Promote understanding of how students can work with diverse cultural, class, and ethnic groups and adapt one's practice to specified groups' needs.
- Develop in students the capacity and capability for exercising leadership in social welfare in public or private institutions and at federal, state, and local levels.
- Develop students' understanding and capacity to collaborate with allied professions and work in interdisciplinary settings.
- Identify emerging and continuing practice areas.
- Promote and support research and knowledge development to improve the effectiveness of social work practice, policies, and programs.
- Provide a curriculum that addresses public welfare issues facing Michigan, the nation, and the world.
- Incorporate curricular content that is relevant to the needs of special populations.

Curriculum Structure

In 1996 the school's M.S.W. program changed the course requirement for the M.S.W. degree from 56 to 60 credit hours for the degree, with 15 fewer hours for students receiving advanced standing based on undergraduate courses. Courses are offered in five content areas: methods, human behavior and social environment, social welfare policy and services, research and evaluation, and field instruction. Foundation courses in these areas are completed in the first and second terms of study, with advanced studies in the second year. Specific objectives for these courses, approved by the faculty in 2006, are listed in the *Report to CSWE* (2007). The foundation objectives focus on the generalist base for social work practice, while the advanced educational objectives highlight the knowledge and skills needed for advanced, specialized social work practice within practice methods.

To earn the M.S.W. degree, students must complete 60 credit hours, which include the foundation curriculum (18 credits), a practice method concentration (6 credits), a practice area concentration (9 credits), evaluation (3 credits), elective courses (9 credits), and 912 hours in field placement (3 foundation field and 12 advanced field credits).

All students are required to complete a dual concentration in a practice method and practice area. The practice method concentration focuses on theories and interventions related to practice with individuals, families, groups, organizations, communities, and/or society. The practice area concentration focuses on selected contexts and domains of practice, with particular attention given to specific policies, procedures, and practice.

All students must select a concentration from one of four practice methods: interpersonal practice, community organization, management of human services, and social policy and evaluation. Students have an option of selecting a minor practice method. Practice area concentrations are aging in families and society, children and youth in families and society, community and social systems, health, and mental health.

The required field instruction courses provide students with experiential opportunities that lead to competent practice by integrating classroom knowledge and social work practice in agency settings.

The school offers a number of certificate and specialization options, including scholarships in geriatric social work and child welfare social work, specialist in aging certificate, Certificate in Jewish Communal Service and Judaic Studies, specialist in social work in public schools, and specialist in social work in the workplace.

Minority Relevant Course Requirement
The school continues its minority relevant course requirement initiated in the 1970s—that is, all M.S.W. students must select one course from the school, or the university at large, that meets the minority relevant course requirement. Courses meet the requirement if they devote fifty percent or more of the readings, lectures, and assignments to minority content. In April 2001 the faculty approved changes in this component of the curriculum, which "stated that all of the courses in the Practice Area Concentrations, plus the Program Evaluation course (683) would intensively focus on PODS (Privilege, Oppression, Diversity, and Social Justice) (PODS Questions/Answers, SSW, 2005).

The *School Bulletin* (2004–05) notes:

The Governing Faculty of the School has mandated that all courses in the curriculum should contain content on multiculturalism, gender, oppression, poverty, sexual orientation and ethics. Multicultural content in courses examines cultural and historical dimensions of African Americans, Arab Americans, Asian Americans, Hispanics, and Native Americans, and focuses on social processes critical to practice with these populations. These processes address various forms of discrimination and oppression (for example, racism, sexism, ageism) applicable to each of these cultural groups. The changing roles of women and men in modern society are the focus of gender related content integrated into the curriculum. The inclusion of content on oppression and poverty reflects the School's continuing interest and historical concerns with these basic societal problems. Increasingly, ethical issues confront social workers and other human service professionals in their delivery of services. Therefore knowledge of ethical dilemmas and concerns is an important component of the social work curriculum. In each of the Practice Area concentration courses, the curriculum provides a more intensive focus on issues of privilege, oppression, diversity, and social justice.

The school's Curriculum Committee and total faculty continued to give attention to the PODS component of the curriculum during the 2004–05 academic year, as well as at a faculty retreat in May 2005. Materials for the retreat included a chart displaying differences in the new intensive focus criteria and the old minority relevant course requirement. During this period a Transgender-Bisexual-Lesbian-Gay (TBLG)Advisory Task Group made recommendations to insure proper inclusion of TBLG individuals and issues at the school, including curriculum matters such as inclusion of course content relative to these groups, as well as review through the course evaluation survey. In response to the task group's recommendations regarding the curriculum, the dean's office gave charges to a number of school committees, including the Multicultural and Gender Affairs Committee, the PODS Committee, and the Curriculum Committee. The *Report to CSWE* (2007) shows advanced concentration practice method and practice area competencies and intensive focus on privilege, oppression, diversity, and social justice competencies.

Alternative Curriculum Schedules
Students have six choices in selecting a curriculum schedule: 16-month, 20-month, advanced standing, extended degree, and part-time option.

Special Certificate/Specialization Programs
In 1993 special programs offered to M.S.W. students included Specialist in Aging Certificate, Certificate in Jewish Communal Service and Judaic

Studies, specialist in social work in the public schools, and specialist in social work in the workplace.

The Sol Drachler Program in Jewish Communal Service (now the Jewish Communal Leadership Program) provides students interested in professional leadership in the Jewish community to earn a certificate in conjunction with the M.S.W. degree. The school offers a Civitas Child and Family Program, directed by Professor Kathleen Faller and designed to prepare specialists in child abuse and neglect, with direct practice experience in a family assessment clinic. Added in 2004–05 was a new certificate option, Interdisciplinary Certificate in International Health and Social Development, allowing study in the Schools of Social Work, Public Health, and Nursing for the certificate. The School of Social Work is also the location for a Nonprofit and Public Management Center, directed by Professor Diane Kaplan Vinokur, and designed to advance and promote understanding of the contributions of nonprofit and public organizations through courses and workshops. The school offers a Certificate in Women's Studies through the Rackham Graduate School and the university's Program in Women's Studies. The school participates, with the School of Business Administration, in the direction of the Institute of Labor and Industrial Relations, an institute created in 1957 to provide a vehicle for research and a focus within the university on issues pertaining to employment and labor relations. A school faculty member, Professor Larry Root, directed the institute through 2008.

Changes in the Curriculum Model: 1996
In 1996 the school's faculty concluded a reexamination of the curriculum by increasing the total credit hour degree requirement for the M.S.W. to 60 hours. The curricular objectives stated for the curriculum model in 1992–93 remained the same for 1996, but a new introduction to the curriculum (*School Bulletin*, 1996) stated:

> In developing its curricular objectives, the Faculty have demonstrated a commitment to four themes which undergird and provide the philosophical and value basis for the curriculum heading into the 21st century:
> 1) commitment to multiculturalism and diversity;
> 2) commitment to social justice and social change;
> 3) commitment to promotion, prevention, treatment and rehabilitation;
> 4) commitment to a knowledge base of behavioral and social science research.
>
> This "new" curriculum model of 1996 called for students to take a "dual concentration"—practice method and practice area. The practice method

concentration focuses on theories and interventions related to practice with individuals, families, and groups. The practice area concentration focuses on selected contexts and domains of practice with particular attention to their specific policies, procedures, and practices.

Two major concepts required by the CSWE curriculum policy statement guided the curriculum: foundation curriculum and advanced social work practice. The foundation curriculum was designed to build on a liberal arts perspective and to provide students with core academic content and competencies in order to be able to function as generalist practitioners. Most students completed almost all courses designated as foundation in the first term of study, with some foundation courses offered in the second term. All students were required to take the following five foundation courses:

(1) Introduction to Social Welfare Policy and Services
(2) Human Differences, Social Relationships, Well-Being, and Change Through the Life Course
(3) Organizational, Community and Societal Structures; Cross-Cutting Skills for Social Work Practice
(4) Basic Social Work Research
(5) In addition, all students were expected to have some field instruction experience at both interpersonal and macro levels of practice.

The advanced social work practice part of the M.S.W. curriculum was built on the foundation courses and was designed to provide the student with the choices of concentrating on one of a set of practice methods and on one of the fields of practice that provide a context for such practice. In this curriculum model, the earlier designation of two practice areas under the terms "interpersonal practice" and "macro methods" was replaced by identification of four practice methods:

(1) interpersonal practice
(2) community organization
(3) management of human services
(4) social policy and evaluation

Under this plan, practice methods formerly labeled social policy and planning, social welfare administration, and research and evaluation were re-conceptualized as stated. Students continued to have the option of electing a minor practice method.

The student's second area of concentration was elected from five practice areas:

(1) adults and elderly in families and society
(2) children and youth in families and society
(3) community and social systems
(4) health
(5) mental health

This concentration required 9 hours of course work in a practice area. Courses in this concentration had formally been conceptualized under the label of "fields of service."

The requirement for content in research was changed from a 4-hour course to two courses, a Basic Social Work Research foundation course (3 credit hours) and an evaluation course (2 credit hours). Credit hours required in field instruction continued to include 4 hours in Foundation Field Instruction and 8 hours in Advanced Field Instruction. Elective hours remained at 9.

A new designation, platform courses, was introduced into this curriculum model. Platform-level courses were intermediate courses in each practice method concentration and were prerequisites for the advanced courses. Particular platform-level and advanced courses depended on the student's concentrations. Platform methods courses included 1 hour of content in Human Behavior and the Social Environment.

Field Instruction

The *School Bulletin* of 2004–05 description of field instruction continues through 2008. As noted in the bulletin, "field instruction provides students with experiential opportunities that lead to competent practice by integrating classroom knowledge and social work practice in agency settings. Students complete a total of 16 credits, 912 field hours (684 for advanced standing students), spread over three or four terms. Field experience provides for the acquisition of knowledge and skills in social work roles and in-depth knowledge in one of the five practice area concentrations. Foundation field instruction, consisting of a seminar and a two-day field placement, is focused on helping students apply foundation knowledge of social work skills, values, and ethics in practice. The goals for competency training in the field experience are the following:

- Technical proficiency in a practice area and practice method
- Application and testing of theory and knowledge in social work settings

- Incorporation of knowledge and skills necessary for understanding and utilizing social work ethics, values, and goals in day-to-day practice
- Refinement of professional awareness, judgment, and decision-making abilities
- Understanding the interdependence of the range of social work roles and skills from interpersonal to macro levels and within various settings and fields of service
- Engagement in practice with diverse cultural, racial, and multiethnic groups

A *Field Instruction Manual* on policies and procedures is provided to all students, faculty, and field instructors, with basic information on field instruction also provided in the *Student Guide*.

Curriculum Model for 2004–07

The curriculum for the academic years 2004–07—including the curricular objectives, structure, and course requirements—remained essentially the same as the model described for the 1996–97 year. Alternative enrollment and curriculum schedule options remained the same. Minor changes included renaming the practice area to aging in families and society, discontinuation of the place of platform courses, modification of the Foundation Field Instruction course to include a field placement and a field seminar, and reduction of credit hours for advanced standing from 16 to 15.

The 60 semester hour program requirements for 2004–07 appear in the chart below.

Courses	Credit Hours
Foundation Method Courses	6
Foundation HBSE Courses	6
Foundation SWPS Course	3
Foundation Research Course	3
Advanced Practice Methods Courses (2)	6
Advanced Practice Area Methods Course	3
Advanced Practice Area HBSE Course	3
Advanced Practice Area SWPS Course	3
Evaluation	3
Foundation Field Instruction/Seminar	3
Electives	9
Advanced Field Instruction	12
Total Credit Hours	60

Advanced Standing

Advanced standing status, initiated in 1977–78, was granted to students with the B.S.W. degree who met the following conditions:

- Attain an undergraduate degree with a major in social work from a program accredited by the Council on Social Work Education, or one that is in candidacy status for this accreditation at the time the degree was awarded.
- Maintained a GPA of 3.5 or above in the equivalent of the final two years of undergraduate study.
- Completed their undergraduate degree within six years of the expected completion of the M.S.W. degree.

Students admitted to the school under the policies regarding advanced standing for B.S.W. candidates were required to complete 44 credit hours for the M.S.W. degree until 2002. At that time the credit hours for the Evaluation (research) course was increased from 2 to 3 hours' credit so that the advanced standing student needed to complete 45 credit hours for the M.S.W. degree.

Curriculum Evaluation and Renewal

A number of evaluation measures for surveys related to the curriculum are presented in the *Report to the Commission on Accreditation* (2007): Foundation Year Measure, PODS, Second Year Competency Exit Measure, Organizational Climate Survey, Alumni Survey, Field Measures, Field Instructor Survey.

Grades

The 1992–94 *School Bulletin* specifies the school's policies on grades as follows:

Letter grades from "A" through "E" are given for class. "A" grades are given for exceptional individual performance, "B" grades are given to students who do all the required work for the course satisfactorily. "B+" and "B-" grades reflect slight variations from this satisfactory level. "C" grades are given when performance definitely falls below requirements for graduate work. "D" grades indicate deficiency, and "E" is failure. Credits toward degree requirements are not earned for courses in which "D" or "E" grades are obtained. "I" (Incomplete) is used when illness or other compelling reasons prevent completion of work, and there is a definite plan and date for completion of course work approved by the Instructor.

The grading system for the Professional Practicum consists of S (satisfactory), M (marginal), and U (unsatisfactory). "S" grades mean that the quality of performance is acceptable. "M" means that performance quality is less than satisfactory but short of failing. "U" grades mean that the quality of performance is inadequate and no credit is granted.

This grading system has continued through 2004–05.

Academic Standing and Discipline

The 2002–03 *School Bulletin* notes: "A student is automatically placed on academic probation for the subsequent term when he or she fails to maintain good academic standing. Failure to maintain good academic standing is defined as: (1) having less than a 'B' average, or (2) having accumulated 9 or more credit hours of 'I' (incomplete) grades, (3) having a grade of U (unsatisfactory) in Field Instruction, or (4) having a grade of (M) marginal in Field Instruction."

A Committee on Academic Difficulty is appointed annually by the school's Executive Committee. It is comprised of three faculty members and is chaired by the associate dean for educational programs. It reviews students in academic difficulty and has the authority to disenroll students or allow them to continue in a probationary status.

Academic Misconduct

The 2002–03 *School Bulletin* notes:

As is traditional in a community of graduate professional education, social work students are held in the highest standards of academic conduct, including a commitment to fairness, openness, honesty, and measured reciprocity. Therefore, deception for the purpose of personal gain is an offense against members of this academic community and is subject to sanction. In addition, students are expected to abide by the National Association of Social Work Code of Ethics and to adhere to established professional norms and values, in their Field Instruction and in the classroom.

Students who have allegedly failed to maintain these standards are subject to review by an Academic Misconduct Hearing Panel, consisting of two members of the Governing Faculty and one student appointed by the Dean. The Hearing Panel has jurisdiction over current and former students related to allegations of ethical misconduct and other violations of professional social work norms and values. In addition, the Hearing Panel has jurisdiction over allegations of deceptive or dishonest academic practices including, but

not limited to, plagiarism, cheating, fabrication, aiding and abetting deception or dishonesty, the falsification of records or official documents, and
the unauthorized or malicious interference or tampering with computer
property.

Non-Degree Student Enrollment
The 2004–05 *School Bulletin* notes:

> Enrolling for graduate level social work courses as a non-degree student
> enables a person to take one or two courses per term in order to help focus
> their interests, to test capabilities in a graduate setting, to increase knowl-
> edge or to improve professional skills. Persons who already hold an MSW
> may enroll for additional graduate level social work credit as non-degree
> students.

Post-MSW Management Certificate Program
A Certificate in Management is available to experienced social workers who
possess an M.S.W. degree from an accredited school of social work. Nine
credit hours of coursework are required for the certificate, with courses focused on knowledge and skills in organizational analysis, program design,
implementation and management; funding, budgeting and fiscal management; management information systems; program evaluation; and executive leadership.

Post-MSW Certificate Program on Work with Infants, Toddlers and Their Families
This program is for professionals with a M.S.W. or another relevant field
who wish to acquire the specialized, advanced knowledge and clinical skills
necessary for practice with at-risk/disabled children under three years of
age and their biological or foster families. The course of study extends over
approximately one year, with seminars scheduled over weekends.

PART FIVE   Summary

The School's Organization, Personnel, and Reaccreditation
Part One identifies the administrative personnel of the school during the
period of 1993, when Paula Allen-Meares became dean, through the winter
term 2008. John E. Tropman served as interim dean in the fall term 2008.
A profile is provided for the new dean of the school, Professor Laura Lein,

who began her term January 1, 2009. The school's committee structure is described, along with the membership of the school's Alumni Society Board and the Visiting Committee. A history of the school's lecture series is included. Student enrollment figures are cited. The school was reaccredited by the Council on Social Work Education in 2008.

The School's Students

The school's admissions policies and procedures remained essentially the same during the period 1993–2007. The school continued to seek a diverse student body. The student full-time M.S.W. enrollment each year during this period ranged from 481 to over 600, with an increase in minority enrollment and an enrollment of women of over 80 percent each year. The enrollment of over 60 percent students in direct practice remained the pattern during this time period.

The School's Faculty

Part Three provides a listing of tenure track and research professors and clinical/research scientist faculty associated with the school during the 2007–08 academic year, along with a list of emeritus/emerita professors. A calendar of arrivals/departures of faculty during the period of 1993 through January 2009 is presented, along with research/teaching interests of new arrivals on the faculty. An extensive list of faculty involved in research activities is presented.

The School's Curriculum

The school's curriculum is described in this part, including attention to curricular objectives, M.S.W. degree requirements, curriculum structure, and major content areas. Alternative curriculum schedules are presented, as well as changes in the curriculum from 1993 to 2008.

The University of Michigan's Joint Interdisciplinary Doctoral Program in Social Work and Social Science: A History

The goals of the University of Michigan—teaching, research, and service, "the warp and woof of the University"—provided a framework for the establishment of the Joint Interdisciplinary Doctoral Program in Social Work and Social Science. The doctoral program allowed the School of Social Work to more fully participate in the achievement of these goals, especially with regard to the strand of research and knowledge development (Peckham, 1994). Contributing to the founding of the program was a long history of interdepartmental, interdisciplinary interaction and collaboration between schools, colleges, and departments within the university. For over one hundred years, prominent faculty members in the social sciences and professional schools have displayed an interest in social work education. As a result, a special relationship of the social sciences and social work emerged that facilitated creation of the Joint Doctoral Program.

Part One of this appendix describes the interests of social science faculty in social work education and the early development at Michigan of educational programs in social work at undergraduate and graduate levels vis-à-vis the social sciences. Part Two presents selected characteristics of the Joint Doctoral Program from its beginning through the year 2007, along with a list of graduates over the past fifty years.

PART ONE   Social Work Education at Michigan—The Early Years

In Part One, the place of the social sciences within social work education at Michigan up to 1957 is discussed in terms of four major stages. First, in the late 1800s and early 1900s, nationally recognized Michigan faculty members in the social sciences called for the training of social workers in higher education and offered courses related to social work. Second, by 1921 these courses, along with social work practice courses, were organized into a curriculum in social work leading to a bachelor's degree in the College of

Literature, Sciences, and the Arts. This curriculum had a strong social science component. Third, a master's degree in social work was offered in 1936 under the auspices of the university's Center for Graduate Study in Detroit. Finally, a School of Social Work was opened in Ann Arbor in 1951, with the addition of social scientists to the faculty who participated in teaching, research, and curriculum development of both the Ph.D. and the M.S.W. programs in the school.

Stage One: Turn of the Century

The University of Michigan has a long tradition of interest and involvement of social scientists in social work education. Prominent among these faculty members, beginning in the late 1890s up to the time of the initiation of a social work curriculum in 1921, were Andrew Dickson White, Henry Carter Adams, Charles Horton Cooley, and Arthur Evans Wood.

Historical documents suggest that Andrew Dickson White was perhaps the first Michigan faculty member interested in education for social workers. Joining the faculty in 1856 as a professor of history, White was a proponent of a "new" scientific education approach fostered at Johns Hopkins, an education focused on "acquiring a knowledge of the history of education, of graduate education, of mental and moral science, of religion, and of the development of history, economics, and psychology as fields of study" (Broadhurst, 1971). In 1863 White left Hopkins to serve as a state senator in New York, hence joining Ezra Cornell in establishing Cornell University in 1867. As president of Cornell, White pushed for instruction in political economy and social science and emphasized the "importance of men receiving education and training in order to fulfill positions of social usefulness." In 1890, as president of the American Social Science Association, White noted the "need for special schools for the study of the science of charity" (Broadhurst, 1971).

Henry C. Adams began his career at the University of Michigan in 1880 as a lecturer in political economy and by 1900 was offering business courses listed under the title of "Political Economy, Industry and Commerce, and Sociology" (Tradition, 2001). Adams had studied at Johns Hopkins, where professors helped create the National Conference of Charities and Correction in 1879. This conference was organized for discussion of common concerns, such as "training workers in urban charity agencies and improving the efficiency of charity administration" (Austin, 1997). While at Michigan, Professor Adams served on a committee at the 1893 International Conference of Charities in Chicago and administered a university fellowship in sociology that included a field assignment in settlement work at Chicago Commons.

Charles Horton Cooley finished his Ph.D. in political economy at Michigan in 1884 and gave the first courses bearing the name "sociology" at the university in the academic year of 1884–85. In these courses, he "discussed the relationship of sociology to charitable work" (Bruno, 1957). In 1904 Professor Cooley served on a Committee on Training for Social Workers organized at the National Conference of Charities and Correction. Committee members were responsible for having papers presented at subsequent conferences on the need for training of social workers, thus demonstrating how "social science and philanthropy had come together in developing education for social work" (Broadhurst, 1971). Cooley taught the first social work course at the University of Michigan, entitled "Seminar in Principles of Social Casework," in 1913. Cooley's interest in social work was apparent in his establishing "the foundations for modern study of child behavior through the case histories of our Child Guidance Clinics" (Wood, 1930). His courses on basic sociology and social process were included in a Curriculum in Social Work established in 1921 in the College of Literature, Science, and the Arts.

Arthur E. Wood joined the Michigan faculty in 1917, teaching courses on social programs and social work in the Department of Economics and Political Economy. Wood taught courses on criminology, community problems, problems of poverty, and the family, and he also arranged field work courses in social agencies. In 1919 Wood and Harry L. Lurie published *Trouble Cases: A Study of the More Difficult Family Problems and the Work Upon Them of the Detroit Social Agencies*. In this book, Wood and Lurie noted that "it is desirable that more and better trained caseworkers be brought into the specialized fields of social service such as the courts and institutions." In 1922 Wood published *The Philosophy of Community Organization,* noting that "fifty years of social work have not been in vain if as a result an increasing number of people have begun to see the community and the value of effort on its behalf."

Stage Two: Curriculum in Social Work

At a meeting of the regents of the university in January 1921, a Committee on Educational Policies "reported that a hearing had been held with representative citizens of the state in regard to the establishment of a School for the training of social and civic workers." The regents resolved "that the President in cooperation with the Deans and other persons concerned make a careful study of the needs for training of social workers in the State of Michigan, and the best methods by which the University could undertake to meet these needs" (Board of Regents, 1921).

Based on this study, in May 1921 the regents authorized the establishment of a Curriculum in Social Work in the College of Literature, Science, and the Arts (LS&A) for the training of social workers. Such curriculum was to include the usual requirements for the bachelor's degree and to be subject to the approval of the dean of the College of LS&A. Dr. A. E. Wood was appointed director of the curriculum for the training of social workers (Board of Regents, 1921).

The University's 1921–22 *Catalogue* announced the Curriculum in Social Work, noting, "It is expected that undergraduates following this curriculum shall do their major work in the social sciences, including Sociology, Political Science, Economics, Biology, Psychology, History, and Philosophy." Courses offered by sociology faculty members included Social Process, Rural Sociology, Social Evolution, and Immigration. Professor Wood taught courses on criminology, family, principles of social work, community problems, and problems of poverty. Social work courses included electives on casework, medical social work, psychiatric social work, child welfare, and supervised field work.

In a text on *Community Problems* (1928), Professor Wood identified a role for social science in social work: "Unless social science has constructive suggestions to make concerning the problems that infest such an area, we might as well return to a mumbling of outworn theological shibboleths. However we are not restricted to such a dreary prospect. The humanized social science of our day is delving to the roots of social maladjustment as it affects both communities and individuals therein. The correlate of social science is social work. The former is normative, giving us a rational basis for community efforts; the latter has an ameliorative purpose, but seeks a scientific basis."

Stage Three: Graduate Social Work Programs: 1935–51

Graduate-level social work education at Michigan was established in 1935 in response to a 1934 report to the regents by a committee of prominent Detroit citizens. These civic leaders believed that "mere apprenticeship on the job was proving inadequate and that departments of sociology could not train students for competent practice in this difficult field" (U-M Announcement, 1946). From 1935 onwards, graduate study in social work at Michigan has been offered under various organizational entities and academic requirements, as follows:

1935:   Institute of the Health and Social Sciences, Detroit, M.A. in social work (24 credits)

1936: Institute of Public and Social Administration, Detroit, M.S.W. (48 credits)
1946: Institute of Social Work, Detroit, M.S.W. (48 credits)
1951: School of Social Work, Ann Arbor, M.S.W. (48 credits); 1960 (M.S.W., 56 credits); 1996–present (M.S.W., 60 credits).

These graduate social work programs were offered at the Horace H. Rackham Educational Building in Detroit prior to the establishment of the new School of Social Work located in Ann Arbor in 1951.

The Institute of the Health and Social Sciences
The Master of Arts in Social Work degree offered in this institute in 1935 involved 24 credit hours plus a semester of field work (no credit). Robert W. Kelso was named director of the institute. Kelso was a 1907 graduate of Harvard University's Law School. Following his practice of law until 1910, Kelso held teaching positions at several institutions, as well as executive positions in a number of social agencies. In 1922 he was president of the National Conference of Social Work. He was recruited as director of the Institute from the Colorado State Relief Administration, a unit of the Federal Emergency Relief Service (Board of Regents Exhibits, 1935). Kelso's publications demonstrated his expertise in the field of social welfare, such as *The History of Public Poor Relief in Massachusetts 1620–1920* (1922) and *The Science of Public Welfare* (1934). In 1936 Kelso authored an article in *Survey* entitled "Tomorrow's Social Work Training," noting that social work education should include "the fundamentals of human relations and sound methods of treatment" for "students already grounded in the theoretical social sciences." Kelso was active in teaching courses in the social work curriculum, including Social Engineering, Law and Social Work, Trends in Social Work, and Housing and Social Welfare.

In addition to Robert Kelso, Arthur Dunham was the other full-time professor in the institute. Dunham came to the institute in 1935 as a professor of community organization, having an A.B. degree from Washington University and a master of political science from the University of Illinois. Prior to coming to Michigan, Dunham held numerous executive positions in social agencies and had teaching appointments in several schools of social work. At Michigan he was active in service projects within local, state, national, and international communities, notably on behalf of the Religious Society of Friends. His published books—including *Community Welfare Organization: Principles and Practice* (1958), *Community Organization in Action* (1959, with E. B. Harper), *Trends in Community Organization* (1963, with M. Heath), and *New Community Organization* (1970)—were widely used in social work education within the United States and internationally.

The Institute of Public and Social Administration
In 1936 the Institute of the Health and Social Sciences was absorbed into the Institute of Public and Social Administration. The M.A. in social work was discontinued, and a two-year program of 48 hours credit for the master of social work degree was initiated. The committee in charge of the master of social work degree program consisted of Professors Max S. Handman (Economics), William Haber (Economics), Robert Kelso (Social Service), Arthur E. Wood (Sociology), Arthur Dunham (Social Work), and Richard Fuller (Sociology). In 1936 these professors were joined by Eleanor Cranefield, the first full-time faculty member with a degree in social work (M.A., University of Chicago School of Social Service Administration). Cranefield taught courses on child welfare, family, social casework, and corrections. In 1941 Ralph Fletcher, a social researcher (M.A. in economics, Washington University) joined the faculty. Clarice Freud, a specialist in child welfare (M.S.S., Western Reserve School of Applied Social Sciences), was appointed in 1942. In 1947 Mary N. Taylor (M.S.W., University of Pennsylvania) was appointed to the faculty. A large number of lecturers taught courses in the social work program, including persons with medical, social science, law, and social work degrees.

The Transition Years: 1949–51
Following Professor Robert Kelso's retirement at the beginning of the academic year of 1949, Professor Dunham was appointed acting director of the Institute of Social Work for the period of 1949–51. The years 1949–51 were transitional, with consideration given to whether or not the Institute of Social Work would remain in Detroit, move to Ann Arbor, or merge with Wayne State's social work program. The regents decided in 1950 to reconstitute the Institute of Social Work as a School of Social Work under the administrative direction of a dean, with the school to be situated in Ann Arbor, to be effective on July 1, 1951. At the time of this action, University President Ruthven stated, "This action by the Board of Regents is a recognition of the importance of social work as a field of public service. . . . This should make possible the further development of a distinctive program related to the over-all interests of the University and the needs of the state" (Board of Regents, 1950).

At their January 1951 meeting, the regents named Fedele Frederick Fauri to be dean of the school and professor of public welfare administration, effective March 1, 1951. Fauri, a native of Crystal Falls, Michigan, and a graduate of the University of Michigan School of Law, had served as director of the Michigan Department of Social Welfare. Prior to this, in Washington D.C., he was senior specialist in social security, general counsel of the U.S. Senate Finance Committee, and chair of the Advisory Council on Public Welfare for the U.S. Department of Health, Education, and Welfare.

Stage Four: School of Social Work in Ann Arbor

The new School of Social Work began operating in Ann Arbor in September 1951 in an old frame house at 320 E. Washington Street. With Fedele Fauri as the dean of the new School of Social Work at Michigan, the stage was set for expansion of the student enrollment, from a size of 91 full-time students in the M.S.W. program to 581 students in 1970, becoming the largest school of social work in the United States at that time. Accompanying this enrollment was an increase in the size of the faculty, from eight in 1951 to sixty in 1970. The growth of the size of the faculty was accompanied by a high level of diversity, especially in representation of faculty with doctorates in social work and social science. Thus in the early years of the school, "Fauri recognized the need to form alliances with the social science disciplines" (Vinter & Sarri, 1997), exemplified by his faculty hiring patterns and his leadership in creating a faculty seminar on the Research Basis of Social Welfare (1953–54) and a Coordinating Committee on Social Welfare Research (1955–70).

As the School of Social Work at Michigan opened in Ann Arbor in 1951, it lacked the presence of social scientists on the faculty. Social casework was the dominant social work practice method taught at the school during the period from 1935 to 1951. Courses in this area relied heavily on psychoanalytic theory, with an emphasis on ego psychology. The specialization in social casework was led by Eleanor Cranefield, Clarice Freud, Mary Taylor, Dorothy Schroeder, and Katherine Reebel. The creation of new practice specializations in social group work, community organization, and social welfare administration was accompanied by new courses and course content from the social sciences, especially in the courses on human behavior and the social environment. Early faculty leaders in this curriculum development were Robert Vinter and Edwin J. Thomas.

While group work courses were offered since 1935, a specialization in group work was first offered in 1955. The turning point in the development of social group work at Michigan came in 1954 with the appointment of Robert D. Vinter to the faculty, with further development of the group work program under Rosemary Sarri, Paul Glasser, and Charles Garvin. Community organization and social welfare administration courses were offered since 1935, with specializations offered in these areas in 1950–51 and with their early development under the leadership of Arthur Dunham, Fedele Fauri, Wilbur Cohen, Patricia Rabinovitz, Jack Rothman (1970, 1976), and Rosemary Sarri (1969, 1971). These practice specializations began with small numbers of students, soon to be developed into nationally recognized programs.

Courses supporting all the practice specializations were classified in terms of human growth and behavior, social welfare policy and services, and social research. The infusion of social science knowledge and theory in these areas came through the appointment in the 1950s of faculty from the fields of psychology, social psychology, sociology, and a mix of social work and one of these fields.

PART TWO   The Joint Interdisciplinary Doctoral Program in Social Work and Social Science

The Russell Sage Foundation

The significant role of the Russell Sage Foundation in the establishment of the doctoral program at Michigan is recognized by Professors Vinter and Sarri (1997), who note that Michigan fits the profile of a university that could successfully launch a doctoral program consistent with one of the goals of the Russell Sage Foundation. The foundation was interested in facilitating "the infusion of social science knowledge into professional curricula, including social work." The foundation viewed the University of Michigan as "a major state university with a positive stance toward the public sector; it supported very strong social science departments with distinguished and visionary leaders; its culture was hospitable to ventures that spanned academic divisions and to research that addressed societal conditions and problems."

Development of the Michigan program came about after the chief executive of the Russell Sage Foundation, Donald Young, "persuaded David G. French, a social worker concerned with strengthening services through research, to remain in Michigan as a foundation fellow to pursue prospects with Dean Fauri" (Vinter & Sarri, 1997). David French had carried out an evaluative research study in 1951 at the School of Social Work at Michigan, sponsored by the Michigan Welfare League and the James Foster Foundation. The study findings were published in *An Approach to Measuring Results in Social Work* (French, 1952).

Seminar in Doctoral Education

Under the leadership of Dean Fedele Fauri and David French, a 1953–54 faculty seminar on the Research Basis of Social Welfare was formed at Michigan, involving 18 leading faculty members of social science departments and the School of Social Work. Members from the School of Social Work were Professors Eleanor Cranefield, Arthur Dunham, Fedele F. Fauri, Ralph C. Fletcher, Clarice Freud, David G. French, and Patricia Rabinovitz. Members from the social science departments and other schools were Professors Robert C. Angell (Sociology), Solomon J. Axelrod (Public Health), Kenneth Boulding (Economics), William Haber (Economics), Amos H. Hawley (Sociology), E. Lowell Kelly (Psychology), Werner Landecker (Sociology), Ronald Lippitt (Sociology, Psychology), William Morse (Education), Theodore Newcomb (Social Psychology, Sociology, Psychology), and Josephine Williams (Sociology).

As Vinter and Sarri (1997) have observed, "There was an elegant logic in the strategic intramural alliances being forged by Fauri and French to gain effective collaboration between social work and the social sciences." As Fauri later noted, "In addition to breaking down the barriers to communication between social work and various other disciplines, the seminar fostered interdisciplinary research and established the climate of opinion necessary for planning a more substantial liaison between social science and social work" (Vinter & Sarri, 1997).

The faculty seminar group proposed the creation of a Coordinating Committee on Social Welfare Research in order to pursue interdisciplinary activities. This coordinating committee functioned from 1955 to 1970. "Underlying the alliance was a premise unique to Michigan: Social science and social welfare should be equal partners based on differing but compatible and mutually reinforcing interests" (Vinter & Sarri, 1997). Committee members consisted of Amos Hawley (chair),* Solomon Axelrod, Arthur Bromage,* Eleanor Cranefield, Fedele F. Fauri, Robert S. Ford,* David French, William Haber,* Roger Heyns, Daniel Katz, Morris Janowitz, E. Lowell Kelly, John Lederle, Ronald Lippitt,* James Morgan, and Dorothy Schroeder. (*Denotes members of the original committee, as membership rotated.)

"This committee formulated arrangements by which the interdisciplinary alliance could be continued along two closely connected lines: (1) creation of a Joint Ph.D. Degree Program in Social Work and Social Science, and (2) stimulating research within the school and between it and the disciplines. The Rackham School's executive committee gave formal assent for a joint interdepartmental Ph.D. Program under the direction of a supervising committee appointed by the Rackham Dean. The Russell Sage Foundation also approved the proposals and awarded funding of $250,000 (equivalent to about $1.5 million in current dollars (1997) for five years, hence renewed in 1961 for another five years" (Vinter & Sarri, 1997). Funding for the joint program was also available from federal government sources, notably the U.S. Public Health Service.

The Proposal for a Program of Advanced Training and Research in Social Work and Social Science, submitted to the Russell Sage Foundation in March 1956, included the following statement:

Distinctive Features of the Program in Advanced Training and Research
1. A Ph.D. Program leading to a joint doctoral degree in social work and in one social science—a single, combined theory and research degree, not a two degree track—with provision for students to obtain the M.S.W. degree if not already possessed;
2. A curriculum providing advanced studies sufficient to meet the basic knowledge and skill requirements of both the profession and the respective discipline (theoretical courses, research methods and supervised training, preliminary exams, and a dissertation relevant to both social work and the discipline), including development of new advanced seminars in social work/social welfare with attention to the integration of such knowledge;
3. A degree program focused on knowledge development and utilization, to equip persons specifically for the task of bringing together the resources and approaches of social science and social work for research, teaching, and practice (not on traditional professional skills except as embodied in prior M.S.W. studies);
4. A location that firmly embedded the Program and its associated activities within the University's structures: administration with all other Ph.D. programs by the Rackham School of Graduate Studies; continuation of the interdepartmental Coordinating Committee on Social Welfare Research to foster ongoing inter-unit collaborative endeavors; and creation of a Joint Program Supervising Committee with faculty representatives from social work and social science departments to oversee admissions, degree requirements, curriculum, and student progress (and formation of a School Doctoral Faculty group); with professional and support staffing for the Program and for the Coordinating and Supervising Committees;
5. Complementary provisions and resources for stimulating and facilitating research and other knowledge development initiatives focused on problems relevant to the profession and field, and to the disciplines (largely through the Coordinating Committee)—i.e., interdisciplinary faculty seminars, research seed funding, faculty released time, student fellowships

and new faculty joint appointments between social work and each of the participating social science departments;

6. A commitment of phased-in University funding to assume full costs to the Program as Foundation grants were spent down, and the School's assurances of procuring other outside support and recruiting more faculty with social science credentials;

7. Pledges to extend social science knowledge and theory into the M.S.W. professional social work curriculum.

Administration of the Program

The strength and uniqueness of the program has been maintained through the years by the leadership of professors in the School of Social Work known as "program heads." Dean Fauri appointed Henry J. Meyer as the first head of the program. Meyer held a joint appointment in sociology and social work. Deans of the school during the years of the doctoral program responsible for appointing the program head have been Fedele F. Fauri, 1951–70; Robert Vinter (acting), 1970–71; Phillip Fellin, 1971–81; Harold R. Johnson, 1981–93; Paula Allen-Meares, 1993–2008; John Tropman (interim), 2008; Laura Lein, 2009–present. The following professors have served as doctoral program heads over the past fifty years:

Henry Meyer, 1957–70
Rosemary Sarri, 1970–77
Yeheskel Hasenfeld, 1977–78
John Tropman, 1978–80
Norma Radin, 1980–82
Sheila Feld, 1982–89
Charles Garvin, 1989–96
Ruth Dunkle, 1996–2001
David Tucker, 2001–05
Lorraine Gutiérrez, 2005–present

The Supervising Committee

The members of the first Supervising Committee of the Joint Doctoral Program, 1956–57, were Morris Janowitz, chair, Sociology; Eleanor G. Cranefield, Social Work; William Haber, Economics; Daniel R. Miller, Psychology; Robert D. Vinter, Social Work; David G. French, Social Work, secretary. A School of Social Work Doctoral Committee was also established at this time, headed by the doctoral program head, with members from the social work faculty. Beginning in 1971, doctoral students were represented on the committee. The students in the doctoral program have their own doctoral student organization.

Members of the Supervising Committee, 2006–07
Ann Lin, Political Science, chair
Lorraine Gutiérrez, Social Work
Julia Paley, Anthropology and Social Work
John Bound, Economics
Kai Cortina, Psychology
Berit Ingersoll-Dayton, Social Work
Rene Anspach, Sociology
Amanda Toler, Doctoral Student Organization
Huei-Wern Shen, Doctoral Student Organization

School of Social Work Doctoral Committee, 2006–07
Lorraine Gutiérrez, chair
Barry Checkoway
Berit Ingersoll-Dayton
Trina Shanks
John Tropman

Description of the Joint Doctoral Program: 1957–58

The doctoral program began with the offering of joint Ph.D. degrees in social work and three social sciences: economics, psychology, and sociology. In 1966 political science was added, and in 1981, anthropology. The 1957–58 *School Bulletin* announced the new Joint Doctoral Program in Social Work and Social Science as follows:

> Beginning in September 1957, the School will co-operate with the Horace H. Rackham School of Graduate Studies in offering a program of study in social work and a related social science leading to the Doctor of Philosophy degree. The program will be administered by a supervising committee drawn from the faculties of the School of Social Work and the Departments of Economics, Psychology, and Sociology. As an interdepartmental degree program, it is designed to enable the student to pursue a course of study which cuts across the subject-matter areas represented in the School of Social Work and the social science departments of the University. The doctoral program is directed toward meeting the need for a more effective relationship between the social sciences and the field of social work. The doctoral program is closely integrated with a research program under the

general oversight of the Coordinating Committee on Social Welfare Research of the Social Science Division of the University. Both the doctoral program and the research activities of the Coordinating Committee have been made possible by a generous grant from the Russell Sage Foundation. (*School of Social Work Bulletin,* 1957–58)

Characteristics of the Doctoral Program in Social Work and Social Science are further described in a special section of the 1957–58 *School Bulletin.*

Admission Requirements. A student seeking admission to the Doctoral Program in Social Work and Social Science must meet the admission requirements of the School of Social Work and the Horace H. Rackham School of Graduate studies. In addition, he must have fulfilled the prerequisites established for doctoral study in the social science department in which he intends to take his work.

Program of Study. The program of study leading to the doctorate provides for substantial work in advanced theory and research in one social science; advanced courses and seminars in the area of social work in which the student wishes to specialize; and a year of seminars and supervised research in collaborative work between social science and social work practice. The student may plan a program of study around one of the methods of social work practice or one of the areas of social service.

The Supervising Committee for the Doctoral Program in Social Work and Social Science has general supervision of the student's academic program. After it has recommended the student for admission, it will appoint a preliminary committee to review and approve the student's program of study and to determine the areas in which he will be expected to take preliminary examinations. Upon completion of the preliminary examinations and language and other requirements, the Supervising Committee will recommend the student for candidacy for the doctoral degree and nominate to the Dean of the Horace H. Rackham School of Graduate Studies members of a doctoral committee for the student. The doctoral committee is responsible for approving the student's dissertation subject, supervising his research, conducting the student's oral examination on the dissertation, and recommending him for the degree.

Requirements for the Doctor of Philosophy Degree in Social Work and Social Science. The general requirements of the Horace H. Rackham

School of Graduate Studies for the Doctor of Philosophy degree with respect to residence, grade-point average, time limit for completion of work, dissertation, and proficiency in two foreign languages must be met (a group of graduate courses totaling nine credit hours may be substituted for one foreign language).

All students must have completed, or must complete during the course of their doctoral study, the requirements for the Master of Social Work degree. Four preliminary examinations must be passed satisfactorily: one major and one minor examination in the social science in which the student is specializing; one in the student's field of specialization in social work; and one in the integration of social science and social work theory. A fifth preliminary examination in research methods is optional. A substitute for this examination is satisfactory completion of the research methods courses prescribed by the social science department in which the student is taking his major.

A dissertation is required as a demonstration of the candidate's ability to investigate a problem in social work through utilizing, and where possible contributing to, theory and research method in the social science in which the student has specialized.

In addition to this interdepartmental program that led to the Ph.D. degree in social work and a social science, a second type of advanced study was available. This was a program of study in one area of social work, which doctoral students in a social science department could elect as a minor field.

Students in the Joint Doctoral Program completed most of their course work in the social science department related to their joint degree, including sociology, psychology, economics, and political science. Students entering the program without the M.S.W. degree were able to take master's degree courses in the School of Social Work, along with selected courses in a social science department. Students with an M.S.W. enrolled in doctoral-level courses in the School of Social Work. Courses offered at the beginning of the program, with instructors listed, were:

Seminar on the Integration of Social Work and Social Science (Henry Meyer)

Social Welfare Policy I and II (Wilbur Cohen, Fedele Fauri, Henry Meyer)

Directed Reading and Research in Social Work and Social Science (Faculty)

Organizational Factors in Treatment Programs (Robert Vinter)

In the first few years of the program, additional doctoral courses were offered by social work faculty:

Seminar on Theoretical Foundations of Casework and Group Work (Mary Burns)

Seminar on Community Cohesion, Social Change, and Local Welfare (Eugene Litwak)

Processes of Interpersonal Influence (Edwin Thomas)

Practice Principles of Casework and Group Work (Mary Burns, Paul Glasser, Jesse Gordon)

Theories and Issues in Community Organization Practice (Jack Rothman)

Empirical Bases of Clinical Practice (Jesse Gordon)

Socio-Behavioral Theory and Interpersonal Helping (Edwin Thomas)

Organizational Factors in Treatment Programs (Rosemary Sarri, Robert Vinter)

Social Welfare Policy (Philip Booth)

Research Designs in Human Service Organizations (Faculty)

Problems in the Economics of Social Services (William Neenan)

Seminars on the Integration of Social Work and Social Science

Full program fees in 1957–58 for the doctoral program complied with the Graduate School fees of $125 for Michigan residents and $300 for nonresidents, per semester. These fees entitled the student to the privileges of the Health Service, Michigan Union or Michigan League, admission to athletic events, and physical education.

Socio/Behavioral Science in the M.S.W. Program

At Michigan the extension of social science knowledge and theory in the professional social work curriculum came about through the addition of new faculty in the 1950s from the fields of psychology, social psychology, and sociology. As Vinter and Sarri (1997) have noted: "Early in this period the school recruited some faculty with both M.S.W. and Social Science Ph.D. degrees; they were called 'hybrids' and shared the dual orientations of the doctoral students. The first of these were Robert D. Vinter (1954) and Edwin J. Thomas (1956). Social scientists without the M.S.W. who were committed to collaboration between the sciences and the profession and to the aims of the joint program were soon also successfully recruited," including Henry J. Meyer and Eugene Litwak. These faculty members taught in both doctoral and master's programs and engaged in research studies.

"During 1958–1970 persons with doctorates explicitly appointed to contribute to the integration of social science within the curriculum, to conduct research, and to qualify for teaching in the doctoral program included, in order of appointment: Paul Glasser, Eugene Litwak, William Neenan (joint with Economics), Rosemary Sarri, Jack Rothman, Phillip Fellin, Charles Garvin, Sheldon Rose, Richard Stuart, John Tropman, Yeheskel Hasenfeld, Tony Tripodi, Thomas Anton, Richard English, Eileen Gambrill, Irwin Epstein, Sheila Feld, Martin Sundel, David Himle, and Norma Radin" (Vinter & Sarri, 1997). Also teaching social science-based courses in the school were faculty from other units of the university, and students were able to take cognate courses in other departments.

An important influence of the early social work/social science faculty was related to changes in the M.S.W. curriculum, cited in "Social Work and Social Welfare" (Meyer, Litwak, Thomas, & Vinter, 1967). By 1965 the faculty began "the process of restructuring the M.S.W. curriculum largely around the organization of knowledge bases that were fundamental to those of the doctoral program." This led to an M.S.W. curriculum framework in 1967 that "explicitly recognized the program's levels of social organization (interpersonal, group and family; organizational; community; and societal)" (Vinter & Sarri, 1997).

> Up to this time, one of the original goals of the Joint Doctoral Program, infusion of social science knowledge and theory into the M.S.W. professional social work curriculum, was the most difficult to advance. Faculty members with both social work and social science credentials first sought to introduce supplementary content on social organization and processes into the traditional four terms of required courses in Human Growth and Behavior, without success. But because a social group work specialization had been authorized in the late 1950s, the faculty became willing to approve two new Human Behavior in the Social Environment courses that drew directly on knowledge mainly from social psychology and sociology, Group Process and Social Organization I and II, to be taken by group work and community organization students in addition to all existing requirements. (Vinter & Sarri, 1997)

At the same time, the traditional practice specializations were strengthened with an increased use of social/behavioral science knowledge by all faculty.

The Idea of Integration and Research Studies

In their insightful discussion of the Michigan doctoral program, Vinter and Sarri (1997) provide a useful chart that displays the doctoral program in context: on the one hand, the social welfare field and the social work profession, and on the other, social science disciplines and social science in society, both operating within the overarching societal context (demographic/economic/political). The origins, founding, and early development of the program are examined within this context.

These elements of context are similar to those used by Thomas (1997) to focus on the idea of "integration" vis-à-vis social work/welfare and social science. Thomas established an Integration Triangle for analyzing problems relating to the integration of social work/welfare and social science: that is, social science (methods, theories, research findings methods), social work and social welfare (policy, administration, services, practice), and social context (social factors, cultural factors, economic factors, political factors, environmental factors, values, and ideology). Thomas also identified various models of integration of social science and social work/welfare: research utilization, social research, action research, developmental research, sociopolitical change, empirical practice, ecological analysis, and education.

In the early years of the Joint Doctoral Program, professors teaching doctoral program courses were actively involved in the conduct of research using social science methods to study social welfare and social work practice issues. Examples follow:

- Professor Edwin J. Thomas and colleagues carried out an experiment in the Michigan Department of Social Services using role theory to focus on staff training, with the findings represented in Edwin J. Thomas, D. McLeod, and colleagues' *In-Service Training and Reduced Workload: Experiments in the State Welfare Department* (1968). Thomas established the foundation for the development of socio-behavioral theory for social work practice in a number of publications, including "Selecting Knowledge from Behavioral Science" in *Building Social Work Knowledge: Report of a Conference* (1964).
- Professor Thomas organized a set of presentations for the Annual Program Meeting of the CSWE, hence published as *The Socio-Behavioral Approach and Applications to Social Work* (1967). Nine faculty members contributed to this publication, including Professors Thomas, Richard Stuart, Sheldon Rose, Roger Lind, Phillip Fellin,

Jack Rothman, and Henry J. Meyer. In 1967 Professor Thomas edited *Behavioral Science for Social Workers,* in which all thirty-three contributions involved at least one faculty member at the University of Michigan School of Social Work. This volume included discussions of research that allowed for the infusion of social science into the social work curriculum.

- Professor Eugene Litwak was principal investigator in a number of research projects at the School, including:

  —Detroit Area Study: A Study of Family–School Relationships in Detroit, Inter-university Consortium for Political and Social Research (1963).

  —School, Family, and Neighborhood: The Theory and Practice of School–Community Relations (with H. J. Meyer, 1974).

- Professors Robert Vinter and Rosemary Sarri were co-directors of several research projects during this period, most notably the National Assessment of Juvenile Corrections. Publications by Vinter and Sarri and others include books such as *Brought to Justice?* (1976) by Sarri and Hasenfeld; *Organization for Treatment* (1966) by Street, Vinter, and Perrow; *A Comparative Study of Juvenile Correctional Institutions* (1962) by Vinter and M. Janowitz; and *Time Out: A National Study of Juvenile Correctional Programs* (1976) by Vinter, Sarri, Newcomb, and Kish (eds.).

- Professor Paul Glasser was active in advising doctoral students and involving them in his research on social group work and family. Examples of this are *Families in Crisis* (ed. with L. Glasser, 1970), including chapters by Professors Paul Glasser, Norma Radin, Fedele Fauri, Richard Stuart, and Edwin J. Thomas; and Paul Glasser, Rosemary Sarri, and Robert Vinter's *Individual Change Through Small Groups* (1974).

- Professor Henry Meyer's involvement in research projects and publications demonstrated his interest in the relationship of social work and social science, including "Professionalization and Social Work" (1959), "Profession of Social Work: Contemporary Characteristics" in the *Encyclopedia of Social Work* (1971), and H. Meyer, E. Litwak, E. Thomas, and R. Vinter's "Social Work and Social Welfare" (1967). This relationship was also described in the *Social Work Education Reporter* by Professor Mary Burns in "Social Science Content in Doctoral Programs" (1965).

Curriculum Development and Changes

A review of curriculum changes in the social work doctoral curriculum is provided by Vinter and Sarri (1997).

> Curriculum change in the 1970s appears to have been more significant in the social sciences than in social work. The minutes of the program's supervising committee reflect the increasing departmental interests in assuring that the joint program students met all of the disciplines' curricular requirements. The shift also reflected a growing emphasis on acquiring very sophisticated competence in research methodology and statistics, especially in economics, political science, and sociology. A major strength in the program has been its rigorous training in research methods. . . . In response to the interests of some students and faculty, the program committee in the 1970s developed and refined a "utilization" internship as an alternative research internship. This was explicitly directed toward developing skills in the utilization of social science knowledge in social work practice.

The April 1971 minutes of the Doctoral Program Committee note: "The purpose of the research internship is to provide supervised study and training, through participation in an on-going research project, that adds to the student's research skills and serves to prepare him more fully for his career objectives."

During 1974–76 major revisions were made in the social work components of the doctoral curriculum. The new framework emphasized foundation courses and foci on specific social problems and on change theories and actions. The curriculum became focused on five components:

> Foundation courses that dealt with individuals, groups, organizations, and society. These were designed to provide students with social science knowledge at the several levels of intervention, but they differed from regular/typical discipline courses because the focus was on social welfare and social work issues.
>
> Social change theory courses were developed for each of the four levels of intervention and were often broader in focus than intervention theory courses.
>
> Social problem areas were selected by the faculty and students for emphasis; these changed depending upon student interest and faculty resources.

Each student was expected to develop special competence in one social problem area.

Knowledge specifically related to integration of social science knowledge and social work practice in social welfare was promoted through special seminars and individual studies.

Advanced seminars were offered on specific timely issues to help to integrate foundation, social problem, and change theory knowledge. These often included social science students and faculty from other departments. With some minor modifications, this curriculum plan/design remained in place until the early 1980s. (Vinter & Sarri, 1997)

The curriculum was modified in 1983 and 1987, and the principles and structure from those changes continue to guide the program, as described in the 2007 curriculum design. The major change came about through the inclusion into the social work course component of four areas: (1) practice, intervention, and policy; (2) social service systems; (3) the social context for practice and policy; and (4) research methods for policy and practice. Curriculum changes from the 1990s to the present are recorded in the school's doctoral program committee minutes, with the final version presented in the current edition of the program guidelines.

The 2007 Curriculum

The basic framework for the current curriculum was established in 1987, with the present curriculum goals and structure specified in the *August 2006 Guidelines to Requirements for Doctoral Study in Social Work and Social Science,* as follows:

1. Basic Assumptions and Principles: Knowledge generation and knowledge transmission is a central focus for the Program and the major basis upon which the Doctoral Program Curriculum is organized. Related to this is a commitment to retain and enhance the unique character of the Doctoral Program, namely, its emphasis on the articulation of social work and social science. The social work component of the program is based on the following principles and assumptions.
   a. Articulation of social work and social science.
   b. Emphasis on knowledge development.
   c. The central role of knowledge development and research related to intervention methods and social service systems.
   d. Recognition of ethical and value issues and commitments relevant to social work and social welfare.
   e. Flexibility in the curriculum to adapt to new developments.

    f. Opportunity for original, specialized study.

2. Curriculum Structure: Four curriculum areas for the social work component of the program include (1) Practice, Intervention, and Policy; (2) Social Service Systems; (3) Research Methods for Practice and Policy; (4) The Social Context for Practice and Policy. Course requirements include a proseminar plus at least five doctoral courses in social work.

3. The Social Work Specialization. Each student will have a specialization in social work that bears a significant and substantial relationship to the curriculum areas of either Practice, Prevention and Policy, or Social Service Systems.

4. The Research Internship. A unique feature of the doctoral program has been to provide a knowledge development orientation to students early in their careers. This is enhanced by the research internship, which has these specific goals: (1) to provide a complete research experience through participation in a supervised research project prior to the dissertation; (2) to involve students in doing research early in their doctoral studies; (3) to increase students' research skills; and (4) to develop skills in writing for publication.

5. The Social Work Preliminary Examination. The purpose of this examination is to enable the student to demonstrate mastery of knowledge in an individualized area of subject matter, including specialization areas.

6. Practicum on Teaching Social Work Methods

7. Doctoral Social Work Practice Internship

Social science requirements are specified in the current *Guidelines*. Over thirty doctoral courses in social work are described in the *Guidelines*.

Characteristics of Doctoral Students and Graduates

Complete data are available in the Doctoral Office on the names of graduates, year of graduation, social science discipline, gender, and dissertation titles. The doctoral program's first entering class consisted of Phillip Fellin, Warren Haggstrom, Lydia Hylton, Roger Lind, Rosemary Conzemius Sarri, and Jean Shores. This document gives a summary of graduates from 1957 to 2008 in terms of gender and social science discipline.

Summary of Graduates by Social Science Discipline

Sociology	(134)	38%
Psychology	(173)	49%
Political Science	(26)	7%
Economics	(9)	3%
Anthropology	(14)	4%
Total	(356)	100%

Graduates by Social Science Discipline by Time Periods

Discipline	1957–70	1971–80	1981–90	1991–00	2000–08
Sociology	49%	45%	34%	31%	33%
Psychology	43%	44%	56%	53%	39%
Political Science	3%	10%	6%	5%	11%
Economics	5%	1%	3%	3%	8%
Anthropology	-	-	1%	8%	9%
N: (356)	(37)	(84)	(88)	(75)	(72)

From 1957 through 1980, the highest percent of graduates were in the social work–sociology program, followed closely by social work–psychology graduates. From 1981 onwards, graduates in psychology had the highest percentage. Graduates in political science ranged from 3% to 12%, economics from 1% to 5%, with anthropology graduates increasing from 1% to 9%.

Summary of Graduates by Gender

Years	Female	Male	Total
1957–1970	30%	70%	37
1971–1980	46%	54%	84
1981–1990	53%	47%	88
1991–2000	65%	35%	75
2001–2008	69%	31%	72
Total	55% (196)	45% (160)	356

Employment of Graduates

From the beginning of the program through 1990, Vinter and Sarri (1997) have observed, "The joint program has thrived and grown extensively. It is recognized nationally and internationally as a leader in the training of social work educators and researchers. Graduates of the joint program now occupy many important leadership roles in the academic and policy community in the United States and internationally. A large number serve as deans or directors of social work programs; many are distinguished scholars whose research and publications have had significant impact upon social work education or in their discipline; and several occupy important policy positions at the federal and state levels." Prominent among graduates in academic settings is Richard A. English, who served as provost of

Howard University and who received the University of Michigan's Alumni Association's 2005 Distinguished Alumni Service Award.

Studies by Hasenfeld and Leon (1979), Jayaratne (1979), Radin, Benbenisky, and Leon (1982), Radin (1983), Thyer and Bentley (1986), Garvin (1994), and Tucker (2004) provide information on the program's graduates. The most recent study by Tucker (2004) involved a survey of 134 graduates, with the finding that over 80 percent were currently employed in university settings. At the present time, thirteen faculty members at the school are graduates of the Michigan program: Letha Chadiha, Kathleen Coulborn Faller, Larry Gant, Lorraine Gutiérrez, Joseph Himle, Berit Ingersoll-Dayton, Srinika Jayaratne, Robert Ortega, Daphna Oyserman, Robert Joseph Taylor, John E. Tropman, Diane Vinokur, and Bradley Zebrack.

Program Evaluation

At the call of the vice president of academic affairs in 1979, an external review of the programs of the School of Social Work was conducted by a team composed of Professors June Hopps, Shanti Khinduka, William Reid, and Eleanor Sheldon. The evaluation team noted: "The School of Social Work enjoys a well deserved eminence and prestige in the profession. . . . The social work–social science Ph.D. program can take legitimate credit for training some of the more productive researchers in social work in the United States" (External Review, 1979).

In 1994–95 an internal review of the doctoral program was conducted by the Rackham School of Graduate Studies in cooperation with the Joint Doctoral Program and the School of Social Work. This review team was led by John D'Arms, vice provost for academic affairs and dean of the Graduate School, along with Elaine Didier, Jacquelynne Eccles, Machree Robinson, Homer Rose, Robert Weisbuch, and Warren Whatley. This team made its report to Professor Charles Garvin, director of the doctoral program, on February 3, 1995. According to Tucker (2004), the findings of this report "strongly affirmed the value of the program to the university but also pointed to the need for improvements in long standing areas of concern such as a low sense of community among students, inadequate student funding, and the need to improve the intellectual integration of social work and social science."

In preparation for an external review of the doctoral program in 2005, David Tucker, as head of the Joint Doctoral Program, prepared a Report of the Interdepartmental Program in Social Work and Social Science in 2004, on behalf of an internal review committee composed of Tucker (Social Work), John Campbell (Political Science), Lorraine Gutiérrez (Social Work,

Psychology), Larry Hirschfeld (Anthropology, Psychology), Karin Martin (Sociology), Scott Paris (Psychology), and David Sommerfeld (doctoral student), and assisted by Bowen McBeath (doctoral student), Fatma Gocek (Sociology), and Arnold Sammeroff (Psychology).

Volume II of the internal committee report includes observations by allied departments, the student organization, and School of Social Work faculty. Tucker notes in this volume that the contributions from these groups "affirm the overall nature of the Joint Program as fluid and dynamic, capable of acknowledging and working with the inevitable differences, tensions, uncertainties and opportunities generated by the complexities of its structure, relationships and context. In the view of the internal review committee, it is this fluid and dynamic nature that has enabled the Program to persist in, and adapt to its challenging and changing internal and external environments while at the same time promoting and achieving excellence in interdisciplinary scholarship and research."

This report was provided to an external review committee formed by the Rackham School to review the doctoral program. The members of this external review committee were:

> Greg J. Duncan, Institute for Policy Research and School of Education, Northwestern University
> Hazel Rose Markus, Department of Psychology, Stanford University
> Martha N. Ozawa, George Warren Brown School of Social Work, Washington University
> Richard P. Taub, The Committee on Human Development and the Department of Sociology, University of Chicago

The *Report of the External Review Committee* in 2005, provided after an on-campus site visit, included the following observations:

> Our committee was asked to conduct an external review of the Joint Program in Social Work and Social Science. Specifically, our charge was to evaluate the program's academic reputation and contributions, assess whether the program's structure is appropriate to meet its long-term goals, determine whether the curriculum prepares students for their chosen careers, discover how current and former students evaluate their graduate experience, determine whether the program's resources are appropriate for the scale and quality of the program, assess the organization of the program, and identify areas of concern that prevent the program from achieving future goals.

The Joint Program in Social Work and Social Science has been a crown jewel of interdisciplinary doctoral training for the University of Michigan for nearly 50 years. It is a key reason for the School of Social Work's current number one ranking. Through their scholarship, teaching, and academic administration, the program's graduates have played key roles in injecting and maintaining academic rigor within schools of social work.

The multidisciplinary structure and quality of the Joint Program reflect well on Rackham's ability to innovate and sustain a unique and highly productive doctoral program that involves a complicated amalgam of a graduate school, an arts and sciences college, and a professional school. (Duncan et al., 2005)

Challenges for the program are identified in the evaluation, leading to a number of committee recommendations, including:

- Fostering of the "jointness" of the Joint Doctoral Program
- Expansion of the efforts to recruit joint program students
- Review and upgrade of core and optional courses in the curriculum
- Faculty development and deployment

In conclusion, the evaluation team noted:

We are impressed by the fine record of this program and the commitment of students, alumni, and faculty to it. We realize that it is difficult to focus effort on it when the number of students in the program is so small compared to the large number of MSW students for whom a solid professional program must be delivered. But the Ph.D. program is, in many ways, a flagship for the entire school and has the potential to be an important source of vitality as it bridges the world of practice and the world of theory and research in the social sciences. Greater effort relating to that world, raising the quality and intensity of the social work part of the program, so it is more a coequal of the elements of the social science degrees, and the broadening recruitment of students and faculty, would go a long way to help the program maintain its preeminence. (Duncan et al., 2005)

Readings on the Establishment of the Doctoral Program
The School's Joint Doctoral Program in Social Work and Social Science was established in 1957, with the program's Ph.D. degree granted through the Horace H. Rackham School of Graduate Studies. Accounts of the development of the doctoral program are presented in an edited volume by

David Tucker, Charles Garvin, and Rosemary Sarri, *Integrating Knowledge and Practice: The Case of Social Work and Social Science* (1997). This volume includes the following topics:

  I. Promises and Problems: Progress and Problems in the Integration of Knowledge and Practice
 II. Social Science to Social Work: How Social Science Contributes to Social Work
III. Social Work to Social Science: Social Work Perspectives on the Integration of Social Work and Social Science
 IV. Themes and Perspectives on Integration and Related Models
  V. A History of Educational Integration in One Program

Contributors from the faculty of the school, including the editors, are Lorraine Gutiérrez, Diane Vinokur-Kaplan, Armand Lauffer, Robert Vinter, and Edwin J. Thomas, along with graduates of the doctoral program at other schools, Eileen Gambrill, Aaron M. Brower, Paula S. Nurius, Susan Lambert, and John F. Longres.

Of special historical interest in the volume are chapters by Robert Vinter and Rosemary Sarri, "Doctoral Education in Social Work and Social Science at Michigan"; Edwin J. Thomas, "Themes and Perspectives on Integration and Related Models"; and Eileen Gambrill, "Making Decisions About Integration." Additional historical accounts of the program can be found in Fellin (2003), *Social Work Education at Michigan;* Tucker (2004), *Self-Study Report of the Interdepartmental Program in Social Work and Social Science;* Duncan et al. (2005), *Report of the External Review Committee for the Joint Program in Social Work and Social Science; School of Social Work Bulletins; School of Social Work* (2006), *Guidelines to Requirements for Doctoral Study in Social Work and Social Science.* These chapters and reports, as is the case of my document, do not represent an "official" school chronicle of the doctoral program.

25th Anniversary of the Doctoral Program
The school celebrated the 25th anniversary of the Joint Doctoral Program in Social Work and Social Science with a special colloquium on May 27–28, 1982. Presentations for the colloquium were compiled by Dean Harold Johnson and Professor John Tropman into a special volume, *Social Work Policy and Practice* (1986). This volume was dedicated to Professor Henry J. Meyer, first head of the doctoral program, and included the following papers, all by graduates of the program.

Social Work Policy and Practice
   I. Research and Practice: Aaron Rosen, Jeanne Marsh
   II. Societal Perspectives: John Longres, C. Aaron McNeece, Lynne Morris
   III. Policy Perspectives: Irvin Garfinkel, John Tropman, Jeannette Jennings
   IV. Community-Based Services and Informal Networks: Jeffrey David-son, Betty Jones, Julianne Oktay
   V. Organizational Perspectives: Michael Sherraden, Suzanne Rinaldo, William Hutchison
   VI. Minority and Gender Concerns: Lawrence Gary, Diane Kravitz, Diane Pearce
   VII. Methodological Advances: Jerry Cates, Bogart Leashore, Martin Sundel, Bruce Thyer

Colloquium program notes included "Reflections on the History of the Program" by Phillip Fellin, first doctoral program graduate, and "The Celebration of Twenty-Five Years" by Henry J. Meyer, the first program head. At the celebration Dean Harold Johnson noted, "This Program represents the first, and most successful, attempt by a University to systematically combine social work knowledge and values with social science theories and research methods in an advanced education program."

Dean Alfred S. Sussman of the Horace H. Rackham School of Graduate Studies stated: "This celebration of the venerable nature of Michigan's Program in Social Work and Social Science should not conceal its continuing uniqueness and modernity. Thus, despite its age, this program remains alone in effecting the convergence of a free-standing School of Social Work and the autonomous departments of Psychology, Sociology, Political Science, Economics, and Anthropology upon the education of students who, for the most part, contribute to social work theory and practice. Its modernity and credibility are assured by the maintenance of the dynamic tension between the disciplinary and professional approaches." Professor Henry J. Meyer concluded the 25th anniversary celebration by asking, "Is the past prologue? Does the interplay of social science and social practice in the thinking and teaching of graduates still represent a viable objective? Are the training and standards reflected in the Joint Doctoral Program worthy of the years to come? The answer rests with the graduates, their students, and their successors in the Program who celebrate and who are celebrated by this anniversary."

50th Anniversary: Solving Problems in Society—People and Ideas
In celebration of the 50th year of the doctoral program, the school sponsored a conference on October 11–12, 2007, with the following events.

Keynote Speaker: Frances Fox Piven, Distinguished Professor of Sociology & Political Science, City University of New York, and president, American Sociological Association

Concurrent Panels with Joint Program Alumni:
- Identifying the Interactions of Structural, Cultural, and Individual Determinants of Social Issues
- Using Policy to Create Effective Cross-System Public Mental Health and Substance Abuse Service Networks
- Scholarship on Aging
- Applied Social Science to Address Social Issues

Luncheon Speaker: Patricia Gurin, Nancy Cantor Distinguished University Professor Emerita, Psychology and Women's Studies, University of Michigan

Concurrent Panels
- The Development of Evidence-Based Practice
- Roundtable on Mixed Methods Research
- Perspectives from Social Work History
- Global and International Perspectives on Social Work and Social Welfare

Closing Plenary Session: The Future of Social Work and Social Work Education

Doctoral Program Graduates: 1957–2008

1962
Phillip A. Fellin (February 1962), Warren C. Haggstrom (June 1962), Rosemary Conzemius Sarri (June 1962)

1963
Roger Murray Lind, Ruth Rittenhouse Morris, Maeda Galinsky, Mukhtar Malik, Aaron Rosen, Marvin Silverman

1965
Eileen Gambrill, Arnold Gurin

1966
Ronald Feldman, C. David Hollister

1967
John E. Tropman, Darrel J. Vorwaller

1968
Clayton T. Shorkey, Shimon E. Spiro, Martin Sundel, Marcia Bok, Shirley Terreberry

1969
Victor L. Schneider, Robert D. Carter, Norma L. Radin, Edward Lowenstein

1970
Lawrence E. Gary, William H. Butterfield, Irwin Garfinkel, Yeheskel Hasenfeld, David P. Himle, Ray H. MacNair, Richard A. English, Dorothy Chave Herberg, David Katz, Diane Kravetz, John F. Longres, Esther Goodman Sales, Carolyn Barnard Pryor

1971
Josefina Figueira McDonough, Lawrence H. Boyd, Carmi Bar-Ilan, James A. Ajemian, Martha Noble Gizynski, Robert S. Keller

1972
David H. Knoke, Arthur J. Frankel, Judith H. Braver, Michael E. Hayes, Josef Katan, Gary R. Hamilton, Edward J. Pawlak, William Joseph Hutchison

1973
Benjamin H. Gottlieb, Julianne S. Oktay

1974
Sheldon Siegel, Kyu-Taik Sung, Kevin W. O'Flaherty, John L. Musick, Jr., Barbara N. McMillian Carter, Diane Ehrenstaft, Nancy R. Hooyman, Stephen F. Burghardt, Rona L. Levy

1975
Claire Lanham, Diane Vinokur, Shirley Vining Brown, Barbara Felton, Srinika Jayaratne, Jeanne Cay Marsh

1976
Prudence Brown, George Downs, Jr., John Louis Ford, Carl Aaron McNeece, Margaret A. Rust, Matthew Black, Michael Joseph Gorodezky, Joyce R. Borkin, Phyllis Day, Fredrick Gutierrez, Lynne Morris, Saeko Murayana, Diana Pearce, Abraham Sagi, Seyoum Selassie, John Spores

1977

Stephen Aigner, Jeffrey Davidson, Harry Finkelstein Keshet, Michael Sosin, Ann Carolyn Woods, Albert E. Benjamin, Jr., Joan P. Bowker, Larry Earl Davis, Beryl Ann Schulman, David Shapiro, Peter Bernard Vaughan, Mark Creekmore, Margaret Olene Nielsen, Helen Rytz, John Anthony Slosar, Mark Krell

1978

Mary Mitchell Hinchman, Alfreda Paulette Iglehart, Roberta Turner

1979

Josephine Allen, Richard Ketterer, Karen Kirkhart, Bogart Raymond Leashore, Lambert Maguire, Elaine Ruth Selo, Sandra Paulette Stokes, Catherine Ann Faver, Michael Wayne Sherraden

1980

Bernard Joseph O'Connell, Eugene Joseph D'Angelo, Clairborne Moore, Barbara Carol Bader, Bonnie Elise Carlson, John Elvin Ferguson, Jeanette Jennings, Susan Murray Partridge, Virginia Elizabeth Richardson

1981

Jerry Ray Cates, Betty Brown Jones, Roger Manela, Suzanne Gelber Rinaldo, Helen Ruth Weingarten, Rami Benbenishty, Ronald Evan Lemley-Masa, Kathleen M. L. Coulborn Faller, Alan Lawrence Gordon, Barton Francis Grossman

1982

Roland Etcheverry, David Guzman, Ingrid Kuhl Martin, Kathleen Pottick, Adnan Abd el Razek, Alfreida Daly, Wendy Wintermute, Berit Ingersoll, Thomas Regulus, Constance Saltz, Bruce Thyer

1983

Robert Taylor, Joel Leon, Paul Cheung, Jeremiah Cotton, Marcia Bombyk, Gary Miller, Moshe Spero

1984

Jose Eli Fresquez, Rosemary Holland, Rebecca Schilit, Chrystal Mills, Paula Nurius, Dianne Dailey, David Demetral, John Woods, Deborah Zinn

1985
Jon Matsuoka, Suzanne Model, Elizabeth Ozanne, H. Roy Partridge, William Barton, Jacques Boulet, Andrea Savage-Abramovitz, Eileen Trzcinski, Aaron Brower, Marylou Davis-Sacks

1986
Larry Maurice Gant, Cathleen Ann Santa, Jacqueline Smith, Joanne Turnbull, Emma Gross, Denise Bronson, Cynthia Loveland Cook, Rena Harold, Andrew Safyer

1987
Audrey Begun, Julie Jaffee Nagel, Dorothy Feeman, Amy Butler, Susan Lambert, Daphna Oyserman, Jay Rathburn

1988
Jon Sager, Harry Cohen, Fred Groskind, Karen Kersten, Joanne Yaffe

1989
Carol Russell, Injeong Lee, Raoul Betancourt, Victor Burke, Letha Chadiha, Henry D'Souza, Lorraine Gutiérrez, Richard Hoefer

1990
Pauline Collins, Elizabeth Robinson, Alfred Winn, Faye Yvonne Abram, Gregory Paul Acs, Roger Simpson, Ann Rosegrant Alvarez, Erica Bell-Lowther, Karin Ann Elliott, Ritsuko Green, Pau-Ching Lu, Manorama Venkatraman

1991
Richard Ager, Elizabeth Chapleski, Cheryl Hyde, Robert Ortega, Janet Shapiro

1992
Jeffrey Butts, Enos Greer Massie, Leslie Sackett, Donna Cochran, Marvella Ford, Neil Guterman, Julia Shaw Holmes

1993
Anna Celeste Burke, Janice Harrington, Kathryn A. Kozaitis, Yolanda Chavez Padilla, Grant Martin Woodard, Jay Mark Callahan, Linda Ann Pertusati

1994
Pamela Dodd, Jann Hoge, David Pollio, Susan Lynch, Carol Kinney, Hiroko Yamada, Linwood Cousins, Laura Dresser, Julia Henly, Diane Marcus

1995
Aixa Cintron, Janet Finn, Andrew Hamid, Edith Williams, Joseph Himle, Rosalind Folman, Yvonne Williams, Kyoung Ja Hyun, David Freiband

1996
Harry Ford, Amy Ai, Ruk Jayakody, Kip Coggins, Ellen DeVoe, Biren Nagda, Rogeair Purnell, Stephanie Robert, Marilyn Wedenoja

1997
James Kunz, James Rollin, Ingrid Phillips Whitaker, Bonnie F. Hatchett, Faith Pratt Hopp, Sybil Cecelia McPherson, Jodi R. Sandfort

1998
Hyun Joo Oh, Ivan Alexandre de la Rosa, Lynn Alice Warner, Gerhard Johann Schwab, Anna Maria Yeakley

1999
Nancy R. Beekman, Theresa Mary McArdle, Peter Adam Newman, Alison Heather Climo, Kimberly S. Roberson, Pilgrim Stewart Spikes, Bradley Jay Zebrack

2000
Lisa G. Colarossi, Daniel Rosen, Sherrill L. Sellers, Erna-Lynne Bogue, James Michael Mandiberg, Sabrina Watson Tyuse, Vivian Loyola Dames, Barbara Ntombi Ngwenya

2001
Jane Mildred, Ronald O'Neal Pitner, Deborah Kay Anderson, John Johnson Kerbs, Izumi Sakamoto, Shirley Ann Thomas, Deborah Megivern, David Crampton

2002
Karen Lincoln, Bill Dethlefs, Edna Brown, Carla Parry, Sang Kahng, Yunju Nam, Lynn M. Nybell, Debra Marguerite Jozefowicz

2003

Valerie Lynn Myers, La Reese Collins, Laina Ya-Hui Bay-Cheng, Belinda Wilburn Nelson, Tracy A. Schroepfer, Michael A. Dover, Amy Robyn Schigelone

2004

R. Khari Brown, Carol A. Plummer, Luke J. Bergmann, E. Summerson Carr, Amelia Ryle Gavin, Beverly Y. Araujo, Melnee D. McPherson, Jordana R. Muroff, Jeffrey James Shook, Katherine L. Hinds, Chantal C. Follett

2005

Ann Marie Conway, Chyrell Denise Bellamy, Jennifer Kellman Fritz, Katherine E. Richards-Schuster, Abigail R. Lawrence, Deborah Alice Willis, Stephanie Boys, Hae-Sook Jeon, Abigail R. Lawrence-Jacobson, Ann P. Rall, Deborah Willis, Yael Harlap, Helen K. Kim, Jennifer B. Lyle, Anthony J. Mallon

2006

Jung-Hwa Ha, Bowen McBeath, Rebecca L. Stotzer, Irene Y. Ng, Nina Rhee, Peregrine C. Silverschanz, Elizabeth Johnson, Diane Miller, Inna Altschul, Michael MacKenzie, William Russell "Skip" Barcy

2007

Juan Chen, Lourdes Gutiérrez Najera, Cristina Beatriz Bares, Alexandra Lee Crampton, Amanda Toler, David Sommerfeld

2008

David S. Dobbie, Kimberly Clum, Jenell Shiyama Clarke, Barbara Carlette Thomas, Joanne Smith-Darden, Melita Vaz

References

Abbott, E. (1937). *Some American pioneers in social welfare*. Chicago: University of Chicago Press.

Abbott, E. (1941). Twenty-one years of university education for the social services, 1920–41. *Social Service Review, 15* (4), 670–705.

Abbott, E. (1942). *Social welfare and professional education* (2nd ed.). Chicago: University of Chicago Press.

Addams, J. (1893). *Philanthropy and social progress*. New York: Crowell.

Addams, J. (1899). The subtle problems of charity. Cited in S. Wenocur, & M. Reisch (1989), *From charity to enterprise: The development of American social work in a market economy*. Urbana: University of Illinois.

Addams, J. (1902). *Democracy and social ethics*. New York: Macmillan.

Addams, J. (1910). *Twenty years at Hull House*. New York: Macmillan.

Alexander, S., & Torkko, T. (2001). Women in social work. *Ongoing*. Ann Arbor: University of Michigan School of Social Work.

Allen-Meares, P., Washington, R. O., & Welsh, B. L. (1999). *Social work services in schools* (3rd ed.). Boston: Allyn-Bacon.

American Association of Social Workers. (1948–53). *Statistics on social work education*. New York: Author.

Anderson, J. (1971, May 6). *Michigan Daily*.

Andriola, J. P. (1940, April 3). *Michigan Daily*.

Angell, R. C. (1936). *The family encounters the depression*. New York: Charles Scribner's Sons.

Angell, R. C. (1951a). The department of sociology. In W. B. Shaw (Ed.), *University of Michigan: An encyclopedic survey*. Ann Arbor: University of Michigan.

Angell, R. C. (1951b). *The moral integration of American cities*. Chicago: University of Chicago.

Angell, R. C. (1954). A research basis for social welfare. *Social Work Journal* (October).

Arnold, M. (2002, February 28). Writers beware: History is an art, not a toaster. *The New York Times*, p. E1.

Austin, D. (2000). *The institutional development of social work education* (long version). Austin, Texas: School of Social Work.

Austin, D. et al. (1991). *Building social knowledge for effective services and policies. A plan for research development.* Austin, TX: Task Force on Social Work Research.

Austin, D. M. (1983). The Flexner myth and the history of social work. *Social Service Review 57*(3), 357–377.

Austin, D. M. (1997). The institutional development of social work education: The first 100 years—and beyond. *Journal of Social Work Education, 33*(3), 599–611.

Bartlett, H. M. (1951). The study of social work education. *Social Work Journal, 32*(3).

Berkowitz, E. D. (1995). *Mr. Social Security: The life of Wilbur J. Cohen.* Lawrence, Kansas: University of Kansas Press.

Bertcher, H. (1979). *Group participation techniques for leaders and members.* Thousand Oaks, CA: Sage Publications.

Bertcher, H. (1988). *Staff development in human service organizations.* Englewood Cliffs, NJ: Prentice-Hall.

Bertcher, H., & Maple, F. (1977). *Creating groups.* Thousand Oaks, CA: Sage Publications.

Bertcher, H., Kurtz, L. F., & Lamont, A. (Eds.). (1999). *Rebuilding communities: Challenges for group work.* Binghamton, NY: Haworth.

Bertcher, H., Maple, F., & Wallace, H. (1971). Group composition: An instructional program. Ann Arbor, MI: Campus Publishers.

Biddle, B. J., & Thomas, E. J. (Eds.). (1966). *Role theory: Concepts and research.* New York: Wiley.

Bidlack, R. E. (1998). *Ann Arbor's first lady.* Ann Arbor: University of Michigan Bentley Historical Library.

Blouin, F. X. (1999). Foreword. In R. M. Warner (Ed.), *Frost-bite, frost-bark.* Ann Arbor: University of Michigan Bentley Historical Library.

Board of Regents. (1921; 1950). *Proceedings.* Ann Arbor: University of Michigan Bentley Historical Library.

Board of Regents. (1935). *Exhibits.* Ann Arbor: University of Michigan Bentley Historical Library.

Board of Regents. (1949–2003). *Proceedings, retirement memoirs.* Ann Arbor: University of Michigan Bentley Historical Library.

Board of Regents. (1949–2003). *Minutes.* Ann Arbor: University of Michigan Bentley Historical Library.

Board of Regents. (2005). *Bylaws.* Ann Arbor: University of Michigan.

Boehm, W. W. (1959). *Objectives of the social work curriculum of the future: The comprehensive report of the curriculum study.* New York: CSWE.

Boehm, W. W. (1959). *Social work curriculum study.* New York: CSWE.

Bohm, H. V., & Pentecost, P. J. (Eds.). (2000). *Reminiscences of Wayne.* Ann Arbor, MI: Cushing-Malloy.

Booth, P. (1967). *California farm workers and disability insurance.* N.p.

Booth, P. (1973). *Social Security in America*. Ann Arbor, MI: Institute of Labor and Industrial Relations.

Borgatta, E. F., Fanshel, D., & Meyer, H. J. (1960). *Social workers' perceptions of clients*. New York: Russell Sage Foundation.

Brabson, H. (1976). Strategies for developing citizen participation in low socio-economic areas. *Social Thought*.

Brackett, J. R. (1901). Present opportunities for training in charitable work. In I. C. Barrows (Ed.), *Proceedings of the National Conference of Charities and Correction*. Boston: George H. Ellis.

Brackett, J. R. (1903). *Supervision and education in charity*. London: MacMillan & Co.

Brackett, J. R. (1904). The worker: Purpose and preparation. In I. C. Barrows (Ed.), *Proceedings of the National Conference of Charities and Correction*. New York: Fred J. Heer.

Brager, C., & Holloway, S. (1978). Changing human service organizations: Politics and practice. New York: Free Press.

Brinkman, F. (Ed.). (1977; 1981). *University of Michigan: An encyclopedic survey*. Ann Arbor: University of Michigan Bentley Historical Library.

Broadhurst, B. P. (1971). *Social thought, social practice and social work education*. Unpublished doctoral dissertation, Columbia University School of Social Work, New York.

Brown, E. L. (1942). *Social work as a profession*. New York: Russell Sage Foundation.

Bruno, F. J. (1944). Twenty-five years of schools of social work. *Social Service Review, 18*(2), 152–164.

Bruno, F. J. (1957). *Trends in social work 1874–1956*. New York: Columbia University Press.

Burns, M. H. (1965a). Criteria for selection of students for advanced study. *Social Work Education Reporter, 13*(1).

Burns, M. H. (1965b). Social science content in doctoral programs. *Social Work Education Reporter, 13*(3).

Burns, M. H. (1965c). Supervision in social work. In H. L. Lurie (Ed.), *Encyclopedia of social work*. New York: NASW.

Burns, M. H., & Glasser, P. H. (1963). Similarities and differences in casework and group work practice. *Social Service Review, 37*, 416–428.

Bushey, P. (1965). Social work practice in public assistance agencies. In H. L. Lurie (Ed.), *Encyclopedia of social work*. New York: NASW.

Cabot, R. C. (1909). *Social service and the art of healing*. New York: Moffat, Yard & Co.

Cabot, R. C. (1919). *Social work: Essays on the meeting-ground between doctor and social worker*. Boston: Houghton Mifflin Company.

Cannon, I. M. (1923). *Social work in hospitals: A contribution to progressive medicine*. New York: Survey Associates, Inc.

Carr, L. J., Valentine, M. A., & Levy, M. H. (1939). *Integrating the camp, the community, and social work*. New York: Association Press.

Channing, A. (1954). The early years of a pioneer school. *Social Service Review,* *28*(4), 430–440.

Churchill, S. et al. (1974a). *A comparison of two models of social group work: The treatment model and the reciprocal model.* Ann Arbor: University of Michigan School of Social Work.

Churchill, S. et al. (1974b). *Diagnosis in group work.* Ann Arbor: University of Michigan School of Social Work.

Churchill, S. et al. (1974c). *Preventive, short-term groups for siblings of child mental hospital patients.* Ann Arbor: University of Michigan School of Social Work.

Churchill, S. et al. (1974d). *Small groups in the mental hospital.* Ann Arbor: University of Michigan School of Social Work.

Cloward, R., & Epstein, I. (1965). *Private social welfare's disengagement from the poor.* Buffalo, NY: University of Buffalo.

Cohen, W. J. (1965a). Federal organizations for social welfare. In H. L. Lurie (Ed.), *Encyclopedia of social work.* New York: NASW.

Cohen, W. J. (1965b). *Social work education and social welfare manpower: Present realities and future imperatives.* New York: CSWE.

Cohen, W. J. (1967). Womanpower policies for the 1970s. An address. Washington, DC: U.S. Department of Labor.

Cohen, W. J. (1969). *Toward a social report.* Washington, DC: U.S. Department of Health, Education, and Welfare.

Cohen, W. J. (1971). Social insurance. In R. Morris (Ed.), *Encyclopedia of social work.* New York: NASW.

Cohen, W. J. (1984). *The New Deal: Fifty years after.* Austin, TX: L. B. J. Library.

Cohen, W. J., & Fauri, F. F. (1958). *The objectives of public welfare administration and the leadership role of the public welfare administrator.* Chicago: American Public Welfare Association.

Cohen, W. J., & Friedman, M. (1972). *Social security: Universal or selective?* Washington: Enterprise Institute for Public Policy Research.

Columbia University School of Social Work. (n.d.). *History.* Retrieved 2001 from www.columbia.edu/cu/ssw.

Coohey, C. (1999). Notes on the origins of social work education [Letter to the editor]. *Social Service Review, 73*(3), 418–422.

Cook, L. & Cook, D. (1963). The law and social work: Compatible conflict. *Buffalo Law Review.*

Cooley, C. H. (1902). *Human nature and the social order.* New York: Scribner.

Cooley, C. H. (1909). *Social organization: A history of the larger mind.* New York: Scribner.

Cooley, C. H. (1918). *The social process.* New York: Scribner.

Council on Social Work Education. (1962). *Official statement of curriculum policy for the master's degree program in graduate professional schools of social work.* New York: Author.

Council on Social Work Education. (1984). Letters to President Harold Shapiro.

Council on Social Work Education. (1972a). *Concentrations and special learning opportunities in the master of social work curricula of graduate schools of social work 1971–72.* New York: Author.

Council on Social Work Education. (1972b). *Statistics on social work education, 1954–1971.* New York: Author.

Council on Social Work Education. (1999). *Self-study.* New York: Author.

Cox, F. et al. (1970a). *Strategies of community organization: A book of readings.* Itasca, IL: Peacock.

Cox, F. et al. (1970b). *Tactics of community organization.* Itasca, IL: Peacock.

Cox, F. et al. (1974). *Community action, planning, development: A casebook.* Itasca, IL: Peacock.

Cox, F. et al. (1977). *Tactics and techniques of community practice.* Itasca, IL: Peacock.

Croxton, T. (1967a). The juvenile court: Some current issues. *Child Welfare.*

Croxton, T. (1967b). The Kent case and its consequences. *Journal of Family Law.*

Croxton, T. (1969). Juvenile court and the code. *Urban Crime and Urban Planning.*

Davies, S. P. (1950). The relation of social science to social welfare. *Social Work Journal.*

Deardorff, N. R. (1925). The place of a professional school in training for social work. *American Academy of Political and Social Science, 121.*

Deardorff, N. R. (1930). Social work as a profession. In F. S. Hall & M. B. Ellis (Eds.), *Social work year book.* New York: Russell Sage Foundation.

Detroit Free Press. (1950). Detroit, Michigan. May 9.

Dillick, S. (1984). *Chronology of social work education at Wayne State University.* Detroit, MI: Wayne State University School of Social Work.

Diner, H. R. (1985). *Service and scholarship. Seventy-five years of the School of Social Service Administration of the University of Chicago. 1908–1983.* Chicago: University of Chicago.

Dinerman, M., & Geismar, L. L. (Eds.). (1984). *A quarter-century of social work education.* Washington, DC: NASW.

Donnelly, W. A., Shaw, N. B., & Gjelsness, R. W. (Eds.). (1953). *University of Michigan: An encyclopedic survey.* Ann Arbor: University of Michigan Bentley Historical Library.

Dore, M. M. (2001). Clinical practice. In R. Feldman & S. Kamerman (Eds.), *The Columbia University School of Social Work.* New York: Columbia University Press.

Duderstadt, J. J. (2003). *On the move: A personal history of The University of Michigan's College of Engineering in modern times.* University of Michigan, Millenium Project.

Duncan, G. J. et al. (2005). *Report of the External Review Committee for the Joint Program in Social Work and Social Science.* Ann Arbor: University of Michigan School of Social Work.

Dunham, A. (1950). Exchange. *Social Work Journal.*

Dunham, A. (1958). *Community welfare organization: Principles and practice.* New York: Crowell.

Dunham, A. (1970). *The new community organization.* New York: Crowell.

Dunham, A., & Harper, E. B. (1959). *Community organization in action.* New York: Association Press.

Dunham, A., & Heath, M. (1963). *Trends in community organization: 1874–1960.* Chicago: University of Chicago Press.

Elbel, L. (1898). *The victors.* Ann Arbor: Regents of the University of Michigan.

Erlich, J. (1966–70). John Erlich Papers. Ann Arbor: University of Michigan Bentley Historical Library Collections.

Erlich, J. (1971). Youth movements. In R. Morris (Ed.), *Encyclopedia of social work.* New York: NASW.

Erlich, J., & Erlich, S. (1971). *Student power, participation, and revolution.* New York: Association Press.

Erlich, J., & Tropman, J. (1969). Student power. *Social Work.*

Esser, B. F., & Freud, C. (1966). *Testing as a tool in the admissions process.* New York: CSWE.

External review. (1979). Ann Arbor: University of Michigan School of Social Work.

Fauri, F. F. (1952). *School of Social Work: Report to the president.* Ann Arbor: University of Michigan Bentley Historical Library.

Fauri, F. F. (1955). The shortage of social workers. *Social Work Journal.*

Fauri, F. F. (1960). Foreword. In E. J. Thomas et al. (Eds.), *In-service training and reduced workloads.* New York: Russell Sage Foundation.

Fauri, F. F. (1966). Achieving the great society: The contribution of social work education. *Social Work Education Reporter.*

Fauri, F. F. (1973). Foreword. In P. Booth, *Social security in America.* Ann Arbor: University of Michigan Institute of Labor & Industrial Relations.

Feld, S., & Radin, N. (1982). *Social psychology for social work and the mental health professions.* New York: Columbia University Press.

Feldman, F. L. et al. (1996). *The evolution of USC social work education.* Los Angeles: University of Southern California.

Feldman, R., & Kamerman, S. B. (Eds.). (2001). *The Columbia University School of Social Work: A centennial celebration.* New York: Columbia University Press.

Fellin Records. (1971–81). Ann Arbor: University of Michigan School of Social Work.

Fellin, P. (1972–80). *Annual reports to the president.* Ann Arbor: University of Michigan Bentley Historical Library.

Fellin, P. (1974). Long-range planning. *Journal of Education for Social Work.*

Fellin, P. (1977). Social work. In F. Brinkman (Ed.), *The University of Michigan: An encyclopedic survey.* Ann Arbor: University of Michigan Bentley Historical Library.

Fellin, P. (1987). *The community and the social worker.* Itasca, IL: Peacock Publishers.

Fellin, P. (1996). *Mental health and mental illness.* Itasca, IL: Peacock Publishers.

Fellin, P. (2001). Social Work Education at Michigan: The First Thirty Years. Personal document.

Fellin, P. (2002). Social Work Education at Michigan: Emeritus/Emerita Faculty Retirement Memoirs. Personal document.

Fellin, P. (2003a). Social Work Education at Michigan: The Fauri Years. Personal document.

Fellin, P. (2003b; 2004a). *Social work education at Michigan.* Ann Arbor: University of Michigan School of Social Work.

Fellin, P. (2004b). Social Work Education at Michigan: The Fellin Years. Personal document.

Fellin, P. (2005a). Social Work Education at Michigan: The Allen-Meares Years. Personal document.

Fellin, P. (2005b). Social Work Education at Michigan: The Johnson Years. Personal document.

Fellin, P., & Vinter, R. D. (1969). Curriculum development for contemporary social work education. In H. Cassidy, *Modes of professional education: Report of a symposium, Feb. 1969.* New Orleans: Tulane University.

Fellin, P., Thomas, E. J., & Freud, C. (1968). Institutes on behavioral science for field instructors. *Journal of Education for Social Work.*

Ferman, L. (Ed.). (1968). *Poverty in America: A book of readings.* Ann Arbor: University of Michigan Press.

Ferman, L. (Ed.). (1979). *Mental health and the economy.* Kalamazoo, MI: W. E. Upjohn.

Fleming, R. W. (1996). *Tempests into rainbows, managing turbulence.* Ann Arbor: University of Michigan Press.

Fletcher, R. C. (1948). Runaway youth to Detroit. *Social Service Review, 22*(3), 349–354.

Fletcher, R. C. (1950). *Historical statistical report of the institute of social work.* Ann Arbor: University of Michigan Bentley Historical Library.

Fletcher, R. C., Schroeder, D., Marshall, A. W., & Marckwardt, J. (1960). *A study of the number of pre-hospital contacts of children committed to two state mental institutions in Michigan.* Ann Arbor: University of Michigan School of Social Work.

Fletcher, R. C., Schroeder, D., Marshall, A. W., & Marckwardt, J. (1960). *Movement of children hospitalized at Ypsilanti State Hospital.* Ann Arbor: University of Michigan School of Social Work.

Flexner, A. (1915). Is social work a profession? *Proceedings of the National Conference of Charities and Correction, 1915.* Chicago: Hildmann.

Folks, H. (1893). College graduates in benevolent work. *Proceedings of the International Congress of Charities, Corrections, and Probation.* Chicago.

Foster, M. (1978). Black organizing: The need for a conceptual model of the ghetto. *Catalyst.*

Foster, M., & Ferman, L. (1982). Minority populations and mental health manpower development. Ann Arbor: University of Michigan.

Fraiberg, S. (1959). *The magic years.* New York: Scribner.

Fraiberg, S. (1977). *Every child's birthright: In defense of mothering.* New York: Basic Books.

Fraiberg, S. (1980). *Clinical studies in infant mental health.* New York: Basic Books.

Frantilla, A. (1998). *Social science in the public interest: A 50th history of the Institute of Social Research.* Ann Arbor: University of Michigan Bentley Historical Library.

French, D. G. (1952). *An approach to measuring results in social work.* New York: Columbia University Press.

French, D. G., & Gordon, W. E. (1952). *Applications for admissions to schools of social work, Fall Term, 1950, and variations among schools in admissions decisions.* New York: American Association of Schools of Social Work.

Gambrill, E. (1977). *Behavioral modification: Handbook of assessment, intervention, and evaluation.* San Francisco: Jossey-Bass.

Gambrill, E. (1983). *Casework: A competency-based approach.* Englewood Cliffs, NJ: Prentice-Hall.

Gambrill, E. (1990). *Critical thinking in clinical practice.* San Francisco: Jossey-Bass.

Gambrill, E. (1997a). Making decisions about integration. In D. Tucker, C. Garvin, & R. C. Sarri (Eds.), *Integrating knowledge and practice: The case of social work and social science.* Westport, CN: Praeger.

Gambrill, E. (1997b). *Social work practice: A critical thinker's guide.* New York: Oxford.

Gardner, J. W. (1965). *Closing the gap in social work manpower.* Washington, DC: Department of Health, Education, Welfare.

Gardner, J. W. (1966). Remarks. *Journal of Education for Social Work.*

Garvin, C. (1973). *Education for generalist practice in social work: A comparative analysis of current modalities.* Paper presented at the annual meeting of the CSWE, San Francisco, CA.

Garvin, C. (1981). *Contemporary group work.* Englewood Cliffs, NJ: Prentice-Hall.

Garvin, C. (1994). *Report to the Doctoral Committee.* Ann Arbor: University of Michigan.

Garvin, C. (1997). Social science to social work. In D. J. Tucker, C. Garvin, & R. Sarri (Eds.), *Integrating knowledge and practice: The case of social work and social science.* Westport, CN: Praeger.

Garvin, C., & Bertcher, H. (1969). *Staff development in social welfare agencies.* Ann Arbor, MI: Campus Publishers.

Garvin, C., & Glasser, P. (1971). Social group work: The preventive and rehabilitative approach. In R. Morris (Ed.), *Encyclopedia of social work.* New York: NASW.

Garvin, C., & Glasser, P. (1974). The bases of social treatment. In P. Glasser, R. Sarri, & R. Vinter (Eds.), *Individual change through small groups.* New York: Free Press.

Garvin, C., & Seabury, B. (1984). *Interpersonal practice in social work.* Englewood Cliffs, NJ: Prentice-Hall.

Garvin, C., & Seabury, B. (1997). *Interpersonal practice in social work*. Needham Heights, MA: Allyn & Bacon.

Garvin, C., & Tolson, E. (1994). *Generalist practice: A task-centered approach*. New York: Columbia University.

Garvin, C., & Tropman, J. (1992). *Social work in contemporary society*. Englewood Cliffs, NJ: Prentice-Hall.

Gary, L. E. (1968). Social work education and the black community: A proposal for curriculum revisions. *Social Work Education Reporter, 16*(5).

Gavrilovich, P. (2001, July 24). Say thanks to the leaders. *Detroit Free Press*.

Glasser, P. (1963). Group services in child welfare. *Child Welfare*.

Glasser, P., & Garvin, C. (1971). Social group work: The preventive and rehabilitative approach. In R. Morris (Ed.), *Encyclopedia of social work*. New York: NASW.

Glasser, P., & Glasser, L. N. (Eds). (1970). *Families in crisis*. New York: Harper & Row.

Glasser, P., Sarri, R. C., & Vinter, R. D. (1974). *Individual change through small groups*. New York: Free Press.

Gordon, J. (1963). *Personality and behavior*. New York: Macmillan.

Gordon, J. (Ed.). (1967). *Handbook of clinical and experimental hypnosis*. New York: Macmillan.

Gordon, W. E. (1950). The research project: Its educational value and its contribution to social work knowledge. *Social Work Journal, 31*(3).

Gottesfeld, M. L., & Pinkus, H. (Eds.). (1977). *Education for clinical social work*. New York: Human Sciences Press.

Green, R. G., Baskind, F. R., & Bellin, M. H. (2002). Results of the doctoral faculty publication project. *Journal of Social Work Education, 38*(1).

Greenwood, E. (1957). The attributes of a profession. *Social Work, 2*, 45–55.

Grosser, C. F. (1976). *New directions in community organizing: From enabling to advocacy*. New York: Praeger.

Gurin, A., & Lauffer, A. (1971). *Community organization curriculum in graduate social work education*. New York: CSWE.

Gurin, G., & Feld, S. (1970). *Marriage and work in America*. New York: Reinhold.

Gurin, G., Veroff, J., & Feld, S. (1960). *Americans view their mental health*. New York: Basic Books.

Haber, W., & Cohen, W. J. (1948). *Readings in social security*. New York: Prentice Hall.

Haber, W., & Cohen, W. J. (1960). *Social security: Programs, problems, and policies*. Homewood, IL: Irwin.

Hagerty, J. E. (1931). *The training of social workers*. New York: McGraw-Hill.

Hall, F. S., & Ellis, M. B. (Eds.). (1930). *Social work year book*. New York: Russell Sage Foundation.

Hamilton, G. (1940). *Theory and practice of social case work*. New York: Columbia University Press.

Harper, E. B., & Dunham, A. (1959). *Community organization in action*. New York: Association Press.

Harris, O., & Janzen, C. (1980). *Family treatment in social work practice*. Itasca, IL: Peacock Publishers.

Hartman, A. (1972). *Casework in crisis 1932–1941*. Unpublished doctoral dissertation. Columbia University School of Social Work, New York.

Hasenfeld, Y., & English, R. (1974). *Human service organizations*. Englewood Cliffs, NJ: Prentice-Hall.

Hasenfeld, Y., & Leon, J. (1979). A profile of doctoral students in social work and social science at the University of Michigan. Unpublished.

Heath, M., & Dunham, A. (1963). *Trends in community organization: 1874–1960*. Chicago: University of Chicago Press.

Hillenbrand, L. (2001). *Seabiscuit*. New York: Ballentine.

Hinsdale, B. A. (1906). *History of the University of Michigan*. Ann Arbor: University of Michigan.

Hollis, E. V., & Taylor, A. L. (1951). *Social work education in the United States*. New York: Columbia University Press.

Hollis, F. (1964). *Casework: A psychosocial therapy*. New York: Random House.

Hourihan, J. P. (1952). *The duties and responsibilities of the visiting teacher*. Unpublished doctoral dissertation, Wayne State University, Detroit.

Hourihan, J. P. (2000). The School of Social Work. In H. V. Bohm & P. J. Pentecost (Eds.), *Reminiscences of Wayne*. Ann Arbor, MI: Cushing-Malloy.

Hunt, J. M., & Kogan, L. S. (1950). *Measuring results in social casework*. New York: Family Service Association of America.

Institute of Social Work. (1935–45). U-M Announcements. Ann Arbor: University of Michigan Bentley Historical Library.

Institute of Social Work. (1946). *First ten years report*. Ann Arbor: University of Michigan.

Jayaratne, S. (1979). An analysis of selected social work journals and productivity rankings among schools of social work. *Journal of Social Work Education, 15*, 72–80.

Johnson, A. (1965). Schools (social work practice in). In H. L. Lurie (Ed.), *Encyclopedia of social work*. New York: NASW Press.

Johnson, H. (1971). Neighborhood services. In R. Morris (Ed.), *Encyclopedia of social work*. New York: NASW.

Johnson, H. R. (1981–97). Annual reports to the University of Michigan president. Ann Arbor: University of Michigan Bentley Historical Library.

Johnson, H. R. (1988). Prospectus for a new building for the school of social work. Ann Arbor: University of Michigan School of Social Work.

Johnson, H. R., & Tropman, J. (Eds.). (1986). *Social work policy and practice*. Ann Arbor: University of Michigan School of Social Work.

Kahn, A. J. (Ed.). (1959). *Issues in American social work*. New York: Columbia University Press.

Kahn, A. J. (Ed.). (1973). *Shaping the new social work*. New York: Columbia University Press.

Kahn, A. J. (1998a). The social work research domain in historical perspective: The first hundred years. In M. Potocky & T. Tripodi (Eds.), *New directions in social work practice research*. New York: NASW.

Kahn, A. J. (1998b). *Themes for a history: The first hundred years of the Columbia University School of Social Work*. Retrieved 2001 from www.columbia.edu/cu/ssw.

Kahn, A. J. (1999). Letter to the Editor. *Social Service Review, 73*(2), 261.

Kahn, A. J. (2000). Letter to the Editor. *Social Service Review, 74*(1), 137–138.

Kahn, A. J. (2001). Themes for a history: The first hundred years. In R. Feldman & S. Kamerman (Eds.), *The Columbia University School of Social Work: A centennial celebration*. New York: Columbia University Press.

Kasius, C. (Ed.). (1950). *A comparison of diagnostic and functional casework concepts*. New York: Family Service Association of America.

Kelso, R. W. (1922). *The history of public poor relief in 1620–1920 in Massachusetts*. Boston: Houghton Mifflin.

Kelso, R. W. (1930). County and city homes. In F. S. Hall & M. B. Ellis (Eds.), *Social work year book*. New York: Russell Sage Foundation.

Kelso, R. W. (1934). *The science of public welfare*. New York: Holt & Co.

Kelso, R. W. (1936). Tomorrow's social work training. *Survey, 72*.

Kelso, R. W. (1942). *The organization and functioning of the system of public welfare services in Michigan*. N. p.

Kendall, K. A. (1966). Issues and problems in social work education. *Social Work Education Reporter, 13*(1).

Kendall, K. A. (1978). *Reflections on social work education 1950–1978*. New York: International Association of Schools of Social Work.

Kendall, K. A. (2002). *Council on Social Work Education*. Alexandria, VA: Council on Social Work Education.

Kidneigh, J. (1965). History of American social work. In H. L. Lurie (Ed.), *Encyclopedia of social work*. New York: NASW Press.

Lauffer, A. (1970). Social activists come to social work. *Journal of Education for Social Workers*.

Lauffer, A. (1973). *The aim of the game: A primer on the use and design of gamed social simulations*. New York: Gamed Simulations.

Lauffer, A. (1977a). *Grantsmanship*. Thousand Oaks, CA: Sage.

Lauffer, A. (1977b). *Practice of community education in the human services*. New York: McGraw-Hill.

Lauffer, A. (1977c). *Understanding your social agency*. Thousand Oaks, CA: Sage.

Lauffer, A. (1977d). *Volunteers*. Thousand Oaks, CA: Sage.

Lauffer, A. (1978). *Social planning at the community level*. Englewood Cliffs, NJ: Prentice-Hall.

Lauffer, A. (1984). *Strategic planning for not-for-profit organizations*. New York: Free Press.

Lazarsfeld, P. F., Sewell, W. H., & Wilensky, H. L. (1967). *The uses of sociology*. New York: Basic Books.

Lee, P. R. (1937). *Social work as cause and function*. New York: Columbia University Press.

Leiby, J. (1978). *A history of social welfare and social work in the United States*. New York: Columbia University Press.

Leighninger, L. (2000). *Creating a new profession: The beginnings of social work education in the United States*. Alexandria, VA: CSWE.

Levy, R., & Jayaratne, S. (1979). *Empirical clinical practice*. New York: Columbia University Press.

Little, R. A. (2001). In memoriam: Henry J. Meyer. *Ongoing*. Ann Arbor: University of Michigan School of Social Work.

Litwak, E. (1963). *Detroit Area Study: A study of family-school relationships in Detroit*. Ann Arbor: University of Michigan School of Social Work.

Litwak, E., & Meyer, H. J. (1966). A balance theory of coordination between bureaucratic organizations and community primary groups. *Administrative Science Quarterly, 11*(1), 31–58.

Litwak, E., & Meyer, H. J. (1974). *School, family, and neighborhood: The theory and practice of school–community relations*. New York: Columbia University Press.

Litwak, E., & Meyer, H. J. (n.d.). *Relationship between school–community coordinating procedures and reading achievement*. Ann Arbor: University of Michigan School of Social Work.

Lubove, R. (1965). *The professional altruist*. Cambridge: Harvard University Press.

Lurie, H. L. (1965). *Encyclopedia of social work*. New York: NASW Press.

Maas, H. (1950). Collaboration between social work and the social sciences. *Social Work Journal, 31*(3).

Maple, F. (1972). *Problem solving through shared decision-making*. Thousand Oaks, CA: Sage.

Maple, F., & Bertcher, H. (1974). Elements and issues in group composition. In P. Glasser, R. C. Sarri, & R. D. Vinter, *Individual change through small groups*. New York: Free Press.

Maple, F., Bertcher, H., & Wallace, H. (1971). *Group composition*. Ann Arbor: Campus Publishers.

Marks, R. (1965). Education for social work. In H. L. Lurie (Ed.), *Encyclopedia of social work*. New York: NASW Press.

McGraw, B. (2001, January 29). Motor City Journal. *Detroit Free Press*.

McKenzie, R. (1951). Department of Sociology. In W. B. Shaw (Ed.), *University of Michigan: An encyclopedic survey*. Ann Arbor: University of Michigan Press.

McVinney, L. D. (2001). Advanced generalist practice and programming. In R. A. Feldman & S. W. Kamerman (Eds.), *The Columbia University School of Social Work: A centennial celebration*. New York: Columbia University Press.

Meier, E. G. (1954). *A history of the New York School of Social Work*. New York: Columbia University Press.

Meyer, C. H. (1976). *Social work practice: The changing landscape*. New York: Free Press.

Meyer, C. H. (Ed.). (1983). *Clinical social work in the eco-systems perspective.* New York: Columbia University Press.

Meyer, C. H. (1986). *Curriculum policy statements in social work education.* Austin: University of Texas School of Social Work.

Meyer, H. J. (1959). Professionalization and social work. In A. J. Kahn (Ed.), *Issues in American social work.* New York: Columbia University Press.

Meyer, H. J. (1971). Profession of social work: Contemporary characteristics. In R. Morris (Ed.), *Encyclopedia of social work.* New York: NASW.

Meyer, H. J., & Borgatta, E. F. (1959). *An experiment in mental patient rehabilitation— Evaluating a social agency program.* New York: Russell Sage Foundation.

Meyer, H. J., Borgatta, E. F., & Jones, W. (1965). *Girls at vocational high. An experiment in social work intervention.* New York: Russell Sage Foundation.

Meyer, H. J., Litwak, E., Thomas, E. J., & Vinter, R. D. (1967). Social work and social welfare. In P. F. Lazarsfeld, W. H. Sewell, & H. L. Wilensky (Eds.), *The uses of sociology.* New York: Basic Books.

Michigan Daily. (1904, October 18). Ann Arbor: University of Michigan.

Miller, J. (1998). *Reflections: Narratives of professional helping.* Long Beach: California State University.

Mills, C. (2003). Bragging, boasting, and crowing: The ethics of sharing one's glad tidings with others. *Philosophy and Public Policy Quarterly, 23*(4), 7–12.

Morris, R. (Ed.). (1971). *Encyclopedia of social work.* New York: NASW.

National Association of Visiting Teachers. (1921). *The visiting teacher in the U.S.* New York: Public Education Association of the City of New York.

Neenan, W. (1967). *A normative evaluation of a public health program.* Ann Arbor: University of Michigan Institute of Public Administration.

Neenan, W. (1972). *Political economy of urban areas.* Chicago: Markham.

Okkelberg, P. (1953). The Institute of Public and Social Administration. In W. A. Donnelly et al. (Eds.), *University of Michigan: An encyclopedic survey.* Ann Arbor: University of Michigan Press.

Ongoing, alumni newsletter/magazine. (1981–92; 2001; 2005). Ann Arbor: University of Michigan School of Social Work.

Peckham, H. H. (1994). *The making of the University of Michigan.* Ann Arbor: University of Michigan Bentley Historical Library.

Peckham, H. H. (with Steneck, M. L., & Steneck, N. H., Eds.). (1994). *The making of the University of Michigan.* Ann Arbor: University of Michigan Bentley Historical Library.

Perlman, H. H. (1953). The basic structure of the casework process. *Social Service Review, 27,* 308–315.

Perlman, H. H. (1957). *Social casework: A problem solving process.* Chicago: University of Chicago Press.

Popple, P. R. (1976). *A voice in the wilderness: Social work education in St. Louis, MO, 1901–1925.* St. Louis: George Warren Brown School of Social Work.

Popple, P. R. (1985). The social work profession: A reconceptualization. *Social Service Review, 59,* 560–577.

Popple, P. R., & Leighninger, L. L. (2001). *The policy-based profession* (2nd ed.). Boston: Allyn & Bacon.

Powell, T. (1987). *Self-help organizations and professional practice*. New York: NASW.

Powell, T. (1990). *Working with self-help*. New York: NASW.

Powell, T. (1994). *Understanding the self-help organization*. Thousand Oaks, CA: Sage.

Proposal for a program of advanced training and research in social work and social science. (1956). Ann Arbor: University of Michigan School of Social Work.

Pumphrey, M. W. (1956). *Mary Richmond and the rise of professional social work in Baltimore: The foundations of a creative career*. Unpublished doctoral dissertation, New York School for Social Work.

Pumphrey, R. E., & Pumphrey, M. W. (Eds.). (1961). *The heritage of American social work: Readings in its philosophical and institutional development*. New York: Columbia University Press.

Radin, N. (1971). Child welfare: Preschool programs. In R. Morris (Ed.), *Encyclopedia of social work*. New York: NASW.

Radin, N. (1983, October). *The success of graduates of two social work doctoral programs and implications for comparable programs*. Paper presented at the Group for the Advancement of Doctoral Education Conference. Tuscaloosa, AL.

Radin, N., Benbenisky, R., & Leon, J. (1982). Predictors of success in a social work doctoral program. *Social Service Review, 56,* 640–658.

Reid, W. J. (1994). The empirical practice movement. *Social Service Review, 68,* 165–184.

Reid, W. J., & Epstein, L. (1972). *Task-centered casework*. New York: Columbia University Press.

Reynolds, B. C. (1934). *Between client and community: A study in responsibility in social case work*. Northhampton, MA: Smith College.

Reynolds, B. C. (1942). *Learning and teaching in the practice of social work*. New York: Rinehart & Co.

Reynolds, B. C. (1963). *An uncharted journey*. New York: The Citadel Press.

Richmond, M. (1897). The need of a training school in applied philanthropy. *Proceedings of the National Conference of Charities and Correction*. Boston: George H. Ellis.

Richmond, M. (1899). *Friendly visiting among the poor*. New York: Macmillan.

Richmond, M. (1911). *First steps in social service treatment: A textbook for caseworkers*. New York: Russell Sage Foundation.

Richmond, M. (1917). *Social diagnosis*. New York: Russell Sage Foundation.

Richmond, M. (1922). *What is social casework?* New York: Russell Sage Foundation.

Robertson, M. E. (1966). Forward. In B. F. Esser & C. Freud (Eds.), *Testing as a tool in the admissions process*. New York: CSWE.

Robinson, V. (1960). The University of Pennsylvania School of Social Work in perspective: 1909–1959. *Journal of Social Work Process, XI.*

Rose, S. D. (1972). *Treating children in groups: A behavioral approach.* San Francisco: Jossey-Bass.

Rose, S. D. (1977). *Group therapy: A behavioral approach.* Englewood Cliffs, NJ: Prentice-Hall.

Rose, S. D. (1980). *A casebook in group therapy: A behavioral-cognitive approach.* Englewood Cliffs, NJ: Prentice-Hall.

Rose, S. D. (1987). *Working with children and adolescents in groups.* San Francisco: Jossey-Bass.

Rose, S. D., & Kravitz, D. (1973). *Contracts in groups.* Dubuque, IA: Kendall/Hunt.

Rothman, J. (1963). *Minority group identity and intergroup relations.* Chicago: Research Institute of Group Work in Jewish Agencies.

Rothman, J. (1977). *Issues in race and ethnic relations.* Itasca, IL: Peacock.

Rothman, J. (1980a). *Social R and D: Research and development in the human services.* Englewood Cliffs, NJ: Prentice-Hall.

Rothman, J. (1980b). *Using research in organizations: A guide to successful application.* Thousand Oaks, CA: Sage.

Rothman, J. (1981). *Changing organizations and community programs.* Thousand Oaks, CA: Sage.

Rothman, J., & Epstein, I. (1971). Social planning and community organization: Social science foundations. In R. Morris (Ed.), *Encyclopedia of social work.* New York: NASW.

Rothman, J., & Jones, W. (1971). *A new look at field instruction.* New York: CSWE.

Rothman, J., & Thomas, E. J. (1994). *Intervention research. Design and development for the human services.* New York: Haworth.

Rothman, J., & Tropman, J. (1970). *Strategies of community organization.* Itasca, IL: Peacock.

Rothman, J., Erlich, J. L., & Teresa, J. G. (1976). *Promoting innovation and change in organizations and communities.* New York: Wiley.

Rothman, J., Erlich, J., & Tropman, J. (Eds.). (1970). *Strategies of community organization.* Itasca, IL: Peacock.

Safire, W. (2005, May 29). Blendwords. *The New York Times.*

Sarri, R. C. (1969). *Updating education for administration.* Paper presented at the annual program meeting of the Council on Social Work Education, Cleveland, OH.

Sarri, R. C. (1971). Administration in social welfare. In R. Morris (Ed.), *Encyclopedia of social work.* New York: NASW.

Sarri, R. C. (1997). Social work to social science. In D. J. Tucker, C. Garvin, & Sarri, R. (Eds.), *Integrating knowledge and practice.* Westport, CN: Praeger.

Sarri, R. C., & Hasenfeld, Y. (1976). *Brought to justice?* Ann Arbor: University of Michigan.

Sarri, R. C., & Maple, F. (Eds.). (1972). *The school and the community.* Washington, DC: NASW.

Schamess, G. (1995, March). *Smith College Studies in Social Work.* N.p.

Schinke, S., & Tripodi, T. (2001). Social research. In R. Feldman & S. Kamerman (Eds.), *The Columbia University School of Social Work: A centennial celebration.* New York: Columbia University Press.

Schrager, J. (1974). *Social work departments in university hospitals—Some issues in manpower utilization.* Syracuse, NY: Syracuse University.

Schroeder, D. (1955). Teaching psychiatric social work. *Proceedings of the Institute.* Atlantic City, NY: American Association of Psychiatric Social Workers.

Schroeder, D. (1963). Integrating social science theory through case discussion. *Social Casework, 44*(7).

Schroeder, D. (1965). Social work practice in mental health and psychiatric services. In H. L. Lurie (Ed.), *Encyclopedia of social work.* New York: NASW.

Shapiro, H. (2001, September 21). *Professional education and the soul of the American research university.* Presented at the University of Michigan School of Social Work's 80th Anniversary Symposium, Ann Arbor.

Shaw, W. B. (Ed.). (1942–51). *University of Michigan: An encyclopedic survey.* Ann Arbor: University of Michigan Press.

Shoemaker, L. M. (1998). Early conflicts in social work education. *Social Service Review, 72*(2), 182–191.

Siegel, S. (1964). *Social work practice with the aging and its implications for mental health.* Proceedings of workshop presented at The University of Michigan School of Social Work, Ann Arbor.

Siegel, S. (1974). *Organization growth: Expansion and diversity in Schools of Social Work.* Unpublished doctoral dissertation, University of Michigan, Ann Arbor.

Site visit team report: University of Michigan School of Social Work. (1983; 1991). New York: Council on Social Work Education.

Social Work Education Reporter. (1966; 2002). Alexandria, VA: Council on Social Work Education.

Soop, E. J. (1977). Extension Service. In F. Brinkman (Ed.), *University of Michigan: An encyclopedic survey.* Ann Arbor: University of Michigan Press.

Stein, H. D., & Cloward, R.A. (Eds.). (1958). *Social perspectives on behavior.* New York: Free Press.

Steiner, J. F. (1921). *Education for social work.* Chicago: University of Chicago Press.

Stewart, M. G. (1951). The economic status of social workers, 1950. *Social Work Journal, 32*(2).

Stillman, E. G. (1920). A medical point of view of hospital social service. *Hospital Social Service Quarterly, II,* 28–34.

Street, D., Vinter, R. D., & Perrow, C. (1966). *Organization for treatment: A comparative study of institutions for delinquents.* New York: Free Press.

Stroup, H. (1986). *Social welfare pioneers.* Chicago: Nelson-Hall.

Stuart, R. B. (1967). Casework treatment of depression viewed as interpersonal disturbance. *Social Work.*

Stuart, R. B. (1969a). *Behavior modification and ideal mental health services.* Presented at the Banff International Conference on Behavior Modification, Calgary, Alberta, Canada.

Stuart, R. B. (1969b). Operant-interpersonal treatment for marital discord. *Journal of Consulting and Clinical Psychology, 33*(6), 675–682.

Stuart, R. B. (1970). *Trick or treatment: How and when psychotherapy fails.* Champaign, IL: Research Press.

Stuart, R. B. (1971b). Research in social work: Social casework and social group work. In R. Morris (Ed.), *Encyclopedia of social work.* New York: NASW.

Stuart, R. B. (1972). *Slim chance in a fat world: Behavioral control of obesity.* Champaign, IL: Research Press.

Sundel, M., Glasser, P., Sarri, R. C., & Vinter, R. D. (1985). *Individual change through small groups.* New York: Free Press.

Sundwall, J. (1953). School of Public Health. In W. A. Donnelly et al. (Eds.), *University of Michigan: An encyclopedic survey.* Ann Arbor: University of Michigan Bentley Historical Library.

Taylor, A. L. (1950). How shall specialization in social work develop? *Social Work Journal, 31*(3).

The Columbia University School of Social Work: A centennial celebration. New York: Columbia University Press.

Thomas, E. J. (1964a). *Building social work knowledge: Report of a conference.* New York: NASW.

Thomas, E. J. (1964b). Selecting knowledge from behavioral science. In *Building social work knowledge: Report of a conference.* New York: NASW.

Thomas, E. J. (1967a). *The socio-behavioral approach and applications to social work.* New York: CSWE.

Thomas, E. J. (Ed.). (1967b). *Behavioral science for social workers.* New York: Free Press.

Thomas, E. J. (Ed.). (1974). *Behavioral modification procedures: A sourcebook.* Chicago: Aldine.

Thomas, E. J. (Ed.). (1984). *Designing intervention for the helping professions.* Thousand Oaks, CA: Sage.

Thomas, E. J. (1997). Themes and perspectives on integration and related models. In D. Tucker, C. Garvin, & R. C. Sarri (Eds.), *Integrating knowledge and practice: The case of social work and social science.* Westport, CN: Praeger.

Thomas, E. J., Carter, R. D., & Walter, C. (1971). *Socio-behavioral techniques for open welfare settings.* Ann Arbor: University of Michigan School of Social Work.

Thomas, E. J., Gambrill, E., & Carter, R. D. (1969). *Utilization and appraisal of socio-behavioral techniques in social welfare.* Ann Arbor: University of Michigan School of Social Work.

Thomas, E. J., & Goodman, E. (Eds.). (1965). *Socio-behavioral theory and interpersonal helping in social work: Lectures and institute proceedings.* Ann Arbor, MI: Campus Publishers.

Thomas, E. J., & McLeod, D. L. (1960). *In-service training and reduced workloads— Experiments in a state department of welfare.* New York: Russell Sage Foundation.

Thomas, E. J., McLeod, D. L. et al. (1968). *In-service training and reduced workloads: Experiments in the State Welfare Department.* New York: Russell Sage.

Thyer, B. A., & Bentley, K. (1986). Academic affiliation of social work authors. *Journal of Social Work Education, 22,* 67–73.

Towle, C. (1952). *Common human needs.* New York: American Association of Social Workers.

Tradition, vision, and change: Business education at the University of Michigan 1900–2000. (2001). Ann Arbor, University of Michigan.

Tripodi, T. (1974). *Uses and abuses of social research in social work.* New York: Columbia University Press.

Tripodi, T., Fellin, P., & Epstein, I. (1969). *Social program evaluation.* Itasca, IL: Peacock Publishers.

Tripodi, T., Fellin, P., & Meyer, H. J. (1969). *The assessment of social research: Guidelines for use of research in social work and social science.* Itasca, IL: Peacock Publishers.

Tropman, J. (1980). *The crucial relationship: Community agencies and community structure.* Alexandria, VA: United Way of America.

Tropman, J. (1984). *Policy management in the human services.* New York: Columbia University Press.

Tropman, J. (1989). *American values and social welfare: Cultural contradictions in the welfare state.* Englewood Cliffs, NJ: Prentice-Hall.

Tropman, J. (1992). *The Catholic ethic and the spirit of community.* Washington, DC: Georgetown University Press.

Tropman, J. (1995). *The Catholic ethic in American society.* San Francisco: Jossey-Bass.

Tropman, J. (1996). *Effective meetings: Improving group decision-making.* Thousand Oaks, CA: Sage.

Tropman, J. (1998). *Do Americans hate the poor?* Westport, CT: Praeger.

Tropman, J. (2001). *The total compensation solution.* San Francisco: Jossey-Bass.

Tropman, J., Dluhy, M., & Lind, R. (Eds.). (1981). *New strategic perspectives on social policy.* New York: Pergamon.

Tropman, J., Dluhy, M., Lind, R., Vasey, W., & Croxton, T. (Eds.). (1976). *Strategic perspectives on social policy.* New York: Pergamon.

Tropman, J., Erlich, J., & Rothman, J. (Eds.). (1995). *Tactics and techniques of community intervention.* Itasca, IL: Peacock Publishers.

Tropman, J., Johnson, H., & Tropman, E. (1979). *The essentials of committee management.* Chicago: Nelson-Hall.

Tropman, J., Johnson, H., & Tropman, E. (1992). *Committee management in the human services.* Chicago: Nelson-Hall.

Tropman, J. et al. (1970). *Tactics of community organization.* Itasca, IL: Peacock Publishers.

Tropman, J. et al. (1974). *Community action, planning, and development.* Itasca, IL: Peacock Publishers.

Tucker, D. (2003; 2004). *Self-study report of the interdepartmental program in social work and social science.* Ann Arbor: University of Michigan School of Social Work.

Tucker, D. J., Garvin, C., & Sarri, R. (Eds.). (1997). *Integrating knowledge and practice. The case of social work and social science.* Westport, CT: Praeger.

U.S. Department of Health, Education, and Welfare. (n.d). *Closing the gap in social work manpower.* Report of the Departmental Task Force on Social Work Education and Manpower.

United Nations, & UNESCO. (1960). *The contributions of social sciences in social work training. A report of a UN/UNESCO meeting of experts.* Paris: Author.

University of Michigan. (1984). Policy statement on sexual orientation. Ann Arbor: Author.

University of Michigan. (2001). *Tradition, vision, & change: Business education at the University of Michigan 1900–2000.* Ann Arbor: Author.

University of Michigan. (1935–50). *University of Michigan announcements.* Ann Arbor: University of Michigan Bentley Historical Library.

University of Michigan. (1921). *University of Michigan catalogue, 1921–22.* Ann Arbor: University of Michigan Bentley Historical Library.

University of Michigan. (1921–28). *University of Michigan catalogues.* Ann Arbor: University of Michigan Bentley Historical Library.

University of Michigan. (2008). *University of Michigan standard practice guide.* Ann Arbor: Author.

University of Michigan Center for Graduate Study. (1935). *Center for Graduate Study.* Detroit: Author.

University of Michigan School of Social Work. (1951–80). *School of Social Work faculty minutes.* Ann Arbor: University of Michigan Bentley Historical Library.

University of Michigan School of Social Work. (1957). *School of Social Work bulletin, 1957–58.* Ann Arbor: Author.

University of Michigan School of Social Work. (1973; 1983). *Council on Social Work Education reports.* Ann Arbor: University of Michigan Bentley Historical Library.

University of Michigan School of Social Work. (1981–92). *School of Social Work bulletins.* Ann Arbor: Author.

University of Michigan School of Social Work. (1982). *Twenty-fifth anniversary conference: Doctoral Program in Social Work and Social Science.* Ann Arbor: Author.

University of Michigan School of Social Work. (1983; 1991). *Self-study report.* Ann Arbor: Author.

University of Michigan School of Social Work. (1990). *A report on faculty research at the University of Michigan, 1988–90.* Ann Arbor: Author.

University of Michigan School of Social Work. (1992). *A report on faculty research at the University of Michigan, 1990–92.* Ann Arbor: Author.

University of Michigan School of Social Work. (2000a). *Building leadership for a changing society.* Ann Arbor: Author.

University of Michigan School of Social Work. (2000b). *A guide to the research interests of the School of Social Work faculty.* Ann Arbor: Author.

University of Michigan School of Social Work. (2003; 2004b; 2006). *Guidelines to requirements for doctoral study in social work and social science.* Ann Arbor: Author.

University of Michigan School of Social Work. (2004a). *Doctoral program guidelines.* Ann Arbor: Author.

University of Michigan School of Social Work. (2004c). *School of Social Work faculty handbook.* Ann Arbor: Author.

University of Michigan School of Social Work. (2004d). *School of Social Work research newsletter, 1 & 2.* Ann Arbor: Author.

University of Michigan School of Social Work. (2005a). *PODS questions/answers.* Ann Arbor: Author.

University of Michigan School of Social Work. (2005b). School of Social Work materials. Ann Arbor: Author.

University of Michigan School of Social Work. (2005c). *School of Social Work student guide.* Ann Arbor: Author.

University of Michigan School of Social Work. (2007). *Faculty research and publications.* Ann Arbor: Author.

Veroff, J., & Feld, S. (1970). *Marriage and work in America.* New York: Van Nostrand Reinhold.

Vinter, R. D. (1965). Social group work. In H. L. Lurie (Ed.), *Encyclopedia of social work.* New York: NASW.

Vinter, R. D. (Ed.), & Sarri, R. C. (1967). *Readings in group work practice.* Ann Arbor, MI: Campus Publishers.

Vinter, R. D., & Janowitz, M. (1962). *A comparative study of juvenile correctional institutions.* Ann Arbor: University of Michigan.

Vinter, R. D., & Kish, R. (1984). *Budgeting for the not-for-profit organizations.* New York: Free Press.

Vinter, R. D., & Sarri, R. C. (1965a). Group treatment strategies in juvenile corrections programs. *Crime and Delinquency.*

Vinter, R. D., & Sarri, R. C. (1965b). Malperformance in the public schools: A group work approach. *Social Work.*

Vinter, R. D., & Sarri, R. C. (1967). *Readings in group work practice.* Ann Arbor: University of Michigan.

Vinter, R. D., & Sarri, R. C. (1997). Doctoral education in social work and social science at Michigan. In D. J. Tucker, C. Garvin, & R. Sarri (Eds.), *Integrating knowledge and practice: The case of social work and social science.* Westport, CT: Praeger.

Vinter, R. D., & Siegel, S. (1971). *Proposal for schools of social work to establish a national information system.* Ann Arbor: University of Michigan School of Social Work.

Vinter, R. D., Sarri, R. C., Newcomb, T., & Kish, R. (Eds.). (1976). *Time out: A national study of juvenile correctional programs*. Ann Arbor: University of Michigan.

Warner, A. (1894). *American charities*. New York: Crowell.

Warner, R. M. (1999). *Frost-bite, frost-bark*. Ann Arbor: University of Michigan Bentley Historical Library.

Warren D. (1971). Neighborhoods in urban areas. *Encyclopedia of social work*. New York: NASW.

Warren, D. (1975). *Black neighborhoods*. Ann Arbor: University of Michigan.

Warren, D., & Warren, R. (1977). *The neighborhood organizer's handbook*. South Bend, IN: University of Notre Dame.

Wenocur, S., & Reisch, M. (1989). *From charity to enterprise: The development of American social work in a market economy*. Urbana: University of Illinois.

White, L. A. (1949). *The science of culture: A study of man and civilization*. New York: Farrar, Straus.

White, L. A. (1959). *The evolution of culture: The development of civilization to the fall of Rome*. New York: McGraw-Hill.

White, L. A. (1973). *The concept of culture*. Minneapolis: Burgess.

Whittman, M. (1950). Psychiatric social work training under the national mental health act. *Social Work Journal*.

Wilensky, H., & Lebeaux, C. (1965). *Industrial society and social welfare*. New York: Russell Sage Foundation.

Williams, B. A. (1998). *Thought and action: John Dewey at the University of Michigan*. Ann Arbor: University of Michigan Bentley Historical Library.

Wolfson, C. (1971). *Strategies in planning and implementing community corrections programs*. Ann Arbor: University of Michigan School of Social Work.

Wolfson, C. (1984). *Social deviance and the human services*. Springfield, IL: C.C. Thomas.

Wood, A. E. (1920). *Some unsolved problems of a university town*. Unpublished doctoral dissertation, University of Pennsylvania, Philadelphia.

Wood, A. E. (1922). *The philosophy of community organization*. N.p.

Wood, A. E. (1928). *Community problems*. New York: Century.

Wood, A. E. (1930). C. H. Cooley: An appreciation. *American Journal of Sociology, 35*(5), 707–717.

Wood, A. E. (1951). Social work. In W. B. Shaw (Ed.), *University of Michigan: An encyclopedic survey*. Ann Arbor: University of Michigan Press.

Wood, A. E., & Lurie, H. L. (1919). *Trouble cases: A study of the more difficult family problems and the work upon them of the Detroit social agencies*. Detroit, MI: Detroit Community Education.

Wright, H. (1954). Three against time: Edith and Grace Abbott and Sophonisba P. Breckinridge. *Social Service Review, 28*(1), 41–53.

Young, D. (1956). Forward. In H. Wilensky & C. Lebeaux (Eds.), *Industrial society and social welfare*. New York: Russell Sage Foundation.

Index of Names

Subject Index

gerontology, 70, 72, 187, 205, 221, 225, 247, 261, 282
grades, 103–104, 181–183, 240–241, 294–295
grants, 54, 55, 62, 67, 96, 126, 127, 139, 144, 146, 172, 185, 186, 187, 193, 221, 225, 227, 231, 247, 248, 253, 256, 258, 269, 283–285, 309, 311, 323
group formation, 82
group work, 34, 36, 54, 56, 63, 70, 73, 76, 78–82, 85–87, 89–90, 92–93, 102, 106, 107, 108–109, 111–112, 113, 114, 117–118, 121, 125, 128, 133, 138, 174, 176, 177, 178, 232, 235, 236, 277, 305, 313–314, 316

health, 6, 7, 11, 18, 19, 28, 35, 40, 68, 70, 71, 72, 74, 78, 85, 89, 90, 95, 96, 97, 109, 111, 118, 126, 128, 139, 144, 155, 158, 162, 163, 165, 166, 167, 171, 172, 176, 178, 179, 184, 185, 187, 188, 199, 200, 205, 214, 217, 218, 219, 221, 222–223, 225–226, 229–230, 231–232, 233, 234, 236, 238, 247, 251, 262, 263, 276, 277, 278, 279, 280, 282, 286, 288, 292, 326
health behavior, 97, 200
health education, 28, 97, 199, 200
human behavior and the social environment, 76, 83, 100, 113, 122–123, 161, 174, 215, 223, 238, 239, 292, 305
human growth and behavior, 54, 100, 105–106, 107, 110, 113, 121, 122–123, 128, 132, 306, 314
human service organizations, 92, 98, 162, 164, 179, 212, 220, 232, 237, 313

Institute of Gerontology, 80, 93, 97, 135, 163, 165, 168, 169, 183, 184, 185, 199, 218, 244, 254
Institute of Health and Social Sciences, 22–44, 135, 255
Institute of Public and Social Administration, 22, 31–32, 34, 44, 304
intergroup relations, 80

interpersonal practice, 83, 84, 86, 90, 91, 98, 113, 134, 165, 166, 167, 172, 174, 175–176, 177, 178, 179, 188, 213, 223, 230, 235, 236, 238, 239, 240, 242, 277, 281, 288, 291
intervention, 74, 80, 95, 110–112, 118, 128, 167, 168, 172, 174, 175–176, 188, 220, 223, 224, 228, 229, 232, 234, 276, 278, 279, 280, 287, 288, 291, 317, 318–319
interviewing, 81, 98, 108, 115, 285

job satisfaction, 98, 232, 234
Joint Doctoral Program in Social Work and Social Science, 1, 33, 66, 74, 175, 247, 256, 299–331
juvenile justice, 73, 78, 90, 145, 147, 223, 225, 232, 234

law and social work, 121–122
lecturers, 30, 32, 40–41, 53, 69–70, 114, 127, 159, 304
library, 49, 54, 55–56, 126, 139–140, 157, 206, 247, 259

marriage, 96, 98, 223, 227, 229, 234, 263
McGregor Foundation, 23
medical social work, 19, 35, 39, 56, 64, 172, 302
mental health, 68, 72, 74, 85, 89, 90, 92, 95, 96, 97, 128, 162, 163, 166, 171, 172, 178, 179, 184, 188, 217, 218, 221, 223, 226, 227, 228, 229–230, 232, 233, 234, 236, 238, 251, 276–282, 288, 292
mental retardation, 97, 160, 170–171
Merrill–Palmer School, 53, 114–115
Miller Analogies Test, 61, 149
minority faculty, 159, 215, 250, 271
minority populations, 113, 131, 147, 160, 179–181, 187, 189, 208, 219, 225, 226, 232, 237–238, 261, 288–289
minority students, 127, 140, 143, 144, 152–153, 155, 192, 193, 209, 212, 251, 267, 297